$\mathscr{A}$ GLOSSARY OF LITERARY TERMS

SIXTH EDITION

A GLOSSARY OF LITERARY TERMS

SIXTH EDITION

M. H. ABRAMS
CORNELL UNIVERSITY

HARCOURT BRACE COLLEGE PUBLISHERS

*Fort Worth, San Diego, Philadelphia, New York, Orlando, Austin, San Antonio
Montreal, Toronto, London, Sydney, Tokyo*

EDITOR IN CHIEF	TED BUCHHOLZ
ACQUISITIONS EDITOR	MICHAEL ROSENBERG
DEVELOPMENTAL EDITORS	CHRISTINE CAPERTON/HELEN TRILLER
PROJECT EDITOR	ANGELA WILLIAMS
PRODUCTION MANAGER	JANE TYNDALL PONCETI
BOOK DESIGNER	GARRY HARMAN

Address for Editorial Correspondence
Harcourt Brace College Publishers, 301 Commerce Street,
Suite 3700, Fort Worth, TX 76102

Address for Orders
Harcourt Brace & Company, 6277 Sea Harbor Drive, Orlando,
FL 32887
1-800-782-4479, or 1-800-433-0001 (in Florida)

ISBN: 0-03-054982-5

Library of Congress Catalogue Number: 92-70632

Printed in the United States of America
5 6 7 8 9 0 1 2 016 9 8 7 6 5 4

$\mathcal{T}$able of Contents

Preface

This book defines and discusses terms, critical theories, and points of view that are commonly applied to the classification, analysis, interpretation, and history of works of literature. The discussions and the guides to further reading are oriented especially toward undergraduate students of English, American, and other literatures; over the decades, however, the book has proved to be a useful reference work for advanced students as well.

The *Glossary* is organized as a series of succinct essays in the alphabetic order of the title word or phrase. Terms that are related but subsidiary, or that designate subclasses, are discussed under the title heading of the primary or generic term, and words that are commonly used in conjunction or as mutually defining contraries (*distance and involvement, empathy and sympathy, narrative and narrotology*) are discussed in the same essay. The alternative organization—a dictionary of terms defined singly—makes dull reading and requires excessive repetition and cross-referencing; it may also be misleading, because the application of many terms becomes clear only in the context of other concepts to which they are related, subordinated, or opposed. Presentation in the form of an essay also makes it feasible to supplement the central definition of a term with enough indications of its changes in meaning over time and of its diversity in current application, to help students steer their way through the shifting references and submerged ambiguities of its uses in literary studies. In addition, the discursive way of treating more or less technical terms provides the author with better opportunities to write discussions that are readable as well as useful. In each essay, **boldface** type indicates the terms for which the essay supplies the principal discussion; *italics* identify other terms that are used in the essay but are treated more fully elsewhere in the *Glossary*.

The new edition has been prepared in order to keep the text current with the rapid and incessant changes in the literary and critical scene, to take into account new books in literary history and criticism, and to take advantage of many suggestions for improvements and additions, some of them solicited by the publisher but many generously volunteered by users of the *Glossary*. All of the essays have been rewritten, and many drastically recast, including those in the section entitled "Modern Theories of Literature and Criticism" (pp. 223–286), which describe and date the innovative, fast-evolving critical theories and procedures of the last six or seven decades, from *archetypal criticism* and *New Criticism* to *deconstruction* and *new historicism*. All of the revisions are designed to make the expositions as clear and precise as possible and also to enlarge the range of references and examples, especially of writings by women and by cultural minorities that have recently achieved prominence. In each essay, the list of suggested readings has been enlarged and brought up to the date of the revision; books originally published in languages other than English are listed in their English translations.

In accordance with requests from a number of users, essays discussing the following terms have been added to this sixth edition: *dialogic criticism, discourse analysis, fiction and truth, hymn, narrative and narratology, new historicism, oral formulaic poetry, palinode, poststructuralism,* and *seven deadly sins.* In addition, a number of other new terms (including *cultural materialism, cultural studies, documentary fiction, foil, free indirect discourse, hagiography, multiculturalism, new pragmatism, sestina,* and *seven cardinal virtues*) have been introduced and discussed within the texts of these and other essays.

Also new in this edition, in chronological order under the heading *Periods of English Literature,* are expanded entries for the various periods of English literature that in earlier editions were dispersed through the *Glossary* in alphabetic order. This move makes the representation of English literature parallel with that in the entry for *Periods of American Literature.* Together, these two essays provide the convenience of a brief, chronological overview of the most prominent movements, authors, and forms in the literatures of England and America, from their beginnings to the present.

How to Use the *Glossary*

To find a literary word or phrase, always look it up in the alphabetic *Index of Terms* at the end of the volume. Although the separate essays in the *Glossary* are in the alphabetic order of their title-terms, by far the larger number of terms are defined and discussed within the body of these essays. In the *Index,* readers will find, in **boldface,** the page number of the principal discussion of the term; this is followed by the page numbers, in *italics,* of the term's occurrences in other essays that serve to exemplify and clarify the way the term functions in actual critical practice. Note that the word referred to by a secondary, italicized entry may be a modified form of the index-term; thus the forms "parodies" and "parodic" are listed under the entry "parody." Note also that those terms in the *Index* (mainly foreign in origin) that are most likely to be mispronounced by a student are followed by simplified guides to pronunciation; the key to these guides is on the first page of the *Index of Terms.*

In the *Index,* some of the more general and inclusive terms are supplemented by a list of specific or analytic terms that are closely related. These supplementary references expedite for the student the fuller exploration of a topic and also make it easy for the teacher to locate items that best serve the needs of a particular course or subject of study. For example, the added references identify the separate essays that deal with particular types and movements of literary *criticism,* the terms most relevant to the analysis of *style,* the separate entries that define and discuss types of *figurative language* or of literary *genres,* and the many essays that deal with the form, component features, history, and critical treatments of the *drama, lyric,* and *novel.*

At the end of the *Index* a number of pages, labeled "Additional Terms," have been provided on which, as the occasion arises, a user may supplement the terms, discussions, and references in the text of the *Glossary*.

Acknowledgments

This edition, like earlier ones, has profited greatly from the suggestions of teachers (and often students as well) at many colleges and universities, who suggested changes that would enhance the usefulness of the *Glossary* to the broad range of courses in American, English, and foreign literatures. In the present instance, I am especially grateful for counsel by A. R. Ammons, Daniel J. Boorstin, Cheryl Fresch, Nelly Furman, Mary Jacobus, Dominick La Capra, Richard Levin, and Joel Porte, and for many detailed suggestions by Charles L. Batten, University of California, Los Angeles; Miles Orvell, Temple University; Sibbie O'Sullivan, University of Maryland, College Park; Philip Rollinson, University of South Carolina at Columbia; and Susan Belasco Smith, Allegheny College. Dianne Ferriss has been indispensable, patient, and cheerful as a research assistant, editor, and word processor. Vernon Jackman supplied the expertise for programming and producing the *Index of Terms*. Michael Rosenberg, Acquisitions Editor, Christine Caperton and Helen Triller, Developmental Editors, and Angela Williams, Project Editor, at Harcourt Brace Jovanovich have with firmness but unfailing tact instigated and supervised this revision. All these friends, advisers, and co-workers have helped me come closer to the goal announced in the original edition: to write the kind of handbook that I would have found most valuable when, as an undergraduate, I was an eager but often bewildered student of literature and criticism.

A Note to the Reader

To find a literary word or phrase, always look it up in the alphabetic *Index of Terms* at the end of this volume. Although the separate essays in the *Glossary* are in the alphabetic order of their title-terms, by far the larger number of terms are defined and discussed within the body of these essays. For explanations of the typographical cues utilized in the text, refer to the section of the Preface entitled "How to Use the *Glossary*."

Absurd, Literature of the. The term is applied to a number of works in drama and prose fiction which have in common the sense that the human condition is essentially and ineradicably absurd, and that this condition can be adequately represented only in works of literature that are themselves absurd. Both the mood and dramaturgy of absurdity were anticipated as early as 1896 in Alfred Jarry's French play *Ubu roi* (*Ubu the King*). The literature has its roots also in the movements of *expressionism* and *surrealism,* as well as in the fiction, written in the 1920s, of Franz Kafka (*The Trial, Metamorphosis*). The current movement, however, emerged in France after the horrors of World War II, as a rebellion against essential beliefs and values both of traditional culture and traditional literature. This earlier tradition had included the assumptions that human beings are fairly rational creatures who live in an at least partially-intelligible universe, that they are part of an ordered social structure, and that they may be capable of heroism and dignity even in defeat. After the 1940s, however, there was a widespread tendency, especially prominent in the *existential philosophy* of men of letters such as Jean-Paul Sartre and Albert Camus, to view a human being as an isolated existent who is cast into an alien universe, to conceive the universe as possessing no inherent truth, value, or meaning, and to represent human life, as it moves from the nothingness whence it came toward the nothingness where it must end, as an existence which is both anguished and absurd. As Camus said in *The Myth of Sisyphus* (1942),

> In a universe that is suddenly deprived of illusions and of light, man feels a stranger. His is an irremediable exile. . . . This divorce between man and his life, the actor and his setting, truly constitutes the feeling of Absurdity.

Or as Eugène Ionesco, a leading French writer of absurd drama, including *The Chairs* (1952), has put it: "Cut off from his religious, metaphysical, and transcendental roots, man is lost; all his actions become senseless, absurd, useless." He also said, in commenting on the mixture of moods in the literature of the absurd: "People drowning in meaninglessness can only be grotesque, their sufferings can only appear tragic by derision."

Samuel Beckett (1906–89), the most eminent and influential of writers in this mode, was an Irishman living in Paris who often wrote in French and then translated his works into English. His plays project the irrationalism, helplessness, and absurdity of life, in dramatic forms that reject realistic settings, logical reasoning, or a coherently evolving plot. *Waiting for Godot* (1955) presents two tramps in a waste place, fruitlessly and all but hopelessly waiting for an unidentified person, Godot, who may or may not exist and with whom they sometimes think they remember that they may have an appointment; as one of them remarks, "Nothing happens, nobody comes, nobody goes, it's awful." Like most works in this mode, the play is "absurd" in the double sense that it is grotesquely comic and also irrational and non-consequential; it is a parody not only of the traditional assumptions of Western culture, but of the conventions and generic distinctions in traditional drama, and even of its own inescapable participation in the dramatic medium. The lucid but eddying and pointless dialogue is often funny, and pratfalls and other modes of slapstick are used to project metaphysical alienation and tragic anguish. Beckett's prose fiction, such as *Malone Dies* (1958) and *The Unnamable* (1960), present an *antihero* who plays out the absurd moves of the end game of civilization in a nonwork which tends to undermine the coherence of its own medium, language itself. But typically, Beckett's characters carry on, even if in a life without purpose, trying to make sense of the senseless and to communicate the uncommunicable.

Another French playwright of the absurd was Jean Genet (who combined absurdism and diabolism); some of the early dramatic works of the Englishman Harold Pinter and the American Edward Albee are in a similar mode. The plays of Tom Stoppard, such as *Rosencrantz and Guildenstern Are Dead* (1966) and *Travesties* (1974), exploit the devices of absurdist drama more for comic than philosophical ends. There are also affinities with this movement in the numerous recent works which exploit **black comedy:** baleful, naive, or inept characters in a fantastic or nightmarish modern world play out their roles in what Ionesco called a "tragic farce," in which the events are often simultaneously comic, horrifying, and absurd. Examples are Joseph Heller's *Catch-22* (1961), Thomas Pynchon's *V* (1963), John Irving's *The World According to Garp* (1978), and some of the novels by the German Günter Grass and the Americans Kurt Vonnegut, Jr., and John Barth.

See *wit, humor, and the comic,* and refer to: Martin Esslin, *The Theatre of the Absurd* (rev., 1968); David Grossvogel, *The Blasphemers: The Theatre of Brecht, Ionesco, Beckett, Genet* (1965); Arnold P. Hinchliffe, *The Absurd* (1969); Charles B. Harris, *Contemporary American Novelists of the Absurd* (1972); and Max F. Schultz, *Black Humor Fiction of the Sixties* (1980).

Act. A major division in the action of a play. Such a division was introduced into England by Elizabethan dramatists, who imitated ancient Roman plays by structuring the represented action so that it fell into five acts. Late in the nineteenth century a number of writers followed the example of Chekhov and Ibsen by constructing plays in four acts. In the present century the most common form for nonmusical dramas has been three acts.

Acts are often subdivided into **scenes,** which in modern plays usually consist of units of action in which there is no change of place or break in the continuity of time. (Some recent plays dispense with the division into acts, and are structured as a sequence of scenes, or episodes.) In the conventional theater with a **proscenium arch** that frames the front of the stage, the end of a scene is usually indicated by a dropped curtain, and the end of an act by a dropped curtain and an intermission.

Aestheticism, or the **Aesthetic Movement,** was a European phenomenon during the latter nineteenth century that had its chief headquarters in France. In opposition to the dominance of scientific thinking, and in defiance of the widespread indifference or hostility of the society of their time to any art that was not useful or did not teach moral values, French writers developed the view that a work of art is the supreme value among human products precisely because it is self-sufficient, and has no use or moral aim outside its own being. The end of a work of art is simply to exist in its formal perfection; that is, be beautiful, and to be contemplated as an end in itself. A rallying cry of Aestheticism became the phrase "l'art pour l'art"—**art for art's sake.**

The historical roots of aestheticism are in the views proposed by the German philosopher Immanuel Kant in his *Critique of Aesthetic Judgment* (1790) that the "pure" aesthetic experience consists of a "disinterested" contemplation of an object that "pleases for its own sake," without reference to reality or to the "external" ends of utility or morality. As a self-conscious movement, however, French aestheticism is often said to date from Théophile Gautier's witty defense of his assertion that art is useless (Preface to *Mademoiselle de Maupin*, 1835). Aestheticism was developed by Baudelaire, who was greatly influenced by Edgar Allan Poe's claim (in "The Poetic Principle," 1850) that the supreme work is a "poem *per se*," a "poem written solely for the poem's sake"; it was later taken up by Flaubert, Mallarmé, and many other writers. In its extreme form, the aesthetic doctrine of art for art's sake veered into the moral and quasi-religious doctrine of life for art's sake, with the artist represented as a priest who renounces the practical and self-profiting canons of ordinary existence in the service of what Flaubert and others called "the religion of beauty."

The views of French Aestheticism were introduced into Victorian England by Walter Pater, with his emphasis on high artifice and stylistic subtlety, his recommendation to crowd one's life with the maximum of exquisite sensations, and his precept of the supreme value of beauty and of "the love of art for its own sake." (See his Conclusion to *The Renaissance*, 1873.) The artistic and moral views of Aestheticism are also expressed by Algernon Charles Swinburne, and by English writers of the 1890s such as Oscar Wilde, Arthur Symons, and Lionel Johnson. The influence of some central ideas stressed in Aestheticism—especially the view of the "autonomy" (self-sufficiency) of a work of art, the emphasis on craft and artistry, and the concept of a poem or novel as an end in itself whose values are "intrinsic"—has been important in the writings of prominent recent authors such as W. B. Yeats, T. E. Hulme, and T. S. Eliot, as well as in the literary theory of the *New Critics*.

For related developments, see *decadence* and *ivory tower*. Refer to: William Gaunt, *The Aesthetic Adventure* (1945, reprinted 1975); Frank Kermode, *Romantic Image* (1957); Enid Starkie, *From Gautier to Eliot* (1960); R. V. Johnson, *Aestheticism* (1969); and for the intellectual and social conditions of the emergence of aesthetic theory, M. H. Abrams, "Art-as-Such: The Sociology of Modern Aesthetics," in *Doing Things with Texts: Essays in Criticism and Critical Theory* (1989). Useful collections of writings in the Aesthetic Movement are Ian Small, ed., *The Aesthetes: A Sourcebook* (1979), and Eric Warner and Graham Hough, eds., *Strangeness and Beauty: An Anthology of Aesthetic Criticism 1848–1910* (2 vols.; 1983). A useful descriptive guide to books on the subject is Linda C. Dowling, *Aestheticism and Decadence: A Selective Annotated Bibliography* (1977).

Affective Fallacy. In an essay published in 1946, W. K. Wimsatt and Monroe C. Beardsley defined the affective fallacy as the error of evaluating a poem by its effects—especially its emotional effects—upon the reader. As a result of this fallacy "the poem itself, as an object of specifically critical judgment, tends to disappear," so that criticism "ends in impressionism and relativism." The two critics wrote in direct reaction to the view of I. A. Richards, in his influential *Principles of Literary Criticism* (1923), that the value of a poem can be measured by the psychological responses of its readers. Beardsley has since modified the earlier claim by the admission that "it does not appear that critical evaluation can be done at all except in relation to certain types of effect that aesthetic objects have upon their perceivers." So modified, the doctrine becomes a claim for *objective criticism,* in which the critic does not describe the effects of a work upon himself, but concentrates upon the analysis of the features, devices, and form of the work by which such effects are achieved. An extreme reaction against the doctrine of the affective fallacy was manifested in the recent development of *reader-response criticism.*

Wimsatt and Beardsley, "The Affective Fallacy," reprinted in W. K. Wimsatt, *The Verbal Icon* (1954); and Monroe C. Beardsley, *Aesthetics: Problems in the Philosophy of Criticism* (1958), p. 491 and Chapter 11. See also Wimsatt and Beardsley's related concept of the *intentional fallacy.*

Allegory. An allegory is a narrative fiction in which the agents and actions, and sometimes the setting as well, are contrived to make coherent sense on the "literal," or primary, level of signification, and at the same time to signify a second, correlated order of agents, concepts, and events.

We can distinguish two main types: (1) Historical and political allegory, in which the characters and actions that are signified literally in their turn represent, or "allegorize," historical personages and events. So in John Dryden's *Absalom and Achitophel* (1681), King David represents Charles II, Absalom represents his natural son the Duke of Monmouth, and the biblical plot allegorizes a political crisis in contemporary England. (2) The allegory of ideas, in which the literal characters represent abstract concepts and the plot exemplifies a doctrine or thesis. Both types of allegory may either be sustained throughout a work, as in *Absalom and Achitophel* and John Bunyan's *The Pilgrim's Progress* (1678), or else serve merely as an episode in a nonallegorical work. A famed example of episodic allegory is the encounter of Satan with his daughter Sin, as well as with Death—who is represented allegorically as the son born of their incestuous relationship—in John Milton's *Paradise Lost,* Book II (1667).

The central device in the second type, the sustained allegory of ideas, is the *personification* of abstract entities such as virtues, vices, states of mind, modes of life, and types of character. In explicit allegories, such reference is specified by the names given to characters and places. Thus Bunyan's *The Pilgrim's Progress* allegorizes the Christian doctrines of salvation by telling how the character named Christian, warned by Evangelist, flees the City of Destruction and makes his way laboriously to the Celestial City; enroute he encounters characters with names like Faithful, Hopeful, and the Giant

Despair, and passes through places like the Slough of Despond, the Valley of the Shadow of Death, and Vanity Fair. A passage from this work will indicate the nature of an explicit allegorical process:

> Now as Christian was walking solitary by himself, he espied one afar off come crossing over the field to meet him; and their hap was to meet just as they were crossing the way of each other. The Gentleman's name was Mr.Worldly-Wiseman; he dwelt in the Town of Carnal-Policy, a very great Town, and also hard by from whence Christian came.

Works which are primarily nonallegorical may introduce **allegorical imagery** (the personification of abstract entities who perform a brief allegorical action) in short passages. Familiar instances are the opening lines of Milton's *L'Allegro* and *Il Penseroso* (1645). This device was exploited especially in the *poetic diction* of authors in the mid-eighteenth century. An example— so brief that it presents an allegoric tableau rather than an action—is the passage in Thomas Gray's "Elegy Written in a Country Churchyard" (1751):

> Can Honour's voice provoke the silent dust,
> Or Flatt'ry soothe the dull cold ear of Death?

Allegory is a narrative strategy which may be employed in any literary form or genre. *The Pilgrim's Progress* is a moral and religious allegory in a prose narrative; Edmund Spenser's *The Faerie Queene* (1590–96) fuses moral, religious, historical, and political allegory in a verse romance; the third book of Jonathan Swift's *Gulliver's Travels*, the voyage to Laputa and Lagado (1726), is an allegorical satire directed mainly against philosophical and scientific pedantry; and William Collins' "Ode on the Poetical Character" (1747) is a lyric poem which allegorizes a topic in literary criticism—the nature, sources, and power of the poet's creative imagination. John Keats makes a subtle use of allegory throughout his ode "To Autumn" (1820), most explicitly in the magnificent second stanza, which represents autumn personified as a female figure amid the scenes and activities of the harvest season.

Sustained allegory was a favorite form in the Middle Ages, when it produced masterpieces—especially in the mode of the *dream vision*, in which the narrator falls asleep and experiences an allegoric dream—including, in the fourteenth century, Dante's *Divine Comedy*, the French *Roman de la Rose*, Chaucer's *House of Fame*, and William Langland's *Piers Plowman*, as well as, early in the sixteenth century, the drama *Everyman*. (See *morality play*.) But sustained allegory has been written in all literary periods, and is the form of such major nineteenth-century poetic works as Goethe's *Faust, Part II*, Shelley's *Prometheus Unbound*, and Thomas Hardy's *The Dynasts;* in the present century the stories and novels of Franz Kafka can be considered instances of allegory.

Various literary *genres* may be classified as types of allegory, in that they all narrate, though in varied forms, one coherent set of circumstances which signify a second order of correlated meanings. A **fable** (also called an **apologue**) is a short narrative, in prose or verse, that exemplifies an abstract moral thesis or principle of human behavior; usually in its conclusion either the narrator or one of the characters states the moral in the form of an *epigram*. Most common is the **beast fable**, in which animals talk and act like the human types they represent. In the familiar fable of the fox and the grapes, the fox—after exerting all his wiles to get the grapes hanging beyond his reach, but in vain—concludes that they are probably sour anyway: the express moral is that human beings belittle what they cannot get. There were beast fables written in classical times; best known is the set attributed to Aesop, a Greek slave of the sixth century B.C. In the seventeenth century a Frenchman, Jean de la Fontaine, wrote a set of witty fables in verse which are the classics of this literary kind. Chaucer's "The Nun's Priest's Tale," the story of the cock and the fox, is a beast fable; the American Joel Chandler Harris (1848–1908) wrote many Uncle Remus stories which are beast fables, told in Black southern dialect and based on Black *folktales;* James Thurber's *Fables for Our Time* (1940) is a recent set of short fables; and in *Animal Farm* (1945) George Orwell expanded the beast fable into a sustained satire on the political and social situation in the mid-twentieth century.

A **parable** is a very short narrative about human beings presented so as to stress the tacit analogy, or parallel, with a general thesis or lesson that the narrator is trying to bring home to his audience. The parable was one of Christ's favorite devices as a teacher; examples are His parables of the good Samaritan and of the prodigal son. Here is Christ's terse parable of the fig tree, Luke 13:6–9:

> He spake also this parable: A certain man had a fig tree planted in his vineyard; and he came and sought fruit thereon, and found none. Then said he unto the dresser of his vineyard, "Behold, these three years I come seeking fruit on this fig tree, and find none: cut it down; why cumbereth it the ground?" And he answering said unto him, "Lord, let it alone this year also, till I shall dig about it, and dung it. And if it bears fruit, well: and if not, then after that thou shalt cut it down."

An **exemplum** is a story told as a particular instance of the general theme of a sermon. The device was popular in the Middle Ages, when extensive collections of exempla were prepared for use by preachers. In Chaucer's "The Pardoner's Tale" the Pardoner, preaching on the theme "Greed is the root of all evil," incorporates as exemplum the tale of the three drunken revelers who set out to find Death and find a heap of gold instead, only after all to find Death when they kill one another in the attempt to gain sole possession of the treasure. By extension the term "exemplum" is also applied to tales used in a formal, though nonreligious, exhortation. Thus Chaucer's Chanticleer, in "The Nun's Priest's Tale," borrows the preacher's technique in the ten exempla he tells in a vain effort to persuade his skeptical wife, Dame Pertelote the hen, that bad dreams forebode disaster.

See *didactic, symbol* (for the distinction between allegory and symbol), and (on the fourfold allegorical interpretation of the Bible) *interpretation: typological and allegorical.* On allegory in general, consult C. S. Lewis, *The Allegory of Love* (1936), Chapter 2; Edwin Honig, *Dark Conceit: The Making of Allegory* (1959); Angus Fletcher, *Allegory: The Theory of a Symbolic Mode* (1964);

Rosemund Tuve, *Allegorical Imagery* (1966); Michael Murrin, *The Veil of Allegory* (1969); Maureen Quilligan, *The Language of Allegory* (1979). On the exemplum, see G. R. Owst, *Literature and Pulpit in Medieval England* (2d ed., 1961), Chapter 4.

Alliteration is the repetition of a speech sound in a sequence of words; the term is usually applied only to consonants and when the recurrent sound occurs in a conspicuous position at the beginning either of a word or of a stressed syllable within a word. In Old English **alliterative meter**, alliteration is the principal organizing device of the verse line; each line is divided into two half-lines of two strong stresses by a decisive pause, or *caesura*, and at least one, and usually both, of the two stressed syllables in the first half-line alliterate with the first stressed syllable of the second half-line. (In this type of versification a vowel was considered to alliterate with any other vowel.) A number of Middle English poems, such as William Langland's *Piers Plowman* and the romance *Sir Gawain and the Green Knight* in the fourteenth century, continued to use and play variations upon the old alliterative meter. (See *strong-stress meters.*) In the opening line of *Piers Plowman*, for example, all four of the stressed syllables alliterate:

> In a sómer séson, whan sóft was the sónne . . .

In later English versification, however, alliteration is used only for special stylistic effects, such as to reinforce the meaning, to link related words, or to provide tone color and enhance the palpability of uttering the words. An example is the repetitions of the *s, th,* and *w* consonants in Shakespeare's Sonnet 30:

> When to the *s*essions of *s*weet *s*ilent *th*ought
> I *s*ummon up remembrance of *th*ings past,
> I *s*igh the lack of many a *th*ing I sought
> And *w*ith old *w*oes new *w*ail my dear time's *w*aste. . . .

Various other repetitions of speech sounds are identified by special terms. **Consonance** is the repetition of a sequence of two or more consonants, but with a change in the intervening vowel: live-love, lean-alone, pitter-patter. W. H. Auden's poem of the 1930s, "'O where are you going?' said reader to rider," makes prominent use of this device; the last stanza reads:

> "Out of this house"—said *rider* to *reader*,
> "Yours never will"—said *farer* to *fearer*,
> "They're looking for you" said *hearer* to *horror*,
> As he left them there, as he left them there.*

Assonance is the repetition of identical or similar vowel sounds—especially in stressed syllables—in a sequence of nearby words. Note the recurrent long *i* in the opening lines of Keats' "Ode on a Grecian Urn" (1820):

* Lines from "O where are you going?" from *W. H. Auden: Collected Poems 1927–1957* by W. H. Auden, ed. by Edward Mendelson. Copyright © 1934 and renewed 1962 by W. H. Auden. Reprinted by permission of Random House, Inc., and Faber & Faber, Ltd.

> Thou still unravished bride of quietness,
> Thou foster child of silence and slow time.

The richly assonantal effect at the beginning of William Collins' "Ode to Evening" (1747) depends on a patterned sequence of both identical and similar vowels:

> If aught of oaten stop or pastoral song,
> May hope, chaste Eve, to soothe thy pensive ear . . .

For a special case of the repetition of vowels and consonants in combination, see *rhyme.*

Allusion in a literary text is a reference, without explicit identification, to a person, place, or event, or to another literary work or passage. In the Elizabethan Thomas Nashe's "Litany in Time of Plague,"

> Brightness falls from the air,
> Queens have died young and fair,
> Dust hath closed Helen's eye,

there is an allusion to Helen of Troy. Most allusions serve to illustrate or clarify or enhance a subject, but some are used in order to undercut it ironically by the discrepancy between the subject and the allusion. In the lines from T. S. Eliot's *The Waste Land* (1922) describing a woman at her modern dressing table,

> The Chair she sat in, like a burnished throne,
> Glowed on the marble,*

the *ironic* allusion, by the indirect mode of echoing Shakespeare's phrasing, is to Cleopatra's magnificent barge in *Antony and Cleopatra* (II. ii. 196 ff.):

> The barge she sat in, like a burnish'd throne,
> Burn'd on the water.

For discussion of a poet who makes persistent and complex use of this device, see Reuben A. Brower, *Alexander Pope: The Poetry of Allusion* (1959); see also John Hollander, *The Figure of Echo: A Mode of Allusion in Milton and After* (1981).

Allusions of course imply a fund of knowledge that is shared by an author and an audience. Most literary allusions are intended to be recognized by the generally educated readers of the author's time, but some are aimed at a special coterie. For example in *Astrophel and Stella*, the Elizabethan *sonnet sequence*, Sir Philip Sidney's punning allusions to Lord Robert Rich, who had married the Stella of the sonnets, were identifiable only by close intimates of the people concerned. (See Sonnets 24 and 37.) Some modern authors, including Joyce, Pound, and Eliot, often include allusions that are very specialized, or else drawn from the author's private reading and experience, in the awareness that few if any readers will recognize them prior to

---

* Lines from "The Waste Land" from *Collected Poems 1909–1962* by T. S. Eliot, copyright 1936 by Harcourt Brace Jovanovich, Inc., copyright © 1964, 1963 by T. S. Eliot. Reprinted by permission of Harcourt Brace Jovanovich and Faber and Faber Ltd.

the detective work of scholarly annotators. The current term *intertextuality* includes literary echoes and allusions as one of the many ways in which any text is interlinked with other texts.

Ambiguity. In ordinary usage "ambiguity" is applied to a fault in style; that is, the use of a vague or equivocal expression when what is wanted is precision and particularity of reference. Since William Empson published *Seven Types of Ambiguity* (1930), however, the term has been widely used in criticism to identify a poetic device: the use of a single word or expression to signify two or more distinct references, or to express two or more diverse attitudes or feelings. **Multiple meaning** and **plurisignation** are alternative terms for this use of language; they have the advantage of avoiding the pejorative association with the word "ambiguity."

When Shakespeare's Cleopatra, exciting the asp to a frenzy, says (*Antony and Cleopatra*, V. ii. 306 ff.),

> Come, thou mortal wretch,
> With thy sharp teeth this knot intrinsicate
> Of life at once untie. Poor venomous fool,
> Be angry, and dispatch,

her speech is richly multiple in significance. For example, "mortal" means "fatal" or "death-dealing," and at the same time may signify that the asp is itself mortal, or subject to death. "Wretch" in this context serves to express both contempt and pity (Cleopatra goes on to refer to the asp as "my baby at my breast, / That sucks the nurse asleep"). And the two meanings of "dispatch"—"make haste" and "kill"—are equally relevant.

A special type of multiple meaning is conveyed by the **portmanteau word.** The term was introduced into literary criticism by Humpty Dumpty, the expert on semantics in Lewis Carroll's *Through the Looking Glass* (1871). He is explicating to Alice the meaning of the opening lines of "Jabberwocky":

> 'Twas brillig, and the slithy toves
> Did gyre and gimble in the wabe.

"Slithy," Humpty Dumpty explained, "means 'lithe and slimy' . . . You see it's like a portmanteau—there are two meanings packed up into one word." That is, a portmanteau word consists of a fusion of two or more existing words. James Joyce exploited this device to the full in order to sustain the multiple levels of meaning throughout his long dream narrative *Finnegans Wake* (1939). An example is his comment on girls who are "yung and easily freudened"; "freudened" fuses "frightened" and "Freud," while "yung" fuses "young" and Sigmund Freud's rival in depth psychology, Carl Jung. (Compare *pun.*) "Différance," a key analytic term of the philosopher of language Jacques Derrida, is a portmanteau noun which he describes as fusing two diverse meanings of the French verb "différer": "to differ" and "to defer." (See *deconstruction.*)

William Empson (who, in analyzing poetic ambiguity, named and enlarged upon a literary phenomenon that had been noted by some earlier critics) helped make current a mode of *explication* which greatly expanded the awareness by readers of the complexity and richness of poetic language. The risk, at times exemplified by Empson, as well as by other recent critics, is that the intensive search for ambiguities will result in **over-reading**: ingenious, overdrawn, and sometimes contradictory explications of a literary word or passage.

For related terms see *connotation and denotation* and *pun*. In addition to Empson, above, refer to Philip Wheelwright, *The Burning Fountain* (1954), especially Chapter 4. For critiques of Empson's theory and practice, see John Crowe Ransom, "Mr. Empson's Muddles," *The Southern Review* 4 (1938), and Elder Olson, "William Empson, Contemporary Criticism and Poetic Diction," in *Critics and Criticism,* ed. R. S. Crane (1952).

Antithesis is a contrast or opposition in the meanings of contiguous phrases or clauses that is emphasized by **parallelism**—that is, a similar order and structure—in the *syntax*. An example is Alexander Pope's description of Atticus in his *Epistle to Dr. Arbuthnot* (1735), "Willing to wound, and yet afraid to strike." In the antithesis in the second line of Pope's description of the Baron's designs against Belinda, in *The Rape of the Lock* (1714), the parallelism in the syntax is made especially prominent by *alliteration* in the correspondent nouns:

> Resolved to win, he meditates the way,
> By *f*orce to ravish, or by *f*raud betray.

In a sentence from Samuel Johnson's prose fiction *Rasselas* (1759), Chapter 26, the antithesis is similarly heightened by the alliteration in the contrasted nouns: "Marriage has many *p*ains, but celibacy has no *p*leasures."

Archaism. The use in literature of words and expressions that have become obsolete in the common speech of an era. Spenser in *The Faerie Queene* (1590–96) deliberately employed archaisms (many of them derived from Chaucer's medieval English) in the attempt to achieve a specialized poetic style appropriate to his revival of the medieval *chivalric romance*. The translators of the King James Version of the Bible (1611) gave weight, dignity, and sonority to their prose by archaic revivals. Both Spenser and the King James Bible have in their turn been major sources of archaisms in Milton and many later authors. When Keats, for example, in his ode (1820) described the Grecian urn as "with *brede* / Of marble men and maidens *overwrought*," he used archaic words for "braid" and "worked [that is, ornamented] all over." Archaism readily becomes a standard resort for *poetic diction*. Until fairly recent times, for example, many poets continued to use "I ween," "methought," "steed," "taper" (for candle), and "morn," but only in their verses, not their everyday speech.

Atmosphere (alternative terms are **mood** and **ambience**) is the emotional tonality pervading a section or the whole of a literary work, which fosters in the reader expectations as to the course of events, whether happy or (more commonly) terrifying or disastrous. Shakespeare establishes the tense and fearful atmosphere of *Hamlet* at the beginning, by the terse and nervous dialogue of the sentinels as they anticipate a reappearance of the ghost; Coleridge engenders a compound of religious and superstitious terror by his description of the initial scene in the narrative poem *Christabel* (1816); and Hardy in his novel *The Return of the Native* (1878) makes Egdon Heath an immense and brooding presence which reduces to pettiness and futility the human struggle for happiness for which it is the setting.

Ballad. A short definition of the **popular ballad** (known also as the **folk ballad** or "traditional ballad") is that it is a song, transmitted orally, which tells a story. Ballads are thus the narrative species of *folk songs*, which originate, and are communicated orally, among illiterate or only partly literate people. In all probability the initial version of a ballad was composed by a single author, but he or she is unknown; and since each singer who learns and repeats an oral ballad is apt to introduce changes in both the text and the tune, it exists in many variant forms. Typically, the popular ballad is dramatic, condensed, and impersonal: the narrator begins with the climactic episode, tells the story tersely by means of action and dialogue (sometimes by means of the dialogue alone), and tells it without self-reference or the expression of personal attitudes or feelings.

The most common stanza form—called the **ballad stanza**—is a *quatrain* in alternate four- and three-stress *iambic* lines; usually only the second and fourth lines rhyme. This is the form of "Sir Patrick Spens"; the first stanza of this ballad also exemplifies the conventionally abrupt opening and the manner of proceeding by third-person narration, curtly sketched setting and action, sharp transition, and spare dialogue:

> The king sits in Dumferling towne,
>   Drinking the blude-red wine:
> "O whar will I get a guid sailor,
>   To sail this schip of mine?"

Many ballads employ set formulas (which helped the singer remember the course of the song) including (1) stock descriptive phrases like "blood-red wine" and "milk-white steed," (2) a *refrain* in each stanza ("Edward," "Lord Randall"), and (3) **incremental repetition**, in which a line or stanza is repeated, but with an addition that advances the story ("Lord Randall," "Child Waters"). (See *oral formulaic poetry*.)

The collecting and printing of popular ballads began in England, then in Germany, during the eighteenth century. In 1765 Thomas Percy published his *Reliques of Ancient English Poetry* which, although most of the contents had been rewritten in the style of that time, did much to inaugurate widespread interest in folk literature. The basic modern collection is Francis J. Child's *English and Scottish Popular Ballads* (1882–98), which includes 305 ballads, many of them in variant versions. Bertrand H. Bronson has edited *The Traditional Tunes of the Child Ballads* (4 vols.; 1959–72). Popular ballads are still being sung—and collected, now with the help of a tape recorder—in the British Isles and remote rural areas of America. To the songs its early settlers inherited from Great Britain, America has added native forms of the ballad, such as those sung by lumberjacks, cowboys, laborers, and social protesters. A number of recent folk singers, from Woody Guthrie to Bob Dylan and Joan Baez, themselves compose ballads; most of these, however, such as "The Ballad of Bonnie and Clyde" (about a notorious gangster and his moll), are closer to the journalistic "broadside ballad" than to the archaic and heroic mode of the popular ballads in the Child collection.

A **broadside ballad** is a ballad that was printed on one side of a single sheet (called a "broadside"), dealt with a current event or person or issue, and was sung to a well-known tune. Beginning with the sixteenth century, these broadsides were hawked in the streets or at country fairs in Great Britain.

The traditional ballad has had immense influence on the form and style of lyric poetry in general, in addition to engendering the **literary ballad,** which is a narrative poem written in deliberate imitation of the form, language, and spirit of the traditional ballad. In Germany, some major literary ballads were written in the latter eighteenth century, including G. A. Bürger's very popular "Lenore" (1774)—which soon became widely read and influential in an English translation—and Goethe's "Erlkönig" (1782). In England, some of the greatest literary ballads were composed in the *Romantic Period:* Coleridge's "Rime of the Ancient Mariner" (which, however, is much longer and has a much more elaborate plot than the folk ballad), Walter Scott's "Proud Maisie," and Keats' "La Belle Dame sans Merci." In the *Lyrical Ballads* of 1798, Wordsworth begins "We Are Seven" by introducing a narrator as an agent and first-person teller of the story—"I met a little cottage girl"—which is probably one reason he called the collection "*lyrical* ballads." Coleridge's "Ancient Mariner," on the other hand, of which the first version also appeared in *Lyrical Ballads,* opens with the abrupt and impersonal third-person narration of the traditional ballad:

> It is an ancient Mariner
> And he stoppeth one of three.

Gordon H. Gerould, *The Ballad of Tradition* (1932); M. J. C. Hodgart, *The Ballads* (2d ed., 1962); John A. and Alan Lomax, *American Ballads and Folk Songs* (1934). For the broadside ballad see *The Common Muse,* eds. V. de Sola Pinto and Allan E. Rodway (1957).

Baroque is a term applied by art-historians (at first derogatorily, but now merely descriptively) to a style of architecture, sculpture, and painting that developed in Italy in the late-sixteenth and seventeenth centuries and then spread to Germany and other countries in Europe. The style employs the classical forms of the *Renaissance,* but breaks them up and intermingles them to achieve elaborate, grandiose, energetic, and highly dramatic effects.

The term has been adopted with reference to literature, in various applications. It may signify any elaborately formal and magniloquent style in verse or prose—for example, some verse passages in Milton's *Paradise Lost*

(1667) and Thomas De Quincey's prose descriptions of his dreams in *Confessions of an English Opium Eater* (1822) have both been called baroque. Occasionally—though oftener on the Continent than in England—it serves as a period term for post-Renaissance literature in the seventeenth century. More frequently it is applied specifically to the elaborate verses and extravagant conceits of the late-sixteenth and early-seventeenth-century poets Giambattista Marino in Italy and Luis de Góngora in Spain. In English literature the metaphysical poems of John Donne are sometimes described as baroque; but the term is more often, and more appropriately, applied to the elaborate style, fantastic conceits, and extreme religious emotionalism of the poet Richard Crashaw, 1612–49. (See under *metaphysical conceit*.)

The term "baroque" is derived from the Spanish and Portuguese name for a pearl that is rough and irregular in shape.

Bathos and Anticlimax. Bathos is Greek for "depth," and it has been an indispensable term to critics since Alexander Pope, *parodying* the Greek Longinus' famous essay *On the Sublime* (that is, "loftiness"), wrote in 1727 an essay *On Bathos: Of the Art of Sinking in Poetry.* With mock solemnity Pope assures his readers that he undertakes "to lead them as it were by the hand . . . the gentle down-hill way to Bathos; the bottom, the end, the central point, the *non plus ultra,* of true Modern Poesy!" The word ever since has been used for an unintentional descent in literature when, straining to be pathetic or passionate or elevated, the writer overshoots the mark and drops into the trivial or the ridiculous. Among his examples Pope records "the modest request of two absent lovers" in a contemporary poem:

> Ye Gods! annihilate but Space and Time,
> And make two lovers happy.

The slogan "For God, for Country, and for Yale!" is bathetic because it moves to intended **climax** (that is, an ascending sequence of importance) in its rhetorical order and to unintended descent in its reference—at least for someone who is not a Yale student. The greatest of poets sometimes fall unwittingly into the same rhetorical figure. In the early version of *The Prelude* (1805; Book IX), William Wordsworth, after recounting at length the tale of the star-crossed lovers Vaudracour and Julia, tells how Julia died, leaving Vaudracour to raise their infant son:

> It consoled him here
> To attend upon the Orphan and perform
> The office of a Nurse to his young Child
> Which after a short time by some mistake
> Or indiscretion of the Father, died.

"Bathos" is occasionally used to identify a figure of speech employed for a deliberate, rather than unintended, rhetorical effect; but the term "anticlimax" is much more common in this unpejorative application. *The Stuffed Owl: An Anthology of Bad Verse,* ed. D. B. Wyndham Lewis and Charles Lee (rev., 1948), is a rich mine of unintended bathos.

Anticlimax is sometimes used as an equivalent of bathos—the writer aims at rhetorical climax but achieves semantic descent. In a second usage, however, "anticlimax" is non-derogatory, and denotes a writer's deliberate drop from the serious and elevated to the trivial and lowly, in order to achieve an intended comic or satiric effect. Thus Thomas Gray in his *mock-heroic* "Ode on the Death of a Favorite Cat" (1748)—the cat had drowned when she tried to catch a goldfish—gravely inserts the moral observation:

> What female heart can gold despise?
> What cat's averse to fish?

And in *Don Juan* (1819–24; I. ix) Byron thus exemplifies the would-be gallantry of Juan's father:

> A better cavalier ne'er mounted horse,
> Or, being mounted, e'er got down again.

Beat Writers identifies a loose-knit group of poets and novelists, writing in the second half of the 1950s, who shared a set of social attitudes—antiestablishment, antipolitical, anti-intellectual, opposed to reigning cultural and moral values, and in favor of unfettered self-realization and self-expression. "Beat" was used to signify both "beaten down" (that is, by the oppressive culture of the time) and "beatific" (many of the Beat writers cultivated ecstatic states by way of Buddhism, Jewish and Christian mysticism, and/or drugs that induced visionary experiences). The group included such diverse figures as the poets Allen Ginsberg, Gregory Corso, and Lawrence Ferlinghetti and the novelists William Burroughs and Jack Kerouac. Ginsberg's *Howl* (1956) is a central Beat achievement in its breathless, chanted celebration of the down-and-out and the subculture of drug addicts, social misfits, and compulsive wanderers, as well as in its representation of the derangement of the intellect and the senses effected by a combination of sexual abandon, drugged hallucinations, and religious ecstasies. (Compare the vogue of *decadence* in the late nineteenth century.) A representative novel of the movement is Jack Kerouac's *On the Road* (1958). While the Beat movement was short-lived, it left its imprint on the subjects and forms of many writers of the 1960s and 1970s; see *counterculture*.

See Lawrence Lipton, *The Holy Barbarians* (1959); Seymour Krim, ed., *The Beats* (1960); Gregory Stephenson, *The Daybreak Boys: Essays on the Literature of the Beat Generation* (1989).

Biography. Late in the seventeenth century, Dryden defined biography neatly as "the history of particular men's lives." The name now connotes a relatively full account of a person's life, involving the attempt to set forth character, temperament, and milieu, as well as the facts of the subject's activities and experiences.

Both the ancient Greeks and Romans produced short, formal lives of individuals. The most famed surviving example is the *Parallel Lives* of Greek and Roman notables by the Greek writer Plutarch, c. 46–120 A.D.; in the translation by Sir Thomas North in 1579, it was the source of Shakespeare's plays on Roman subjects. Medieval authors wrote generalized chronicles of the deeds of a king, as well as **hagiographies:** the stylized lives of Christian saints, often based much more on pious legends than on fact. In England, the fairly detailed secular biography appeared in the seventeenth century; the greatest instance is Izaak Walton's *Lives* (including short biographies of the poets John Donne and George Herbert), written between 1640 and 1678.

The eighteenth century in England is the age of the distinguished practice of the full-scale biography, and also of the emergence of the theory of biography as a special literary *genre.* It was the century of Samuel Johnson's *Lives of the English Poets* (1779–81) and of James Boswell's *Life of Samuel Johnson* (1791), which many readers hold to be the greatest of all biographies. In our own time it has become one of the most popular of literary forms, and usually there is at least one biographical title high on the best-seller list. The recent increase of interest in notable women has led to a number of biographies of such pioneers of *feminism* as Mary Wollstonecraft in England and Margaret Fuller in America. (See also *psychobiography.*)

Autobiography is a biography written by the subject about himself or herself. It is to be distinguished from the **memoir**, in which the emphasis is not on the author's developing self but on the people and events that the author has known or witnessed, and also from the private **diary** or **journal**, which is a day-to-day record of the events in a person's life, written for personal use and pleasure, with little or no thought of publication. Examples of the latter type are the seventeenth-century diaries of Samuel Pepys and John Evelyn, and the eighteenth-century journals of James Boswell. The first fully developed autobiography is also one of the greatest: the *Confessions* of St. Augustine, written in the fourth century. The design of this profound and subtle **spiritual autobiography** centers on what became the crucial experience in Christian autobiography: the author's anguished mental crisis and a recovery in which he discovers his Christian identity and religious vocation. Some later spiritual histories of the self, like Augustine's, are religious confessions of crisis and conversion such as John Bunyan's *Grace Abounding to the Chief of Sinners* (1666). Others are secular works in which the crisis is resolved by the author's discovery of his identity and vocation, not as a Christian, but as a poet or artist; examples are Wordsworth's autobiography in verse, *The Prelude* (completed 1805, published in revised form 1850), or the partly autobiographical works of prose fiction such as Marcel Proust's *À la recherche du temps perdu* (1913–27) and James Joyce's *Portrait of the Artist as a Young Man* (1915).

Notable American and British autobiographies are those by Benjamin Franklin, John Stuart Mill, Anthony Trollope, Henry Adams, and Sean O'Casey. Among the great achievements of this genre in other languages are Rousseau's *Confessions*, written 1764–70, and Goethe's *Dichtung und Wahrheit* ("Poetry and Truth"), written 1810–31.

On biography: Donald A. Stauffer, *English Biography before 1700* (1930), and *The Art of Biography in Eighteenth-Century England* (1941); Leon Edel, *Literary Biography* (1957); Richard D. Altick, *Lives and Letters: A History of Literary Biography in England and America* (1965); David Novarr, *The Lines of Life: Theories of Biography, 1880–1970* (1986). On autobiography: Wayne

Shumaker, *English Autobiography* (1954); Roy Pascal, *Design and Truth in Autobiography* (1960); Estelle C. Jellinek, ed., *Women's Autobiography: Essays in Criticism* (1980); James Olney, *Metaphors of Self: The Meaning of Autobiography* (1981). John N. Morris, in *Versions of the Self: Studies in English Autobiography from John Bunyan to John Stuart Mill* (1966), deals both with religious and secular spiritual autobiographies. M. H. Abrams, in *Natural Supernaturalism* (1971), narrates the history of spiritual autobiography and the wide ramifications of the form in philosophy and literature, as well as the autobiographical genre itself.

Blank Verse consists of lines of *iambic pentameter* (five-stress iambic verse) which are unrhymed—hence the term "blank." Of all English verse forms it is closest to the natural rhythms of English speech, yet flexible and adaptive to diverse levels of discourse; as a result it has been more frequently and variously used than any other type of versification. Soon after blank verse was introduced by the Earl of Surrey in his translations of Books 2 and 4 of Virgil's *The Aeneid* (about 1540), it became the standard meter for Elizabethan and later poetic drama; a free form of blank verse is still the medium in such recent verse plays as those by Maxwell Anderson and T. S. Eliot. John Milton used blank verse for his epic *Paradise Lost* (1667), James Thomson for his descriptive and philosophical *Seasons* (1726–30), William Wordsworth for his autobiographical *Prelude* (1805), Alfred, Lord Tennyson for the narrative *Idylls of the King* (1891), Robert Browning for *The Ring and the Book* (1868–69) and many dramatic monologues, and T. S. Eliot for much of *The Waste Land* (1922). A large number of meditative lyrics, from the *Romantic Period* to the present, have also been written in blank verse, including Coleridge's "Frost at Midnight," Wordsworth's "Tintern Abbey," Tennyson's "Tears, Idle Tears" (in which the blank verse is divided into five-line stanzas), and Wallace Stevens' "Sunday Morning."

Divisions in blank verse poems, used to set off a sustained passage, are called **verse paragraphs.** See, for example, the great verse paragraph of twenty-six lines which initiates Milton's *Paradise Lost,* beginning with "Of man's first disobedience" and ending with "And justify the ways of God to men," or the opening verse paragraph of twenty-two lines in Wordsworth's "Tintern Abbey" (1798).

See *meter,* and refer to Moody Prior's critical study of blank verse in *The Language of Tragedy* (1964).

Bombast denotes a verbose and inflated diction that is greatly disproportionate to the matter that it signifies. The high style of even so fine a poet as Christopher Marlowe is at times inappropriate to its sense, as when Faustus declares (*Dr. Faustus,* 1604; III. i. 47 ff.):

> Now by the kingdoms of infernal rule,
> Of Styx, Acheron, and the fiery lake
> Of ever-burning Phlegethon I swear
> That I do long to see the monuments
> And situation of bright-splendent Rome;

which is to say: "By Hades, I'd like to see Rome!" Bombast is a frequent component in the *heroic drama* of the late seventeenth and early eighteenth centuries. The pompous language of that drama is parodied in Henry Fielding's *Tom Thumb the Great* (1731), as in the famous opening of Act II. v, in which the diminutive male lover cries:

> Oh! Huncamunca, Huncamunca, oh!
> Thy pouting breasts, like kettle-drums of brass,
> Beat everlasting loud alarms of joy;
> As bright as brass they are, and oh! as hard;
> Oh! Huncamunca, Huncamunca, oh!

Fielding points out in a note that this parody was inspired by James Thomson's lines in *The Tragedy of Sophonisba* (1730):

> Oh! Sophonisba, Sophonisba, oh!
> Oh! Narva, Narva, oh!

"Bombast" originally meant "cotton stuffing," and in Elizabethan times became used as a metaphor for an over-elaborate style.

Bowdlerize. To expurgate from an edition of a literary work passages considered by the editor to be indecent or indelicate. The word derives from the Reverend Thomas Bowdler, who tidied up his *Family Shakespeare* in 1815 by omitting, as he put it, "whatever is unfit to be read by a gentleman in a company of ladies." Jonathan Swift's *Gulliver's Travels* (1726), Shakespeare's plays, and *The Arabian Nights* are often bowdlerized in editions intended for the young, and until recent decades, when the standards of propriety were drastically liberalized, some compilers of anthologies for college students availed themselves of Bowdler's prerogative in editing Chaucer.

Burlesque has been succinctly defined as "an incongruous imitation"; that is, it imitates the manner (the form and style) or else the matter of a serious literary work or of a literary *genre*, but makes the imitation amusing by a ridiculous disparity between the manner and the subject matter. The burlesque may be written for the sheer fun of it; usually, however, it is a form of *satire*. The butt of the satiric ridicule may be the particular work or the genre that is being imitated, or else the subject matter to which the imitation is incongruously applied, or (often) both of these together.

"Burlesque," "parody," and "travesty" are sometimes applied interchangeably; simply to equate these terms, however, is to surrender useful critical distinctions. It is better to follow the critics who use "burlesque" as the generic name and use the other terms to discriminate species of burlesque. The application of these terms will be clearer if we make two preliminary distinctions: (1) In a burlesque imitation, the form and style may be either lower or higher in level and dignity than the subject to which it is incongruously applied. (See the discussion of levels under *style*.) If the form and style are elevated but the subject is low or trivial, we have "high burlesque;" if the subject is high in status and dignified but the style and manner of treatment are low and undignified, we have "low burlesque." (2) A burlesque may also be distinguished according to whether it imitates a general type or genre, or a particular work or author. Applying these two distinctions, we get the following species of burlesque.

I   Varieties of high burlesque:

1)   A **mock epic** or **mock-heroic** poem imitates the elaborate form and ceremonious style of the *epic* genre, but applies it to a commonplace or trivial subject matter. In a masterpiece of this type, *The Rape of the Lock* (1714), Alexander Pope views through the grandiose epic perspective a quarrel between the belles and elegants of his day over the theft of a lady's curl. The story includes such elements of traditional epic protocol as supernatural *machinery,* a voyage on board ship, a visit to the underworld, and a heroically scaled battle between the sexes—although with metaphors, hatpins, and snuff for weapons. The term *mock-heroic* is often applied to other dignified poetic forms which are purposely mismatched to a lowly subject; for example, to Thomas Gray's comic "Ode on the Death of a Favorite Cat" (1748); see under *bathos and anticlimax.*

2)   A **parody** imitates the serious manner and characteristic features of a particular literary work, or the distinctive style of a particular author, or the typical stylistic and other features of a serious literary genre, and applies the imitation to a lowly or comically inappropriate subject. John Phillips' "The Splendid Shilling" (1705) parodied the epic style of John Milton's *Paradise Lost* (1667) by exaggerating its high formality and applying it to the description of a tattered poet composing in a drafty attic. Henry Fielding in *Joseph Andrews* (1742) parodied Samuel Richardson's novel *Pamela* (1740–41) by putting a hearty male hero in place of Richardson's sexually beleaguered heroine. Here is Hartley Coleridge's parody of the first stanza of William Wordsworth's "She Dwelt among the Untrodden Ways," which he applies to Wordsworth himself:

> He lived amidst th' untrodden ways
> To Rydal Lake that lead,
> A bard whom there were none to praise,
> And very few to read.

From the early nineteenth century to the present, parody has been the favorite form of burlesque. Among the gifted parodists of the present century have been Max Beerbohm in England (see his *A Christmas Garland,* 1912) and such American writers for *The New Yorker* as James Thurber, Robert Benchley, and E. B. White.

II   Varieties of low burlesque:

1)   The **Hudibrastic poem** takes its name from Samuel Butler's *Hudibras* (1663), which satirized rigid Puritanism by describing the adventures of a Puritan knight, Sir Hudibras. Instead of the doughty deeds and dignified style of the traditional genre of the *chivalric romance,* however, we find the knightly hero experiencing mundane and humiliating misadventures which are described in *doggerel* verses and a ludicrously colloquial idiom.

2)   The **travesty** mocks a particular work by treating its lofty subject in a jocular and grotesquely undignified manner and style. As Boileau put it,

describing a travesty of Virgil's *Aeneid,* "Dido and Aeneas are made to speak like fishwives and ruffians."

The term **lampoon** is applied to a short satirical work, or to a passage in a longer work, which describes the appearance and character of a particular person in a way that makes them ridiculous. It typically employs **caricature,** which in a verbal description (as in graphic art) exaggerates or distorts, for comic effect, a person's distinctive physical features or other characteristics. John Dryden's *Absalom and Achitophel* (1681) includes a famed twenty-five-line lampoon of Zimri (Dryden's contemporary the Duke of Buckingham), which begins:

> In the first rank of these did Zimri stand;
> A man so various, that he seemed to be
> Not one, but all mankind's epitome:
> Stiff in opinions, always in the wrong;
> Was everything by starts, and nothing long. . . .

The modern sense of "burlesque" as a theater form derives, historically, from plays which mocked serious types of drama by an incongruous imitation. John Gay's *Beggar's Opera* (1728)—which in turn became the model for the German *Threepenny Opera,* by Bertolt Brecht and Kurt Weill (1928)—was a high burlesque of Italian opera, applying its dignified formulas to a company of beggars and thieves; a number of the musical plays by Gilbert and Sullivan in the Victorian era also burlesqued grand opera.

George Kitchin, *A Survey of Burlesque and Parody in English* (1931); Richmond P. Bond, *English Burlesque Poetry, 1700-1750* (1932). Anthologies: Walter Jerrold and R. M. Leonard, eds., *A Century of Parody and Imitation* (1913); Robert P. Falk, ed., *The Antic Muse: American Writers in Parody* (1955); Dwight MacDonald, ed., *Parodies: An Anthology* (1960).

Canon of Literature. The Greek word "kanon," signifying a measuring rod or a rule, was extended to denote a list or catalogue, then came to be applied to the list of books in the Hebrew Bible and the New Testament which were designated by church authorities as comprising the genuine Holy Scriptures. A number of writings related to those in the Scriptures, but not admitted into the canon, are called **apocrypha;** eleven books which have been included in the Roman Catholic biblical canon are considered apocryphal by Protestants.

The term "canon" was later used in a literary application, to signify the list of secular works accepted by experts as genuinely written by a particular author. We speak thus of "the Chaucer canon" and "the Shakespeare canon," and refer to other works that have sometimes been attributed to an author, but on evidence judged to be inadequate or invalid, as "apocryphal." In recent decades the phrase **literary canon** has come to designate—in world literature, or in European literature, but most frequently in a national literature—those authors who, by a cumulative consensus of critics, scholars, and teachers, have come to be widely recognized as "major," and to have written works often hailed as literary *classics*. These canonical writers are the ones which, at a given time, are most kept in print, most frequently and fully discussed by literary critics and historians, and most likely to be included in anthologies and taught in college courses with titles such as "World Masterpieces," "Major English Authors," or "Great American Writers."

The use of the term "canon" with reference both to the Bible and to secular writings obscures important differences in the two applications. The biblical canon has been established by church authorities vested with the power to make such a decision, and is enforced by authorities with the power to impose religious sanctions; the canonical list is explicit and closed, permitting no deletions or additions; and the interpretation of many crucial passages in the canonical books is limited by the established creed of a particular church or sect. The canon of literature, on the other hand, emerges by way of a gradual and unofficial consensus; it is tacit rather than explicit, very loose-boundaried, and subject to changes in its inclusions; while the texts in the canon are open to, and constantly subjected to, diverse and often conflicting interpretations and evaluations.

The social process by which an author comes to be tacitly and durably recognized as canonical is called "canon formation." The factors in this formative process are complex and disputed. It seems clear, however, that the process involves, among other things, the wide concurrence of critics, scholars, and authors with diverse viewpoints and sensibilities; the persistent influence of, and reference to, an author in the work of other authors; the frequent reference to an author within the discourse of a cultural community; and the widespread assignment of an author or text in school and college curricula. Such factors are of course mutually interactive, and they need to be sustained over a period of time. In his "Preface to Shakespeare" (1765) Samuel Johnson said that a century is "the term commonly fixed as a test of literary merit." It seems, however, that some authors who wrote within the present century such as Marcel Proust, Franz Kafka, Thomas Mann, and James Joyce—perhaps even a writer so recent as Vladimir Nabokov—already have achieved the prestige, influence, and persistence of reference in literary discourse to establish them in the European canon; others, including Yeats, T. S. Eliot, Virginia Woolf, and Robert Frost seem already secure in their national canons, at least.

At any time, the boundaries of a canon remain indefinite, while inside those boundaries some authors are central and others marginal. Occasionally an earlier author who was for long on the fringe of the canon, or even outside it, gets transferred to a position of eminence. A conspicuous recent example was John Donne, who from the eighteenth century on was regarded mainly as an interestingly eccentric poet. T. S. Eliot, followed by Cleanth Brooks and other *New Critics* in the 1930s and later, made Donne's writings the very paradigm of the self-ironic and paradoxical poetry they most admired, and so helped elevate him to prominence in the English canon. (See *metaphysical poets*.) Once firmly established as a central figure, an author shows considerable resistance to being disestablished by adverse criticism and changing literary preferences. For example many New Critics, together with the influential F. R. Leavis in England, while lauding Donne, vigorously attacked the Romantic poet Shelley as embodying the poetic qualities they strongly condemned; but although a considerable number of critics joined in this derogation of Shelley, the long-term effect was to aggrandize the critical attention and discussion, whether in praise or dispraise, that helps sustain the place of an author in the canon.

Discussions of the process of canon formation, and opposition to established literary canons, have recently become a leading concern in critics of diverse viewpoints, whether deconstructive, feminist, Marxist, or new-historicist (see *poststructuralism*). The debate often focuses on the practical issue of what books to assign in college curricula, especially in required "core courses" in the humanities and in Western civilization. A widespread charge is that the standard canon of great books, not only in literature but in all areas of *humanistic* study, has been formed in accordance with the *ideology* and political interests and values of an élite and privileged class that was white, male, and European, with the result that the canon consists mainly of works that manifest racism, *patriarchy*, and imperialism, and either marginalize or exclude the interests and accomplishments of Blacks, Hispanics, and other ethnic minorities, of women, of the working class, of popular culture, of homosexuals, and of non-European civilizations. The frequent demand is "to open the canon" so as to make it *multicultural* instead of "Eurocentered" and to make it represent adequately the concerns and literary achievements of women and of ethnic, non-heterosexual, and other minority groups. Another demand is that the standard canon be stripped of its élitism and its "hierarchism"—that is, its built-in discriminations between works that are better or worse, higher or lower—in order to include such cultural products as everyday Hollywood films, television serials, popular songs, and fiction written for a mass audience. There is also a radical wing of revisionist theorists who, on behalf of the political aim to transform the existing power-structures, demand not merely the opening, but the abolition of the standard canon and its replacement by hitherto marginal and excluded groups and texts.

The views of defenders of the standard canon, like those of its attackers, range from moderate to extreme. The position of many moderate defenders might be summarized as follows. Whatever has been the influence of class, gender, and other special interests in forming the existing canon, this is far from the whole story. The canon is the result of the concurrence of a great many (often unexpressed) norms and standards, and among these, one crucial factor has been the high intellectual and artistic quality of the canonical works themselves and their attested power to appeal to widely shared and lasting human concerns and values. Moderate defenders agree to the desirability of enlarging the canon of texts that are required or assigned frequently in academic courses in order to make it more broadly representative of diverse ethnic groups, classes, and interests, while pointing out that this would not be a drastic innovation, since the educational canon has constantly been subject to deletions and additions. They emphasize that the existing Western, English, and American canons include strong advocates and exemplars of skepticism about established ways of thinking, self-criticism, political radicalism, and the toleration of dissent—aspects of the accepted canons of which the present theorists and proponents of change are, clearly, both the inheritors and the beneficiaries. And however a canon is enlarged to represent other cultures and classes, moderate defenders insist on the indispensability of a continuing scrutiny of and dialogue with the diverse and long-lasting works of intellect and imagination that have shaped Western civilization and constitute much of Western culture. They also remark that many theorists who challenge the traditional literary canon, when they turn from theory to applied criticism, attend preponderantly to established major authors—above all Shakespeare, as well as Spenser, Milton, Jane Austen, Wordsworth, George Eliot, and many others—and so recognize and confirm in practice the canon that they in theory oppose.

Discussions of the nature and formation of the literary canon: the collection of essays edited by Robert von Hallberg, *Canons* (1984); John Guillory, "Canon," in *Critical Terms for Literary Study,* ed. Frank Lentricchia and Thomas McLaughlin (1990); and Wendell V. Harris, "Canonicity," *PMLA,* 106 (1991), pp. 110–21. Questioners or opponents of the traditional canon: Leslie A. Fiedler and Houston A. Baker, Jr., eds., *English Literature: Opening Up the Canon* (1981); Jane Tompkins, *Sensational Designs: The Cultural Work of American Fiction, 1790-1860* (1985); Jonathan Culler, *Framing the Sign: Criticism and Its Institutions* (1988), Chapter 2, "The Humanities Tomorrow;" and Darryl L. Gless and Barbara H. Smith, eds., *The Politics of Liberal Education* (1990). Defenses of the traditional canon: Frank Kermode, "Prologue" to *An Appetite for Poetry* (1989); and the contributors to *The Changing Culture of the University,* a special issue of *Partisan Review* (Spring 1991).

Carpe Diem, meaning "seize the day," is a Latin phrase from one of Horace's *Odes* (I. xi) which has become the name for a very common literary *motif,* especially in lyric poetry. The speaker in a carpe diem poem emphasizes that life is short and time is fleeting in order to enjoin his auditor—who is often represented as a virgin reluctant to change her state—to make the most of present pleasures. A frequent emblem of the brevity of physical beauty and the finality of death is the rose, as in Edmund Spenser's *The Faerie Queene,* 1590–96 (II. xii. 74–75: "Gather therefore the Rose, whilst yet is prime"), and in the seventeenth century, Robert Herrick's "To the Virgins, to Make Much of Time" ("Gather ye rosebuds, while ye may") and Edmund Waller's "Go, Lovely Rose." The more complex poems of this kind communicate the poignant sadness—or else desperation—of the pursuit of pleasures under the sentence of inevitable death; see Andrew Marvell's "To His Coy Mistress" (1681) and the set of variations on the carpe diem motif *The Rubáiyát of Omar Khayyám* by the Victorian poet Edward FitzGerald. In 1747 the early *feminist* Lady Mary Wortley Montagu wrote "The Lover: A Ballad," a brilliant counter to the carpe diem poems written by male poets, in which the woman explains to her importunate lover why she finds him utterly resistible.

Celtic Revival, also known as the **Irish Literary Renaissance,** identifies the very creative period in Irish literature from about 1885 to the death of William Butler Yeats in 1939. The aim of Yeats and other early leaders of the movement was to create a distinctively national literature by going back to Irish history, legend, and folklore, as well as to native literary models. The major writers, however, wrote not in the native Irish (one of the Celtic languages) but in English, and under the influence of various non-Irish literary forms; a number of them also turned increasingly for their subject matter to modern Irish life rather than to the ancient past.

Notable poets in addition to Yeats were AE (George Russell) and Oliver St. John Gogarty. The dramatists included Yeats himself, as well as Lady Gregory (who was also an important patron and publicist for the movement), John Millington Synge, and later Sean O'Casey. Among the novelists were George Moore and James Stephens, as well as James Joyce, who, although he abandoned Ireland for Europe and ridiculed some of the excesses of the nationalist writers, adverted to Irish subject matter and characters in all his writings. As these names indicate, the Celtic Revival produced some of the greatest poetry, drama, and prose fiction written in English during the first four decades of the twentieth century.

See E. A. Boyd, *Ireland's Literary Renaissance* (1916, rev. 1922); Herbert Howarth, *The Irish Writers* (1958); Phillip L. Marcus, *Yeats and the Beginning of the Irish Renaissance* (1970), and "The Celtic Revival: Literature and the Theater," in *The Irish World: The History and Cultural Achievements of the Irish People* (1977).

Character and Characterization. (1) **The character** is the name of a literary *genre;* it is a short, and usually witty, sketch in prose of a distinctive type of person. The genre was inaugurated by Theophrastus, a Greek author of the second century B.C., who wrote a lively book called *Characters.* The form had a great vogue in the earlier seventeenth century; the books of characters then written by Joseph Hall, Sir Thomas Overbury, and John Earle influenced later writers of the essay, history, and fiction. The titles of some of Overbury's sketches will indicate the nature of the form: "A Courtier," "A Wise Man," "A Fair and Happy Milkmaid." See Richard Aldington's anthology *A Book of "Characters"* (1924).

(2) **Characters** are the persons presented in a dramatic or narrative work, who are interpreted by the reader as being endowed with moral, dispositional, and emotional qualities that are expressed in what they say—the **dialogue**—and by what they do—the **action.** The grounds in the characters' temperament, desires, and moral nature for their speech and actions are called their **motivation.** A character may remain essentially "stable," or unchanged in outlook and disposition, from beginning to end of a work (Prospero in *The Tempest,* Micawber in Charles Dickens' *David Copperfield,* 1849–50), or may undergo a radical change, either through a gradual process of motivation and development (the title character in Jane Austen's *Emma,* 1816) or as the result of a crisis (Shakespeare's *King Lear,* Pip in Dickens' *Great Expectations*). Whether a character remains stable or changes, the

reader of a traditional and realistic work expects "consistency"—the character should not suddenly break off and act in a way not plausibly grounded in his or her temperament as we have already come to know it.

E. M. Forster, in *Aspects of the Novel* (1927), introduced popular new terms for an old distinction by discriminating between flat and round characters. A **flat character** (also called a **type**, or "two-dimensional"), Forster says, is built around "a single idea or quality" and is presented without much individualizing detail, and therefore can be fairly adequately described in a single phrase or sentence. A **round character** is complex in temperament and motivation and is represented with subtle particularity; such a character therefore is as difficult to describe with any adequacy as a person in real life, and like real persons, is capable of surprising us. Almost all dramas and narratives, properly enough, have some characters who serve merely as functionaries and are not characterized at all, as well as other characters who are left relatively flat: there is no need, in Shakespeare's *Henry IV, Part I,* for Mistress Quickly to be as globular as Falstaff. The degree to which, in order to be regarded as artistically successful, characters need to be three-dimensional depends on their function in the plot; in many types of narrative, such as in the detective story or adventure novel or farce comedy, even the protagonist usually is two-dimensional. Sherlock Holmes and Long John Silver do not require, for their own excellent literary roles, the roundness of a Hamlet, a Becky Sharp, or a Jay Gatsby. In his *Anatomy of Criticism* (1957), Northrop Frye has proposed that even lifelike characters are identifiable variants, more or less individualized, of stock types that were inherited from old literary genres; examples in the comic genre are the self-deprecating "eiron," the boastful "alazon," and the "senex iratus," or choleric old father. (See *stock characters.*)

A broad distinction is frequently made between alternative methods for **characterizing** (i.e., establishing the distinctive characters of) the persons in a narrative: showing and telling. In **showing** (also called "the dramatic method"), the author presents the characters talking and acting and leaves the reader to infer what motives and dispositions lie behind what they say and do. In **telling**, the author intervenes authoritatively in order to describe, and often to evaluate, the motives and dispositional qualities of the characters. For example, in the terse and splendid opening chapter of *Pride and Prejudice* (1813), Jane Austen first shows us Mr. and Mrs. Bennet as they talk to one another about the young man who has just rented Netherfield Park, then (in the quotation below) tells us about them, and so confirms and expands the inferences that the reader has already begun to make from what has been shown.

> Mr. Bennet was so odd a mixture of quick parts, sarcastic humour, reserve, and caprice, that the experience of three-and-twenty years had been insufficient to make his wife understand his character. *Her* mind was less difficult to develop. She was a woman of mean understanding, little information, and uncertain temper.

Especially since the novelistic theory and practice of Flaubert and Henry James, a critical tendency has been to consider "telling" a violation of artistry and to recommend only the technique of "showing" characters; authors, it is often said, should totally efface themselves in order to write "objectively," "impersonally," or "dramatically." Such judgments, however, glorify a modern kind of artistic limitation which is suited to particular novelistic effects, and decry an alternative method of characterization which all the greatest novelists, until recently, have employed to produce masterpieces. (See *point of view.*)

Innovative writers in the present century—including novelists from James Joyce to French writers of the *new novel,* and authors of the dramas and novels of the *absurd* and other experimental forms—often present the persons in their works in ways which run counter to the earlier way of presenting them so that they will be apprehended by readers as lifelike characters who manifest in what they say and do a consistent substructure of individuality. Recent structuralist critics have undertaken to dissolve even the lifelike characters of traditional realistic novels into a system of literary conventions and codes which are *naturalized* by the readers; that is, readers project lifelikeness upon them by assimilating them to their prior conceptions of individuals in real life. The readers' prior conceptions, and the resulting interpretations of the convincing lifelikeness of literary characters, however, are in turn analyzed by a thoroughgoing structuralist as consisting of nothing more than intersections, or "nodes," of cultural stereotypes and conventions. See *structuralist criticism* and *text and writing (écriture),* and refer to Jonathan Culler, *Structuralist Poetics* (1975), Chapter 9, "Poetics of the Novel."

Refer to *plot.* On the traditional problems and methods of characterization, including discussions of showing and telling, see in addition to E. M. Forster (above), Percy Lubbock, *The Craft of Fiction* (1926); Wayne C. Booth, *The Rhetoric of Fiction* (1961), especially Chapters 1–4; W. J. Harvey, *Character and the Novel* (1966); Robert Scholes and Robert Kellogg, *The Nature of Narrative* (1966).

Chivalric Romance (or **medieval romance**) is a narrative form which developed in twelfth-century France, spread to the literatures of other countries, and displaced the various *epic* and heroic forms of narrative. ("Romance" originally signified a work written in the French language, which evolved from a dialect of the Roman language, Latin.) Romances were at first written in verse, but later in prose as well. The **romance** is distinguished from the epic in that it represents, not a heroic age of tribal wars, but a courtly and chivalric age, often one of highly developed manners and civility. Its standard plot is that of a quest undertaken by a single knight in order to gain a lady's favor; frequently its central interest is *courtly love,* together with tournaments fought and dragons and monsters slain for the damsel's sake; it stresses the chivalric ideals of courage, loyalty, honor, mercifulness to an opponent, and exquisite and elaborate manners; and it delights in wonders and marvels. Supernatural events in the epic had their causes in the will and actions of the gods; romance shifts the supernatural to this world, and makes much of the mysterious effect of magic, spells, and enchantments.

The recurrent materials of medieval romances have been divided by scholars into four classes of subjects: (1) "The Matter of Britain" (that is, Celtic subject matter, especially stories centering on the court of King Arthur); (2) "The Matter of Rome" (stories based on the history and legends of classical antiquity, including the exploits of Alexander the Great and of the heroes of the Trojan War); (3) "The Matter of France" (Charlemagne and his knights); and (4) "The Matter of England" (concerned with heroes such as King Horn and Guy of Warwick). The cycle of tales which developed around the pseudohistorical British King Arthur produced many of the finest romances, some of them (stories of Sir Perceval and the quest for the Holy Grail) with a religious instead of a purely secular interest. Chrétien de Troyes, the great twelfth-century French poet, wrote Arthurian romances; *Sir Gawain and the Green Knight* is a superb **metrical romance** (that is, a romance written in verse) about an Arthurian knight, composed in fourteenth-century England; and Thomas Malory's *Morte d'Arthur* (fifteenth century) is an English version in prose of the cycle of earlier metrical romances about Arthur and his Knights of the Round Table.

See *prose romance,* and refer to W. P. Ker, *Epic and Romance* (1897); L. A. Hibbard, *Medieval Romance in England* (rev., 1961); R. S. Loomis, *The Development of Arthurian Romance* (1963), and *The Grail* (1963); and the anthology *Medieval Romances,* ed. R. S. and L. H. Loomis (1957). For modern adaptations and extensions of the concept of the romance genre, see *myth critics;* also Eleanor T. Lincoln, *Pastoral and Romance: Modern Essays in Criticism* (1969).

Chorus. Among the ancient Greeks the chorus was a group of people, wearing masks, who sang or chanted verse while performing dancelike maneuvers at religious festivals. A similar chorus played a part in Greek tragedies, where (in the plays of Aeschylus and Sophocles) they served mainly as commentators on the characters and events who expressed traditional moral, religious, and social attitudes; beginning with Euripides, however, the chorus assumed primarily a lyrical function. The Greek ode, as developed by Pindar, was also chanted by a chorus; see *ode.*

Roman playwrights such as Seneca took over the chorus from the Greeks, and in the mid-sixteenth century some English dramatists (for example, Norton and Sackville in *Gorbuduc*) imitated the Senecan chorus. The classical type of chorus was never widely adopted by English dramatic writers. John Milton, however, included a chorus in *Samson Agonistes* (1671), Shelley in *Prometheus Unbound* (1820), and Thomas Hardy in *The Dynasts* (1904–08); more recently, T. S. Eliot made effective use of the classical chorus in his religious tragedy *Murder in the Cathedral* (1935).

During the Elizabethan Age the term "chorus" was applied also to a single person who spoke the prologue and epilogue to a play, and sometimes introduced each act as well. This character served as the author's vehicle for commentary on the play, as well as for exposition of its subject, time, and setting, and of events happening offstage; see Christopher Marlowe's *Dr.*

Faustus and Shakespeare's *Henry V.* In Shakespeare's *Winter's Tale*, the fifth act begins with "Time, the Chorus," who asks the audience that they "impute it not a crime / To me or my swift passage that I slide / O'er sixteen years" since preceding events, then summarizes what has happened during those years and announces that the setting for this present act is Bohemia. A modern and extended use of a chorus in this sense is the Stage Manager in Thornton Wilder's *Our Town* (1938).

Modern scholars use the term **choral character** to refer to a person within the play itself who stands largely apart from the action and by his comments provides the audience with a special perspective (often an *ironic* perspective) through which to view the other characters and events. Examples in Shakespeare are the Fool in *King Lear*, Enobarbus in *Antony and Cleopatra*, and Thersites in *Troilus and Cressida*; a modern instance is Seth Beckwith in O'Neill's *Mourning Becomes Electra* (1931). "Choral character" is sometimes applied also to one or more persons in a novel who represent the point of view of a community or of a cultural group, and so provide norms by which to judge other characters and what they do; instances are Thomas Hardy's peasants and the old Black women in some of William Faulkner's novels.

For the alternative use of the term "chorus" to signify a recurrent stanza in a song, see *refrain.* Refer to A. W. Pickard-Cambridge, *Dithyramb, Tragedy and Comedy* (1927), and *The Dramatic Festivals of Athens* (1953); T. B. L. Webster, *Greek Theater Production* (1956).

Chronicle. Chronicles, the predecessors of modern histories, were accounts, in prose or verse, of national or worldwide events over a considerable period of time. If the chronicles deal with events year by year, they are often called **annals.** Unlike the modern historian, most chroniclers tended to take their information as they found it, and made little attempt to separate fact from legend. The most important English chronicles are the *Anglo-Saxon Chronicle*, started by King Alfred in the ninth century and continued until the twelfth century, and the *Chronicles of England, Scotland, and Ireland* (1577–87) by Raphael Holinshed and other writers; the latter documents were important sources of materials for Elizabethan drama.

Chronicle Plays were dramatic works based on the historical materials in the English *Chronicles* by Raphael Holinshed and others. They achieved high popularity late in the sixteenth century, when the patriotic fervor following the defeat of the Spanish Armada in 1588 fostered a demand for plays dealing with English history. The early chronicle plays presented a loosely knit series of events during the reign of an English king and depended for effect mainly on a bustle of stage battles, pageantry, and spectacle. Christopher Marlowe, however, in his *Edward II* (1592) selected and rearranged materials from Holinshed's *Chronicles* to compose a unified drama of character, and Shakespeare's series of chronicle plays, encompassing the succession of English kings from Richard II to Henry VIII, includes such major artistic achievements as *Richard II, Henry IV, Parts 1 and 2*, and *Henry V.*

The Elizabethan chronicle plays are often called **history plays.** This latter term is also applied more broadly to any drama based mainly on historical materials, such as Shakespeare's Roman plays *Julius Caesar* and *Antony and Cleopatra,* and including such recent examples as Arthur Miller's *The Crucible* (1953), which treats the Salem witch trials of 1692, and Robert Bolt's *A Man for All Seasons* (1962), about the sixteenth-century judge, author, and martyr Sir Thomas More.

E. M. Tillyard, *Shakespeare's History Plays* (1946); Lily B. Campbell, *Shakespeare's "Histories"* (1947); Irving Ribner, *The English History Play in the Age of Shakespeare* (rev., 1965); Max M. Reese, *The Cease of Majesty: A Study of Shakespeare's History Plays* (1962). For a recent *new-historicist* treatment of Shakespeare's *Henry IV, 1 and 2* and *Henry V,* see Stephen Greenblatt, "Invisible Bullets," in *Political Shakespeare: New Essays in Cultural Materialism,* ed. Jonathan Dollimore and Alan Sinfield (1985).

Cliché, which is French for the stereotype used in printing, signifies an expression which deviates enough from ordinary usage to call attention to itself and has been used so often that it is felt to be hackneyed or cloying. "I beg your pardon" or "sincerely yours" are standard usages which do not call attention to themselves; but "point with pride," "my better half," "the eternal verities," and "lock, stock, and barrel" are accounted as clichés, as are indiscriminate uses in ordinary talk of terms taken from specialized vocabularies such as "alienation," "identity crisis," and "interface." Some clichés are foreign phrases which are used as an arch or elegant equivalent for a common English term ("aqua pura," "terra firma"); others are hackneyed literary echoes. "The cup that cheers" is an inaccurate quotation from William Cowper's *The Task* (1785), referring to tea—"the cups / That cheer but not inebriate."

> Come, and trip it as you go
> On the light fantastic toe

was charming in John Milton's "L'Allegro," but "to trip the light fantastic" has by now become a hackneyed substitute for "to dance." In his *Essay on Criticism* (II, ll. 350 ff.) Alexander Pope comments satirically on some clichés which early eighteenth-century **poetasters** (untalented pretenders to the poetic art) used in order to eke out their rhymes:

> Where'er you find "the cooling western breeze,"
> In the next line it "whispers through the trees";
>
> If crystal streams "with pleasing murmurs creep,"
> The reader's threatened (not in vain) with "sleep."

See Eric Partridge, *A Dictionary of Clichés* (4th ed., 1950).

Comedy. In the most common literary application, a comedy is a work in which the materials are selected and managed primarily in order to interest, involve, and amuse us: the characters and their discomfitures engage our pleasurable attention rather than our profound concern, we are made to feel confident that no great disaster will occur, and usually the action turns out happily for the chief characters. The term "comedy" is customarily applied only to plays for the stage or to motion pictures; it should be noted, however, that the comic form, so defined, also occurs in prose fiction and narrative poetry.

Within the very broad spectrum of dramatic comedy, the following types are frequently distinguished:

1) **Romantic comedy** was developed by Shakespeare on the model of contemporary *prose romances* such as Thomas Lodge's *Rosalynde* (1590), the source of Shakespeare's *As You Like It* (1599). Such comedy represents a love affair that involves a beautiful and engaging heroine (sometimes disguised as a man); the course of this love does not run smooth, yet overcomes all difficulties to end in a happy union. Many of the boy-meets-girl plots of later writers are instances of romantic comedy. In *The Anatomy of Criticism* (1957), Northrop Frye points out that some of Shakespeare's romantic comedies manifest a movement from the normal world of conflict and trouble into "the green world"—the Forest of Arden in *As You Like It,* or the fairy-haunted wood of *A Midsummer Night's Dream*—in which the problems and injustices of the ordinary world are dissolved, enemies reconciled, and true lovers united. Frye regards that phenomenon (together with other aspects of these comedies, such as their festive conclusion in the social ritual of a wedding, a feast, a dance) as evidence that comic plots reflect primitive myths and rituals that celebrated the victory of spring over winter. (See *archetypal criticism.*)

2) **Satiric comedy** ridicules political policies or philosophical doctrines, or else attacks deviations from the social order by making ridiculous the violators of its standards of morals or manners. (See *satire.*) The early master of satiric comedy was the Greek Aristophanes, c. 450–c. 385 B.C., whose plays mocked political, philosophical, and literary matters of his age. Shakespeare's contemporary, Ben Jonson, wrote satiric or (as it is often called) "corrective comedy." In his *Volpone* and *The Alchemist,* for example, the greed and ingenuity of one or more intelligent but rascally swindlers, and the equal greed but stupid gullibility of their victims, are made grotesquely or repulsively ludicrous rather than lightly amusing.

3) The **comedy of manners** originated in the **New Comedy** of the Greek Menander, c. 342–292 B.C. (as distinguished from the **Old Comedy** represented by Aristophanes), and was developed by the Roman dramatists Plautus and Terence in the third and second centuries B.C. Their plays dealt with the vicissitudes of young lovers and included what became the *stock characters* of much later comedy, such as the clever servant, old and stodgy parents, and the wealthy rival. The English comedy of manners was early exemplified by Shakespeare's *Love's Labour's Lost* and *Much Ado about Nothing,* and was given a high polish in **Restoration comedy** (1660–1700). The Restoration form owes much to the brilliant dramas of the French writer Molière, 1622–73. It deals with the relations and intrigues of men and women living in a sophisticated upper-class society, and relies for comic effect in large part on the wit and sparkle of the dialogue—often in the form of *repartee,* a witty conversational give-and-take which constitutes a kind of verbal fencing match—and to a lesser degree, on the violations of social conventions and decorum by would-be wits, jealous husbands, conniving rivals, and foppish dandies. Excellent examples are William Congreve's *The Way of the World* and William Wycherley's *The Country Wife*. A middle-class reaction against the immorality of situation and what came to be considered the indecency of dialogue in the courtly Restoration comedy resulted in the *sentimental comedy* of the eighteenth century. In the latter part of the century, however, Oliver Goldsmith (*She Stoops to Conquer*) and his contemporary Richard Brinsley Sheridan (*The Rivals* and *A School for Scandal*) revived the wit and gaiety, but deleted the indecency, of Restoration comedy. The comedy of manners lapsed in the early nineteenth century, but was revived by many skillful practitioners, from A. W. Pinero and Oscar Wilde (*The Importance of Being Earnest,* 1895), through George Bernard Shaw and Noel Coward, to Neil Simon, Alan Ayckbourn, Wendy Wasserstein, and other writers of the present era.

4) **Farce** is a type of comedy designed to provoke the audience to simple, hearty laughter—"belly laughs," in the parlance of the theater. To do so it commonly employs highly exaggerated or caricatured types of characters, puts them into improbable and ludicrous situations, and makes free use of sexual mix-ups, broad verbal humor, and physical bustle and horseplay. Farce was a component in the comic episodes in medieval *miracle plays,* such as the Wakefield plays "Noah" and the "Second Shepherd's Play," and constituted the matter of the Italian *commedia dell'arte* in the Renaissance. In the enduring English drama, farce is usually an episode in a more complex form of comedy—examples are the knockabout scenes in Shakespeare's *The Taming of the Shrew* and *The Merry Wives of Windsor.* Brandon Thomas' *Charley's Aunt,* however, an American play of 1892 which has often been revived, is a true farce throughout, as are some of the current plays of Tom Stoppard. Many of the movies by such comedians as Charlie Chaplin, Buster Keaton, W. C. Fields, and Woody Allen are excellent farce. Farce is often employed in single scenes of musical revues, and is the standard fare of television "situation comedies." It should be noted that the term "farce," or sometimes "farce comedy," is applied also to plays—a supreme example is Oscar Wilde's *The Importance of Being Earnest* (1895)—in which exaggerated character-types find themselves in ludicrous situations in the course of an improbable plot, but which achieve their comic effects not by broad humor and bustling action, but by the brilliance and wit of the dialogue. (See Robert Metcalf Smith and H. G. Rhoads, eds., *Types of Farce Comedy,* 1928.)

A distinction is often made between high and low comedy. **High comedy**, as described by George Meredith in the classic essay *The Idea of Comedy* (1877), evokes "intellectual laughter"—thoughtful laughter from spectators who remain emotionally detached from the action—at the spectacle of folly, pretentiousness, and incongruity in human behavior. Meredith finds its highest form within the comedy of manners, in the combats of wit (sometimes identified now as the "love duels") between such intelligent, highly verbal, and well-matched lovers as Benedick and Beatrice in Shakespeare's *Much Ado about Nothing* (1598–99) and Mirabell and Millamant in Congreve's *The Way* *of the World* (1700). **Low comedy,** at the other extreme, has little or no intellectual appeal, but undertakes to arouse laughter by jokes, or "gags," and by slapstick humor and boisterous or clownish physical activity; it is, therefore, one of the common components of farce.

See also *comedy of humours, tragicomedy,* literature of the *absurd,* and *wit, humor, and the comic.* On comedy and its varieties: H. T. E. Perry, *Masters of Dramatic Comedy* (1939); G. E. Duckworth, *The Nature of Roman Comedy* (1952); Louis Kronenberger, *The Thread of Laughter* (1952); W. K. Wimsatt, ed., *English Stage Comedy* (1954); Leo Hughes, *A Century of English Farce* (1956); Elder Olson, *The Theory of Comedy* (1968); Allan Rodway, *English Comedy* (1975). On the relation of comedy to myth and ritual: Northrop Frye, *Anatomy of Criticism* (1957), pp. 163–86; C. L. Barber, *Shakespeare's Festive Comedy* (1959). On the history of low comedy and farce from the Greeks to the present: Anthony Caputi, *Buffo: The Genius of Vulgar Comedy* (1978). On television comedy: Horace Newcomb, *Television: The Most Popular Art* (1974), Chapter 2.

Comedy of Humours. A type of comedy developed by Ben Jonson, the Elizabethan playwright, based on the ancient physiological theory of the **four humours** that was still current in Jonson's time. The "humours" were held to be the four primary fluids—blood, phlegm, choler (or yellow bile), and melancholy (or black bile)—whose "temperament," or mixture, was held to determine both a person's physical condition and character type. An imbalance of one or another humour in a temperament was said to produce four kinds of disposition, whose names have survived the underlying theory: sanguine (from the Latin "sanguis," blood), phlegmatic, choleric, and melancholic. In Jonson's comedy of humours each of the major characters, instead of being a well-balanced individual, has a preponderant humour that gives him a characteristic distortion or eccentricity of disposition. Jonson expounds his theory in the "Induction" to his play *Every Man in His Humour* (1598) and exemplifies the mode in his later comedies as well. The Jonsonian type of humours character remained influential in the *comedies of manners* by William Wycherley, Sir George Etheredge, William Congreve, and other dramatists of the English *Restoration,* 1660–1700.

Comic Relief is the introduction of comic characters, speeches, or scenes in a serious or tragic work, especially a dramatic work. Such elements were almost universal in *Elizabethan* tragedy. Sometimes they occur merely as episodes of dialogue or horseplay for purposes of alleviating tension and adding variety; in more carefully wrought plays, however, they are also integrated with the plot, in a way that counterpoints and enhances the serious or tragic significance. Examples of such complex uses of comic elements are the gravediggers in *Hamlet* (V. i), the scene of the drunken porter after the murder of the king in *Macbeth* (II. iii), the Falstaff scenes in *Henry IV, Part 1,* and the roles of Mercutio and the old nurse in *Romeo and Juliet.*

See Thomas De Quincey's classic essay "On the Knocking at the Gate in *Macbeth*" (1823).

Commedia dell'Arte was a form of comic drama developed about the mid-sixteenth century by guilds of professional Italian actors. These actors, playing *stock characters,* largely improvised the dialogue around a given **scenario**—a term that still denotes a brief outline of a drama, indicating merely the entrances of the main characters and the general course of the action. In a typical play, a pair of young lovers outwit a rich old father ("Pantaloon"), aided by a clever and intriguing servant ("Harlequin"), in a plot enlivened by the buffoonery of "Punch" and other clowns. Wandering Italian troupes played in all the large cities of Renaissance Europe and influenced various writers of comedies in Elizabethan England and, later, Molière in France. The modern puppet shows of Punch and Judy are descendants of this old Italian comedy.

See Kathleen M. Lea, *Italian Popular Comedy, 1560–1620* (2 vols.; 1934).

Conceit. Originally meaning a concept or image, "conceit" came to be the term for figures of speech which establish a striking parallel—usually an elaborate parallel—between two very dissimilar things or situations. English poets of the sixteenth and seventeenth centuries adapted the term from the Italian "concetto" and used it (as we still do) both in a pejorative way and as a neutral identifier of a kind of *figurative language.* Two types of conceit are often distinguished by specific names:

1) The **Petrarchan conceit** is a type of figure used in love poems which had been novel and effective in the Italian poet Petrarch, but became hackneyed in some of his imitators among the *Elizabethan* sonneteers. The figure consists of detailed, ingenious, and often exaggerated comparisons applied to the disdainful mistress, as cold and cruel as she is beautiful, and to the distresses and despair of the worshipful lover. (See *courtly love.*) Sir Thomas Wyatt (1503–42), for example, in his sonnet "My Galley Chargèd with Forgetfulness" that he translated from Petrarch, circumstantially compares the lover's state to a ship laboring in a storm. Another sonnet of Petrarch's translated by Wyatt begins with a familiar conceit, an *oxymoron* describing the simultaneous fever and chills experienced by a courtly sufferer from the disease of love:

> I find no peace; and all my war is done;
> I fear and hope; I burn and freeze in ice.

Shakespeare (who at times employed this type of conceit himself) *parodied* some standard comparisons by Petrarchan sonneteers in his Sonnet 130, beginning

> My mistress' eyes are nothing like the sun;
> Coral is far more red than her lips' red:
> If snow be white, why then her breasts are dun;
> If hairs be wires, black wires grow on her head.

2) The **metaphysical conceit** is a characteristic figure in John Donne (1572–1631) and other *metaphysical poets* of the seventeenth century. It was described by Samuel Johnson, in a famed passage in his "Life of Cowley" (1779–81), as "wit" which is a kind of *discordia concors;* a combination of dissimilar images, or discovery of occult resemblances in things apparently unlike. . . . The most heterogeneous ideas are yoked by violence together.

The metaphysical poets exploited all knowledge—commonplace or esoteric, practical, theological, or philosophical, true or fabulous—for the vehicles of these figures; and their comparisons, whether succinct or expanded, were novel, witty, and at their best startlingly effective. In sharp contrast to both the concepts and figures of conventional Petrarchism is John Donne's "The Flea," a poem that uses a flea who has bitten both lovers as the basic reference for its argument against the lady's resistance against an importunate lover. In Donne's "The Canonization," as the poetic argument develops, the comparisons for the relationship between lovers move from the area of commerce and business, through various actual and mythical birds and diverse forms of historical memorials, to a climax which equates the sexual acts and the moral status of worldly lovers with the ascetic life and heavenly destination of unworldly saints. The most famous sustained conceit is Donne's parallel (in "A Valediction: Forbidding Mourning") between the continuing relationship of his and his lady's soul, despite their physical parting, and the coordinated movements of the two feet of a draftsman's compass. An oft-cited instance of the chilly *hyperbolic* ingenuity of the metaphysical conceit when it is overdriven is Richard Crashaw's description, in his mid-seventeenth-century poem "Saint Mary Magdalene," of the tearful eyes of the repentant Magdalene as

> two faithful fountains
> Two walking baths, two weeping motions,
> Portable and compendious oceans.

Following the great revival of interest in the metaphysical poets during the early decades of the twentieth century, a number of modern poets exploited this type of conceit. Examples are T. S. Eliot's comparison of the evening to "a patient etherized upon a table" in "The Love Song of J. Alfred Prufrock," and the series of startling figurative vehicles in Dylan Thomas' "In Memory of Ann Jones." The vogue for such conceits extended even to popular love songs, in the 1920s and later, by well-educated composers such as Cole Porter: "You're the Cream in My Coffee" and "You're the Top."

Refer to Rosemond Tuve, *Elizabethan and Metaphysical Imagery* (1947); K. K. Ruthven, *The Conceit* (1969).

Concrete and Abstract. In standard philosophical usage a "concrete term" is a word which denotes a particular person or thing, and an "abstract term" is a noun (such as "brightness," "beauty," "evil," "despair") which denotes qualities that exist only as attributes of particular persons or things. A sentence, accordingly, is said to be concrete if it makes an assertion about a particular subject (T. S. Eliot's "Grishkin is nice . . ."), and abstract if it makes an assertion about an abstract subject (Alexander Pope's "Hope springs eternal in the human breast"). Critics of literature, however, often use these terms in an extended way: a passage is called abstract if it represents its subject matter in general or nonsensuous words or with only a thin realization of its experienced qualities; it is called concrete if it represents its subject matter with striking particularity and sensuous detail. In his "Ode to Psyche" (1820) John Keats'

> 'Mid hush'd, cool-rooted flowers, fragrant-eyed,
> Blue, silver-white, and budded Tyrian

is a concrete description of a locale which interinvolves qualities that are perceived by four different senses: hearing, touch, sight, and smell. And in the opening of his "Ode to a Nightingale," Keats communicates concretely, by a combination of literal and figurative language, how it feels to experience the full-throated song of the nightingale:

> My heart aches, and a drowsy numbness pains
> My sense, as though of hemlock I had drunk,
> Or emptied some dull opiate to the drains . . .

It is frequently asserted that "poetry is concrete," or, as John Crowe Ransom put it in *The World's Body* (1938), that its proper subject is "the rich, contingent materiality of things." Most poetry is certainly more concrete than other modes of language, especially in its use of *imagery*. It should be kept in mind, however, that poets do not hesitate to use abstract language when the situation or area of reference or artistic purpose calls for it. Keats, though he was one of the most concrete of poets, began *Endymion* with a sentence composed of abstract terms:

> A thing of beauty is a joy forever:
> Its loveliness increases; it will never
> Pass into nothingness; . . .

And some of the most moving and memorable passages in poetry are not concrete; for example, the statement about God in Dante's *Paradiso*, "In His will is our peace," or the bleak comment by Edgar in the last act of *King Lear*,

>   Men must endure
> Their going hence, even as their coming hither;
> Ripeness is all.

See John Crowe Ransom, *The World's Body* (1938); Richard H. Fogle, *The Imagery of Keats and Shelley* (1949), Chapter 5.

Concrete Poetry is a recent term for an ancient type, called **pattern poems**, which experiment with the visual shape in which a text is presented on the page. Some Greek poets, beginning in the third century B.C., shaped a text in the form of the object which the poem describes or suggests. In the Renaissance and seventeenth century a number of poets composed such patterned forms, in which the lines vary in length in such a way that their printed shape is in the outline of the subject of the poem; familiar examples in English are George Herbert's "Easter Wings" and "The Altar." Prominent later experiments with pictorial or suggestive typography include Stéphane Mallarmé's *Un Coup de dés* ("A Throw of Dice," 1897) and Guillaume Apollinaire's

Calligrammes (1918); in the latter publication, for example, Apollinaire printed the poem "Il pleut" ("It rains") so that the component letters trickle down the page.

The current vogue for **concrete poetry** is a worldwide movement that was largely inaugurated in 1953 by the Swiss poet Eugen Gomringer. The practice of such poetry varies widely, but the common feature is the use of a radically reduced language, typed or printed in such a way as to force the visible text on the reader's attention as an object which is itself to be perceived as a whole. Many concrete poems, in fact, cannot be read at all in the conventional way, since they consist of a single word or phrase which is subjected to systematic alterations in the order and position of the component letters, or else are composed of fragments of words, or of nonsense syllables, or even of single letters, numbers, and marks of punctuation. In their shaped patterns, concrete poets often use a variety of type fonts and sizes and different colors of type, and sometimes supplement the text with drawings or photographs, while some of their shapes, called "kinetic," evolve as we turn the pages.

America had its native tradition of pattern poetry in the typographical experiments of Ezra Pound, and especially E. E. Cummings; see, for example, Cummings' "r-p-o-p-h-e-s-s-a-g-r," in which, as a textual representation of the way we at first perceive vaguely, then identify, the leaping insect, scrambled sequences of letters gradually shape themselves into the word "grasshopper." Prominent recent practitioners of pattern poems in the shape of the things they describe or meditate upon are Mary Swenson (*Iconographie*, 1970) and John Hollander (*Types of Shape*, 1991). Other Americans who have been influenced by the international vogue for concrete poetry include Emmett Williams, Jonathan Williams, and Mary Ellen Solt.

Collections of concrete poems in a variety of languages are Emmett Williams, ed., *An Anthology of Concrete Poetry* (1967); Mary Ellen Solt, ed. (with a useful historical introduction), *Concrete Poetry: A World View* (1968). For a noted early-eighteenth-century attack on pattern poems, see Addison's comments on "false wit" in the *Spectator*, Nos. 58 and 63.

Confessional Poetry designates a type of narrative and lyric verse, given impetus by Robert Lowell's *Life Studies* (1959), which deals with the facts and intimate mental and physical experiences of the poet's own life. It differs in subject matter from poems of the *Romantic Period* about the poet's own circumstances, experiences, and feelings, such as William Wordsworth's "Tintern Abbey" and Samuel Taylor Coleridge's "Dejection: An Ode," in the candor and detail—and sometimes the *psychoanalytic* insight—with which the poet reveals private or clinical matters about himself or herself. Confessional poems have been written by Allen Ginsberg, Theodore Roethke, Sylvia Plath, Anne Sexton, John Berryman, and other recent American poets. See Diane Middlebrook, *Anne Sexton: A Biography* (1991).

Confidant (the feminine form is "confidante") is a character in a drama or novel who plays only a minor role in the action, but serves the protagonist as a trusted friend to whom he or she confesses intimate thoughts, problems, and feelings. In drama the confidant provides the playwright with a plausible device for communicating to the audience the knowledge, state of mind, and intentions of a principal character without the use of stage devices such as the *soliloquy* or the *aside;* examples are Hamlet's friend Horatio in Shakespeare's *Hamlet,* and Cleopatra's maid Charmion in his *Antony and Cleopatra.*

In prose fiction a famed confidant is Dr. Watson in Arthur Conan Doyle's stories about Sherlock Holmes (1887 and following). The device is particularly useful to modern writers who, like Henry James, have largely renounced the novelist's earlier privileges of having access to a character's state of mind and of intruding in order to address information directly to the reader. (See *point of view*.) To the confidant James also applied the term **ficelle,** French for the string by which the puppeteer manages his puppets. Discussing Maria Gostrey, Strether's confidante in *The Ambassadors,* James remarks that she is a "ficelle" who is not, "in essence, Strether's friend. She is the reader's friend much rather" (James, *The Art of the Novel,* ed. R. P. Blackmur, 1934, pp. 321–22).

See W. J. Harvey, *Character and the Novel* (1966).

Connotation and Denotation. In literary usage, the **denotation** of a word is its primary significance or reference, such as a dictionary mainly specifies; its **connotation** is the range of secondary or associated significances and feelings which it commonly suggests or implies. Thus "home" denotes the house where one lives, but connotes privacy, intimacy, and coziness; that is the reason real estate agents like to use "home" instead of "house" in their advertisements. "Horse" and "steed" denote the same quadruped, but "steed" has a different connotation, deriving from the chivalric or romantic narratives in which this word was often used.

The connotation of a word is only a potential range of shared secondary significance; which of these connotations are evoked depends on the way a word is used in a particular context. Poems typically establish contexts which bring into play some part of the connotative as well as the denotative meaning of words. In his poem "Virtue" George Herbert wrote,

> Sweet day, so cool, so calm, so bright,
> The bridal of the earth and sky. . .

The denotation of "bridal"—a union between human beings—serves as part of the *ground* for applying the word as a *metaphor* to the union of earth and sky; but the specific poetic context in which the word occurs also evokes such connotations of "bridal" as sacred, joyous, and ceremonial. (Note that "marriage," although metrically and denotatively equivalent to "bridal," would have been less richly significant in this context, because more commonplace in its connotation.) Even the way a word is spelled may alter its connotation. John Keats, in a passage of his "Ode to a Nightingale" (1819),

> Charmed magic casements, opening on the foam
> Of perilous seas, in *faery* lands forlorn,

altered his original spelling of "fairy" to the older form "faery" in order to evoke the connotations of antiquity and of the magic world of Spenser's *The Faerie Queene.*

On connotation and denotation see Isabel C. Hungerland, *Poetic Discourse* (1958), Chapter 1, and Monroe C. Beardsley, *Aesthetics: Problems in the Philosophy of Criticism* (1958), Chapter 3.

Conventions. *1)* In one sense of the term, conventions (derived from the Latin term for "coming together") are necessary, or at least convenient, devices, accepted by tacit agreement between author and audience, for solving the problems in representing reality that are posed by a particular artistic medium. In watching a modern production of a Shakespearean play, for example, the audience accepts without question the convention by which a *proscenium* stage with three walls (or if it is a **theater in the round,** with no walls) represents a room with four walls. It also accepts the convention of characters speaking in *blank verse* instead of prose, and uttering their private thoughts in *soliloquies* and *asides,* as well as the convention by which actions presented on a single stage in less than three hours may represent events which take place in a great variety of places, and over a span of many years.

2) In a second sense of the term, conventions are conspicuous features of subject matter, form, or technique which occur repeatedly in works of literature. Conventions in this sense may be recurrent types of character, turns of plot, forms of versification, or kinds of diction and style. *Stock characters* such as the Elizabethan braggart soldier, or the languishing and fainting heroine of Victorian fiction, or the sad young men of the lost-generation novels of the 1920s, were among the conventions of their literary eras. The abrupt reform of the villain at the end of the last act was a common convention of *melodrama. Euphuism* in prose, and the *Petrarchan* and *metaphysical conceits* in verse, were conventional devices of style. It is now just as much a literary convention to be outspoken on sexual matters as it was to be reticent in the age of Charles Dickens and George Eliot.

3) In the most inclusive sense, common in structuralist criticism, all literary works, no matter how seemingly realistic, are held to be entirely constituted by literary conventions, or "codes"—of genre, plot, character, language, and so on—which a reader *naturalizes,* by assimilating these conventions to the world of discourse and experience which, in the reader's particular time and place, are regarded as real, or "natural." (See *structuralist criticism* and *character and characterization.*)

Invention was originally a term used in theories of *rhetoric,* and later in literary criticism, to signify the "finding" of the subject matter by an orator or a poet; it then came to be used to signify innovative elements in a work, in contrast to the deliberate "imitation" of the forms and subjects of prior literary models. (See *imitation.*) At the present time, "invention" is often opposed to "convention" (in sense 2, above) to signify the inauguration by a writer of an unprecedented subject or theme or form or style, and the resulting work is said to possess **originality.** The history of literature shows a repeated process in which innovative writers such as John Donne or William Wordsworth or James Joyce or Samuel Beckett rebel against reigning conventions of their time to produce highly original works, only to have their inventions imitated by other writers, who thereby convert literary novelties into an additional set of literary conventions.

There is nothing either good or bad in the extent or obviousness of conformity to pre-existing conventions; all depends on the kind and effectiveness of the use an individual writer makes of them. The *pastoral elegy*, for example, is one of the most conspicuously convention-bound of literary forms, yet in "Lycidas" (1638) John Milton achieved what, by wide critical agreement, ranks as one of the greatest lyrics in the language. He did this by employing the ancient pastoral rituals with freshness and power, so as to absorb an individual's death into the experience of the human race and to add to his own voice a resonance achieved by echoing earlier pastoral laments for a poet who died young.

See E. E. Stoll, *Poets and Playwrights* (1930); M. C. Bradbrook, *Themes and Conventions of Elizabethan Tragedy* (1935); Harry Levin, "Notes on Convention," in *Perspectives of Criticism* (1950); and the issues *On Convention of New Literary History*, vols. 13–14 (1981 and 1983). On convention and originality see John L. Lowes, *Convention and Revolt in Poetry* (1919); Graham Hough, *Reflections on a Literary Revolution* (1960).

Courtly Love. A doctrine about love between the sexes, including an elaborate code governing the relations of aristocratic lovers, which was widely represented in the lyric poems and *chivalric romances* of western Europe during the Middle Ages. The development of the *conventions* of courtly love is usually attributed to the **troubadours** (poets of Provence, in Southern France), in the period from the latter eleventh century through the twelfth century. In this doctrine, love, with its erotic and physical aspects spiritualized, is regarded as the noblest passion this side of heaven. The courtly lover idealizes and idolizes his beloved, and subjects himself to her every whim. (This love is often that of a bachelor knight for another man's wife, as in the stories of Tristan and Isolde or of Lancelot and Guinevere; it must be remembered that marriage among the medieval upper classes was usually a kind of business contract, for economic and political purposes.) The lover suffers agonies and sickness of body and spirit at the caprices of his imperious sweetheart, but remains devoted to her, manifesting his honor by his unswerving fidelity and his adherence to a rigorous code of behavior, both in knightly battles and in the complex ceremonies of courtly speech and conduct.

The origins and development of courtly love have been traced to a serious reading of the Roman poet Ovid's mock-serious book *The Remedies of Love;* to an imitation in lovers' relations of the politics of feudalism (the lover is a vassal, and both his lady and the god of love are his lords); and to an importation into amatory situations of Christian concepts and ritual, especially from the cult of the Virgin Mary. Thus, the lady is exalted and worshiped; the lover sins and repents; and if his faith stays steadfast, he may be admitted at last into the lover's heaven through his lady's "gift of grace."

From southern France the doctrines of courtly love spread to Chrétien de Troyes (flourished 1170–90) and other poets and romance writers in northern France, to Dante (*La Vita Nuova,* 1290–94), Petrarch, and other writers in fourteenth-century Italy, and to the love poets of Germany and northern Europe. To the reader of English literature the conventions of courtly love are best known by their occurrence in the medieval romance *Sir Gawain and the Green Knight,* in Chaucer's *Troilus and Criseyde,* and later in the Petrarchan subject matter and the *Petrarchan conceits* of the Elizabethan sonneteers. There has long been a debate as to whether medieval courtly love was a set of purely literary conventions and a topic for elegant conversation at courts, or whether to some degree it reflected the actual sentiments and conduct of aristocratic life of the time. What is clear is that its views of the intensity and the ennobling power of love as "the grand passion," of the special sensibility and spiritual status of women, and of the complex decorum governing relations between the sexes have profoundly affected not only the literature of love but also the actual experience of "being in love" in the Western world, through the nineteenth century and (though to a diminished extent) even into our own day of sexual candor, freedom, and the *feminist* movement for gender-equivalence in the relations between the sexes.

C. S. Lewis, *The Allegory of Love* (1936); A. J. Denomy, *The Heresy of Courtly Love* (1947); M. J. Valency, *In Praise of Love* (1958); F. X. Newman, ed., *The Meaning of Courtly Love* (1968); Denis de Rougemont, *Love in the Western World* (rev., 1974); Roger Boase, *The Origin and Meaning of Courtly Love: A Critical Study of European Scholarship* (1977). For skeptical views of some commonly held opinions, see Peter Dronke, *Medieval Latin and the Rise of European Love-Lyric* (1965–66); E. Talbot Donaldson, "The Myth of Courtly Love," in *Speaking of Chaucer* (1970). For a feminist reappraisal of the role of women in the tradition, see Andrée Kahn Blumstein, *Misogyny and Idealization in the Courtly Romance* (1977).

Criticism is the overall term for studies concerned with defining, classifying, analyzing, interpreting, and evaluating works of literature. **Theoretical criticism** proposes a **theory** of literature, in the sense of general principles, together with a set of terms, distinctions, and categories, to be applied to identifying and analyzing works of literature, as well as the **criteria** (the standards, or norms) by which these works and their writers are to be evaluated. The earliest great work of theoretical criticism was Aristotle's *Poetics* (fourth century B.C.). Especially influential works of theoretical criticism in the first half of the present century are I. A. Richards, *Principles of Literary Criticism* (1924); Kenneth Burke, *The Philosophy of Literary Form* (1941, rev. 1957); Eric Auerbach, *Mimesis* (1946); R. S. Crane, ed., *Critics and Criticism* (1952); and Northrop Frye, *Anatomy of Criticism* (1957). Since the 1970s there has been a flood of writings, Continental, American, and English, proposing diverse novel and radical forms of critical theory. These are discussed in the section of the *Glossary* titled "Modern Theories of Literature and Criticism," beginning on p. 223; see especially *poststructuralism* in that section, for a description of the special sense of the term "theory" in current usage.

Practical criticism, or **applied criticism,** concerns itself with the discussion of particular works and writers; in an applied critique, the theoretical principles controlling the mode of the analysis, interpretation, and evaluation are often left implicit, or brought in only as the occasion demands. Among the more influential works of applied criticism in England are the literary essays of Dryden in the *Restoration,* Dr. Johnson's *Lives of the English Poets* (1779–81), Coleridge's chapters on the poetry of Wordsworth in *Biographia Literaria* (1817) and his lectures on Shakespeare, Matthew Arnold's *Essays in Criticism* (1865 and following), I. A. Richards' *Practical Criticism* (1930), T. S. Eliot's *Selected Essays* (1932), and the many critical essays by Virginia Woolf, F. R. Leavis, and Lionel Trilling. Cleanth Brooks' *The Well Wrought Urn* (1947) is an instance of the "close reading" of single texts which was the typical mode of practical criticism in the American *New Criticism.*

Practical criticism is sometimes distinguished into impressionistic and judicial criticism:

Impressionistic criticism attempts to represent in words the felt qualities of a particular passage or work, and to express the responses (the "impression") that the work directly evokes from the critic. As William Hazlitt put it in his essay "On Genius and Common Sense" (1824): "You decide from feeling, and not from reason; that is, from the impression of a number of things on the mind . . . though you may not be able to analyze or account for it in the several particulars." And Walter Pater later said that in criticism "the first step toward seeing one's object as it really is, is to know one's own impression as it really is, to discriminate it, to realise it distinctly," and posed as the basic question, "What is this song or picture . . . to *me* ?" (Preface to *Studies in the History of the Renaissance,* 1873). At its extreme this mode of criticism becomes, in Anatole France's phrase, "the adventures of a sensitive soul among masterpieces."

Judicial criticism, on the other hand, attempts not merely to communicate, but to analyze and explain the effects of a work by reference to its subject, organization, techniques, and style, and to base the critic's individual judgments on general standards of literary excellence. Rarely are these two modes of criticism sharply distinct in practice, but good examples of primarily impressionistic commentary can be found in the Greek Longinus (see the characterization of the *Odyssey* in his essay *On the Sublime*), Hazlitt, Walter Pater (the locus classicus of impressionism is his description of Leonardo's Mona Lisa in *The Renaissance,* 1873), and some of the twentieth-century critical essays of E. M. Forster and Virginia Woolf.

Types of traditional critical theories and applied criticism can be usefully classified according to whether, in explaining and judging a work of literature, they refer the work primarily to the outer world, or to the reader, or to the author, or else treat the work as an entity in itself:

1) **Mimetic criticism** views the literary work as an imitation, or reflection, or representation of the world and human life, and the primary criterion applied to a work is that of the "truth" of its representation to the subject matter that it represents, or should represent. This mode of criticism, which first appeared in Plato and (in a qualified way) in Aristotle, remains characteristic of modern theories of literary realism. (See *imitation.*)

2) **Pragmatic criticism** views the work as something which is constructed in order to achieve certain effects on the audience (effects such as aesthetic pleasure, instruction, or kinds of emotion), and it tends to judge the value of the work according to its success in achieving that aim. This approach, which largely dominated literary discussion from the versified *Art of Poetry* by the Roman Horace (first century B.C.) through the eighteenth century, has been revived in recent *rhetorical criticism,* which emphasizes the artistic strategies by which an author engages and influences the responses of readers to the matters represented in a literary work, as well as by those *structuralists* who analyze a literary text as a systematic play of **codes** which effect the interpretative responses of the reader.

3) **Expressive criticism** treats a literary work primarily in relation to its author. It defines poetry as an expression, or overflow, or utterance of feelings, or as the product of the poet's imagination operating on his or her perceptions, thoughts, and feelings; it tends to judge the work by its sincerity, or its adequacy to the poet's individual vision or state of mind; and it often looks in the work for evidences of the particular temperament and experiences of the author who, consciously or unconsciously, has revealed himself in it. Such views were developed mainly by romantic critics in the early nineteenth century and remain current in our own time, especially in the writings of *psychological and psychoanalytic critics* and in *critics of consciousness* such as George Poulet and the Geneva School.

4) **Objective criticism** approaches a work of literature as something which stands free from what is often called "extrinsic" reference to the poet, or to the audience, or to the environing world. Instead it describes the literary product as a self-sufficient and autonomous object, or else as a world-in-itself, which is to be analyzed and judged solely by "intrinsic" criteria such as its complexity, coherence, equilibrium, integrity, and the interrelations of its component elements. The general viewpoint was presented in Kant's *Critique of Aesthetic Judgment* (1790)—see *distance and involvement*—was taken up by proponents of *art for art's sake* in the latter part of the nineteenth century, and has been elaborated in detailed modes of applied criticism by a number of important critics since the 1920s, including the *New Critics,* the *Chicago School,* and proponents of European *formalism.*

An essential literary enterprise that the ordinary reader takes for granted is **textual criticism,** whose aim is to establish as accurately as possible what an author actually wrote, or intended to be the final version of each work. The textual critic **collates** (that is, puts side by side for comparison) the printed texts of a work, together with any surviving manuscripts, in order to detect variants, to trace the changes made by an author at various stages of a work, and to identify and correct sources of error; a *variorum edition* of a text reprints the variants as well as the author's last version. For problems and current methods, see Fredson Bowers, *Textual and Literary Criticism* (1959);

James Thorpe, *Principles of Textual Criticism* (1972); G. T. Tanselle, "Textual Scholarship," in Joseph Gibaldi, ed., *Introduction to Scholarship in Modern Language and Literature* (1981); and Jerome McGann, *A Critique of Modern Textual Criticism* (1983).

It is also common to distinguish types of criticism which bring to bear upon literature various special areas of knowledge and theory, in the attempt to identify the conditions and influences which determine the particular characteristics of a literary work. Accordingly, we have "historical criticism," "biographical criticism," "sociological criticism" (see *sociology of literature* and *Marxist criticism*), *psychological criticism* (a subspecies is *psychoanalytic criticism*), and *archetypal* or *myth criticism* (which undertakes to explain the formation of types of literature by reference to the theories of myth and ritual in modern cultural anthropology).

For detailed discussion and application of the classification of traditional theories represented in this essay, see M. H. Abrams, *The Mirror and the Lamp* (1953), Chapter 1, and "Types and Orientations of Critical Theories" in *Doing Things with Texts: Essays in Criticism and Critical Theory* (1989). On types of critical approaches, refer also to René Wellek and Austin Warren, *Theory of Literature* (rev., 1970). Histories of criticism: *Classical Criticism*, ed. George A. Kennedy (1989); Bernard Weinberg, *A History of Literary Criticism in the Italian Renaissance* (2 vols.; 1963); W. K. Wimsatt and Cleanth Brooks, *Literary Criticism: A Short History* (1957); René Wellek, *A History of Modern Criticism, 1750–1950* (7 vols.; 1955 ff.). On criticism in the earlier nineteenth century see Abrams, *The Mirror and the Lamp,* and on twentieth-century criticism, S. E. Hyman, *The Armed Vision* (1948); Murray Krieger, *The New Apologists for Poetry* (1956); Jonathan Culler, *Structuralist Poetics* (1975); Grant Webster, *The Republic of Letters: A History of Postwar American Literary Opinion* (1979); Frank Lentricchia, *After the New Criticism* (1980). Convenient anthologies of literary criticism: A. H. Gilbert and G. W. Allen, *Literary Criticism, Plato to Croce* (2 vols.; 1940–41); W. J. Bate, *Criticism: The Major Texts* (1952); Lionel Trilling, *Literary Criticism: An Introductory Reader* (1970). Anthologies of recent and current criticism: Hazard Adams and Leroy Searle, eds., *Critical Theory since 1965* (1986); Vassilis Lambropoulos and David Neal Miller, eds., *Twentieth-Century Literary Theory: An Introductory Anthology* (1987); David Lodge, ed., *Modern Criticism and Theory* (1988); Robert Con Davis and Ronald Schleifer, *Contemporary Literary Criticism* (rev., 1989). Suggested readings in present day critical "theories" are listed under each essay in the section of this *Glossary* on "Modern Theories of Literature and Criticism," which begins on p. 223.

Decadence. In the latter nineteenth-century in France, some proponents of the doctrines of *Aestheticism,* especially Charles Baudelaire, also espoused views and values which developed into a movement called "the Decadence." This term (not viewed by its exponents as derogatory) was based on qualities attributed to the literature of Hellenistic Greece in the last three centuries B.C., and of Roman literature after the death of the Emperor Augustus in 14 A.D. These literatures were said to possess the high refinements and subtle beauties of a culture and art which have passed their vigorous prime, but manifest a special, sweet savor of incipient decay. Such was also held to be the state of European civilization, especially French civilization, as it approached the end of the nineteenth century.

Many of the precepts of the Decadence were summarized by Théophile Gautier in the "Notice," describing Baudelaire's poetry, that he prefixed to an edition of Baudelaire's *Les Fleurs du mal* ("Flowers of Evil") in 1868. Central to the movement was the view that art is totally opposed to "nature," in the sense both of biological nature and of the standard, or "natural," norms of morality and sexual behavior. The thoroughgoing Decadent writer cultivates high artifice in his style and, often, the bizarre in his subject matter, recoils from the fecundity and exuberance of the organic and instinctual life of nature, prefers elaborate dress over the living form and cosmetics over the natural hue, and sometimes sets out to violate what is commonly held to be "natural" in human experience by resorting to drugs, deviancy, or sexual experimentation in the attempt to achieve (in a phrase echoed from the French poet Arthur Rimbaud) "the systematic derangement of all the senses." The movement reached its height in the last two decades of the century; extreme products were the novel *À rebours* ("Against the Grain"), written by J. K. Huysmans in 1884, and some of the paintings of Gustave Moreau. This period is also known as the **fin de siècle** (end of the century); the phrase connotes the lassitude, satiety, and ennui expressed by many writers of the Decadence.

In England the ideas, moods, and activities of Decadence are manifested, beginning in the 1860s, in the poems of Algernon Charles Swinburne, and in the 1890s by writers such as Oscar Wilde, Arthur Symons, Ernest Dowson, and Lionel Johnson; the notable English artist of the Decadence was Aubrey Beardsley. In the search for strange sensations, a number of English Decadents of the '90s experimented with drugs and illicit, or what were conventionally held to be extra-natural, modes of sexual experience; several of them died young. Representative literary productions are Wilde's novel *The Picture of Dorian Gray* (1891), his play *Salomé* (1893), and the poems of Ernest Dowson.

The emphases of the Decadence on drugged perception, sexual experimentation, and the deliberate inversion of conventional moral, social, and artistic norms reappeared, with modern variations, in the *Beat* poets and novelists of the 1950s and in the *counterculture* of the next two decades.

Mario Praz, *The Romantic Agony* (1933); A. E. Carter, *The Idea of Decadence in French Literature, 1830–1900* (1958); Karl Beckson, ed., *Aesthetes and Decadents of the 1890s* (1966); Richard Gilman, *Decadence: The Strange Life of an Epithet* (1979); and the collection by Ian Fletcher, ed., *Decadence and the 1890s* (1979). A useful descriptive guide to books on the subject is Linda C. Dowling, *Aestheticism and Decadence: A Selective Annotated Bibliography* (1977).

Decorum, as a term in literary criticism, designates the view that there should be propriety, or fitness, in the way that a literary *genre*, its subject matter, characters, and actions, and the style of its narration and its dialogue, are matched to one another. The doctrine had its roots in classical theory, especially in the versified essay *Art of Poetry* by the Roman Horace in the first century B.C., and it achieved an elaborate form in the criticism and practice of literature in the Renaissance and the *Neoclassic* age, when (as John Milton put it in his essay *Of Education,* 1644) decorum became "the grand masterpiece to observe." In the strictest application of this concept, literary forms, characters, and style were all ordered in hierarchies, or "levels," from high through middle to low, and all these had to be matched to one another. Thus comedy must not be mixed with tragedy, and the highest and most serious genres (epic and tragedy) must represent characters of the highest social classes (kings and nobility) acting in a way appropriate to their status and speaking in the *high style.* A number of critics in this period, however, especially in England, maintained the theory of decorum only in qualified ways.

See *neoclassic and romantic, poetic diction,* and *style,* and refer to Vernon Hall, *Renaissance Literary Criticism: A Study of Its Social Content* (1945). Erich Auerbach's *Mimesis* (1953) describes the sustained conflict in postclassical Europe between the reigning doctrines of literary decorum and the example of the Bible, in which the highest and most serious matters, including the sublime tragedy of the life and passion of Christ, are intermingled with base characters and humble narrative detail and are treated with what seemed to a classical taste a blatant indecorum of style. For Wordsworth's deliberate inversion of traditional poetic decorum at the beginning of the nineteenth century, by investing the common, the lowly, and the trivial with the highest dignity and sublimity, see M. H. Abrams, *Natural Supernaturalism* (1971), pp. 390–408.

Deus ex Machina is Latin for "a god from a machine." It describes the practice of some Greek playwrights (especially Euripides) to end a drama with a god who was lowered to the stage by a mechanical apparatus and, by his judgment and commands, solved the problems of the human characters. The phrase is now used for any forced and improbable device—a telltale birthmark, an unexpected inheritance, the discovery of a lost will or letter— by which a hard-pressed author resolves a plot. Notorious examples occur even in major novels like Charles Dickens' *Oliver Twist* (1837–38) and Thomas Hardy's *Tess of the D'Urbervilles* (1891). The German playwright Bertolt Brecht *parodies* the abuse of such devices in the madcap conclusion of his *Threepenny Opera* (1928). See *plot.*

Didactic Literature. The adjective "didactic," which means "intended to give instruction," is applied to works of literature which are designed to expound a branch of theoretical or practical knowledge, or else to embody, in imaginative or fictional form, a moral, religious, or philosophical doctrine or *theme.* Such works are commonly distinguished from essentially imaginative works (sometimes called "mimetic," or "representational") in which the materials are organized and rendered, not in order to present and to enhance their appeal as knowledge or doctrine, but primarily in order to enhance their human interest and their capacity to move and give artistic pleasure to their audience. In the first century B.C. the Roman Lucretius wrote his didactic poem *De Rerum Natura* ("On the Nature of Things") to expound and make persuasive and appealing his naturalistic philosophy and ethics, and in the same era Virgil wrote his *Georgics* on the practical subject of how to manage a farm. Most medieval and much Renaissance literature was didactic in intention. In the eighteenth century, a number of poets wrote **georgics** (on the model of Virgil) expounding such utilitarian arts as sheepherding, running a sugar plantation, and making cider. Alexander Pope's *Essay on Criticism* and his *Essay on Man* are eighteenth-century didactic poems on the subjects of literary criticism and of moral philosophy.

Such works for the most part directly expound a branch of knowledge or art, or else argue an explicit doctrine by proofs and examples. Didactic literature, however, may also take on the attributes of imaginative works, by embodying the doctrine in a narrative or dramatic form that is intended to enhance its interest and persuasive force, as well as to add a dimension of pleasure in the artistry. In the various forms of *allegory*, for example, including Edmund Spenser's *The Faerie Queene* and John Bunyan's *The Pilgrim's Progress*, the purpose of enhancing and adding force to the incorporated doctrine is a primary determinant of the choice of characters, the evolution of the plot, and the choice of fictional details. The various forms of *satire* are didactic in that they are designed, by various devices of ridicule, to alter the reader's attitudes toward certain types of people, institutions, products, and modes of conduct. Dante's *Letter to Can Grande* tells us that he planned his fourteenth-century *Divine Comedy* to represent, in the mode of a visionary narrative, the major Christian truths and the way to avoid damnation and achieve salvation. And John Milton's *Paradise Lost* (1667) can also be called didactic to the extent that the narrative is in fact organized, as Milton claimed in his opening invocation, around his "great argument" to "assert Eternal Providence,/And justify the ways of God to men." It will be seen from these examples that "didactic literature," as here defined, is a technical distinction and not a derogatory term. Some literary masterpieces are didactic and others (Shakespeare's *King Lear,* Jane Austen's *Emma,* James Joyce's *Ulysses*)—even though their plots involve moral concerns and imply criteria for moral judgments—are essentially, to adopt a phrase by Samuel Taylor Coleridge, works "of pure imagination."

The term **propagandist literature** is sometimes used as the equivalent of didactic literature, but it is much more useful to reserve the term for that species of didactic work which patently is written to move the reader to assume a specific attitude toward, or to take direct action on, a pressing social, political, or religious issue of the time at which the work is written. Prominent and effective examples of such works are Harriet Beecher Stowe's *Uncle Tom's Cabin* (1852; attacking slavery in the South), Upton Sinclair's *The Jungle* (on the horrors of the unregulated slaughtering and meat-packing industry in Chicago in 1906), and Clifford Odets' *Waiting for Lefty* (1935; a play directed against the strong-arm tactics used to suppress a taxicab drivers' union).

See *fiction,* and refer to John Chalker, *The English Georgic: A Study in the Development of a Form* (1969). On a useful way to distinguish between didactic and primarily imaginative, or "mimetic," literature, see R. S. Crane, ed., *Critics and Criticism* (1952), especially pp. 63–68 and 589–94.

Dissociation of Sensibility is a phrase introduced by T. S. Eliot in his essay "The Metaphysical Poets" (1921). Eliot's claim was that the *metaphysical poets* of the earlier seventeenth century, like the Elizabethan and Jacobean dramatists, "possessed a mechanism of sensibility which could devour any kind of experience." They manifested "a direct sensuous apprehension of thought," and felt "their thought as immediately as the odour of a rose." "A thought to John Donne was an experience; it modified his sensibility." But "in the seventeenth century a dissociation of sensibility set in, from which we have never recovered." This dissociation of intellection from emotion and sensuous perception, according to Eliot, was greatly aggravated by the influence of John Milton and John Dryden; and most later poets in English either thought or felt, but did not think and feel as an act of unified sensibility.

Eliot's vaguely defined distinction had a great vogue, especially among American *New Critics.* The dissociation of sensibility was taken to be the characteristic feature that weakened most poetry between Milton and the later writings of W. B. Yeats, and was attributed to a variety of causes, but particularly to the development in the seventeenth century of the scientific conception of the world as a material universe stripped of human values and feeling. (See, for example, Basil Willey, *The Seventeenth Century Background,* 1934.) Especially since 1950, however, Eliot's doctrine of a sudden but persisting dissociation of sensibility has come in for strong criticism, on the ground that it is an invalid historical claim which was largely contrived to support Eliot's disapproval (as a political and social conservative) of the course of English intellectual, political, and religious history after the Civil War of 1642, as well as to rationalize Eliot's particular poetic preferences.

See T. S. Eliot, "The Metaphysical Poets," *Selected Essays* (2d ed., 1960), and "Milton II," *On Poetry and Poets* (1957). Attacks on the validity of the doctrine are Leonard Unger, *Donne's Poetry and Modern Criticism* (1950); F. W. Bateson, "Dissociation of Sensibility," in the journal *Essays in Criticism,* 1 (1951) and 2 (1952); and Frank Kermode, *Romantic Image* (1957), Chapter 8.

Distance and Involvement. In his *Critique of Aesthetic Judgment* (1790), Immanuel Kant analyzed the experience of an aesthetic object as an act of "contemplation" which is "disinterested" (that is, independent of one's personal interests and desires) and free from all reference to its reality, moral effect, or utility. Various philosophers of art developed this concept into attempts to distinguish "aesthetic experience" from all other kinds of experience, on the basis of the impersonality and disinterestedness with which we contemplate an object or work of art. Writing in 1912, Edward Bullough introduced the term "distance" into this type of theory. He points, for example, to the difference between our ordinary experience of a dense fog at sea, with its strains, anxiety, and fear of invisible dangers, and the aesthetic experience, in which we attend with delight to the "objective" features and sensuous qualities of the fog itself. He accounts for this aesthetic mode of experiencing the fog as the effect of "psychical distance," which "is obtained by separating the object and its appeal from one's own self, by putting it out of gear with practical needs and ends." The extent of this psychical distance varies according to the nature of the artistic object which we contemplate, and also in accordance with an "individual's capacity for maintaining a greater or lesser degree" of such distance.

In recent literary criticism the term **aesthetic distance**, or simply **distance**, is often used not only to define the nature of literary and aesthetic experience in general, but also to analyze the many devices by which authors control the degree of a reader's distance, or "detachment"—in inverse relationship to the degree of a reader's **involvement**, or "concern"—with the actions and fortunes of one or another character represented within a work of literature. See, for example, Wayne C. Booth's detailed analysis of the control of distance in Jane Austen's *Emma,* in *The Rhetoric of Fiction* (1961), Chapter 9.

In his *epic theater* of the 1920s and later, the German dramatist Bertolt Brecht adapted the *Russian formalist* concept of "defamiliarization" into what he called **estrangement effects** (sometimes translated also as **alienation effects**), which are used to make familiar aspects of reality seem strange, and so to prevent the emotional identification or involvement of the audience with the characters and subject matter of the play. His aim was to effect and sustain a critical attitude on the part of the audience in order to arouse them to take action against, rather than simply to accept, the social reality represented on the stage. (On Brecht, see under *Marxist criticism.*)

See Edward Bullough, "Psychical Distance as a Factor in Art and an Aesthetic Principle," *British Journal of Psychology* 5 (1912), reprinted in Melvin Rader, ed., *A Modern Book of Aesthetics* (rev., 1952), and partially reprinted in Eliseo Vivas and Murray Krieger, *The Problems of Aesthetics* (1963). A useful review of theories of the aesthetic attitude and of aesthetic distance is Jerome Stollnitz, *Aesthetics and the Philosophy of Art Criticism* (1960), Chapter 2. For the view that such theories are mistaken, see George Dickie, *Art and the Aesthetic* (1974), Chapters 4 and 5.

Doggerel. A term applied to rough, heavy-footed, and jerky versification. It is usually the result of ineptitude on the part of the versifier, but is sometimes deliberately employed by poets for satiric, comic, or rollicking effect. John Skelton (1460?–1529) wrote in short lines of two or three stresses, intentionally rough and variable in meter, which have come to be called **Skeltonics;** as he both described and exemplified his own versification in *Colin Clout:*

> For though my rhyme be ragged,
> Tattered and jagged,
> Rudely rain-beaten,
> Rusty and moth-eaten,
> If ye take well therewith,
> It hath in it some pith.

The tumbling, broken, and comically grotesque *octosyllabic couplets,* often using double, triple, and imperfect rhymes, which were developed by Samuel Butler for his satiric poem *Hudibras* (1663–78) are a form of deliberate doggerel which came to be called **Hudibrastic verse:**

> Besides, he was a shrewd philosopher,
> And had read every text and gloss over;
> Whate'er the crabbed'st author hath,
> He understood b'implicit faith.

See *meter.*

Drama. The form of composition designed for performance in the theater, in which actors take the roles of the characters, perform the indicated action, and utter the written dialogue. (The common alternative name for a dramatic composition is a **play.**) In **poetic drama** the dialogue is written in verse, which in English is usually *blank verse* and in French is the twelve-syllable line called an *Alexandrine;* almost all the *heroic dramas* of the English Restoration Period, however, were written in *heroic couplets* (iambic pentameter lines rhyming in pairs). A **closet drama** is written in the form of a drama, with dialogue, indicated settings, and stage directions, but is intended by the author to be read rather than to be performed in the theater; examples are Milton's *Samson Agonistes* (1671), Byron's *Manfred* (1817), Shelley's *Prometheus Unbound* (1820), and Hardy's *The Dynasts* (1904–08).

For the types and components of plays, see the Index under *drama.*

Dramatic Monologue. A monologue is a lengthy speech by a single person. In a play, when a character utters a monologue that expresses his or her private thoughts, it is called a *soliloquy.* A **dramatic monologue,** however, is not a component in a play, but a type of *lyric poem* that was perfected by Robert Browning. In its fullest form, as represented in Browning's "My Last Duchess," "The Bishop Orders His Tomb," "Andrea del Sarto," and many other poems, the dramatic monologue has the following features: (1) A single person, who is patently *not* the poet, utters the entire poem in a specific situation at a critical moment: the Duke is negotiating with an emissary for a second wife; the Bishop lies dying; Andrea once more attempts wistfully to believe his wife's lies. (2) This person addresses and interacts with one or more other people; but we know of the auditors' presence and what they say and do only from clues in the discourse of the single speaker. (3) The main principle controlling the poet's choice and organization of what the lyric speaker says is to reveal to the reader, in a way that enhances its interest, the speaker's temperament and character.

Even Browning, in monologues such as "Soliloquy of the Spanish Cloister" and "Caliban upon Setebos," omits the second feature, the presence of a silent auditor; but features (1) and (3) are essential distinctions between the dramatic monologue and the **dramatic lyric,** which is also a monologue uttered in an identifiable situation at a dramatic moment. John Donne's "The Canonization" and "The Flea" (1613), for example, are dramatic lyrics that, although very close to the dramatic monologue, lack one essential feature: the focus of interest is primarily on the speaker's elaborately ingenious argument, rather than on the character he inadvertently reveals in the course of arguing. And although Wordsworth's "Tintern Abbey" (1798) is spoken by one person to a silent auditor (his sister) in a specific situation at a significant moment in his life, it is not a dramatic monologue proper, both because we are invited to identify the speaker with the poet himself, and because the organizing principle and focus of interest is not the revelation of the speaker's distinctive temperament so much as the evolution of his observation, memories, and thought toward the resolution of an emotional problem.

Tennyson wrote "Ulysses" (1842) and other dramatic monologues, and the form has been used by Robert Frost, E. A. Robinson, Ezra Pound, Robert Lowell, and other poets of this century. The best-known modern instance is T. S. Eliot's "The Love Song of J. Alfred Prufrock" (1915).

See Benjamin Fuson, *Browning and His English Predecessors in the Dramatic Monologue* (1948); Robert Langbaum, *The Poetry of Experience: The Dramatic Monologue in Modern Literary Tradition* (1957); Ralph W. Rader, "The Dramatic Monologue and Related Lyric Forms," *Critical Inquiry* 3 (1976); and Adena Rosmarin, *The Power of Genre* (1985), Chapter 2, "The Dramatic Monologue."

Dream Vision. A mode of narrative widely employed by medieval poets: the narrator falls asleep, usually in a spring landscape, and dreams the events he goes on to relate; often he is led by a guide, human or animal, and the events which he dreams are at least in part an *allegory*. A very influential medieval example is the thirteenth-century French poem *Roman de la Rose;* the greatest of medieval poems, Dante's *Divine Comedy*, is also a dream vision. In fourteenth-century England, it is the narrative mode of the fine elegy *The Pearl,* of Langland's *Piers Plowman,* and of Chaucer's *The Book of the Duchess* and *The House of Fame.* After the Middle Ages the vogue of the dream allegory diminished, but it never died out, as Bunyan's prose narrative *The Pilgrim's Progress* (1678) and Keats' verse narrative *The Fall of Hyperion: A Dream* (1819) bear witness. Lewis Carroll's *Alice's Adventures in Wonderland* (1865) is in the form of a dream vision, and James Joyce's *Finnegans Wake* (1939) consists of an immense cosmic dream on the part of an archetypal dreamer.

See C. S. Lewis, *The Allegory of Love* (1938); and Howard Rollin Patch, *The Other World according to Descriptions in Medieval Literature* (1950, reprinted 1970).

Elegy. In Greek and Roman literature, "elegy" denoted any poem written in **elegiac meter** (alternating *hexameter* and *pentameter* lines); the term was also used to refer to the subjects and moods frequently expressed in the elegiac verse form, especially complaints about love. In Europe and England the word continued to have a variable application through the Renaissance; John Donne's *Elegies,* for example, are love poems. In the course of the seventeenth century, however, the term **elegy** began to be limited to its present usage: a formal and sustained lament in verse for the death of a particular person, usually ending in a consolation. Examples are Alfred, Lord Tennyson's *In Memoriam* (1850), on the death of Arthur Hallam, and W. H. Auden's "In Memory of W. B. Yeats" (1940). Occasionally the term is used in a broader sense for somber meditations such as the *Old English* "elegies" ("The Wanderer," "The Seafarer") and Thomas Gray's "Elegy Written in a Country Churchyard" (1751), which deal generally with the mortality of human beings and the passing of things they value. The *Duino Elegies* (1912–22) of the German poet Rainer Maria Rilke are also elegies in this broader sense; their subject is the transience both of poets and of the earthly objects which they write about in their poems.

The **dirge** also is a versified expression of grief on the occasion of a particular person's death, but differs from the elegy in that it is short, is less formal, and is usually represented as a text to be sung; examples are Shakespeare's "Full Fathom Five Thy Father Lies" and William Collins' "A Song from Shakespeare's *Cymbeline*" (1749). **Threnody** is now used mainly as an equivalent for "dirge," and **monody** for an elegy or dirge which is presented as being the utterance of a single person. John Milton describes his "Lycidas" (1638) in the subtitle as a "monody" in which "the Author bewails a learned Friend," and Matthew Arnold called his elegy on A. H. Clough "Thyrsis: A Monody" (1866).

An important subspecies of the elegy is the **pastoral elegy**, which represents both the mourner and the one he mourns—who is usually also a poet—as shepherds (the Latin word for shepherd is "pastor"). This poetic form was originated by the Sicilian Greek poet Theocritus, was continued by the Roman Virgil, was developed in various European countries during the Renaissance, and remained current in English poetry throughout the nineteenth century. Notable English pastoral elegies are Milton's "Lycidas" (1638), Shelley's "Adonais" (1821), and in the Victorian age, Arnold's "Thyrsis." The pastoral elegists, from the Greeks through the Renaissance, developed elaborate *conventions*, which are illustrated here by reference to "Lycidas." In addition to the fictional representation of both mourner and subject as shepherds tending their flocks (lines 23–36 and elsewhere), we usually find these conventions:

1) The lyric speaker begins by invoking the muses, and goes on to make frequent reference to other figures from classical mythology (lines 15–22, and later).

2) All nature joins in mourning the shepherd's death (lines 37–49). (Recent critics who stress the mythic and ritual origins of poetic genres claim that this feature is a survival from primitive laments for the death of Thammuz, Adonis, or other vegetational deities who died in the autumn to be reborn in the spring. See *myth critics*.)

3) The mourner charges with negligence the nymphs or other guardians of the dead shepherd (lines 50–63).

4) There is a procession of appropriate mourners (lines 88–111).

5) The poet raises questions about the justice of fate, or Providence, and adverts to the corrupt conditions of his own times (lines 64–84,

113–31). Such passages, though sometimes called "digressions," are integral to the evolution of the mourner's thought in "Lycidas."

6) Post-Renaissance elegies often include an elaborate passage in which appropriate flowers are brought to deck the hearse (lines 133–51).

7) There is a closing consolation. In Christian elegies, the lyric reversal from grief and despair to joy and assurance occurs when the elegist suddenly realizes that death in this world is the entry to a higher life (lines 165–85).

In his *Life of Milton* (1779), Samuel Johnson, who disapproved both of pastoralism and mythology in modern poetry, decried "Lycidas" for "its inherent improbability," but in Milton and other major poets the ancient rituals are in fact structural elements on which they play variations with originality and power. Some of the pastoral conventions, although adapted to an industrial age and a non-Christian worldview, are still manifest in Walt Whitman's great elegy on Lincoln, "When Lilacs Last in the Dooryard Bloom'd" (1866).

See *conventions* and *pastoral*. On the elegy: Mary Lloyd, *Elegies, Ancient and Modern* (1903); T. P. Harrison, Jr., and H. J. Leon, eds., *The Pastoral Elegy: An Anthology* (1939); Peter Sacks, *The English Elegy: Studies in the Genre from Spenser to Yeats* (1985). On "Lycidas": C. A. Patrides, ed., *Milton's "Lycidas": The Tradition and the Poem* (rev., 1983), which includes a number of recent critical essays; and Scott Elledge, ed., *Milton's "Lycidas"* (1966), which reprints classical and Renaissance pastoral elegies and other texts by way of background to Milton's poem.

Empathy and Sympathy. German theorists in the nineteenth century developed the concept of "Einfühlung" ("feeling into"), which has been translated as **empathy**. It signifies an identification with a perceived person or object which is so close that the observer seems to participate in the posture, motion, and sensations that he or she perceives. Empathy is often described as "an involuntary projection of ourselves into an object," and is commonly explained as the result of an "inner mimicry" on the part of the observer; that is, the observer of an object manifests incipient muscular movements which are not experienced as one's own sensations, but as if they were attributes of the outer object. The object may be human, or non-human, or even inanimate. In thoroughly absorbed contemplation we seem empathically to pirouette with a ballet dancer, soar with a hawk, bend with the movements of a tree in the wind, and even share the strength, ease, and grace with which a well-proportioned arch appears to support a bridge. When John Keats said that he became "a part of all I see," and that "if a sparrow comes before my window I take part in its existence and pick about the gravel," he was describing an habitual experience of his intensely empathic nature, long before the word was coined.

In literature we call "empathic" a passage which conspicuously evokes from the reader this sense of participation with the pose, movements, and physical sensations of the object that the passage describes. An example is Shakespeare's description, in his narrative poem *Venus and Adonis,* of

> the snail, whose tender horns being hit,
> Shrinks backward in his shelly cave with pain.

Another is the description of the motion of a wave in Keats' *Endymion* (1818),

> when heav'd anew
> Old ocean rolls a lengthen'd wave to the shore,
> Down whose green back the short-liv'd foam, all hoar,
> Bursts gradual, with a wayward indolence.

Sympathy, as distinguished from empathy, denotes fellow-feeling: not feeling-into the physical state, but feeling-along-with the mental state and emotions of another human being, or of nonhuman beings to whom we attribute human emotions. We "sympathize," for example, with the emotional experience of a child in his first attempt to recite a piece in public; we may also "empathize" as he falters in his speaking or makes an awkward gesture. Robert Burns' "To a Mouse" (1786) is an engaging expression of his quick sympathy with the terror of the "wee, sleekit, cow'rin, tim'rous beastie" whose nest he has turned up with his plow.

The engagement and control of a reader's sympathy with certain characters, and the establishment of "antipathy" toward others, is essential to the traditional literary artist. In Shakespeare's *King Lear,* we sympathize with Cordelia, for example, and progressively with King Lear, but feel horror and antipathy toward his "pelican daughters," Goneril and Regan. Our attitude in the same play toward the villainous Edmund, the bastard son of Gloucester, as managed by Shakespeare, is more complex—antipathetic, yet with some element of sympathetic understanding of his distorted personality. (See *distance and involvement.*) Bertolt Brecht's *estrangement effects* were designed to inhibit the sympathy of an audience with the protagonists of his plays, in order to encourage a critical attitude to the social realities that the plays represent.

Refer to H. S. Langfeld, *The Aesthetic Attitude* (1920)—the section on empathy is reprinted in *Problems of Aesthetics* (1963), ed. Eliseo Vivas and Murray Krieger. For detailed analyses of empathic passages in literature, see Richard H. Fogle, *The Imagery of Keats and Shelley* (1949), Chapter 4.

Enlightenment. The name applied to an intellectual movement and cultural ambience which developed in western Europe during the seventeenth century and reached its height in the eighteenth. The common element was a trust in human reason as adequate to solve the crucial problems and to establish the essential norms in life, together with the belief that the application of reason was rapidly dissipating the darkness of superstition, prejudice, and barbarity, was freeing humanity from its earlier reliance on mere authority and unexamined tradition, and had opened the prospect of progress toward a life in this world of universal peace and happiness. (See the idea of *progress.*) For some thinkers the model for "reason" was the inductive procedure of science, which develops by reasoning from the facts of experience to general laws; for others (especially Descartes and his followers), the model for "reason" was primarily geometrical—the deduction of particular truths from clear and distinct ideas which are known intuitively, by "the light of reason." Many thinkers relied on reason in both these senses.

In England, the thought and the world outlook of the Enlightenment are usually traced from Francis Bacon (1561–1626) through John Locke (1632–1704) to late-eighteenth-century thinkers such as William Godwin; in France, from Descartes (1596–1650) through Voltaire (1694–1778) to Diderot and other editors of the great twenty-volume *Encyclopédie* (1751–72); in Germany, from Leibniz (1646–1716) to what is often described as the highest product of the Enlightenment, the "critical philosophy" of Immanuel Kant (1724–1804). In his famous essay "What Is Enlightenment?" written in 1784, Kant defined it as "the liberation of mankind from his self-caused state of minority" and the achievement of a state of maturity which is exemplified in his "determination and courage to use [his understanding] without the assistance of another."

A typical manifestation of the Enlightenment was the widespread mode of religious thought known as **deism**, which has been described as "religion without revelation." Many thinkers assimilated elements of deism but remained professing Christians. The thoroughgoing deist, however, renounced, as violating reason, all "revealed religion"—that is, all particular religions, including Christianity, which are based on faith in the truths and mysteries revealed in special scriptures at a certain time and place and to a particular individual or group. The deist instead relied on those truths which, it was claimed, prove their accord with universal human reason by the fact that they are to be found in all religions, everywhere, at all times. Therefore the basic tenets of deism—for example, that there is a deity, discoverable by reasoning from the creation to the creator, who deserves our worship and sanctions all moral values—were, in theory, the common elements of all particular, or "positive," religions. Alexander Pope, without renouncing his Catholicism, expressed succinctly the basic tenets of deism in his poem "The Universal Prayer" (1738), which begins

> Father of all! in every age,
>   In every clime adored,
> By saint, by savage, and by sage,
>   Jehovah, Jove, or Lord!

See *neoclassicism* and *romanticism;* and refer to Ernst Cassirer, *The Philosophy of the Enlightenment* (1932); A. O. Lovejoy, *Essays in the History of Ideas* (1948); Basil Willey, *The Eighteenth Century Background* (1950); Peter Gay, *The Enlightenment: An Interpretation* (1966).

Epic. In its standard sense, the term **epic** or **heroic poem** is applied to a work that meets at least the following criteria: it is a long narrative poem on a serious subject, told in a formal and elevated style, and centered on a heroic or quasi-divine figure on whose actions depends the fate of a tribe, a nation, or (in the instance of John Milton's *Paradise Lost*) the human race.

There is a standard distinction between traditional and literary epics. The "traditional epics" were written versions of what had originally been oral poems about a tribal or national hero that developed in a warlike age. (See *oral formulaic poetry*.) Among these traditional epics are the *Iliad* and *Odyssey* that the Greeks ascribed to Homer, the Anglo-Saxon *Beowulf*, and the twelfth-century French epic the *Chanson de Roland*. "Literary epics" were composed by individual poetic craftsmen in deliberate imitation of the traditional form. Of this kind is Virgil's Latin poem the *Aeneid*, which later served as the chief model for Milton's literary epic *Paradise Lost* (1667); *Paradise Lost* in turn became, in the Romantic Period, a model for John Keats' fragmentary epic *Hyperion*, as well as for William Blake's several epics, or "prophetic books" (*The Four Zoas, Milton, Jerusalem*), which translated into Blake's own mythic terms the biblical narrative which had served as Milton's subject matter.

The epic was ranked by the Greek theorist Aristotle as second only to tragedy, and by many Renaissance critics as the highest of all *genres*. The literary epic is certainly the most ambitious of poetic enterprises, making immense demands on a poet's knowledge, invention, and skill to sustain the scope, grandeur, and variety of a poem that tends to encompass the world of its day and a large portion of its learning. Despite numerous attempts in many languages over nearly three thousand years, we possess no more than a half-dozen epic poems of indubitable greatness. Literary epics are highly conventional poems which usually share the following features, derived by way of the *Aeneid* from the traditional epics of Homer:

1)   The hero is a figure of great national or even cosmic importance. In the *Iliad* he is the Greek warrior Achilles, who is the son of the sea-nymph Thetis; and Virgil's Aeneas is the son of the goddess Aphrodite. In *Paradise Lost*, Adam and Eve are the progenitors of the entire human race, or if we regard Christ as the protagonist, He is both God and man. Blake's primal figure is "the Universal Man" Albion, who incorporates, before his fall, humanity and God and the cosmos as well.

2)   The setting of the poem is ample in scale, and may be worldwide, or even larger. Odysseus wanders over the Mediterranean basin (the whole of the world known at the time), and in Book XI he descends into the underworld (as does Virgil's Aeneas). The scope of *Paradise Lost* is the entire universe, for it takes place in heaven, on earth, in hell, and in the cosmic space between. (See *Ptolemaic universe*.)

3)   The action involves superhuman deeds in battle, such as Achilles' feats in the Trojan War, or a long, arduous, and dangerous journey intrepidly accomplished, such as the wanderings of Odysseus on his way back to his homeland, despite the opposition of some of the gods. *Paradise Lost* includes the revolt in heaven by the rebel angels against God, the journey of Satan through chaos to discover the newly created world, and his desperately audacious attempt to outwit God by corrupting mankind, in which his success is ultimately frustrated by the sacrificial action of Christ.

4)   In these great actions the gods and other supernatural beings take an interest or an active part—the Olympian gods in Homer, and Jehovah, Christ, and the angels in *Paradise Lost*. These supernatural agents were in the *Neoclassic Age* called the **machinery**, in the sense that they were part of the literary contrivances of the epic.

5) An epic poem is a ceremonial performance, and is narrated in a ceremonial style which is deliberately distanced from ordinary speech and proportioned to the grandeur and formality of the heroic subject and epic architecture. Hence Milton's **grand style**—his diction and elaborate and stylized syntax, which are often modeled on Latin poetry, his sonorous lists of names and wide-ranging *allusions,* and his imitation of Homer's *epic similes* and *epithets.*

There are also widely used epic *conventions,* or formulas, in the choice and ordering of episodes; prominent among them are these features, as exemplified in *Paradise Lost:*

1) The narrator begins by stating his **argument**, or epic theme, invokes a muse or guiding spirit to inspire him in his great undertaking, then addresses to the muse the **epic question**, the answer to which inaugurates the narrative proper (*Paradise Lost,* I, 1–49).

2) The narrative starts **in medias res**, that is "in the middle of things," at a critical point in the action. *Paradise Lost* opens with the fallen angels in hell, gathering their forces and determining on revenge. Not until Books V–VII does the angel Raphael relate to Adam the events in heaven which led to this situation; while in Books XI–XII, after the fall, Michael foretells to Adam future events up to Christ's second coming. Thus Milton's epic, although its action focuses on the temptation and fall of man, encompasses all time from the creation to the end of the world.

3) There are catalogues of some of the principal characters, introduced in formal detail, as in Milton's description of the procession of fallen angels in Book I of *Paradise Lost.* These characters are often given set speeches which reveal their diverse temperaments and moral attitudes; an example is the debate in Pandemonium, Book II.

The term "epic" is often applied, by extension, to narratives which differ in many respects from this model but manifest the epic spirit and grandeur in the scale, the scope, and the profound human importance of their subjects. In this broad sense Dante's fourteenth-century *Divine Comedy* and Edmund Spenser's late-sixteenth-century *The Faerie Queene* (1590–96) are often called epics, as are conspicuously large-scale and wide-ranging works of prose fiction such as Herman Melville's *Moby-Dick* (1851) and Leo Tolstoy's *War and Peace* (1863–69). In a still more extended application, the Marxist critic Georg Lukács uses the term **bourgeois epic** for all novels which, in his view, reflect the social reality of their capitalist age on a broad scale; and in the 1920s the German playwright Bertolt Brecht identified his plays as **epic theater**. By this term Brecht signified primarily his attempt to emulate on the stage the objectivity of epic narrative; his aim was to prevent the spectators' emotional involvement with the characters and their actions, and so to encourage them to criticize, rather than passively to accept, the social conditions that the play represents (see *estrangement effects*).

See *mock epic* and refer to W. W. Lawrence, *Beowulf and Epic Tradition* (1928); H. T. Swedenborg, *The Theory of the Epic in England, 1650–1800* (1944); C. M. Bowra, *From Vergil to Milton* (1945), and *Heroic Poetry* (1952);

E. M. W. Tillyard, *The English Epic and Its Background* (1954); C. S. Lewis, *A Preface to "Paradise Lost"* (1942); Brian Wilkie, *Romantic Poets and Epic Tradition* (1965). For an *archetypal* conception of the epic, see Northrop Frye, *Anatomy of Criticism* (1957), pp. 315–26.

Epic Similes are formal and sustained similes in which the secondary subject, or "vehicle," is developed far beyond its specific points of close parallel to the primary subject, or "tenor," to which it is compared (see *figurative language*). This figure was imitated from Homer by Virgil, Milton, and other writers of literary epics, who employed it to enhance the ceremonial quality and wide range of reference of the narrative style. So in the epic simile in *Paradise Lost* I, lines 768 ff., Milton describes his primary subject, the fallen angels thronging toward their new-built palace of Pandemonium, by an elaborate comparison to the swarming of bees:

> As Bees
> In spring time, when the Sun with Taurus rides,
> Pour forth their populous youth about the Hive
> In clusters; they among fresh dews and flowers
> Fly to and fro, or on the smoothèd Plank,
> The suburb of their Straw-built Citadel,
> New rubb'd with Balm, expatiate and confer
> Their State affairs. So thick the aery crowd
> Swarm'd and were strait'n'd; . . .

Epigram is the term applied to any very short poem—whether amatory, elegiac, meditative, complimentary, anecdotal, or satiric—which is polished, terse, and pointed; often an epigram ends with a surprising or witty turn of thought. Martial, the Roman epigrammatist, established the enduring model for one of its chief types, the caustically satiric epigram.

The epigram is a species of *light verse* which was much cultivated in England in the late sixteenth and seventeenth centuries by such poets as John Donne, Ben Jonson, and Robert Herrick. The form flourished especially in the eighteenth century, the time that Austin Dobson described as the age "of wit, of polish, and of Pope." Matthew Prior is one of the most accomplished English epigrammatists, and many of Alexander Pope's closed couplets are detachable epigrams. In the same century, when the exiled Stuarts were still pretenders to the English throne, John Byrom proposed this epigrammatic toast:

> God bless the King—I mean the Faith's defender!
> God bless (no harm in blessing) the Pretender!
> But who pretender is or who is king—
> God bless us all! that's quite another thing.

And here is one of Samuel Taylor Coleridge's epigrams, to show that Romanticism did not preclude wit:

> *On a Volunteer Singer*
> Swans sing before they die—'twere no bad thing
> Should certain people die before they sing!

Many of the short poems of Walter Savage Landor (1775–1864) were fine examples of the nonsatirical epigram. Boileau and Voltaire excelled in the epigram in France, as did Lessing, Goethe, and Schiller in Germany. The form has continued to be cultivated by Robert Frost, Ezra Pound, Roy Campbell, Ogden Nash, and other poets in the present century.

Since approximately the end of the eighteenth century, the term "epigram" has come to be applied to neat and witty statements in prose as well as verse; for the analysis of prose examples see *wit, humor, and the comic.* Refer to T. K. Whipple, *Martial and the English Epigram* (1925); E. B. Osborn, ed., *The Hundred Best Epigrams* (1928); Kingsley Amis, ed., *The New Oxford Book of Light Verse* (1978); Russell Baker, ed., *The Norton Book of Light Verse* (1986).

Epiphany means "a manifestation," and by Christian thinkers was used to signify a particular manifestation of God's presence within the created world. In the early draft of *A Portrait of the Artist as a Young Man* entitled *Stephen Hero* (published posthumously in 1944), James Joyce adapted the term to secular experience, to signify a sudden sense of radiance and revelation that one may feel while perceiving a commonplace object. "By an epiphany [Stephen] meant a sudden spiritual manifestation." "Its soul, its whatness, leaps to us from the vestment of its appearance. The soul of the commonest object . . . seems to us radiant. The object achieves its epiphany." Joyce's short stories and novels include a number of epiphanies; a climactic one is the revelation Stephen experiences at the sight of the young girl wading on the shore of the sea in *A Portrait of the Artist,* Chapter 4.

"Epiphany" has become the standard term for the description, frequent in modern poetry and prose fiction, of the sudden flare into revelation of an ordinary object or scene. Joyce, however, had merely substituted this word for what earlier authors had called "the **moment.**" Thus Shelley, in his *Defense of Poetry* (1821), described the "best and happiest moments . . . arising unforeseen and departing unbidden," "visitations of the divinity" which poetry "redeems from decay." William Wordsworth was a pre-eminent poet of what he called "moments," or in more elaborate cases, "spots of time." For examples of his short poems which represent a moment of revelation, see Wordsworth's "The Two April Mornings" and "The Solitary Reaper." Wordsworth's *Prelude,* like some of Joyce's narratives, is constructed as a sequence of such visionary encounters. Thus in Book VIII, lines 543–54 (1850 ed.), Wordsworth describes the "moment" when he for the first time passed in a stagecoach over the "threshold" of London and the "trivial forms/ Of houses, pavement, streets" suddenly manifested a profound power and significance:

> 'twas a moment's pause,—
> All that took place within me came and went
> As in a moment; yet with Time it dwells,
> And grateful memory, as a thing divine.

See Irene H. Chayes, "Joyce's Epiphanies," reprinted in *Joyce's "Portrait": Criticisms and Critiques,* ed. T. E. Connolly (1962); Morris Beja, *Epiphany in the Modern Novel* (1971); Ashton Nichols, *The Poetics of Epiphany* (1987). On the history of the traditional "moment" in sacred and secular writings since St. Augustine and the modern literary epiphany see M. H. Abrams, *Natural Supernaturalism: Tradition and Revolution in Romantic Literature* (1971), Chapters 7–8.

Epithalamion, or in the Latin form "epithalamium," is a poem written to celebrate a marriage. Among its classical practitioners were the Greeks Sappho and Theocritus and the Romans Ovid and Catullus. The term in Greek means "at the bridal chamber," for the verses were originally written to be sung outside the bedroom of a newly married couple. The form flourished among the Neo-Latin poets of the Renaissance, who established the model that was followed by writers in the vernacular languages. Sir Philip Sidney wrote the first English instance in about 1580, and fifteen years later Edmund Spenser wrote his great lyric "Epithalamion," a celebration of his own marriage that he composed as a wedding gift to his bride. Spenser's poem follows, in elaborately contrived numbers of stanzas and lines, the sequence of the hours during his wedding day and night and combines, with unfailing grace and dignity, the inherited pagan topics and mythology, Christian ritual and beliefs, and the local Irish setting. John Donne, Ben Jonson, Robert Herrick, and many other Renaissance poets composed wedding poems that were solemn or ribald, according to the intended audience and the poet's temperament. Sir John Suckling's "A Ballad upon a Wedding" is a good-humored *parody* of this upper-class poetic form, which he applies to a lower-class wedding. The tradition persists. Shelley composed an "Epithalamium"; Tennyson's *In Memoriam*, although it opens with a funeral, closes with an epithalamion; A. E. Housman spoke in the antique idiom of the bridal song in "He Is Here, Urania's Son"; and W. H. Auden wrote an "Epithalamion" in 1939.

See Robert H. Case, *English Epithalamies* (1896); Virginia J. Tufte, *The Poetry of Marriage* (1970); and (on the elaborate construction of the stanzas and lines in Spenser's "Epithalamion" to correspond with measurements of the passage of time on his wedding day) A. Kent Hieatt, *Short Time's Endless Monument* (1960).

Epithet. As a term in criticism, **epithet** denotes an adjective or adjectival phrase used to define a distinctive quality of a person or thing; an example is John Keats' *"silver snarling* trumpets" in *The Eve of St. Agnes*. The term is also applied to an identifying phrase that stands in place of a noun; thus Alexander Pope's "the *glittering forfex*" is a heroic epithet for the scissors with which the Baron performs his heinous act in *The Rape of the Lock* (1714). The frequent use of derogatory adjectives and phrases in *invective* has led to the mistaken notion that an "epithet" is always uncomplimentary.

Homeric epithets are adjectival terms—usually a compound of two words—like those which Homer in his epic poems used as formulas in referring to someone or something: *"fleet-footed* Achilles," *"bolt-hurling* Zeus," "the *wine-dark* sea." Buck Mulligan in James Joyce's *Ulysses* parodied the formula in his reference to "the snot-green sea." We often use fixed, or "conventional," epithets in identifying historical or legendary figures, as in Charles *the Great,* Lorenzo *the Magnificent, Patient* Griselda.

Essay. Any short composition in prose that undertakes to discuss a matter, express a point of view, or persuade us to accept a thesis on any subject. The essay differs from a "treatise" or "dissertation" in its lack of pretension to be a systematic and complete exposition, and in being addressed to a general rather than a specialized audience; as a consequence, the essay discusses its subject in nontechnical fashion, and often with a liberal use of such devices as anecdote, striking illustration, and humor to augment its appeal.

A useful distinction is that between the formal and informal essay. The **formal essay,** or **article,** is relatively impersonal: the author writes as an authority, or at least as highly knowledgeable, and expounds the subject in an orderly way. Examples will be found in various scholarly journals, as well as among the serious articles on current topics and issues in any of the magazines addressed to a thoughtful audience—*Harper's, Commentary, Scientific American,* and so on. In the **informal essay** (or "familiar" or "personal essay"), the author assumes a tone of intimacy with his audience, tends to deal with everyday things rather than with public affairs or specialized topics, and writes in a relaxed, self-revelatory, and sometimes whimsical fashion. Accessible modern examples are to be found in any issue of *The New Yorker.*

The Greeks Theophrastus and Plutarch and the Romans Cicero and Seneca wrote essays long before the genre was given what became its standard name by Montaigne's great French *Essais* in 1580. The title signifies "attempts," and was meant to indicate the tentative and unsystematic nature of Montaigne's discussions, in contrast to formal and technical treatises on the same subjects. Francis Bacon, late in the sixteenth century, inaugurated the English use of the term in his own *Essays;* most of them are short commentaries on such subjects as "Of Truth," "Of Adversity," "Of Marriage and the Single Life." Alexander Pope adopted the term for his expository compositions in verse, the *Essay on Criticism* (1711) and the *Essay on Man* (1733), but the verse essay has had few important exponents after the eighteenth century. In the early eighteenth century Joseph Addison and Sir Richard Steele's *Tatler* and *Spectator,* with their many successors, gave to the essay written in prose its standard modern vehicle, the literary periodical (earlier essays had been published in books). In the early nineteenth century the founding of new types of magazines, and their steady proliferation, gave great impetus to the writing of essays and made them a major department of literature. This was the age when William Hazlitt, Thomas De Quincey, and Charles Lamb brought the English essay—and especially the personal essay—to a level that has not been surpassed. Major American essayists in the nineteenth century include Washington Irving, Ralph Waldo Emerson, James Russell Lowell, and Mark Twain. In our own era the many periodicals pour out scores of essays every week. Most of them are formal in type; Virginia Woolf, George Orwell, E. M. Forster, James Thurber, and E. B. White, however, are notable recent practitioners of the informal essay.

See Hugh Walker, *The English Essay and Essayists* (1915, reprinted 1923); Robert Scholes and Carl H. Klaus, *Elements of the Essay* (1969). W. F. Bryan and R. S. Crane, eds., *The English Familiar Essay* (1916), has an excellent introduction to this literary form.

Euphemism. An inoffensive expression used in place of a blunt one that is felt to be disagreeable or embarrassing. Euphemisms are used frequently with reference to such topics as death ("pass away" instead of "die"), bodily functions ("comfort station" instead of "toilet"), and sex ("to sleep with" instead of "to have intercourse with"). Elizabethans used a euphemism when they exclaimed "Zounds!" in place of swearing by "God's wounds," and we now use a euphemism in saying "Gosh darn!" for "God damn!"

On the extraordinary number and variety of sexual euphemisms see Eric Partridge, *Shakespeare's Bawdy* (1960).

Euphony and Cacophony. Euphony is a term applied to language which strikes the ear as smooth, pleasant, and musical, as in these lines from John Keats' *The Eve of St. Agnes* (1820),

> And lucent syrops, tinct with cinnamon;
> Manna and dates, in argosy transferred
> From Fez; and spicèd dainties, every one,
> From silken Samarcand to cedar'd Lebanon.

Analysis of the passage, however, will show that what seems to be a purely auditory agreeableness is due more to the meaning of the words, and to the ease of uttering the sound combinations, than to the melodiousness of the speech sounds themselves. The American critic John Crowe Ransom illustrated this fact by altering Alfred, Lord Tennyson's euphonious "The murmur of innumerable bees" to "The murder of innumerable beeves"; the euphony is destroyed, not by the change in two of the speech sounds, but by the change in reference.

Similarly, in **cacophony**, or **dissonance**—language which seems harsh, rough, and unmusical—the discordancy is the combined effect of meaning and difficulty of pronunciation, as well as sound. Cacophony may be inadvertent, through a lapse in the writer's attention or skill, as in the unfortunate line of Matthew Arnold's fine poem "Dover Beach" (1867), "Lay like the folds of a bright girdle furled." But cacophony may also be deliberate and functional: for humor, as in Robert Browning's "Pied Piper" (1842),

> Rats!
> They fought the dogs and killed the cats . . .
> Split open the kegs of salted sprats,
> Made nests inside men's Sunday hats;

or else for other purposes, as in Thomas Hardy's attempt, in his poem "In Tenebris I," to mimic, as well as describe, dogged endurance, by the difficulty of uttering the transition from each stressed monosyllable to the next:

> I shall not lose old strength
> In the lone frost's black length.
> Strength long since fled!

For other sound effects see *alliteration* and *onomatopoeia*. Refer to G. R. Stewart, *The Technique of English Verse* (1930), and Northrop Frye, ed., *Sound and Poetry* (1957).

Euphuism. A conspicuously formal and elaborate prose style which had a vogue in the 1580s. It takes its name from the moralistic prose romance *Euphues: The Anatomy of Wit,* which John Lyly wrote in 1578. In the dialogues of this work and of *Euphues and His England* (1580), as well as in his stage comedies, Lyly exaggerated and used persistently a kind of stylized prose which other writers had developed earlier. The style is sententious (that is, full of moral maxims), relies persistently on syntactical balance and *antithesis,* reinforces the structural parallels by heavy and elaborate patterns of *alliteration* and *assonance,* exploits the *rhetorical question,* and is addicted to long similes and learned allusions which are often drawn from mythology and the habits of legendary animals. Here is a brief example from *Euphues;* the character Philautus is speaking:

> I see now that as the fish *Scholopidus* in the flood Araris at the waxing of the Moon is as white as the driven snow, and at the waning as black as the burnt coal, so Euphues, which at the first encreasing of our familiarity, was very zealous, is now at the last cast become most faithless.

Shakespeare good-humoredly *parodied* this self-consciously elegant style in *Love's Labour's Lost* and other plays; nonetheless he, like other authors of the day, profited from Lyly's explorations of the formal and rhetorical possibilities of English prose.

See *style;* also Jonas A. Barish, "The Prose Style of John Lyly," *English Literary History* 23 (1956), and G. K. Hunter, *John Lyly* (1962).

Expressionism. A German movement in literature and the other arts (especially the visual arts) which was at its height between 1910 and 1925—that is, in the period just before, during, and after World War I. Its chief precursors were artists and writers who had in various ways departed from realistic depictions of life and the world, by expressing in their art visionary or powerfully emotional states of mind. Among these precursors, in painting, were Vincent Van Gogh, Paul Gauguin, and the Norwegian Edvard Munch—Munch's lithograph "The Cry" (1894) depicting, against a bleak background, a tense figure with distorted face uttering a scream of pure horror, is often taken to epitomize what became the expressionist mode. Prominent among the literary precursors of the movement in the nineteenth century were the French poets Charles Baudelaire and Arthur Rimbaud, the Russian novelist Fyodor Dostoevsky, the German philosopher Friedrich Nietzsche, and above all the Swedish dramatist August Strindberg.

Expressionism itself was never a concerted or well-defined movement. It can be said, however, that its central feature is a revolt against the artistic and literary tradition of *realism,* both in subject matter and in style. The expressionist artist or writer undertakes to express a personal vision—usually a troubled or tensely emotional vision—of human life and human society. This is done by exaggerating and distorting what, according to the norms of artistic realism, are objective features of the outer world, and by embodying violent extremes of mood and feeling. Often the work implies that what is depicted or described represents the experience of an individual standing alone and afraid in an industrial, technological, and urban society which is disintegrating into chaos. Expressionists who were radical in their politics also projected utopian views of a future community in a regenerate world.

Expressionist painters tended to use jagged lines to depict contorted objects and forms, as well as to substitute arbitrary, often lurid colors, for natural hues; among these painters were Emil Nolde, Franz Marc, Oskar Kokoschka, and, for a time, Wassily Kandinsky. Expressionist poets (including the Germans Gottfried Benn and Georg Trakl) departed from standard meter, syntax, and poetic structure to organize their works around symbolic images. Expressionist writers of prose narratives (most eminently Franz Kafka) abandoned standard modes of characterization and plot for symbolic figures involved in an obsessive world of nightmarish events.

Drama was a prominent and widely influential form of expressionist writing. Among the better-known German playwrights were Georg Kaiser *(Gas, From Morn to Midnight),* Ernst Toller *(Mass Man),* and in his earlier productions, Bertolt Brecht. Expressionist dramatists tended to represent anonymous human types instead of individualized characters, to replace plot by episodic renderings of intense and rapidly oscillating emotional states, often to fragment the dialogue into exclamatory and seemingly incoherent sentences or phrases, and to employ masks and abstract or lopsided and sprawling stage sets. The producer Max Reinhardt, although not himself in the movement, directed a number of plays by Strindberg and by German expressionists; in them he inaugurated such modern devices as the revolving stage and special effects in lighting and sound. This mode of German drama had an important influence on the American theater. Eugene O'Neill's *The Emperor Jones* (1920) projected, in a sequence of symbolic episodes, the individual and racial memories of a terrified modern Black protagonist, and Elmer Rice's *The Adding Machine* (1923) used nonrealistic means to represent a mechanical, sterile, and frightening world as experienced by Mr. Zero, a tiny and helpless cog in the impersonal system of big business. The flexible possibility of the medium made the motion picture an important vehicle of German expressionism. Robert Wiene's early expressionist film *The Cabinet of Dr. Caligari* (1920)—representing, in ominously distorted settings, the machinations of the satanic head of an insane asylum—as well as Friedrich Murnau's *Nosferatu* (1922) and Fritz Lang's *Metropolis* (1926) are often shown in current revivals of films.

Expressionism had begun to flag by 1925 and was finally suppressed in Germany by the Nazis in the early 1930s, but it has continued to exert influence on English and American, as well as European, art and literature. We recognize its effects, direct or indirect, on the writing and staging of such plays as Thornton Wilder's *The Skin of Our Teeth* and Arthur Miller's *Death of a Salesman,* as well as on the theater of the *absurd;* on the poetry of Allen Ginsberg and other *Beat* writers; on the prose fiction of Samuel Beckett and Thomas Pynchon; and on a number of films, manifesting the distorted perceptions and fantasies of disturbed characters, by such directors as Ingmar Bergman, Federico Fellini, and Michelangelo Antonioni.

Richard Samuel and R. H. Thomas, *Expressionism in German Life, Literature and the Theater, 1910–1924* (1939); Walter H. Sokel, *The Writer in Extremis: Expressionism in Twentieth-Century German Literature* (1959); John Willett, *Expressionism* (1970). On the expressionist cinema: Siegfried Kracauer, *From Caligari to Hitler: A Psychological History of the German Film* (1947); Lotte Eisner, *The Haunted Screen: Expressionism in the German Cinema and the Influence of Max Reinhardt* (1969).

Fabliau. The medieval fabliau was a short comic or satiric tale in verse dealing realistically with middle-class or lower-class characters and delighting in the ribald; its favorite theme is the cuckolding of a stupid husband. (Professor Douglas Bush neatly characterized the type as "a short story broader than it is long.") The fabliau flourished in France in the twelfth and thirteenth centuries and became popular in England during the fourteenth century. Chaucer, who wrote one of the greatest serious short stories in verse, the account of Death and the rioters in "The Pardoner's Tale," also wrote one of the best fabliaux, the hilarious "Miller's Tale."

See Joseph Bédier, *Les Fabliaux* (5th ed., 1928); and *Fabliaux: Ribald Tales from the Old French,* trans. Robert Hellman and Richard O'Gorman (1976).

Fancy and Imagination. The distinction between fancy and imagination was a key element in Samuel Taylor Coleridge's theory of poetry, as well as in his general theory of the mental processes. In earlier discussions, "fancy" and "imagination" had for the most part been used synonymously to denote a faculty of the mind which is distinguished from "reason," "judgment," and "memory," in that it receives "images" that have been perceived by the senses and reorders them into new combinations. In the thirteenth chapter of *Biographia Literaria* (1817), Coleridge attributes this reordering function of the sensory images to the lower faculty he calls **fancy:** "Fancy . . . has no other counters to play with, but fixities and definites. The Fancy is indeed no other than a mode of Memory emancipated from the order of time and space." To Coleridge, that is, the fancy is a mechanical process which receives the elementary images—the "fixities and definites" which come to it ready-made from the senses—and, without altering the parts, reassembles them into a different spatial and temporal order from that in which they were originally perceived. The **imagination** that produces a higher order of poetry, however,

> dissolves, diffuses, dissipates, in order to re-create; or where this process is rendered impossible, yet still at all events it struggles to idealize and unify. It is essentially *vital,* even as all objects (*as* objects) are essentially fixed and dead.

Coleridge's imagination, that is, is able to "create" rather than merely reassemble, by dissolving the fixities and definites—the mental pictures, or images, received from the senses—and unifying them into a new whole. And while the fancy is merely mechanical, the imagination is "vital"; that is, it is an organic faculty which operates not like a sorting machine, but like a living and growing plant. As Coleridge says elsewhere, the imagination "generates and produces a form of its own," while its rules are "the very powers of growth and production." And in the fourteenth chapter of the *Biographia* Coleridge adds his famous statement that the "synthetic" power which is the "imagination . . . reveals itself in the balance or reconciliation of opposite or discordant qualities: of sameness, with difference; of the general, with the concrete; the idea, with the image. . . ." The faculty of imagination, in other words, assimilates and synthesizes the most disparate elements into an organic whole—that is, a newly generated unity, constituted by a living interdependence of parts whose identity cannot survive their removal from the whole. (See *organic form*.)

Most critics after Coleridge who distinguished fancy from imagination tended to make fancy simply the faculty that produces a lesser, lighter, or humorous kind of poetry, and to make imagination the faculty that produces a higher, more serious, and more passionate poetry. And the concept of "imagination" itself is as various as the modes of psychology that critics have adopted (associationist, Gestalt, *Freudian, Jungian*), while its processes vary according to the way in which a critic conceives of the nature of a poem (as essentially realistic or essentially visionary, as "object" or as "myth," as "pure poetry" or as a work designed to produce effects on an audience).

See I. A. Richards, *Coleridge on Imagination* (1934); M. H. Abrams, *The Mirror and the Lamp* (1953), Chapter 7; Richard H. Fogle, *The Idea of Coleridge's Criticism* (1962).

Fiction and Truth. In an inclusive sense, **fiction** is any literary *narrative,* whether in prose or verse, which is invented instead of being an account of events that in fact happened. In a narrower sense, however, fiction denotes only narratives that are written in prose (the *novel* and *short story*), and sometimes is used simply as a synonym for the novel. Literary prose narratives in which the fiction is to a prominent degree based on biographical, historical, or contemporary facts and events are often referred to by compound names such as "fictional biography," the *historical novel,* and the *nonfiction novel.*

Both philosophers and literary critics have concerned themselves with the logical analysis of the types of sentences which constitute a fictional text, and especially with the question of their **truth,** or what is sometimes called their "truth-value"—that is, whether, and in just what way, they are subject to the criterion of truth or falsity. Some thinkers have asserted that "fictional sentences" should be regarded as referring to a special world, "created" by the author, which is analogous to the real world, but possesses its own setting, beings, and mode of coherence. (See M. H. Abrams, *The Mirror and the Lamp,* 1953, pp. 272–85, "The Poem as Heterocosm"; James Phelan, *Worlds from Words: A Theory of Language in Fiction,* 1981.) Others, and most notably I. A. Richards, have held that fiction is a form of **emotive language,** composed of **pseudostatements;** and that whereas a statement in "referential language" is "justified by its truth, i.e., its correspondence . . . with the fact to which it points," a pseudostatement "is justified entirely by its effect in releasing or organizing our attitudes" (I. A. Richards, *Science and Poetry,* 1926). Most current theorists, however, present an elaborated logical version of what Sir Philip Sidney long ago proposed in his *Apology for Poetry* (published 1595), that a poet "nothing affirmes, therefore never lyeth. For, as I take it, to lye is to affirm that to be true which is false." Current versions of this view hold that fictive sentences are meaningful according to the rules of ordinary, nonfictional discourse, but that, in accordance with conventions implicitly shared by the author and reader of a work of fiction, they are not put forward as assertions of fact, and therefore are not subject to the criterion of truth or falsity as these apply to sentences in nonfictional discourse. See Margaret MacDonald, "The Language of Fiction" (1954), reprinted in W. E. Kennick, ed., *Art and Philosophy* (rev., 1979).

In *speech act theorists,* a related view takes the form that a writer of fiction only "pretends" to make assertions, or "imitates" the making of assertions, and so suspends the "normal illocutionary commitment" of the writer of such utterances to the claim that what he asserts is true. See John R. Searle, "The Logical Status of Fictional Discourse," in *Expression and Meaning: Studies in the Theory of Speech Acts* (1979, reprinted 1986). We find in a number of other theorists the attempt to extend the concept of "fictive utterances" to include all the genres of literature—poems, narratives, and dramas, as well as novels; all these forms, it is proposed, are imitations, or fictive representations, of some type of "natural" discourse. A novel, for example, not only is made up of fictional utterances, but is itself a fictive utterance, in that it "*represents* the verbal action of a man [i.e., the narrator] reporting, describing, and referring." See Barbara Hernnstein Smith, "Poetry as Fiction," in *Margins of Discourse* (1978), and Richard Ohmann, "Speech Acts and the Definition of Literature," *Philosophy and Rhetoric* 4 (1971).

Most modern theorists, whatever their persuasion, make an important distinction between the fictional scenes, persons, events, and dialogue that a narrator reports or describes and the narrator's own assertions about the world, human life, or the human situation; the central, or controlling, generalizations of the latter sort are said to be the *theme* or **thesis** of a work. These assertions by the narrator may be explicit (for example, Thomas Hardy's statement at the end of *Tess of the D'Urbervilles,* "The President of the immortals had had his sport with Tess"; or Tolstoy's philosophy of history at the end of *War and Peace*). Many such assertions, however, are said to be merely "implied," "suggested," or "inferrable" from the narrator's choice and control of the fictional characters and plot of the narrative itself. It is often claimed that such generalizations by the narrator within a fictional work, whether expressed or implied, function as assertions which claim to be true about the world, and that they thereby serve to relate the fictional narrative to the factual and moral world of actual experience. See John Hospers, "Implied Truths in Literature" (1960), reprinted in W. E. Kennick, ed., *Art and Philosophy* (rev., 1979).

A much-discussed topic, related to the question of an author's assertions and truth claims in narrative fiction, is that of the role of the **beliefs** of the reader. The problem raised is the extent to which a reader's moral, religious, and social convictions, as they coincide with or diverge from those explicitly asserted, or else implicitly put forth in a work, determine the interpretation, imaginative acceptability, and evaluation of that work by the reader. For the history and discussions of this problem in literary criticism, see William Joseph Rooney, *The Problem of "Poetry and Belief" in Contemporary Criticism* (1949); M. H. Abrams, editor and contributor, *Literature and Belief* (1957); Walter Benn Michaels, "Saving the Text: Reference and Belief," *Modern Language Notes* 93 (1978).

A review of theories concerning the relevance of the criterion of truth to fiction is Monroe C. Beardsley's *Aesthetics: Problems in the Philosophy of Criticism* (1958), pp. 409–19; see also René Wellek, "Literature, Fiction, and Literariness," in *The Attack on Literature and Other Essays* (1982). For an analysis and critique of theories of emotive language see Max Black, "Questions about Emotive Meaning," in *Language and Philosophy* (1949), Chapter 9. Gerald Graff defends propositional truth in poetry in *Poetic Statement and Critical Dogma* (1970), Chapter 6.

Figurative Language is a departure from what users of the language apprehend as the standard meaning of words, or else the standard order of words, in order to achieve some special meaning or effect. Such figures were long described as primarily poetic "ornaments," but they are integral to the functioning of language, and indispensable not only to poetry, but to all modes of discourse.

Modern classifications and analyses are based on the treatment of figurative language by classical rhetoricians; the fullest and most influential treatment is in the Roman Quintilian's *Institutes of Oratory* (first century A.D.), Books VIII and IX. Since that time, figurative language has often been divided into two classes: (1) "Figures of thought," or **tropes** (meaning "turns," "conversions"), in which words or phrases are used in a way that effects a conspicuous change in what we take to be their standard meaning. The standard meaning, as opposed to its meaning in the figurative use, is called the **literal meaning.** (For a philosophical analysis of standard, or literal, meaning, see John R. Searle, *Expression and Meaning,* 1979, Chapter 5, and "The Background of Meaning," in *Speech Act Theory and Pragmatics,* ed. John R. Searle, 1980.) (2) "Figures of speech," or "rhetorical figures," or **schemes** (from the Greek word for "form"), in which the departure from standard usage is not primarily in the meaning of the words, but in the syntactical order or pattern of the words. This distinction is not a sharp one, nor do all critics agree on its application. For convenience of exposition, however, the most common tropes are treated here, and the most common figures of speech are collected in the article *rhetorical figures.* A number of other deviations from the standard significance or order of words, treated in individual articles of the *Glossary* but often classified as tropes, are listed at the end of this essay.

In a **simile,** a comparison between two distinctly different things is indicated by the word "like" or "as." A simple example is Robert Burns' "O my love's like a red, red rose." The following simile from Samuel Taylor Coleridge's "The Rime of the Ancient Mariner" also specifies the feature ("green") in which icebergs are similar to emerald:

> And ice, mast-high, came floating by,
> As green as emerald.

See also *epic similes.*

In a **metaphor,** a word or expression which in literal usage denotes one kind of thing or action is applied to a distinctly different kind of thing or action, without asserting a comparison. For example, if Burns had said "O my love is a red, red rose" he would have uttered, technically speaking, a metaphor instead of a simile. Here is a more complex metaphor from the contemporary poet Stephen Spender, in which he describes the eye as it perceives a landscape:

> Eye, gazelle, delicate wanderer,
> Drinker of horizon's fluid line.*

For the distinction between metaphor and symbol, see *symbol.*

It should be noted that in these examples we can distinguish two elements, the metaphorical term, and its metaphorical signification or subject. In a widely adopted usage, I. A. Richards introduced the name **tenor** for the subject that the metaphor is applied to ("my love" in the altered line from Burns, and "eye" in Spender's lines), and the name **vehicle** for the metaphorical term itself ("rose" in Burns, and the three words "gazelle," "wanderer," and "drinker" in Spender). In an **implicit metaphor,** the tenor is not itself specified, but only implied; thus, if one were to say, while discussing someone's death, "That reed was too frail to survive the storm of its sorrows," the situational and verbal context of the term "reed" indicates that it is the vehicle for an unspecified tenor, a human being, while "storm" is the vehicle for an aspect of a specified tenor, "sorrows." Those aspects, properties, or common associations of a vehicle which, in a given context, apply to a tenor (specified or implicit) are called by Richards the **grounds** of a metaphor. (See I. A. Richards, *Philosophy of Rhetoric,* 1936, Chapters 5–6.)

All the metaphoric terms, or vehicles, cited so far have been nouns, but other parts of speech may also be used metaphorically. The metaphoric use of a verb occurs in Shakespeare's *Merchant of Venice,* V. i. 54, "How sweet the moonlight *sleeps* upon this bank"; and the metaphoric use of an adjective occurs in Andrew Marvell's "The Garden" (1681):

> Annihilating all that's made
> To a *green* thought in a green shade.

Theories or explanations of the nature and workings of metaphor fall roughly into two broad classes. The most common, introduced by Aristotle

---

* Lines from "Not palaces, an era's crown," from *Collected Poems, 1928–1953,* by Stephen Spender. Copyright 1934 by The Modern Library, Inc., and renewed 1962 by Stephen Spender. Reprinted by permission of Random House, Inc., and Faber & Faber Ltd.

in the fourth century B.C., maintains that a metaphor involves an implicit comparison or similarity between a literal object and a metaphoric object; in this view, a metaphor is an elliptical form of simile. I. A. Richards proposed in 1936 the alternative view that the meaning of a metaphor is the product of an "interaction" between the meanings of the vehicle and the tenor of a metaphor. In an influential essay, the philosopher Max Black refined and expanded this notion of interaction by specifying that the vehicle of a metaphor involves a system of "implications," or "associated common-places" that serve as a filter through which we view the topic, or subject, of the metaphor, and so reorganize the way we ordinarily conceive it. Recently John Searle has rejected both the comparison and interaction views as inadequate, on the grounds that at best they serve to explain, and that only in part and in a misleading way, how some metaphors come to be produced and to be understood. Searle, in consonance with his overall *speech act theory*, proposes that to explain metaphor we must distinguish between "word, or sentence meaning" (the literal meaning of the spoken or written expression) and "utterance meaning" (the metaphorical meaning that a speaker or writer uses the word or sentence, with their literal meaning, to express). He goes on to present a set of implicit principles, shared by the speaker and interpreter, to explain how we are able both to produce and to understand metaphorical utterances, as well as to clarify the variety of the relations that may obtain between a literal sentence meaning and the metaphorical utterance meaning of diverse figurative utterances. (For the writings on metaphor by Black and Searle, see the list of readings below.)

A **mixed metaphor** combines two or more diverse metaphoric vehicles. When used inadvertently, without sensitivity to the possible incongruity of the vehicles, the effect can be ludicrous: "Girding up his loins, the chairman plowed through the mountainous agenda." Densely figurative poets such as Shakespeare, however, often mix metaphors in a functional way. Examples are Hamlet's expression of his troubled state of mind in his *soliloquy* (III. i. 59–60), "to take arms against a sea of trouble,/And by opposing end them," and the involvement of metaphor within metaphor in Shakespeare's Sonnet 65:

> O, how shall summer's honey breath hold out
> Against the wrackful siege of battering days?

A **dead metaphor** is one which, like "the leg of a table" or "the heart of the matter," has been so long used and become so common that we have ceased to be aware of the discrepancy between vehicle and tenor. A dead metaphor, however, is only moribund, and can readily be brought back to life. Someone asked Groucho Marx, "Are you a man or a mouse?" He answered, "Throw me a piece of cheese and you'll find out." The history of language indicates that most words that we now take to be literal were, in the distant past, metaphors.

Some tropes, sometimes classified as species of the class "metaphor," are more frequently given names of their own:

In **metonymy** (Greek for "a change of name"), the literal term for one thing is applied to another with which it is closely associated, because of contiguity in common experience. Thus "the crown" or "the scepter" can be used to stand for a king and "the turf" for horse racing; "Milton" can be used to signify the writings of Milton ("I have read all of Milton"); and typical attire to signify the male and female sexes: "doublet and hose ought to show itself courageous to petticoat" (Shakespeare, *As You Like It*, II. iv. 6). (For the influential distinction by the linguist Roman Jakobson between the meta-phoric, or "vertical," and the metonymic, or "horizontal," dimension of lin-guistic usage, and its application to many aspects of the functioning of lan-guage, see under *linguistics in literary criticism.*)

In **synecdoche** (Greek for "taking together"), a part of something is used to signify the whole, or (more rarely) the whole is used to signify a part. We use the term "ten *hands*" for ten workmen, or "a hundred *sails*" (for ships); and Milton refers to the corrupt clergy in "Lycidas" as "blind *mouths.*"

Another figure related to metaphor is **personification,** or in the Greek term, **prosopopeia,** in which either an inanimate object or an abstract con-cept is spoken of as though it were endowed with life or with human attri-butes or feelings (compare *pathetic fallacy*). Milton wrote in *Paradise Lost* (IX, 1002–3), as Adam bit into the fatal apple,

> Sky lowered, and muttering thunder, some sad drops
> Wept at completing of the mortal sin.

The second stanza of Keats' "To Autumn" finely personifies the season, autumn, as a woman carrying on the rural chores of that time of year. The personification of abstract terms was standard in eighteenth-century *poetic diction,* where it sometimes became a thoughtless formula. Coleridge cited an eighteenth-century ode celebrating the invention of inoculation against smallpox which began with this *apostrophe* to the personified subject of the poem:

> Inoculation! heavenly Maid, descend!

See Steven Knapp, *Personification and the Sublime* (1986).

The term **kenning** denotes the standard use, in the Anglo-Saxon *Beowulf* and poems written in other Old Germanic languages, of a descriptive phrase in place of the ordinary name for something. This type of *periphrasis,* which at times becomes a stereotyped expression, is an indication of the origin of these poems in oral tradition (see *oral formulaic poetry*). Some kennings are instances of *metonymy* ("the whale road" for the sea, and "the ring-giver" for a king); others of *synecdoche* ("the ringed prow" for a ship); still others describe salient or picturesque features of the object referred to ("foamy-necked floater" for a ship under sail, "storm of swords" for a battle).

Other deviations from the standard use of words, often classified as tropes, are treated elsewhere in this *Glossary: aporia, conceit, epic similes, hyperbole, irony, litotes, paradox, periphrasis, pun, understatement.* In recent decades, especially in the *New Criticism, Russian formalism, deconstruction,* and Harold Bloom's theory of the *anxiety of influence,* there has been a strong revival of interest in the classification and function of figurative language, which was once thought to be largely the province of pedantic rhetoricians.

Metaphor especially has become a focus of attention and analysis, by professional philosophers as well as by linguists and literary critics.

A clear summary of the standard classification of figures, inherited from the classical past, is Edward P. J. Corbett, *Classical Rhetoric for the Modern Student* (3d ed., 1990). Sister Miriam Joseph's *Shakespeare's Use of the Arts of Language* (1947) treats the conventional analysis of figures in the Renaissance. René Wellek and Austin Warren, in *Theory of Literature* (rev., 1970), summarize, with bibliography, diverse treatments of figurative language; and Jonathan Culler, in *Structuralist Poetics* (1975) and *The Pursuit of Signs* (1981), discusses more recent developments. Influential philosophical analyses of metaphor, discussed above, are Max Black, "Metaphor," in *Models and Metaphor* (1962), and "More About Metaphor," in *Metaphor and Thought,* ed. Edward Ortney (1979); and John R. Searle, *Expression and Meaning* (1979), Chapter 4, "Metaphor"; see also Paul Ricoeur, *The Rule of Metaphor* (1977); and Mark Johnson, ed., *Philosophical Perspectives on Metaphor* (1981). Sheldon Sacks, ed., *On Metaphor* (1979), includes recent essays by Black, Ricoeur, and other philosophers, as well as by literary critics. Eva Feder Kittay, in *Metaphor: Its Cognitive Force and Linguistic Structure* (1987), elaborates and refines Black's theory of interaction.

On the role of root metaphors in philosophical systems, see Stephen C. Pepper, *World Hypotheses* (1942); and on the constitutive metaphors that underlie and structure diverse theories in literary criticism, M. H. Abrams, *The Mirror and the Lamp* (1953). A comprehensive bibliography of discussions of metaphor up to the time of its publication is Warren A. Shibles, *Metaphor: An Annotated Bibliography and History* (1971).

Folklore, since the mid-nineteenth century, has been the collective name applied to sayings, verbal compositions, and social rituals that have been handed down solely, or at least primarily, by word of mouth and by example rather than in written form. Folklore developed, and continues even now to flourish, in communities where few if any people can read or write. It includes legends, superstitions, songs, tales, proverbs, riddles, spells, and nursery rhymes; pseudoscientific lore about the weather, plants, and animals; customary activities at births, marriages, and deaths; and traditional dances and forms of drama which are performed on holidays or at communal gatherings. Elements of folklore have at all times entered into sophisticated written literature. For example, the choice among the three caskets in Shakespeare's *Merchant of Venice* (II. ix) and the superstition about a maiden's dream which is central to Keats' *Eve of St. Agnes* (1820) are both derived from folklore.

The following forms of folklore have been of special importance for later written literature:

Folk drama originated in primitive rites of song and dance, especially in connection with agricultural activities, which centered on vegetational deities and goddesses of fertility. Some scholars maintain that Greek *tragedy* developed from such rites, which celebrated the life, death, and rebirth of the vegetational god Dionysus. Folk dramas survive in England in such forms as the St. George play and the **mummers' play** (a "mummer" is a masked actor). Thomas Hardy's *The Return of the Native* (Book II, Chapter 5) describes the performance of a mummers' play, and a form of this drama is still performed in America in the Kentucky mountains. See Edmund K. Chambers, *The English Folk-Play* (1933).

Folk songs include love songs, Christmas carols, work songs, sea chanties, religious songs, drinking songs, children's game-songs, and many other types of lyric, in addition to the narrative song, or traditional *ballad.* (See *oral formulaic poetry.*) All forms of folk song have been assiduously collected since the late eighteenth century, and have inspired many imitations by writers of lyric poetry. Robert Burns collected and edited Scottish folk songs, restored or rewrote them, and imitated them in his own lyrics. His "A Red, Red Rose" and "Auld Lang Syne," for example, both derive from one or more folk songs, and his "Green Grow the Rashes, O" is a tidied-up version of a bawdy folk song. See J. C. Dick, *The Songs of Robert Burns* (1903); Cecil J. Sharp, *Folk Songs of England* (5 vols.; 1908–12); and Alan Lomax, *The Folk Songs of North America* (1960).

The **folktale**, strictly defined, is a short narrative in prose of unknown authorship which has been transmitted orally. The term, however, is often extended to include stories invented by a known author—such as "The Three Bears" by Robert Southey (1774–83) and Parson Mason L. Weems' story of George Washington and the cherry tree—which have been picked up and repeatedly narrated by word of mouth as well as in printed form. Folktales are found among peoples everywhere in the world. They include *myths, fables,* tales of heroes (whether historical like Johnny Appleseed, or legendary like Paul Bunyan), and fairy tales. Many so-called "fairy tales" (the German word **Märchen** is frequently used for this type of folktale) are not stories of fairies but of various kinds of marvels; examples are "Snow White" and "Jack and the Beanstalk." Another type of folk tale, the set "joke," or comic (often bawdy) *anecdote,* is the most abundant and persistent of all; new jokes, or new versions of very old jokes, continue to be a staple of contemporary social exchange, wherever people congregate in a relaxed mood.

The same, or closely similar, oral stories have turned up in Europe, Asia, and Africa, and have been embodied in the narratives of many writers. Chaucer's *Canterbury Tales* includes a number of folktales; "The Pardoner's Tale" of Death and the three rioters, for example, was of Eastern origin. See Benjamin A. Botkin, *A Treasury of American Folklore* (1944), and Vladimir Propp, *Morphology of the Folktale* (1970). The standard catalogue of the recurrent *motifs* in folktales throughout the world is Stith Thompson's *Motif-Index of Folk-Literature* (1932–37).

Form and Structure. "Form" is one of the most frequently used terms in literary criticism, but also one of the most diverse in its meanings. It is often used merely to designate a *genre* or literary type ("the lyric form," "the short story form"), or for patterns of meter, lines, and rhymes ("the verse form," "the stanza form"). It is also, however—in a meaning descended from the Latin "forma," which was equivalent to the Greek "idea"—the term for a central critical concept. In this application, the **form** of a work is the principle that determines its organization; critics, however, differ greatly in their descriptions of this principle. All agree that "form" is not simply a fixed container, like a bottle, into which the "content" or "subject matter" of a work is poured; but beyond this, the definition of form varies according to a critic's particular assumptions and theoretical orientation (see *criticism*).

Many *neoclassic* critics, for example, thought of the form of a work as a combination of component parts, matched to each other according to the principle of *decorum,* or mutual fittingness. In the early nineteenth century Samuel Taylor Coleridge, following the lead of the German critic A. W. Schlegel, distinguished between **mechanic form**, which is a fixed, preexistent shape such as we impose on wet clay by a mold, and **organic form,** which, as Coleridge says, "is innate; it shapes as it develops itself from within, and the fullness of its development is one and the same with the perfection of its outward form." To Coleridge, in other words, as to other **organicists** in literary criticism, a good poem is like a growing plant which evolves, by an internal energy, into the organic unity which constitutes its achieved form. (See *fancy and imagination.*) Many *New Critics* use the word **structure** interchangeably with "form," and regard it as primarily an equilibrium, or an interaction, or an ironic and paradoxical tension, of diverse words and images in an organized totality of "meanings." Various exponents of *archetypal* theory regard the form of a literary work as one of a limited number of plot-shapes which it shares with myths, rituals, dreams, and other elemental and recurrent patterns of human experience. And *structuralist critics* conceive a literary structure on the model of the systematic way that a language is structured.

In an influential critical enterprise, R. S. Crane, a leader of the **Chicago School** of criticism, has revived and developed the concept of form in Aristotle's *Poetics.* Crane distinguishes between "form" and "structure." The form of a literary work is (in the Greek term) the "dynamis," the particular "working" or "emotional 'power'" that the composition is designed to effect, which functions as its "shaping principle." This formal principle controls and synthesizes the "structure" of a work—that is, the order, emphasis, and rendering of all its component materials and parts—into "a beautiful and effective whole of a determinate kind." See R. S. Crane, *The Languages of Criticism and the Structure of Poetry* (1953), Chapters 1 and 4; also Wayne C. Booth, "Between Two Generations: The Heritage of the Chicago School," in *Profession 82* (Modern Language Association, 1982).

Refer to René Wellek, "Concepts of Form and Structure in Twentieth-Century Criticism," in *Concepts of Criticism* (1963).

Format of a Book. **Format** signifies the size, shape, and other physical features of a book. The printer begins with a large "sheet"; if the sheet is folded once so as to form two "leaves" of four pages, the book is a **folio** (the Latin word for "leaf"). When we refer to "the first Shakespeare folio," for example, we mean a volume published in 1623, the first edition of Shakespeare's collected plays, the leaves of which were made by a single folding of the printer's sheets. A sheet folded twice into four leaves makes a **quarto**; a sheet folded a third time into eight leaves makes an **octavo**. In a **duodecimo** volume, a sheet is folded so as to make twelve leaves. The more leaves into which a single sheet is divided, the smaller the leaf, so that these terms indicate the dimensions of a book, but only approximately, because the size of the full sheet varies, especially in modern printing. It can be said, however, that a folio is a very large book; a quarto is the next in size, with a leaf that is nearly square. The third in size, the octavo, is the most frequently used in modern printing.

As this book is open in front of you, the page on the right is called a **recto**, and the page on the left is called a **verso**.

The **colophon** in older books was a note at the end stating such facts as the title, author, printer, and date of issue. In modern books the colophon is ordinarily in the front, on the title page. With reference to modern books, "colophon" has come to mean, usually, the publisher's emblem, such as a torch (Harper), an owl (Holt), or a ship (Viking).

The term **incunabula** (the singular is "incunabulum") signifies books published in the infancy of printing. The terminal date is 1500, about fifty years after the German printer Johann Gutenberg invented movable printing type. (The word "incunabula" is Latin for "swaddling clothes.")

The word **edition** now designates the total copies of a book that are printed from a single setting of type. The various "printings" or "reprints" of an edition—sometimes with a few minor changes in the text—may be spaced over a period of years. We now identify as a "new edition" a printing in which substantial changes have been made in the text. A text may be revised and reprinted in this way many times, hence the terms "second edition," "third edition," etc.

A **variorum edition** designates either (1) an edition of a work that lists all the textual variants in an author's manuscripts and printed revisions; an example is *The Variorum Edition of the Poems of W. B. Yeats,* ed. Peter Allt and Russell K. Alspach (1957); or (2) an edition of a text that includes a selection of annotations and commentaries on the text by earlier editors and critics. *The New Variorum Edition of Shakespeare,* still in process, is a variorum edition in both senses of the word.

See *textual criticism*. The classic work on bookmaking and printing is Ronald B. McKerrow, *An Introduction to Bibliography* (rev., 1965). Also, Fredson Bowers, *Principles of Bibliographical Description* (1949); Philip Gaskell, *A New Introduction to Bibliography* (1972); G. Thomas Tanselle, *The History of Books as a Field of Study* (1981).

Free Verse is also known as "open form" verse, or by the French term **vers libre**. Like traditional verse, it is printed in short lines instead of with the continuity of prose, but it differs from such verse by the fact that its rhythmic pattern is not organized into meter—that is, into feet, or recurrent units of weak- and strong-stressed syllables. (See *meter*.) Most free verse also has irregular line lengths and lacks *rhyme*.

Within these broad boundaries, there is a great diversity in the measures that are labeled free verse. An approximation to one modern form occurs in the King James translation of the biblical Psalms and Song of Solomon, which imitates in English prose the parallelism and cadences of the Hebrew poetry. In the nineteenth century, William Blake and Matthew Arnold experimented with departures from regular meters; and in 1855, Walt Whitman startled the literary world with his *Leaves of Grass* by using verse lines of varying length which depended for rhythmic effects not on recurrent metric feet, but on cadenced units and on the repetition, balance, and variation of words, phrases, clauses, and lines. French *Symbolist* poets in the later nineteenth century, and American and English poets of the present century, especially after World War I, began the present era of the intensive use of free verse. It has been employed by Rainer Maria Rilke, Jules Laforgue, T. S. Eliot, Ezra Pound, William Carlos Williams, and numberless other poets in all the Western languages. Most of the verse in English that is published today is nonmetrical.

Among the many modes of open versification in English, we can make a broad distinction between the long-lined and often orotund verses of poets like Whitman and Allen Ginsberg, of which a principal origin is the translated poetry of the Hebrew Bible, and the shorter-lined, conversational, often ironic forms employed by the majority of writers in free verse. Such poets yield up the drive, beat, and song achievable by traditional meters in order to exploit other rhythmic possibilities. A poem by E. E. Cummings will illustrate the effects that became available when the verse is released from a regular line and reiterative beat. Instead, Cummings uses conspicuous visual cues—the variable positioning, spacing, and length of words, phrases, and lines—to control pace, pause, and emphasis in the reading, and also to achieve an alternation of suspension and relief, in accordance as the line-ends work against or coincide with the pull toward closure of the units of syntax.

> *Chanson Innocente* *
>
> in Just-
> spring   when the world is mud-
> luscious the little
> lame balloonman
>
> whistles   far   and wee
>
> and eddieandbill come
> running from marbles and
> piracies and it's
> spring
>
> when the world is puddle-wonderful
>
> the queer
> old balloonman whistles
> far   and   wee
> and bettyandisbel come dancing

---

from hop-scotch and jump-rope and

its
spring
and
    the

       goat-footed

balloonMan   whistles
far
and
wee

A very short poem by A. R. Ammons exemplifies the unobtrusive way in which, even as he departs from them, a free-verse poet can recall and exploit traditional stanza forms and meters:

Small Song *
The reeds give
way to the

wind and give
the wind away

The visual pattern of the printed poem signals that we are to read it as consisting of four equal lines of three words each, and as divided into two stanzaic *couplets*. The first line of each stanza ends with the same word "give," not only to achieve tension and release in the suspended syntax of each of the verb-phrases, but also, by means of the parallelism, to enhance our surprise at the shift of meaning from "give way" (surrender) to "give . . . away" (reveal, with a suggestion also of yield up). The poet also adapts standard metric feet to his special purposes: the poem is framed by opening and closing with a regular iambic foot, yet is free to mimic internally the resistance to the wind in the recurrent strong stresses in the first stanza (Thĕ réeds gíve/wáy) and the graceful yielding to the wind in the succession of light iambs in the second stanza (Ănd gíve/thĕ wínd ăwáy).

See Percy Mansell Jones, *The Background of Modern French Poetry* (1951); Donald Wesling, "The Prosodies of Free Verse," in *Twentieth-Century Literature in Retrospect,* ed. Reuben A. Brower (1971); Paul Fussell, *Poetic Meter and Poetic Form* (rev., 1979); Charles O. Hartman, *Free Verse: An Essay on Prosody* (1980). Timothy Steele's *Missing Measures: Modern Poetry and the Revolt against Meter* (1990) is a history of free verse by a writer who argues for a return to metrical versification.

Genre. A term, French in origin, that denotes a recurring type of literature, or as we now often call it, a "literary form." The genres into which works of

* "Small Song" is reprinted from *The Really Short Poems of A. R. Ammons,* by permission of W. W. Norton & Company, Inc. Copyright © 1990 by A. R. Ammons.

literature have been classified at different times are very numerous, and the criteria on which the classifications have been based are highly variable. Since the writings of Plato and Aristotle, however, there has been an enduring division of the overall literary domain into three large generic classes, in terms of who speaks in the work: *lyric* (uttered throughout in the first person), *epic* or *narrative* (in which the narrator speaks in the first person, then lets his characters speak for themselves); and *drama* (in which the characters do all the talking). A similar tripartite scheme was elaborated by German critics in the late eighteenth and early nineteenth centuries, was echoed by James Joyce in his *Portrait of the Artist as a Young Man* (1916), Chapter 5, and is still recognizable in general critical discourse and in the widespread division of college courses, and of anthologies of literature, into poetry, novels, and drama.

Within this overarching division, Plato, Aristotle, and other classical critics identified a number of more limited genres. Many of the ancient names, including *epic, tragedy, comedy,* and *satire,* have remained current to the present day; to them have been added, over the last three centuries, such newcomers as *biography, essay,* and *novel.* A glance at the articles listed in the Index under *genre* will indicate the criss-crossing diversity of the classes and sub-classes to which individual works of literature have been assigned.

Through the Renaissance and much of the eighteenth century, the recognized genres—or poetic "kinds" as they were then called—were widely thought to be fixed literary types, somewhat like species in the biological order of nature. Many *neoclassic* critics insisted that each kind must remain "pure" (there must, for example, be no "mixing" of tragedy and comedy), and also proposed *rules* which specified the subject matter, structure, style, and emotional effect proper to each kind. At that time the genres were also commonly ranked in a hierarchy (related to the ranking of social classes, from royalty and the nobility down to peasants—see *decorum*), ranging from epic and tragedy at the top to the pastoral, short lyric, epigram, and other types, then considered to be minor genres, at the bottom. Shakespeare satirized the pedantic classifiers of his era in Polonius' catalogue (*Hamlet,* II. ii) of types of drama: "tragedy, comedy, history, pastoral, pastoral-comical, historical-pastoral, tragical-historical, tragical-comical-historical-pastoral . . ."

In the course of the eighteenth century the emergence of new literary types—such as the novel, and the poem which combined natural description, philosophy, and narrative (James Thomson's *Seasons,* 1726–30)—helped weaken confidence in the fixity and stability of genres. And in the latter eighteenth and early nineteenth century, the extraordinary rise in the prominence and prestige of the short lyric poem, and the concurrent shift in the basis of critical theory to an *expressive* orientation, effected a drastic alteration both in the conception and ranking of literary genres, with the lyric replacing epic and tragedy as the quintessentially poetic type. From the Romantic Period on, a decreasing emphasis on the generic conception of literature was indicated by the widespread use of criteria for evaluating literature which—unlike those in neoclassic criticism, which tended to be specific to a particular genre—were broadly applicable to all literary works: criteria such as "sincerity," "intensity," "organic unity," and "high seriousness." In the *New Criticism* of the mid-twentieth century, with its ruling concept of the uniqueness of each literary work, genre ceased to play more than a subordinate role in critical analysis and evaluation. For the changes in the nineteenth century in the classification and ranking of the genres, see M. H. Abrams, *The Mirror and the Lamp* (1953), especially Chapters 1, 4, and 6; on the continuance, as well as changes, of writings in the traditional genres during the Romantic Period, see Stuart Curran, *Poetic Form and British Romanticism* (1986).

Since 1950 or so, genre theory has been revived by some critical theorists, although on varied principles of classification. R. S. Crane and other *Chicago critics* have defended the utility for practical criticism of a redefined distinction among genres, based on the principles of classification in Aristotle's *Poetics;* see Crane, ed., *Critics and Criticism* (1952), pp. 12–24, 546–63, and refer to the *Chicago school* in this *Glossary.* Northrop Frye has proposed an *archetypal* theory in which the four major genres (comedy, romance, tragedy, and satire) are held to manifest the permanent forms bodied forth by the human imagination, as represented in the archetypal myths correlated with the four seasons (*Anatomy of Criticism,* 1957, pp. 158–239). Other current theorists conceive genres on the model of social institutions, such as the state or church, rather than on the model of biological species. By *structuralist critics* a genre is conceived as a set of constitutive conventions and codes, altering from age to age, but shared by a kind of implicit contract between writer and reader. These codes make possible the writing of a particular literary text, though the writer may play against, as well as with, the prevailing generic conventions. For the reader, such conventions function as a set of expectations, which may be controverted rather than satisfied, but enable the reader to make the work intelligible—that is, to *naturalize* it, by relating it to the world as defined and ordered by the prevailing culture.

For most critics at the present time, however, genres are widely conceived to be rather arbitrary ways of classifying literature, yet convenient in critical discussions. Some critics have applied to generic classes the philosopher Ludwig Wittgenstein's concept of **family-resemblances.** That is, they propose that, in the loosely grouped family of works that make up a genre, there are no essential defining features, but only a set of family resemblances; each member shares some of these resemblances with some, but not all, of the other members of the genre. (For a description and discussion of Wittgenstein's view, see Maurice Mandelbaum, "Family Resemblances and Generalization Concerning the Arts," *American Philosophical Quarterly,* Vol. 2, 1965, pp. 219–28.) There has also been interest, in recent discussions, in the role that generic assumptions have played both in shaping the work that an author composes, and in establishing expectations that alter the way that a reader will interpret and respond to a particular work. Whatever the present skepticism, however, about the old belief that genres constitute inherent classes in the realm of literature, the fact that generic distinctions remain indispensable in literary discourse is attested by the unceasing publication of books whose titles announce that they deal with tragedy, the lyric, pastoral, the novel, or another of the many types into which literature has for centuries been classified.

Reviews of traditional theories of genre are René Wellek and Austin Warren, *Theory of Literature* (rev., 1970), Chapter 17; and the readable short survey by Heather Dubrow, *Genre* (1982). For recent developments see Paul Hernadi, *Beyond Genre: New Directions in Literary Classification* (1972); Alastair Fowler, *Kinds of Literature* (1982); Adena Rosmarin, *The Power of Genre* (1986).

Gothic Novel. The word "Gothic" originally referred to the Goths, a Germanic tribe, then came to signify "germanic," then "medieval." "Gothic architecture" now denotes the medieval type of architecture, characterized by the use of the pointed arch and vault, which spread through western Europe between the twelfth and sixteenth centuries. The **Gothic novel,** or "Gothic romance," is a type of prose fiction which was inaugurated by Horace Walpole's *The Castle of Otranto: A Gothic Story* (1764)—the subtitle refers to its setting in the middle ages—and flourished through the early nineteenth century. Following Walpole's example, authors of such novels set their stories in the medieval period, often in a gloomy castle furnished with dungeons, subterranean passages, and sliding panels, focused on the sufferings imposed on an innocent heroine by a cruel and lustful villain, and made bountiful use of ghosts, mysterious disappearances, and other sensational and supernatural occurrences (which in a number of novels turned out to have natural explanations). The principal aim of such novels was to evoke chilling terror by exploiting mystery and a variety of horrors. Many of them are now enjoyed mainly as period pieces, but the best opened up to fiction the realm of the irrational and of the perverse impulses and the nightmarish terrors that lie beneath the orderly surface of the civilized mind. Examples of Gothic novels are William Beckford's *Vathek* (1786)—the setting of which is both medieval and Oriental and the subject both erotic and sadistic—Ann Radcliffe's *The Mysteries of Udolpho* (1794) and other highly successful Gothic romances, and Matthew Gregory Lewis' *The Monk* (1796), which exploited, with considerable literary skill, the shock-effects of a narrative involving rape, incest, murder, and diabolism. Jane Austen made good-humored fun of the more decorous instances of the Gothic vogue in *Northanger Abbey* (written 1798, published 1818).

The term "Gothic" has also been extended to a type of fiction which lacks the medieval setting but develops a brooding atmosphere of gloom and terror, represents events which are uncanny or macabre or melodramatically violent, and often deals with aberrant psychological states. In this extended sense the term "Gothic" has been applied to William Godwin's *Caleb Williams* (1794), Mary Shelley's remarkable and influential *Frankenstein* (1817), and the novels and tales of terror by the German E. T. A. Hoffmann; still more loosely, "Gothic" has been used to describe elements in such later works as Emily Brontë's *Wuthering Heights*, Charlotte Brontë's *Jane Eyre*, Charles Dickens' *Bleak House* (for example, Chapters 11, 16, 47) and *Great Expectations* (the Miss Havisham episodes). America, especially southern America, has been fertile in Gothic fiction in this extended sense, from the novels of Charles Brockden Brown (1771–1810) and the terror tales of Edgar Allan Poe to William Faulkner's *Sanctuary* and *Absalom, Absalom!* and some of the fiction of Truman Capote. The nightmarish realm of uncanny terror, violence, and cruelty opened by the Gothic novel continues to be exploited by writers of horror fiction such as H. P. Lovecraft and Stephen King, and by the writers and directors in the current vogue of horror movies.

See Eino Railo, *The Haunted Castle* (1927); Montagu Summers, *The Gothic Quest* (1938); Lowry Nelson, Jr., "Night Thoughts on the Gothic Novel," *Yale Review* 52 (1963), reprinted in part in *Pastoral and Romance,* ed. Eleanor T. Lincoln (1969); G. R. Thompson, ed., *The Gothic Imagination: Essays in Dark Romanticism* (1974); and William Patrick Day, *In the Circles of Fear and Desire* (1985). On "American Gothic"—and especially the "southern Gothic"—see Chester E. Eisinger, "The Gothic Spirit in the Forties," *Fiction in the Forties* (1963). In recent decades *feminist critics* have drawn attention to the host of women writers who wrote Gothic fiction, have explored the mode as revealing results of the suppression of female sexuality in a patriarchal society, and have analyzed the way this fiction challenged the sexual hierarchy and values of a male-dominated culture. See the collection of essays in Juliann E. Fleenor, ed., *The Female Gothic* (1983); also Sandra Gilbert and Susan Gubar, *The Madwoman in the Attic* (1979).

Graveyard Poets. A term applied to eighteenth-century poets who wrote meditative poems, usually set in a graveyard, on the theme of human mortality, in moods which range from elegiac pensiveness to profound gloom. Examples are Thomas Parnell's "Night-Piece on Death" (1721), Edward Young's long *Night Thoughts* (1742), and Robert Blair's "The Grave" (1743). The vogue resulted in one masterpiece, Thomas Gray's "Elegy Written in a Country Churchyard" (1751). The writing of graveyard poems spread from England to Continental literature in the second part of the century.

See Amy Louise Reed, *The Background of Gray's Elegy* (1924). Edith M. Sickels, in *The Gloomy Egoist* (1932), follows the evolution of graveyard and other melancholy verse through the Romantic Period. For the vogue in Europe, refer to Paul Von Tieghem, *Le Pré-romantisme* (3 vols.; 1924–47).

Great Chain of Being. The conception of the Great Chain of Being is grounded in ideas about the nature of God, or the First Cause, in the Greek philosophers Plato, Aristotle, and Plotinus, and was developed by later thinkers into an inclusive philosophy of the origin, types, and relationships of living things in the universe. This worldview was already prevalent in the Renaissance, but was refined and greatly developed by the German philosopher Gottfried Leibniz early in the eighteenth century, and then adopted by a number of thinkers of the *Enlightenment.* In its comprehensive eighteenth-century form, the Great Chain of Being was based on the idea that the essential "excellence" of God consists in His limitless creativity—that is, in an unstinting overflow of His own being into the fullest possible variety of beings. From this premise were deduced three consequences:

1) Plenitude. The universe is absolutely full of every possible kind and variety of life; no conceivable species of being remains unrealized.

2) Continuity. Each species differs from the next by the least possible degree, and so merges all but imperceptibly into the species most nearly related to it.

3) Gradation. The existing species exhibit a hierarchy of status, and so compose a great chain, or ladder, of being, extending from the lowliest condition of the merest existence up to God Himself. In this chain human beings occupy the middle position between the animal kinds and the angels, or purely spiritual beings.

On these concepts Leibniz and other thinkers also grounded what is called the doctrine of **philosophical optimism**—the view that this is "the best of all possible worlds"; but only in the special sense that this is the best world whose existence is logically possible. The reasoning underlying this claim is that, since God's bountifulness consists in His creation of the greatest possible variety of graded beings, that which to a limited human point of view seems to be deficiency and evil can be recognized, from an overall cosmic viewpoint, to follow necessarily from the very excellence of the divine nature, which logically entails that there be a progressive set of limitations, hence increasing "evils," as we move farther down along the chain of being. As Voltaire ironically summarized this mode of optimism: "This is the best of all possible worlds, and everything in it is a necessary evil."

With his incomparable precision and economy, Alexander Pope compressed the concepts that make up the Great Chain of Being into a half-dozen or so *heroic couplets,* in Epistle I of his *Essay on Man* (1732–34):

> Of systems possible, if 'tis confessed
> That Wisdom Infinite must form the best,
> Where all must full or not coherent be,
> And all that rises rise in due degree;
> Then in the scale of reasoning life, 'tis plain,
> There must be, somewhere, such a rank as man. . . .
> See, through this air, this ocean, and this earth,
> All matter quick, and bursting into birth. . . .
> Vast Chain of Being! which from God began,
> Natures ethereal, human, angel, man,
> Beast, bird, fish, insect, what no eye can see,
> No glass can reach! from Infinite to thee,
> From thee to nothing. . . .

Philosophical optimism is one form of what is known as a **theodicy.** This term, compounded of the Greek words for "God" and "right," designates any system of thought which sets out to reconcile the assumption that God is perfectly good with the fact that evil exists. Milton's "great argument" in *Paradise Lost,* by which he undertakes to "assert Eternal Providence /And justify the ways of God to men" (I, 24–26) is an example of a traditional Christian theodicy.

See A. O. Lovejoy's classic work in the history of ideas, *The Great Chain of Being* (1936); also E. M. W. Tillyard, *The Elizabethan World Picture* (1943), Chapters 4–5, which deals with the prevalence of the concept in Shakespeare's lifetime.

Heroic Couplet. Lines of iambic pentameter (see *meter*) which rhyme in pairs: *aa, bb, cc,* and so on. The adjective "heroic" was applied in the later seventeenth century because of the frequent use of such couplets in "heroic" (that is, *epic*) poems and plays. This verse form was introduced into English poetry by Geoffrey Chaucer (in *The Legend of Good Women* and most of *The Canterbury Tales*), and has been used constantly ever since. From the age of John Dryden through that of Samuel Johnson, the heroic couplet was the predominant English measure for all the poetic kinds; some poets, including Alexander Pope, used it almost to the exclusion of other meters.

In that era, usually called the *Neoclassic Period,* the poets wrote in **closed couplets,** in which the end of each couplet tends to coincide with the end either of a sentence or of a self-sufficient unit of syntax. The sustained employment of the closed heroic couplet meant that two lines had to serve something of the function of a stanza. In order to maximize the interrelations of the component parts of the couplet, neoclassic poets often used an end-stopped first line (that is, made the end of the line coincide with a pause in the syntax), and also broke many single lines into subunits by balancing the line around a strong *caesura,* or medial pause in the syntax.

The following passage from John Denham's *Cooper's Hill* (which he added in the version of 1655) is an early instance of the artful management of the closed couplet which fascinated later neoclassic poets; they quoted it and commented upon it again and again, and used it as a model for exploiting the possibilities of this verse form. Note how Denham achieves diversity within the straitness of his couplets by shifts in the position of the caesuras, by the use of rhetorical balance and *antithesis* between the single lines and between the two halves within a single line, and by the variable positioning of the adjectives in the second couplet. Note also the framing and the emphasis gained by inverting the iambic foot that begins the first line and the last line, and by manipulating similar and contrasting vowel and consonant sounds. The poet is addressing the River Thames:

> O could I flow like thee, and make thy stream
> My great example, as it is my theme!
> Though deep, yet clear; though gentle, yet not dull;
> Strong without rage, without o'erflowing full.

And here is a passage from Alexander Pope, the greatest master of the metrical, syntactical, and rhetorical possibilities of the closed heroic couplet ("Of the Characters of Women," 1735, lines 243–48):

> See how the world its veterans rewards!
> A youth of frolics, an old age of cards;
> Fair to no purpose, artful to no end,
> Young without lovers, old without a friend;
> A fop their passion, but their prize a sot;
> Alive, ridiculous, and dead, forgot!

Compare these closed neoclassic couplets with the "open couplets" quoted from Keats' *Endymion* in the entry on *meter.* In the latter, the pattern of stresses varies often from the iambic norm, the syntax is unsymmetrical, and the couplets run on freely, with the rhyme serving to color rather than to stop the verse.

See George Williamson, "The Rhetorical Pattern of Neoclassical Wit," *Modern Philology* 33 (1935); W. K. Wimsatt, "One Relation of Rhyme to Reason (Alexander Pope)," in *The Verbal Icon* (1954); William Bowman Piper, *The Heroic Couplet* (1969).

Heroic Drama was a form mainly specific to the *Restoration Period,* though instances continued to be written in the early eighteenth century. As John Dryden then defined it: "An heroic play ought to be an imitation, in little, of an heroic poem; and consequently . . . love and valour ought to be the subject of it" (Preface to *The Conquest of Granada,* 1672). By "heroic poem" he meant *epic,* and the plays attempted to emulate the epic by employing as protagonist a large-scale warrior whose actions involve the fate of an empire, and by having all the characters speak in an elevated and elaborate style, usually cast in the epigrammatic form of the closed *heroic couplet.* A noble hero and heroine are typically represented in a situation in which their passionate love conflicts with the demands of honor and with the hero's patriotic duty to his country; if the conflict ends in disaster, the play is called an **heroic tragedy.** Often the central dilemma is patently contrived and the characters are statuesque and unconvincing, while the attempt to sustain a high epic style swells sometimes into *bombast,* as in Dryden's *Love Triumphant* (1693): "What woods are these? I feel my vital heat / Forsake my limbs, my curdled blood retreat."

Dryden's *Conquest of Granada* is one of the better heroic tragedies, but his highest achievement is *All for Love* (1678), which is an adaptation to the heroic formula of Shakespeare's *Antony and Cleopatra.* Other heroic dramatists were Nathaniel Lee (*The Rival Queens*) and Thomas Otway, whose *Venice Preserved* is a fine tragedy that transcends the limitations of the form. We also owe indirectly to heroic tragedy two very amusing *parodies* of the type: the Duke of Buckingham's *The Rehearsal* (1672) and Henry Fielding's *The Tragedy of Tragedies, or the Life and Death of Tom Thumb the Great* (1731).

See Bonamy Dobrée, *Restoration Tragedy* (1929); Allardyce Nicoll, *Restoration Drama* (1955); Arthur C. Kirsch, *Dryden's Heroic Drama* (1965).

Humanism. In the sixteenth century the word **humanist** was coined to signify one who taught or worked in the "studia humanitatis," or **humanities** —that is, grammar, rhetoric, history, poetry, and moral philosophy, as distinguished from fields less concerned with the moral and imaginative aspects and activities of man, such as mathematics, natural philosophy, and theology. At that time, these studies focused on classical, and above all, Latin, culture; and they put great emphasis on learning to speak and write good Latin. Scholarly humanists recovered, edited, and expounded many ancient texts in Greek and Latin, and so contributed greatly to the store of materials and ideas of the European *Renaissance.* These humanists also wrote many works concerned with educational, moral, and political problems, based largely on classical writers such as Aristotle, Plato, and above all, Cicero. In the nineteenth century a new word, **humanism**, came to be applied to the view of human nature, the general values, and the educational ideas common to many Renaissance humanists, as well as to a number of later writers in the same tradition.

Typically, Renaissance humanism assumed the dignity and central position of human beings in the universe; emphasized the importance of the study of classical imaginative and philosophical literature, although with emphasis on its moral and practical rather than its aesthetic values; and insisted on the primacy, in ordering human life, of reason (considered the distinctively human faculty) as opposed to the instinctual appetites and the "animal" passions. Many humanists also stressed the need for a rounded development of an individual's diverse powers, physical and mental, artistic and moral, as opposed to merely technical or specialized training.

In our time "humanist" often connotes a person who bases truth on human experience and bases values on human nature and culture, as distinct from people who regard religious revelation as the guarantor of all truth and values. With few exceptions, however, Renaissance humanists were pious Christians who incorporated the concepts and ideals inherited from pagan antiquity into the frame of the Christian creed. The result was that they tended to emphasize the values achievable by human beings in this world, and to minimize the earlier Christian emphasis on innate corruption and on the ideals of asceticism and of withdrawal from this world in a preoccupation with the world hereafter. It has recently become common to refer to this synthesis of classical and Christian views, typical of writers such as Sir Philip Sidney, Edmund Spenser, and John Milton, as **Christian humanism.**

The rapid advance in the achievements and prestige of the natural sciences and technology after the Renaissance sharpened, in later heirs of the humanistic tradition, the need to defend the role of the humanities in a liberal education against the encroachments of the sciences and the practical arts. As Samuel Johnson, the eighteenth-century humanist who had once been a schoolmaster, wrote in his *Life of Milton:*

> The truth is, that the knowledge of external nature, and the sciences which that knowledge requires or includes, are not the great or the frequent business of the human mind. . . . We are perpetually moralists, but we are geometricians only by chance. . . . Socrates was rather of opinion that what we had to learn was, how to do good, and avoid evil.

Matthew Arnold, the notable proponent of humanism in the *Victorian Period,* strongly defended the central role of humane studies in general education. Many of Arnold's leading ideas are adaptations of the tenets of the older humanism—his view, for example, that culture is a perfection "of our humanity proper, as distinguished from our animality," and consists of "a harmonious expansion of *all* the powers which make the beauty and worth of human nature"; his emphasis on knowing "the best that is known and thought in the world," and assumption that much of what is best is in the writers of classical antiquity; and his conception of poetry as essentially "a criticism of life."

In our own century the American movement of 1910–33 known as the **New Humanism,** under the leadership of Irving Babbitt and Paul Elmer More, argued strongly for a return to a primarily humanistic education, and for a conservative view of moral, political, and literary values that is grounded mainly on classical literature. (See Irving Babbitt, *Literature and the American College,* 1908; and Norman Foerster, ed., *Humanism and America,* 1930.) But in the present age of shifting educational standards and proliferating demands for specialists in the sciences, technology, and the practical arts, the broad humanistic base for a general education has been greatly eroded. In most colleges the earlier humanistic theory of education survives mainly in the requirement that all students in the liberal arts must take at least six hours in the loosely defined group called "the humanities."

It is noteworthy that the writings of the influential German philosopher Martin Heidegger (1889–1976), as well as much recent structuralist and post-structuralist philosophical and critical theory, are expressly antihumanistic, not only in the sense that they undertake to subvert many of the values proposed by traditional humanism, but in the more radical sense that they undertake to "decenter," or to eliminate entirely, the focus on the human being, or "subject," as the major object of study and the major agency in effecting scientific, cultural, and literary achievements. "Man," as Michel Foucault has put it in a widely quoted affirmation, "is a simple fold in our language" who is destined to "disappear as soon as that knowledge has found a new form." In the realm of literary and critical theory, *structuralists* conceive of a human author as simply a "space" in which linguistic and cultural codes come together to effect a text; *deconstructionists* tend to reduce the human subject to one of the "effects" engendered by the differential play of language; and a number of *Marxist* and *new-historicist* critics describe the subject as produced and positioned by the ideological or cultural "discursive formations" that the author-as-subject incorporates and transmits in his or her own literary product. (See *poststructuralism.*) For critiques of antihumanist views in criticism, see Charles Altieri, *Act and Quality: A Theory of Literary Meaning and Humanistic Understanding* (1981); M. H. Abrams, "How to Do Things with Texts," in *Doing Things with Texts* (1989); Richard Levin, "Bashing the Bourgeois Subject," in *Textual Practice* 3 (1989); James L. Battersby, *Paradigms Regained: Pluralism and the Practice of Criticism* (1991).

On the history of humanism: Douglas Bush, *The Renaissance and English Humanism* (1939); P. O. Kristeller, *The Classics and Renaissance Thought* (1955); H. I. Marrou, *A History of Education in Antiquity* (1956); R. S. Crane, *The Idea of the Humanities* (2 vols.; 1967). On the New Humanism in the early twentieth century: Claes G. Ryn, *Will, Imagination and Reason: Irving Babbitt and the Problem of Reality* (1986).

Hymn in current usage denotes a song that celebrates God or expresses religious feelings and is primarily intended to be sung as part of a religious service. (See *lyric.*) The term derives from the Greek *hymnos,* which originally signified songs of praise that were for the most part addressed to the gods, but in some instances to human heroes or to abstract concepts. The early Christian Churches, following classical examples, introduced the singing of hymns as part of the liturgy; some of these consisted of the texts or para-phrases of Old Testament psalms, but others were composed as songs of wor-ship by churchly authors of the time. The writing of original religious lyric poems set to music continued through the Middle Ages and into the Protestant Reformation; Martin Luther himself (1483–1546) composed both the words and music of hymns, including "A Mighty Fortress Is Our God," which is now sung by almost all Christian denominations.

The writing of religious hymns, some of them metrical versions of the psalms and others original, continued through the Renaissance and was sup-plemented by a revival of "literary hymns" on secular or even pagan sub-jects—a classical type which had been kept alive through the Middle Ages by a number of neo-Latin poets, and was now composed to be read rather than sung. Edmund Spenser's *Fowre Hymns* (1596) are distinguished examples of such literary hymns; the first two celebrate earthly love and beauty, and the second two celebrate heavenly (that is, Christian) love and beauty. The tradi-tion of writing hymns on secular subjects continued into the nineteenth century, and produced such notable examples as James Thomson's "A Hymn on the Seasons" (1730), Keats' "Hymn to Apollo," and Shelley's "Hymn of Apollo" and "Hymn of Pan"; the last three of these hymns, it should be noted, like many original Greek hymns, are addressed to pagan gods.

The secular hymns were often long and elaborate compositions which verged closely upon another form of versified praise, the *ode*. These hymns, as well as many religious instances such as the great "Hymn" that constitutes all but the brief introduction of Milton's "On the Morning of Christ's Nativity" (1629), were formal compositions that were intended only to be read. The short religious lyric written for public singing was revived, and developed into its modern form, during the eighteenth century by the great hymnists of personal religious emotions, including Isaac Watts, Charles and John Wesley, and William Cowper; a successor in the next century was John Henry Newman, author of "Lead, Kindly Light." In America the poets John Greenleaf Whittier, Oliver Wendell Holmes, and Henry Wadsworth Longfellow wrote hymns, but the greatest American devotional songs are the anonymous *African-American* type that we call **spirituals**.

See the *New Oxford Book of Christian Verse,* ed. Donald Davie (1982), and refer to: C. S. Phillipe, *Hymnody Past and Present* (1937); Louis F. Benson, *The English Hymn* (1962); P. S. Diehl, *The Medieval European Religious Lyric* (1985); and the article "Hymn" in *The Princeton Encyclopedia of Poetry and Poetics* (rev., 1974).

Hyperbole and Understatement. The figure of speech, or *trope*, called **hyperbole** (Greek for "overshooting") is bold overstatement, or the extrava-gant exaggeration of fact or of possibility; it may be used either for serious or ironic or comic effect. Iago says gloatingly of Othello (III. iii. 330 ff.):

> Not poppy nor mandragora,
> Nor all the drowsy syrups of the world,
> Shall ever medicine thee to that sweet sleep
> Which thou ow'dst yesterday.

Famed examples in the seventeenth century are Ben Jonson's gallantly hyperbolic compliments to his lady in "Drink to me only with thine eyes," and the ironic hyperboles in "To His Coy Mistress," by which Andrew Marvell attests how slow his "vegetable love should grow"—if he had "but world enough and time." The "tall talk" or "tall tale" of the American West is a form of mainly comic hyperbole. There is the story of a cowboy in an eastern restaurant who ordered a steak well done. "Do you call this well done?" he roared at the waitress. "I've seen critters hurt worse than that get well!"

The contrary figure is **understatement** (the Greek term is **meiosis**, "lessening"), which deliberately represents something as much less in magnitude or importance than it really is, or is ordinarily considered to be. The effect is usually ironic—savagely ironic in Jonathan Swift's *A Tale of a Tub*, "Last week I saw a woman flayed, and you will hardly believe how much it altered her person for the worse," and comically ironic in Mark Twain's comment that "The reports of my death are greatly exaggerated." (See *irony*.) Some critics extend "meiosis" to the use in literature of a simple, unemphatic statement to enhance the effect of a deeply pathetic or tragic event; an example is the line at the close of the narrative in Wordsworth's *Michael* (1800): "And never lifted up a single stone."

A special form of understatement is **litotes** (Greek for "plain" or "simple"), the assertion of an affirmative by negating its contrary: "He's not the brightest man in the world" meaning "He is stupid." The figure is frequent in Anglo-Saxon poetry, where the effect is usually one of grim irony. In *Beowulf*, after Hrothgar has described the ghastly mere where the monster Grendel dwells, he comments, "That is not a pleasant place."

Imagery. This term is one of the most common in modern criticism, and one of the most variable in meaning. Its applications range all the way from the "mental pictures" which, it is sometimes claimed, are experienced by the reader of a poem, to the totality of the components which make up a poem. An example incorporating this range of usage is C. Day Lewis' statements, in his *Poetic Image* (1948), pp. 17–18, that an image "is a picture made out of words," and that "a poem may itself be an image composed from a multiplicity of images." Three discriminable uses of the word, however, are especially frequent; in all these senses imagery is said to make poetry *concrete*, as opposed to *abstract:*

1) "Imagery" (that is, "images" taken collectively) is used to signify all the objects and qualities of sense perception referred to in a poem or other work of literature, whether by literal description, by allusion, or in the *vehicles* (the secondary references) of its similes and metaphors. In William Wordsworth's "She Dwelt among the Untrodden Ways" (1800), the imagery in this broad sense includes the literal objects the poem refers to ("ways," "maid," "grave"), as well as the "violet" and "stone" of the metaphor and the "star" and "sky" of the simile in the second stanza. The term "image" should not be taken to imply a visual reproduction of the object referred to; some readers of the passage experience visual images and some do not; and among those who do, the explicitness and details of the pictures vary

greatly. Also, "imagery" in this usage includes not only visual sense qualities, but also qualities that are auditory, tactile (touch), thermal (heat and cold), olfactory (smell), gustatory (taste), and kinesthetic (sensations of movement). In his *In Memoriam* (1850), No. 101, for example, Alfred, Lord Tennyson's imagery encompasses not only things that are visible, but also qualities that are smelled or heard, together with a suggestion, in the adjective "summer," of warmth:

> Unloved, that beech will gather brown, . . .
> And many a rose-carnation feed
> With summer spice the humming air. . . .

2) Imagery is used, more narrowly, to signify only descriptions of visible objects and scenes, especially if the description is vivid and particularized, as in Samuel Taylor Coleridge's "The Rime of the Ancient Mariner" (1798):

> The rock shone bright, the kirk no less,
> That stands above the rock:
> The moonlight steeped in silentness
> The steady weathercock.

3) Most commonly in recent usage, imagery signifies *figurative language,* especially the vehicles of metaphors and similes. Critics after the 1930s, and notably the *New Critics,* went far beyond earlier commentators in stressing imagery, in this sense, as the essential component in poetry, and as a major factor in poetic meaning, structure, and effect.

Caroline Spurgeon, in *Shakespeare's Imagery and What It Tells Us* (1935), made statistical counts of the subjects of this third type of imagery in Shakespeare, and used the results as clues to Shakespeare's personal experiences, interests, and temperament. Following the lead of several earlier critics, she also pointed out the frequent occurrence in Shakespeare's plays of image-clusters (recurrent groupings of metaphors and similes), and presented evidence that a number of the individual plays have characteristic image *motifs* (for example, animal imagery in *King Lear,* and the figures of disease, corruption, and death in *Hamlet*); she claimed that these elements established the overall tonality of a play. Many critics in the next few decades joined Spurgeon in the search for images, image patterns, and "thematic imagery" in works of literature. By some New Critics the implicit interaction of the imagery, rather than explicit statements by the author or the overt speeches and actions of the characters, was held to be the way that the subject, or *theme,* worked itself out in many plays, poems, and novels. See, for example, the critical writings of G. Wilson Knight, Cleanth Brooks on *Macbeth* in *The Well Wrought Urn* (1947), Chapter 2, and Robert B. Heilman, *This Great Stage: Image and Structure in "King Lear"* (1948).

See H. W. Wells, *Poetic Imagery* (1924); Owen Barfield, *Poetic Diction* (1928); June E. Downey, *Creative Imagination* (1929); Richard H. Fogle, *The Imagery of Keats and Shelley* (1949); Norman Friedman, "Imagery: From Sensation to Symbol," *Journal of Aesthetics and Art Criticism* 12 (1953).

Imagism   was a poetic vogue that flourished in England, and even more vigorously in America, between the years 1912 and 1917. It was planned and exemplified by a group of English and American writers in London, partly under the influence of the poetic theory of T. E. Hulme, as a revolt against what Ezra Pound called the "rather blurry, messy . . . sentimentalistic mannerish" poetry at the turn of the century. Pound, the first leader of the movement, was soon succeeded by Amy Lowell; after that Pound referred to the movement, slightingly, as "Amygism." Other leading participants, for a time, were H. D. (Hilda Doolittle), D. H. Lawrence, William Carlos Williams, John Gould Fletcher, and Richard Aldington. The Imagist proposals, as voiced by Amy Lowell in her Preface to the first of three anthologies called *Some Imagist Poets* (1915–17), were for a poetry which, abandoning conventional poetic materials and versification, is free to choose any subject and to create its own rhythms, uses common speech, and presents an image that is hard, clear, and concentrated.

The typical Imagist poem is written in *free verse* and undertakes to render as precisely and tersely as possible, and without comment or generalization, the writer's response to a visual object or scene; often the impression is rendered by means of metaphor, or by juxtaposing a description of one object with that of a second and diverse object. This famed example by Ezra Pound exceeds other Imagist poems in the degree of its concentration:

> *In a Station of the Metro**
> The apparition of these faces in the crowd,
> Petals on a wet, black bough.

In this poem Pound, like a number of other Imagists, was influenced by the Japanese **haiku** (or **hokku**), a lyric form that represents the poet's impression of a natural object or scene, viewed at a particular season or month, in exactly seventeen syllables. See Earl R. Miner, *The Japanese Tradition in British and American Literature* (1958).

Imagism was too restrictive to endure long as a concerted movement, but it turned out to be the inauguration of modern poetry. Almost every major poet up to the recent past, including W. B. Yeats, T. S. Eliot, and Wallace Stevens, manifests the influence of the Imagist experiments with the representation of precise, clear images that are juxtaposed without specifying their interconnection.

See T. E. Hulme, *Speculations,* ed. Herbert Read (1924); Stanley K. Coffman, *Imagism* (1951); *The Imagist Poem,* ed. William Pratt (1963).

Imitation.   In literary criticism the word **imitation** has two frequent but diverse applications: (1) to define the nature of literature and the other arts, and (2) to indicate the relation of one literary work to another literary work which served as its model.

---

* Lines from "In a Station of the Metro" from *Personae* by Ezra Pound. Copyright 1926 by Ezra Pound. Reprinted by permission of New Directions Publishing Corporation and Faber & Faber Ltd.

1) In his *Poetics,* Aristotle defines poetry as an imitation (in Greek, **mimesis**) of human actions. By "imitation" he means something like "representation," in its root sense: the poem imitates by taking an instance of human action and re-presenting it in a new "medium," or material—that of words. By distinguishing differences in the artistic media, in the kind of actions imitated, and in the manner of imitation (for example, dramatic or narrative), Aristotle first distinguishes poetry from other arts, and then makes distinctions between the various poetic kinds, such as drama and epic, tragedy and comedy. From the sixteenth through the eighteenth century the term "imitation" was a central term in discussing the nature of poetry; critics differed radically, however, in their concept of the nature of the mimetic relationship, and of the kinds of things in the external world that works of literature imitate, or ought to imitate. With the emergence in the early nineteenth century of the romantic view that poetry is essentially an expression of the poet's feelings or imaginative process, imitation tended to be displaced from its central position in literary theory (see *criticism*). In the last half-century, however, the use of the term has been revived, especially by R. S. Crane and other *Chicago critics,* who ground their theory on the analytic method and basic distinctions of Aristotle's *Poetics.* Many *Marxist critics* also hold a view of literature as an imitation, or, in their preferred term, "reflection," of reality.

2) Ancient rhetoricians and critics often recommended that a poet should "imitate" the established models in a particular literary genre. The notion that the proper procedure for poets, with the rare exception of an "original genius," was to imitate the normative forms and styles of the Greek and Roman masters continued to be influential through the eighteenth century; all the major critics, however, also insisted that mere copying was not enough—that a good literary work must imitate the form and spirit rather than the detail of the classic models, and that it can be achieved only by a poet who possesses an innate poetic talent.

In a specialized use of the term in this second sense, "imitation" was also used to describe a literary work which deliberately echoed an older work but adapted it to subject matter in the writer's own age, usually in a satirical fashion. In the poems that Alexander Pope called *Imitations of Horace* (1733 and following), for example, an important part of the intended effects depend on the reader's recognition of the resourcefulness, wit, and subtlety with which Pope accommodated to contemporary circumstances the structure, details, and even the wording of one or another of Horace's Roman satires.

On "imitation" as a term used to define literature see R. S. Crane, ed., *Critics and Criticism* (1952), and M. H. Abrams, *The Mirror and the Lamp* (1953), Chapters 1–2. On Pope's "imitations" of Horace and other ancient masters see R. A. Brower, *Alexander Pope: The Poetry of Allusion* (1959). For denials, on various grounds, that literature can be claimed to imitate reality, see *Russian formalism, structuralist criticism, deconstruction, new historicism,* and *text and writing (écriture).* Among modern defenses of the view that literature is mimetic, in the broad sense that it has reference beyond the text to the world of human experience, see Gerald Graff, *Literature against Itself* (1979); A. D. Nuttall, *A New Mimesis: Shakespeare and the Representation of Reality* (1983); and Robert Alter, "Mimesis and the Motives for Fiction," in his *Motives for Fiction* (1984).

Intentional Fallacy signifies what is claimed to be the error of interpreting and evaluating a literary work by reference to evidence, outside the text itself, for the intention—the design and purposes—of its author. The term was proposed by W. K. Wimsatt and Monroe C. Beardsley in "The Intentional Fallacy" (1946), reprinted in Wimsatt's *The Verbal Icon* (1964). They asserted that an author's intended aims and meanings in writing a literary work—whether these are asserted by the author or merely inferred from our knowledge of the author's life and opinions—are irrelevant to the literary critic, because the meaning, structure, and value of a text are inherent within the finished, freestanding, and public work of literature itself. Reference to the author's supposed purposes, or else to the author's personal situation and state of mind in writing a text, is held to be a harmful mistake, because it diverts our attention to such "external" matters as the author's biography, or psychological condition, or creative process, which we substitute for the proper critical concern with the "internal" constitution and inherent value of the literary product.

This claim, which was central in the *New Criticism*, has been strenuously debated, and has been reformulated by both of its original proponents. (See Wimsatt, "Genesis: An Argument Resumed," in *Day of the Leopards*, 1976; and Beardsley, *Aesthetics*, 1958, pp. 457–61, and *The Possibility of Criticism*, 1970, pp. 16–37.) A view acceptable to many traditional critics (but not to *structuralist* and *poststructuralist* theorists), is that in the exceptional instances—for example, in Henry James' prefaces to his novels—where we possess an author's express statement about his artistic intentions in a literary work, that statement should constitute evidence for an interpretive hypothesis, but should not in itself be determinative. If the author's stated intentions do not accord with the text, it should be qualified or rejected in favor of an alternative interpretation that conforms more closely to the shared, or "public," conventions incorporated within the text itself.

For diverse views of the role of authorial intention in establishing and interpreting the meanings of a text, see *interpretation and hermeneutics*, below; compare also *affective fallacy*. A detailed objection to Wimsatt and Beardsley's original essay is E. D. Hirsch's "Objective Interpretation" (1960), reprinted as an appendix to his *Validity in Interpretation* (1967). An anthology of discussions of this topic in criticism is David Newton-de Molina, *On Literary Intention* (1976). Ronald Dworkin discusses parallels between the role of intention in legal interpretation and literary interpretation, in "Law as Interpretation," *The Politics of Interpretation*, ed. W. J. T. Mitchell (1983).

Interpretation and Hermeneutics. In the narrow sense, to interpret a work of literature is to specify the meanings of its language by analysis, paraphrase, and commentary; usually such **interpretation** focuses on especially obscure, ambiguous, or figurative passages. In the broad sense, to interpret is to make clear the artistic features and purport of the overall literary work of which language is the medium; interpretation in this sense includes the analysis of such matters as the work's genre, component elements, structure, theme, and effects (see *criticism*).

The term **hermeneutics** originally designated the formulation of principles of interpretation that apply specifically to the Bible; these incorporated both the rules governing a valid reading of the biblical text, and **exegesis**, or commentary on the application of the meanings expressed in the text. Since the nineteenth century, however, "hermeneutics" has come to designate the theory of interpretation in general—that is, a formulation of the principles and methods involved in getting at the meaning of all written texts, including legal, historical, and literary, as well as biblical texts.

The German theologian Friedrich Schleiermacher in a series of lectures in 1819 was the first to frame a theory of "general hermeneutics" as "the art of understanding" texts of every kind. Schleiermacher's views were developed in the 1890s by the influential philosopher Wilhelm Dilthey (1833–1911), who proposed a science of hermeneutics designed to serve as the basis for interpreting all forms of writing in the "human sciences": that is, in the humanities and the social sciences, as distinguished from the natural sciences. Dilthey regarded the human sciences as ways of dealing with temporal, concrete, "lived experience." He proposed that whereas the aim of the natural sciences is to achieve "explanation" by means of static, reductive categories, the aim of hermeneutics is to establish a general theory of "understanding." The understanding of a verbal text consists in "the interpretation of *works,* works in which the texture of inner life comes fully to expression."

In formulating the way in which we come to understand the meaning of a text, Dilthey gave the name the **hermeneutic circle** to a procedure Schleiermacher had earlier described. That is, in order to understand the determinate meanings of the verbal parts of any linguistic whole, we must approach them with a prior sense of the meaning of the whole; yet we can know the meaning of the whole only by knowing the meanings of its constituent parts. This circularity of the interpretive process applies to the interrelations between the single words within any sentence and the sentence as a whole, as well as to interrelations between all the single sentences and the work as a whole. Dilthey maintained, however, that the hermeneutic circle is not a vicious circle, in that we can achieve a valid interpretation by a mutually qualifying interplay between our evolving sense of the whole and our retrospective understanding of its component parts.

Interest in the theory of interpretation strongly revived in the 1950s and 1960s, concurrently with the turn of philosophy to focus on the uses and meanings of language, and the turn of literary criticism—exemplified by the *New Criticism* in America—to the conception of a literary work as a linguistic object and to the view that the primary task of criticism is to interpret its verbal meanings and their interrelations. There have been two main lines of development in recent hermeneutics:

(1) One development, represented notably by the Italian theorist Emilio Betti and the American E. D. Hirsch, takes off from Dilthey's claim that a reader is able to achieve an objective interpretation of an author's expressed meaning. In his *Validity in Interpretation* (1967), followed by *The Aims of Interpretation* (1976), Hirsch asserts that "a text means what its author meant," specifies that this meaning is "the verbal meaning which an author intends," and undertakes to show that such verbal meaning is in principle determinate (even if in some instances determinately ambiguous, or multiply significant), that it remains stable through the passage of time, and that it is in principle reproducible by each competent reader. The author's verbal **intention** is not the author's state of consciousness at the time of writing, but only the intention to mean something which, by making use of the potentialities of pre-existing linguistic conventions and norms, gets actualized in words, and so may be shared by readers who are competent in the same conventions and norms and know how to employ them in their interpretive practice. If a text is read independently of reference to the author's intentions, it remains indeterminate—that is, capable of an indefinite diversity of meanings. A reader arrives at a determinate interpretation by using an implicit logic of validation (capable of being made explicit by the hermeneutic theorist), which serves to specify the author's intention, by reference not only to the general norms of language, but also to all evidence, whether internal or external to the text, concerning "relevant aspects in the author's outlook" or "horizon." Relevant external references include the author's cultural milieu and personal prepossessions, as well as the literary and generic conventions that were available to the author at the time when the work was composed.

Hirsch reformulates Dilthey's concept of the hermeneutic circle as follows: a competent reader forms an "hypothesis" as to the meaning of a part or whole of a text which is "corrigible"—that is, the hypothesis can be either confirmed or disconfirmed by continuing reference to the text; if disconfirmed, it is replaced by an alternative hypothesis which conforms more closely to all the components of the text. Since the interpreted meanings of the components of a text are to some degree constituted by the hypotheses one brings to their interpretation, such a procedure can never achieve absolute certainty as to a text's correct meaning. The most a reader can do is to arrive at the most probable meaning of a text; but this logic of highest probability, Hirsch insists, is adequate to yield objective knowledge, confirmable by other competent readers, concerning the determinate and stable meanings both of the component passages and of the artistic whole in a work of literature.

Hirsch follows traditional hermeneutics in making an essential distinction between verbal meaning and significance. The **significance** of a text to a reader is the relation of its verbal meaning to other matters, such as the personal situation, beliefs, and responses of the individual reader, or the prevailing cultural milieu of the reader's own era, or a particular set of concepts or values, and so on. The **verbal meaning** of a text, Hirsch asserts—the meaning intended by the writer—is determinate and stable; its significance, however—what makes the text alive and resonant for diverse readers in diverse times—is indeterminate and ever-changing. Verbal meaning is the particular concern of hermeneutics; textual significance, in its many aspects, is one of the concerns of literary criticism.

(2) The second line of development in recent hermeneutics takes off from Dilthey's view that the genuine understanding of literary and other humanistic texts consists in the re-experiencing by the reader of the "inner life" that the texts express. A primary thinker in this development is Martin Heidegger, whose *Being and Time* (1927, trans. 1962) incorporated the act of interpretation into an **existential philosophy**—that is, a philosophy centered on "Dasein," or what it is to-be-in-the-world. Heidegger's student Hans Georg Gadamer adapted Heidegger's philosophy into an influential theory of textual interpretation, *Truth and Method* (1960, trans. 1975). The philosophical premise is that temporality and historicality—a stance in one's present that looks back to the past and anticipates the future—is inseparably a part of each individual's being; that the process of understanding something, involving an act of interpretation, goes on not only in reading verbal texts but in all aspects of human experience; and that language, like temporality, pervades all aspects of that experience. In applying these philosophical assumptions to the understanding of a literary text, Gadamer translates the traditional hermeneutic circle into the metaphors of dialogue and fusion. A reader brings to a text a "pre-understanding" which is constituted by his own temporal and personal "horizons." He should not, as a "subject," attempt to analyze and dissect the text as an autonomous "object." Instead he, as an "I," addresses questions to the text as a "Thou," but with a receptive openness that simply allows the matter of the text—by means of their shared heritage of language—to speak in responsive dialogue with the reader, and to readdress its own questions to him. The understood meaning of the text is an event which is always the product of a "fusion of the horizons" which a reader brings to the text and which the text brings to the reader.

Gadamer insists that (unlike many theories of interpretation, including Hirsch's) this hermeneutics is not an attempt to establish norms or rules for a correct interpretation, but an attempt simply to describe how we in fact succeed in understanding texts. Nonetheless his descriptive theory has the consequence that the search for a determinate meaning of a text which remains stable through the passage of time becomes a will-o'-the-wisp. Since the meaning of a text "is always codetermined" by the particular temporal and personal horizon of the individual reader, there cannot be one stable "right interpretation"; the meaning of a text is always to an important extent its meaning that it has here, now, for me. To Gadamer's view that the historical and personal relativity of meaning is inescapable, Hirsch replies that a reader in the present, by reconstructing the linguistic, literary, and cultural conditions of its author, is often able adequately to determine the original and unchanging verbal meaning intended by the writer of a text in the past; and that insofar as Gadamer is right about the unbridgeable gap between the meaning of a text then and its meaning now, he is referring to the ever-alterable "significance" contributed by each reader, in his or her time and personal and social circumstances, to the text's stable verbal meaning.

Traditional literary critics had tacitly assumed that to interpret a text correctly is to approximate the meaning intended by its author, long before theorists such as Hirsch undertook to define and justify this view. Even the *New Critics* took for granted that the meaning of a text is the meaning that the author intended; what some of these critics called the *intentional fallacy* merely designates the supposed error, in interpreting a text, of employing clues concerning an author's intention which are "external" to the "internal" realization of that intention in the language of the text itself. Most traditional philosophers, including current "ordinary language philosophers," have also held that to understand an utterance involves reference to the writer's intention, which we infer from our awareness of the writer's linguistic assumptions. H. P. Grice, for example, proposed in the 1950s an influential account of verbal meaning as a speaker's intention in an utterance to produce some effect in a hearer, by means of the hearer's recognition of the speaker's intention in making that utterance. In *Speech Acts* (1970), John Searle accepted this description, with the qualification that the speaker can express, and so enable the hearer to recognize, his intention only insofar as the expression conforms to the conventions or rules of their common language. In a later refinement of this view, Searle makes a distinction between the speaker's intention which determines the kind and meaning of a *speech act,* and the speaker's intention to communicate that meaning to a hearer; see his *Intentionality* (1983), Chapter 6.

A radical departure from the traditional author-oriented views of a determinate intended meaning occurs in a number of current *structural* and *poststructural* theories. Some theorists, rejecting any control by reference to an author, or subject, and his or her intention, insist that the meanings of a text are rendered "undecidable" by the self-conflicting workings of language itself, or else that meanings are entirely relative to the particular interpretive strategy that is brought into play by the reader. (See *deconstruction* and *reader-response criticism.*) Other current theorists, although they may admit that the manifest meanings of a text are determined by the intentions of the author, regard such meanings merely as disguises, or displacements, of the real meanings, which are the unconscious motives and needs of the author, or the suppressed political realities and power-relations of the social structure of an historical era. (See *psychoanalytic criticism, Marxist criticism, new historicism.*)

In addition to the titles listed above, refer to Richard E. Palmer, *Hermeneutics: Interpretation Theory in Schleiermacher, Dilthey, Heidegger, and Gadamer* (1969), an informative review of the history and conflicting theories of interpretation from the standpoint of an adherent to Gadamer's theory; *The Conflict of Interpretations: Essays in Hermeneutics* (1974) by the French philosopher Paul Ricoeur; Charles Altieri, *Act and Quality: A Theory of Literary Meaning and Understanding* (1981); the anthology of essays *Hermeneutics: Questions and Prospects,* ed. Gary Shapiro and Alan Sica (1984); and Wendell V. Harris, *Interpretive Acts: In Search of Meaning* (1988).

Interpretation: Typological and Allegorical. The typological (or **figural**) mode of interpreting the Bible was inaugurated by St. Paul and developed by the early Church Fathers as a way of reconciling the history, prophecy, and laws of the Hebrew Scriptures with the narratives and teachings of the New Testament. As St. Augustine expressed its principle: "In the Old Testament the New Testament is concealed; in the New Testament the Old Testament is revealed." In typological theory, that is, the key persons, actions, and events in the Old Testament are viewed as "figurae" (Latin for "figures") which are historically real themselves, but also "prefigure" those persons, actions, and events in the New Testament that are similar to them. Often the Old Testament figures are called **types** and their later correlatives in the New Testament are called **antitypes.** The Old Testament figure or type is held to be a prophecy or promise of the higher truth that is "fulfilled" in the New Testament, according to a plan which is eternally present in the mind of God but manifests itself to human beings only in the two scriptural revelations separated by a span of time.

Among the numberless examples of typological interpretation, Adam was said to be a figure (or in alternative terms, a "type," "image," or "shadow") of Christ; one of the analogies cited between prefiguration and fulfillment was that between the creation of Eve from Adam's rib and the flow of blood from the side of the crucified Christ; another was the analogy between the tree that bore the fruit occasioning Adam's original sin and the cross which bore as its fruit Christ, the Redeemer of that sin. In a similar fashion the manna provided the children of Israel in the wilderness (Exodus 16) was held to prefigure the Eucharist, and the relation between the Egyptian servant girl Hagar and Sarah (Genesis 16) to prefigure the relation between the earthly Jerusalem of the Old Testament and the heavenly Jerusalem of the New Testament. By some interpreters, elements of New Testament history were represented as in their turn prefiguring the events that will come to be fulfilled in "the last days" of Christ's Second Coming and Last Judgment.

The **allegorical interpretation** of the Bible had its roots in Greek and Roman thinkers who treated classical myths as allegorical representations of abstract cosmological, philosophical, or moral truths. (See *allegory*.) The method was applied to Old Testament narratives by the Jewish philosopher Philo (died A.D. 50) and was adapted to Christian interpretation by Origen in the third century. The fundamental distinction in the allegorical interpretation of the Bible is between the "literal" (or "historical," or "carnal") meaning of the text—the historical truth that it expressly signifies—and the supplemental "spiritual" or "mystical" or "allegoric" meaning that it signifies by analogy.

The spiritual aspect of a text's literal meaning was often in turn subdivided into two or more levels; some interpreters specified as many as seven, or even twelve levels. By the twelfth century, however, biblical interpreters widely agreed in finding a **fourfold meaning** in many biblical passages. A typical set of distinctions, as proposed by St. Thomas Aquinas and others, is that between: (1) the literal or historical meaning, which is a narrative of what in fact happened; (2) the allegorical meaning proper, which is the New Testament truth, or else the prophetic reference to the Christian Church, that is signified by a passage in the Old Testament; (3) the tropological meaning, which is the moral truth or doctrine signified by the same passage; and (4) the anagogic meaning, or reference of the passage to Christian **eschatology**, that is, the events that are to come in "the last days" of Christ's judgment and the life after death of individual souls.

We can distinguish between the typological and allegorical mode of interpretation by saying that typology is horizontal, in that it relates items in two texts (the Old and New Testament) that are separated in time, while allegorical interpretation is vertical, in that it uncovers multiple significances in a single textual item. The two interpretive methods, however, were often applied simultaneously, and in many instances fused, by biblical exegetes. Both methods flourished into the eighteenth century, and recur recognizably in later periods. They were employed in biblical allusions in sermons and in a great variety of writings on religious matters, and were adapted to **iconography**—that is, representations of biblical persons and events intended to have symbolic significance—in painting and sculpture. Medieval and later poets sometimes adopted the typological and allegorical methods of biblical interpretation in constructing their own writings on religious subjects. Dante, for example, in a letter written in 1319 to his friend and patron Can Grande della Scala, announced that his *Divine Comedy* has a double subject, literal and allegorical, and that the allegorical subject can be subdivided into allegorical, moral, and anagogical meanings. Scholars have analyzed the adaptation of typological and allegorical procedures by many later poets who wrote on religious themes, including Edmund Spenser, George Herbert, John Milton, and (in a late and highly individual revival of the mode) William Blake.

In the last half-century, the American scholar D. W. Robertson and others have proposed that not only religious writings but many seemingly secular poems of the Middle Ages—including the *Roman de la Rose,* the works of Chaucer and Chrétien de Troyes, and medieval love lyrics—were expressly written to incorporate typological and allegorical modes of theological and moral references. The validity, however, of extending these interpretive modes to secular literature is strongly disputed; see the suggested readings below. In *The Genesis of Secrecy: On the Interpretation of Narrative* (1979), the English critic Frank Kermode adapted the ancient interpretive distinction between carnal and spiritual meanings to his analysis of recent works of prose fiction.

On the various modes of biblical interpretation, see F. W. Farrar, *History of Interpretation* (1886), and Beryl Smalley, *The Study of the Bible in the Middle Ages* (rev., 1952). A classic discussion of typological, or figural, interpretation is Erich Auerbach's "Figura," in his *Scenes from the Drama of European Literature* (1959). Philip Rollinson, in *Classical Theories of Allegory and Christian Culture* (1981), relates early medieval interpretation of the Bible to modes of literary interpretation in classical times. A surviving American application in the eighteenth century of the old interpretive modes is Jonathan Edwards' *Images or Shadows of Divine Things*, ed. Perry Miller (1948). For uses of typological and allegoric materials by various literary authors, see Rosemund Tuve, *A Reading of George Herbert* (1952), and

Allegorical Imagery (1966); J. H. Hagstrum, *William Blake: Poet and Painter* (1964); P. J. Alpers, *The Poetry of "The Faerie Queene"* (1967); and the essays on a number of authors in Paul Miner, ed., *Literary Uses of Typology* (1977). For the extension of typological and allegoric methods to the analysis of secular medieval poems, see D. W. Robertson, Jr., "Historical Criticism," in *English Institute Essays, 1950,* ed. A. S. Downer (1951), and *A Preface to Chaucer: Studies in Medieval Perspectives* (1962). The validity of such an extension is debated by several scholars in *Critical Approaches to Medieval Literature,* ed. Dorothy Bethurum (1960), and by R. S. Crane, "On Hypotheses in 'Historical Criticism,'" in *The Idea of the Humanities* (1967, Vol. 2, pp. 236–60). On the relating of biblical allegorization to later literary forms see, in addition to Kermode (above), Northrop Frye, *The Great Code: The Bible and Literature* (1982); and Stephen Prickett, ed., *Reading the Text: Biblical Criticism and Literary Theory* (1991).

Irony. In Greek comedy the character called the *eiron* was a "dissembler," who characteristically spoke in understatement and deliberately pretended to be less intelligent than he was, yet triumphed over the *alazon*—the self-deceiving and stupid braggart. In most of the modern critical uses of the term "irony" there remains the root sense of dissembling or hiding what is actually the case; not, however, in order to deceive, but to achieve special rhetorical or artistic effects.

   Verbal irony (which was traditionally classified as one of the *tropes*) is a statement in which the meaning that a speaker implies differs sharply from the meaning that is ostensibly expressed. The ironic statement usually involves the explicit expression of one attitude or evaluation, but with indications in the overall speech-situation that the speaker intends a very different, and often opposite, attitude or evaluation. Thus in Canto IV of Alexander Pope's *The Rape of the Lock* (1714) after Sir Plume, egged on by the ladies, has stammered out his incoherent request for the return of the stolen lock of hair, the Baron answers:

> "It grieves me much," replied the Peer again,
> "Who speaks so well should ever speak in vain."

This is a straightforward case of an ironic reversal of the surface statement (of which one effect is to give pleasure to the reader) because there are patent clues, in the circumstances established by the preceding narrative, that the Peer is not in the least aggrieved and does not think that poor Sir Plume has spoken at all well. A more complex instance of irony is the famed sentence with which Jane Austen opens *Pride and Prejudice* (1813): "It is a truth universally acknowledged that a single man in possession of a good fortune must be in want of a wife"; part of the ironic implication is that a single woman is in want of a rich husband. Sometimes the use of irony by Pope and other masters is very complicated: the meaning and evaluations may be subtly qualified rather than simply reversed, and the clues to the ironic counter-meaning under the surface statement—or even to the fact that the author intends the statement to be understood ironically—may be oblique and unobtrusive. That is why recourse to irony by an author tends to convey an implicit compliment to the intelligence of readers, who are invited to associate themselves with the author and the knowing minority who are not taken in by the ostensible meaning. That is also why many literary ironists are misinterpreted and sometimes (like Daniel Defoe and Jonathan Swift in the eighteenth century) get into serious trouble with the obtuse authorities. Following the intricate and shifting maneuvers of great ironists like Plato, Swift, Austen, or Henry James is an ultimate test of skill in reading between the lines.

Some literary works exhibit **structural irony;** that is, the author, instead of using an occasional verbal irony, introduces a structural feature which serves to sustain a duplicity of meaning and evaluation throughout the work. One common literary device of this sort is the invention of a **naive hero,** or else a naive narrator or spokesman, whose invincible simplicity or obtuseness leads him to persist in putting an interpretation on affairs which the knowing reader—who penetrates to, and shares, the implied point of view of the authorial presence behind the naive *persona*—just as persistently is called on to alter and correct. (Note that verbal irony depends on knowledge of the speaker's ironic intention which is shared both by the speaker and the reader; structural irony depends on a knowledge of the author's ironic intention which is shared by the reader, but is not intended by the speaker.) One example of the naive spokesman is Swift's well-meaning but insanely rational economist who writes the "Modest Proposal" (1729) to convert the excess children of the oppressed and poverty-stricken Irish into a financial and gastronomical asset. Other examples are Swift's stubbornly credulous Gulliver, the self-deceiving and paranoid monologuist in Browning's "Soliloquy of the Spanish Cloister" (1842), and the insane editor, Kinbote, in Vladimir Nabokov's *Pale Fire* (1962). A related device for sustaining ironic qualification is the use of the *fallible narrator,* in which the teller of the story is a participant in it. Although such a narrator may be neither stupid, credulous, nor demented, he nevertheless manifests a failure of insight, viewing and appraising his own motives, and the motives and actions of other characters, through what the reader is intended to recognize as the distorting perspective of the narrator's prejudices and private interests. (See *point of view.*)

In *A Rhetoric of Irony* (1965) Wayne Booth identifies as **stable irony** that in which the speaker or author offers the reader an assertion or position which, whether explicit or implied, serves as a firm ground for subverting the surface meaning. **Unstable irony,** on the other hand, offers no fixed standpoint which is not itself undercut by further ironies. The literature of the *absurd* typically presents such a regression of ironies. At an extreme, as in Samuel Beckett's drama *Waiting for Godot* (1955) or his novel *The Unnamable* (1960), there is an endless regress of ironic undercuttings. Such works suggest a denial that there is any secure evaluative standpoint, or even any rationale, in the human situation.

Irony can be differentiated from some related uses of language:

Invective is direct denunciation by the use of derogatory *epithets;* so Prince Hal, in *Henry IV, Part 1,* calls the rotund Falstaff "this sanguine coward, this bedpresser, this horseback-breaker, this huge hill of flesh." (In the context of the play, there is in this instance of invective an ironic undertone of affection, as often when friends, secure in an intimacy which guarantees that they will not be taken literally, resort to derogatory name-calling in the exuberance of their esteem.) In his *Discourse Concerning Satire* (1693) Dryden described the difference in efficacy, as a put-down, between direct invective and the indirectness of irony, in which the ironist maintains the advantage of seeming detachment by leaving it to the circumstances to convert his bland compliments into insults:

> How easy is it to call rogue and villain, and that wittily! But how hard to make a man appear a fool, a blockhead, or a knave, without using any of those opprobrious terms. . . . There is . . . a vast difference between the slovenly butchering of a man, and the fineness of a stroke that separates the head from the body, and leaves it standing in its place.

Sarcasm in ordinary parlance is sometimes used as an equivalent for irony, but it is better to restrict it to the crude and taunting use of apparent praise for dispraise: "Oh, you're God's great gift to women, you are!" Sarcasm, to which an added clue is an exaggerated inflection of the speaker's voice, is a common form of irony in dormitory persiflage.

The term "irony," qualified by an adjective, is used to identify various literary devices and modes of organization:

Socratic irony takes its name from the fact that, as he is represented in Plato's dialogues (fourth century B.C.), the philosopher Socrates usually assumes a pose of ignorance, an eagerness to be instructed, and a modest readiness to entertain adverse opinions proposed by others; although these, upon his continued questioning, always turn out to be ill-grounded or to lead to absurd consequences.

Dramatic irony involves a situation in a play or a narrative in which the audience or reader shares with the author knowledge of present or future circumstances of which a character is ignorant; in that situation, the character unknowingly acts in a way we recognize to be grossly inappropriate to the actual circumstances, or expects the opposite of what we know that fate holds in store, or says something that anticipates the actual outcome, but not at all in the way that the character intends. Writers of Greek tragedy, who based their plots on legends whose outcome was already known to their audience, made frequent use of this device. Sophocles' *Oedipus,* for example, is a very complex instance of **tragic irony**, for the king ("I, Oedipus, whom all men call great") engages in a hunt for the incestuous father-murderer who has brought a plague upon Thebes; the object of the hunt turns out (as the audience, but not Oedipus, has known right along) to be the hunter himself, and the king, having achieved a vision of the terrible truth, penitently blinds himself. Dramatic irony occurs also in comedy. An example is the scene in *Twelfth Night* (II. v) in which Malvolio struts and preens in anticipation of a good fortune which the audience knows is based on a fake letter; the dramatic irony is heightened for the audience by Malvolio's ignorance of the presence of the hidden hoaxers, who gleefully comment on his ludicrously complacent speech and actions.

Cosmic irony (or "the irony of fate") is attributed to literary works in which a deity, or destiny, or the course of the universe, is represented as though deliberately manipulating events so as to lead the protagonist to false hopes, only to frustrate and mock them. This is a favorite structural device of Thomas Hardy. In his *Tess of the D'Urbervilles* (1891) the heroine, having lost her virtue because of her innocence, then loses her happiness because of her honesty, finds it again only by murder, and having been briefly happy, is hanged. Hardy concludes: "The President of the Immortals, in Aeschylean phrase, had ended his sport with Tess."

Romantic irony is a term introduced by Friedrich Schlegel and other German writers of the late eighteenth and early nineteenth centuries to designate a mode of dramatic or narrative writing in which the author builds up the illusion of representing reality, only to shatter it by revealing that the author, as artist, is the arbitrary creator and manipulator of the characters and their actions. The concept owes much to Laurence Sterne's use of a self-conscious and willful narrator in his *Tristram Shandy* (1759–67). Byron's great narrative poem *Don Juan* (1819–24) persistently uses this device for ironic and comic effect, letting the reader into the narrator's confidence, and so revealing the latter to be a fabricator of fiction who is often at a loss for matter to sustain his story and undecided about how to continue it. This type of irony, involving a *self-conscious narrator,* has become a standard mode in the modern form of *involuted fiction.*

A number of writers associated with the *New Criticism* used "irony," although in a greatly extended sense, as a general criterion of literary value. This use is based largely on two literary theorists. T. S. Eliot praised a kind of "wit" characteristic, in his view, of seventeenth-century *metaphysical poets* but absent in the romantic poets, which is an "internal equilibrium" that implies the "recognition," in dealing with any one kind of experience, "of other kinds of experience which are possible." ("Andrew Marvell," 1921, in *Selected Essays,* 1960.) And I. A. Richards defined irony in poetry as an equilibrium of opposing attitudes and evaluations (*Principles of Literary Criticism,* 1924, Chapter 32):

> Irony in this sense consists in the bringing in of the opposite, the complementary impulses; that is why poetry which is exposed to it is not of the highest order, and why irony itself is so constantly a characteristic of poetry which is.

Such observations were developed by Robert Penn Warren, Cleanth Brooks, and other New Critics into the claim that poems in which the writer commits himself or herself unreservedly to a single attitude or outlook, such as love or admiration or idealism, are of an inferior order because vulnerable to the reader's ironic skepticism; the greatest poems, on the other hand, are invulnerable to external irony because they already incorporate the poet's own "ironic" awareness of opposite and complementary attitudes. See Robert Penn Warren, "Pure and Impure Poetry" (1943), in *Critiques and Essays in Criticism,* ed. Robert W. Stallman (1949); Cleanth Brooks, "Irony as a Principle of Structure" (1949), in *Literary Opinion in America,* ed. M. W. Zabel (1951).

J. A. K. Thomson, *Irony: An Historical Introduction* (1926); A. R. Thompson, *The Dry Mock: A Study of Irony in Drama* (1948); D. C. Muecke, *The Compass of Irony* (1969), and *Irony* (1970); A. E. Dyson, *The Crazy Fabric, Essays in Irony* (1965); Wayne C. Booth, *A Rhetoric of Irony* (1965). A suggestive and wide-ranging earlier exploration of the mode is Søren Kierkegaard's *The Concept of Irony* (1841), trans. Lee M. Capel (1965).

Ivory Tower. A phrase taken from the biblical Song of Songs 7:4, in which it is said of the beloved woman, "Thy neck is as a tower of ivory." In the 1830s the French critic Sainte-Beuve applied the phrase "tour d'ivoire" to the stance of the poet Alfred de Vigny, to signify his isolation from everyday life and his exaltation of art above all practical concerns. Since then "ivory tower" has been frequently used (often in a derogatory way) as a term for an attitude or way of life which is indifferent or hostile to practical affairs and the everyday world, and especially for a theory and practice of art which insulates it from moral, political, and social concerns or effects. (See *aestheticism*.)

Jeremiad. A term derived from the Old Testament prophet Jeremiah, who in the seventh century B.C. attributed the calamities of Israel to its abandonment of the covenant with Jehovah and return to pagan idolatry, denounced with lurid and gloomy eloquence its religious and moral iniquities, and called on the people to repent and reform in order that Jehovah might restore them to His favor and renew the ancient covenant. As a literary term, **jeremiad** is applied to any work which, with a magniloquence like that of the Old Testament prophet (although it may be in secular rather than religious terms), accounts for the misfortunes of an era as a just penalty for great social and moral evils, but holds out hope for changes that will bring a happier future.

In the *Romantic Period*, powerful passages in William Blake's "prophetic poems" constitute short jeremiads, and the term is often applied to those of Thomas Carlyle's writings in which he uses a biblical style and rhetoric to denounce the social and economic misdeeds of the *Victorian Period* and to call for drastic reforms. The jeremiad, in its original religious mode, was a familiar genre in the sermons and writings of the *Colonial Period* in America, at a time when it was a commonplace that the colonies in New England were the "New Israel" with which God had covenanted a glorious future. The misfortunes of the colonists, accordingly, were attributed to deviations from the divine commands and described as punishments inflicted by God on His chosen people for their own ultimate benefit. In the words of Increase Mather, "God does not punish . . . other Nations until they have filled up the Measure of their sins, and then he utterly destroyeth them; but if our Nation forsake the God of their Fathers never so little," He punishes us in order "that so he may prevent our destruction" (*The Day of Trouble Is Near*, 1674). Since that era the prophetic stance and denunciatory rhetoric of the jeremiad has been manifested by many orators and writers, religious and secular, into the present time. See Sacvan Bercovitch, *The American Jeremiad* (1978), and George P. Landow, *Elegant Jeremiahs: The Sage from Carlyle to Mailer* (1986).

Lai. A name originally applied to a variety of poems by medieval French writers in the latter twelfth and the thirteenth centuries. Some lais were lyric, but most of them were short romantic narratives written in *octosyllabic couplets*. Marie de France, who wrote in the French language although at the English court of King Henry II, composed a number of charming poems of this sort; they are called "Breton lais" because their narratives are drawn for the most part from Arthurian and other Celtic legends. ("Breton" refers to Brittany, which was a Celtic part of France; see *chivalric romance*.) The Anglicized term "Breton lay" was applied in the fourteenth century to English poems written on the model of the narratives of Marie de France; they included *Sir Orfeo*, the *Lay of Launfal*, and Chaucer's "The Franklin's Tale." Later still, **lay** was used by English poets simply as a synonym for song, or as an archaic word for a fairly short narrative poem (for example by Sir Walter Scott in his *Lay of the Last Minstrel*, 1805).

See Roger S. Loomis, ed., *Arthurian Literature in the Middle Ages* (1959), and the Introduction by Charles W. Dunn to *Lays of Courtly Love*, trans. Patricia Terry (1963).

Light Verse is a term applied to a great variety of poems that use an ordinary speaking voice and a relaxed manner to treat their subjects gaily, or playfully, or wittily, or with a good-natured satire. Its subjects may be serious or petty; the defining quality is the *tone* of voice used, and the attitude of the lyric or narrative speaker toward the subject. Thomas Love Peacock's "The War Song of Dinas Vawr" (1829) begins

> The mountain sheep are sweeter,
> But the valley sheep are fatter;
> We therefore deemed it meeter
> To carry off the latter.

And it ends

> We brought away from battle,
> And much their land bemoaned them,
> Two thousand head of cattle,
> And the head of him who owned them:
> Ednyfed, king of Dyfed,
> His head was borne before us;
> His wine and beasts supplied our feasts,
> And his overthrow, our chorus.

The dispassionate attitude, brisk colloquialism, and pat rhymes convert what might have been matter for epic or tragedy into a comic narrative.

Vers de société ("society verse") is the very large subclass of light verse that deals with the relationships, concerns, and doings of polite society. It is often satiric, but in the mode of badinage rather than severity; and when it deals with love it does so as a sexual game, or flirtatiously, or in the mode of elegant and witty compliment, rather than with passion or high seriousness. The tone is usually urbane, the style deft, and the form polished and sometimes contrived with technical virtuosity; most poems using intricate French stanza forms, such as the *villanelle,* are society verse.

Nursery rhymes and other children's verses are another type of light verse. Edward Lear ("The Jumblies," "The Owl and the Pussy Cat") and Lewis Carroll ("Jabberwocky," *The Hunting of the Snark*) made children's nonsense verses into a Victorian specialty. Lear also popularized the five-line **limerick,** rhyming *aabba* which, whether in its ribald or decorous mode, is a form of light verse that everyone knows and many of us have practiced.

Some other fine artificers of light and society verse are the *Cavalier poets* of the early seventeenth century, and John Dryden, Matthew Prior, Alexander Pope, W. S. Gilbert, and Austin Dobson. Modern practitioners include Ezra Pound, W. H. Auden, E. E. Cummings, Ogden Nash, Marianne Moore, Edna St. Vincent Millay, Dorothy Parker, Morris Bishop, John Betjeman, and Ishmael Reed.

See *epigram.* Refer to *Worldly Muse: An Anthology of Serious Light Verse,* ed. A. J. M. Smith (1951); *The Fireside Book of Humorous Poetry,* ed. W. Cole (1959); *The New Oxford Book of Light Verse,* ed. Kingsley Amis (1978); *The Norton Book of Light Verse,* ed. Russell Baker (1986).

Linguistics in Literary Criticism. Linguistics is the systematic study of the elements of language and the principles governing their combination and organization. Through the nineteenth century the study of language was known as "philology" and was mainly "comparative" (the analysis of similarities and differences within a family of related languages) and "historical" (the analysis of the evolution of a family of languages, or of changes within a particular language, over a long course of time). This latter study of the changes in language over a span of time has come to be called **diachronic;** the important developments in twentieth-century linguistics came with the shift to the **synchronic** study of the systematic interrelations of the components of a single language at a particular time. A major contributor to modern synchronic linguistics was Ferdinand de Saussure, a French-speaking Swiss whose lectures on language as a self-sufficient system, delivered 1907–11, were published from students' notes in 1916, three years after Saussure's death; these lectures have been translated as *Course in General Linguistics* (1916). Important contributions were also made by American "descriptive" or "structural" linguists, notably Edward Sapir and Leonard Bloomfield, who set out to devise a linguistic theory and vocabulary adequate to analyze, as modes of verbal "behavior," the current state of various American Indian languages; a basic text in American linguistics is Bloomfield's *Language* (1933).

Both Continental and American linguistics have been applied to the analysis of the distinctive uses of language in literary texts (see *Russian formalism* and *stylistics*), and Saussure's concepts and procedures in analyzing a language have been adopted as a model for analyzing the forms and organization of large-scale literary structures (see *structuralist criticism*). The following linguistic terms and concepts are often employed by current critics and theorists of literature.

Saussure introduced a crucial distinction between langue and parole. A **parole** is any particular meaningful utterance, spoken or written. The **langue** is the implicit system of elements, of distinctions and oppositions, and of principles of combination, which make it possible, within a language community, for a speaker to produce and the auditor to understand a particular parole. The linguist's primary concern, in Saussure's view, is to establish the nature of the underlying linguistic system, the langue. Noam Chomsky has substituted for Saussure's langue and parole the distinction between **competence** (the tacit knowledge on the part of native speakers who have mastered, or "internalized," the implicit conventions and rules of a language system which make possible the production and understanding of well-formed and meaningful sentences) and **performance** (the actual utterance of particular sentences). Competent speakers know how to produce such sentences, without being able to specify the conventions and rules that enable them to do so; the function of the linguist is to identify and make explicit the system of linguistic conventions and rules that the speaker unknowingly puts into practice.

Modern linguists commonly distinguish three aspects which together constitute the **grammar**—the components and principles of order—in any "natural language" (e.g., English, French, Japanese, and so on): (1) **phonology**, the study of the elementary speech sounds; (2) **morphology**, the study of the organization of speech sounds into the smallest meaningful groups (morphemes and words); and (3) **syntax**, the study of the way that sequences of words are ordered into phrases, clauses, and sentences. Structural linguists usually represent these three aspects as manifesting parallel principles of distinctions and ordering, although on successively higher and more complex levels of organization. A fourth aspect of language sometimes included within the area of linguistics is **semantics**, the study of the meaning of words and of word combinations in phrases and sentences. In this last area, Saussure introduced the terminology of the *sign* (a single word) as constituted by an inseparable union of **signifier** (the speech sounds or written marks composing the sign) and **signified** (the conceptual meaning of the sign).

1) One branch of phonology is **phonetics**, the physical description of the elementary speech sounds in all known languages and the way they are produced by the vocal apparatus; the "phonetic alphabet" is a standardized set of symbols for representing in written form these speech sounds. Another branch is "phonemics," which deals with **phonemes**: the smallest units of speech sound which, within any one natural language, are functional—that is, which cannot vary without changing the word of which they are a part into a different word. Thus in the English word represented by the spelling "pin," if we change only the initial speech sound, we get three different words, pin-tin-din; if we change only the medial sound, we get pin-pen-pun; if we change only the final sound, we get pin-pit-pill. From the matrix of such changes, we determine that each of the individual units represented by the spelling p, t, d; i, e, u; and n, t, l function as differentiating phonemes within the English language. Each language has its own phonemic system, which both overlaps with and diverges from the phonemic system of any other language. The imperfect success that a native speaker in one language, such as German, manifests in adapting his habitual pronunciations to the phonemic system of a different language, such as English, is a major feature of what we identify as a "foreign accent."

Even within a single language, however, a native speaker will vary the pronunciation of a single phonemic unit within different combinations of speech sounds, and will also vary the pronunciation from one utterance to another. Even greater phonetic differences are apparent between two native speakers, especially if they speak the **dialects** of diverse regions, or of diverse social groups. Saussure proposed the principle that what we identify as "the same phoneme" within a language is not determined by the physical features of the speech sound itself, but by its **difference** from all other phonemes in that language—that is, by the differentiability, within a given language, between a particular speech unit and all other functional speech units. Saussure's important claim is that the principle of difference, rather than any "positive" property, functions to establish identity not only for phonemes, but for units on all levels of linguistic organization, including morphemes, words, syntax, and semantic significations. All these types of items, then, are systemic facts that achieve an identity only within a particular language, and vary between one language and another. (This claim, that seeming identities are in fact constituted by networks of differences, has been adopted as a central feature in *structuralism, semiotics,* and *deconstruction.*)

2) The next level of analysis, after phonology, is morphology—the combination of phonemes into morphemes and into words. A **morpheme** is the smallest meaningful unit of speech sounds within any one language; that is, a morphemic unit, composed of one or more phonemes, is a unit that recurs in a language with the same, or at least similar, meaning. Some morphemes, such as "man," "open," and "run" in English, constitute complete words; others, however, occur only as parts of words. For example the noun "grace" is a word that is a single morpheme. If we prefix to the root element, "grace," the morpheme "dis-," it becomes a different word with a sharply different meaning: "disgrace"; if we add to the root the morphemic suffix "-ful," the noun functions as an adjective, "graceful"; if we add to these two morphemes the further suffix, "-ly," the resulting word functions as an adverb, "gracefully"; if we prefix to this form either the morphemic "dis-" or "un-," we get the adverbial words, each composed of four morphemes, "disgracefully" and "ungracefully."

We find also an interesting set of phoneme combinations which do not constitute specific morphemes, yet are experienced by speakers of English as having a common, though very loose-boundaried, area of meaning. Examples are the initial sounds represented by "fl-" in the set of words "flash, flare, flame, flicker, flimmer," all of which signify a kind of moving light; while in the set "fly, flip, flap, flop, flit, flutter," the same initial sounds all signify a kind of movement in air. The terminal sounds represented by "-ash," as they occur in the set "bash, crash, clash, dash, flash, gash, mash, slash," have an overlapping significance of sudden or violent movement. Such combinations of phonemes are sometimes called "phonetic intensives," or else instances of **sound-symbolism**; they are important components in the type of words, exploited especially by poets, in which the sounds of the words seem peculiarly appropriate to their significance. See *onomatopoeia,* and refer to Leonard Bloomfield, *Language* (1933), pp. 244–46; I. A. Richards, *The Philosophy of Rhetoric* (1936), pp. 57–65.

Phonemes, morphemes, and words are all said to be "segments" of the stream of the speech sounds which constitute an utterance. Linguists also distinguish a **suprasegmental** feature of language, consisting of stress, juncture, and intonation, all of which function morphemically, in that they alter the identity and significance of the segments in an utterance. A shift in **stress**—that is, of relative forcefulness, or loudness, of a component element in an utterance—from the first to the second syllable converts the noun "ínvalid" into the adjective "inválid," and the noun "cónvict" into the verb "convíct." **Juncture** denotes the transition between adjacent speech sounds in an utterance, whether within a word, between words, or between groups of words. Linguists distinguish various functional classes of junctures in English utterances. **Intonation** is the variation of pitch, or voice-melody, in the course of an utterance. We utter the assertion "He is going home" with a different intonation from that of the question "Is he going home?"; and the use of the question intonation even with the assertive sequence of words "He is going home" will make the sentence function to an auditor not as an assertion, but as a question. Uttering the following three words so as to alter the relative stress in the ways indicated, and at the same time using a variety of intonation patterns and pauses, will reveal the extent to which suprasegmental features can affect the significance of a sentence constituted by the same words: "Í like you." "I líke you." "I like yóu."

3) The third level of analysis (after the level of phonemes and the level of the combination of phonemes into morphemes and words) is syntax: the combination of words into phrases, clauses, and sentences. Analysis of speech performances (paroles) in any language reveals regularities in such constructions, which are explained by postulating syntactic **rules** that are operative within the linguistic system, or langue, which has been mastered by competent speakers and auditors. (These purely "descriptive" rules, or general regularities, of syntax are to be distinguished from the "prescriptive" rules of grammar which are presented in school handbooks designed to teach the "correct usage" of upper-class standard English.) A widely used distinction, developed by Roman Jakobson, is that between the rules governing **paradigmatic** relations (the "vertical" relations between any single word in a sentence and other words that are phonologically, syntactically, or semantically similar, which can be substituted for it), and **syntagmatic** relations (the "horizontal" relations which determine the possibilities of putting words in a sequence so as to make a well-formed syntactic unit). On the phonemic and morphemic levels, a similar distinction is made between paradigmatic relations among single elements and syntagmatic relations of sequences of elements. This paradigmatic-syntagmatic distinction parallels the distinction between metaphoric (vertical) and metonymic (horizontal) relations in analyzing *figurative language.*

Noam Chomsky in *Syntactic Structures* (1951) initiated what is known as "generative-transformational grammar." Chomsky's persistent emphasis is on the central feature he calls "creativity" in language—the fact that a competent native speaker can produce a meaningful sentence which has no exact precedent in the speaker's earlier linguistic experience, as well as the fact that competent auditors can understand the sentence immediately, though it is equally new to them. To explain this "rule-bound creativity" of a language, the linguist proposes that native speakers' and listeners' competence consists in their mastery of a set of generative and transformational rules. This mode of linguistics is called **generative** in that it undertakes to establish a finite system of rules which will suffice to "generate"—in the sense that it will adequately account for—the totality of syntactically "well-formed" sentences that are possible in a given language. It is **transformational** in that it postulates, in the **deep structure** of a language system, a set of "kernel sentences" (such as "John is building a house") which, in accordance with diverse rules of transformation, serve to produce a great variety of sentences on the **surface structure** of a language system (e.g., the passive form "The house is being built by John" and the question form "Is John building a house?" as well as a large number of more complex derivatives from the simple kernel sentence).

For diverse applications of the concepts and methods of modern linguistics to literature, see *deconstruction, Russian formalism, semiotics, structuralism,* and *stylistics.* For Saussure's theories refer to Ferdinand de Saussure, *Course in General Linguistics,* trans. Wade Baskin (1966), and the concise analysis by Jonathan Culler, *Ferdinand de Saussure* (rev., 1986). For American linguistics: Leonard Bloomfield, *Language* (1933); Zellig S. Harris, *Structural Linguistics* (2d ed., 1960); George L. Trager and Henry Lee Smith, Jr., *An Outline of English Structure* (1957). On "generative-transformational grammar": Noam Chomsky, *Selected Readings,* ed. J. P. B. Allen and Paul Van Buren (1971); *The Structure of Language,* ed. Jerry A. Fodor and Jerrold J. Katz (1964); John Lyons, *Noam Chomsky* (1970). Useful reviews of Continental and American linguistics and of their applications in literary criticism are included in Karl D. Uitti, *Linguistics and Literary Theory* (1969); William H. Youngren, *Semantics, Linguistics, and Criticism* (1972); Jonathan Culler, *Structuralist Poetics* (1975), and *The Pursuit of Signs* (1981); Roger Fowler, *Linguistic Criticism* (1986). See also Roman Jakobson's influential essay "Linguistics and Poetics," in *Style in Language,* ed. Thomas A. Sebeok (1960), and the expansion of Jakobson's basic distinction between the horizontal and vertical dimensions of language in David Lodge, *The Modes of Modern Writing: Metaphor, Metonymy, and the Typology of Modern Literature* (1977).

Local Color. The detailed representation in prose fiction of the setting, dialect, customs, dress, and ways of thinking and feeling which are distinctive of a particular region, such as Thomas Hardy's "Wessex" or Rudyard Kipling's India. After the Civil War a number of American writers exploited the literary possibilities of local color in various parts of America; for example, the West (Bret Harte), the Mississippi region (Mark Twain), the South (George Washington Cable), the Midwest (E. W. Howe, Hamlin Garland), and New England (Sarah Orne Jewett). The term "local color writing" is often applied to works which, like O. Henry's or Damon Runyon's stories set in New York City, rely for their interest mainly on a sentimental or comic representation of the surface particularities of a region, instead of on more general human characteristics and problems.

Lyric. In the most common use of the term, a **lyric** is any fairly short poem, consisting of the utterance by a single speaker, who expresses a state of mind or a process of perception, thought, and feeling. Many lyric speakers represented as musing in solitude. In *dramatic lyrics,* however, the lyric speaker is represented as addressing another person in a specific situation; instances are John Donne's "Canonization" and William Wordsworth's "Tintern Abbey."

Although the lyric is uttered in the first person, the "I" in the poem need not be the poet who wrote it. In some lyrics, such as John Milton's sonnet "When I consider how my light is spent" and Samuel Taylor Coleridge's "Frost at Midnight," the references to the known circumstances of the author's life make it clear that we are to read the poem as a personal expression. Even in such personal lyrics, however, both the character and utterance of the speaker may be shaped by the author in a way that is conducive to the desired artistic effect. In a number of lyrics, the speaker is a conventional period-figure, such as the long-suffering suitor in the Petrarchan sonnet (see *Petrarchan conceit*), or the courtly, witty lover of the *Cavalier* poems. And in some types of lyrics, the speaker is obviously an invented figure remote from the poet in character and circumstance. (See *persona, confessional poetry,* and *dramatic monologue* for distinctions between personal and invented lyric speakers.)

The lyric genre comprehends a great variety of utterances. Some, like Ben Jonson's "To the Memory of . . . William Shakespeare" and Walt Whitman's ode "O Captain, My Captain," are ceremonial poems uttered in a public voice on a public occasion. Among the lyrics uttered in a more private mode, some are simply a brief, intense expression of a mood or state of feeling; for example, Shelley's "To Night," or Emily Dickinson's "Wild Nights, Wild Nights," or this fine medieval song:

> Fowles in the frith,
> The fisshes in the flood,
> And I mon waxe wood:
> Much sorwe I walke with
> For best of bone and blood.

But the genre also includes extended expressions of a complex evolution of mind, as in the long elegy and the meditative ode. And within a lyric, the process of observation, thought, memory, and feeling may be organized in a variety of ways. For example, in "love lyrics" the speaker may simply express his state of mind in an ordered form, as in Robert Burns' "O my love's like a red, red rose"; or he may gallantly elaborate a compliment to his lady (Ben Jonson's "Drink to me only with thine eyes"); or he may deploy an argument to persuade his mistress to take advantage of fleeting youth and opportunity (Andrew Marvell's "To His Coy Mistress"). In other kinds of lyrics the speaker manifests and justifies a particular disposition and set of values (John Milton's "L'Allegro" and "Il Penseroso"); or expresses a sustained process of observation and meditation, in which he tries to resolve an emotional problem (Wordsworth's "Ode: Intimations of Immortality," Arnold's "Dover Beach"); or is exhibited as making and justifying the choice of a way of life (Yeats' "Sailing to Byzantium").

In the original Greek, "lyric" signified a song rendered to the accompaniment of a lyre. In some current usages, lyric still retains the sense of a poem written to be set to music; the *hymn,* for example, is a lyric on a religious subject that is intended to be sung. The adjectival form "lyrical" is sometimes applied to an expressive, song-like passage in a narrative poem, such as Eve's declaration of love to Adam, "With thee conversing I forget all time," in Milton's *Paradise Lost,* IV. 639–56.

See *genre* for the broad distinction between the three major genres of drama, narrative, and lyric, and also for the sudden elevation of lyric, in the Romantic period, to the status of the quintessentially poetic mode. For subclasses of the lyric see *aubade, dramatic monologue, elegy, epithalamion, hymn, ode, sonnet.* Refer to Ernest Rhys, *Lyric Poetry* (1913); Norman Maclean, "From Action to Image: Theories of the Lyric in the 18th Century," in *Critics and Criticism,* ed. R. S. Crane (1952); William E. Rogers, *The Three Genres and the Interpretation of Lyric* (1983); W. R. Johnson, *The Idea of Lyric* (1982); Chaviva Hosek and Patricia Parker, eds., *Lyric Poetry: Beyond New Criticism* (1985); David Lindley, *Lyric* (1985). In the present century the lyric has become by far the preponderant poetic mode; see, for example, M. L. Rosenthal, *The Modern Poets* (1960), and *The New Poets* (1967).

Malapropism is a type of **solecism** (that is, the conspicuous and unintended violation of standard usage in a language) which mistakenly uses a word in place of another that it resembles; the effect is usually comic. The term derives from Mrs. Malaprop in Richard Brinsley Sheridan's comedy *The Rivals* (1775), who in the attempt to display a copious vocabulary said things such as "a progeny of learning," "as headstrong as an allegory on the banks of the Nile," and "he is the very pineapple of politeness."

Masque. The masque (a variant spelling of "mask") was inaugurated in Renaissance Italy and flourished in England during the reigns of Elizabeth I, James I, and Charles I. In its full development, it was an elaborate form of court entertainment that combined poetic drama, music, song, dance, splendid costuming, and stage spectacle. A plot—often slight, and mainly mythological and allegorical—served to hold together these diverse elements. The speaking characters, who wore masks (hence the title), were often played by amateurs who belonged to courtly society. The play concluded with a dance in which the players doffed their masks and were joined by the aristocratic audience.

In the early seventeenth century in England the masque drew upon the finest artistic talents of the day, including Ben Jonson for the poetic script (for example, *The Masque of Blacknesse* and *The Masque of Queens*) and Inigo Jones, the architect, for the elaborate sets, costumes, and stage machinery. Each lavish production cost a fortune; it was literally the sport of kings and queens, until both court and drama were abruptiy ended by the Puritan triumph of 1642. The two examples best known to modern readers are the masque-within-a-play in the fourth act of Shakespeare's *The Tempest,* and Milton's sage and serious revival of the form, *Comus,* which was presented at Ludlow Castle in 1634.

The **antimasque** was a form developed by Ben Jonson. In it the characters were grotesque and unruly, the action ludicrous, and the humor broad; it served as a foil and countertype to the elegance, order, and ceremony of the masque proper, which preceded it in a performance.

See Enid Welsford, *The Court Masque* (1927); Allardyce Nicoll, *Stuart Masques and the Renaissance Stage* (1937). Stephen Orgel and Roy Strong, in *Inigo Jones: The Theatre of the Stuart Court* (2 vols.; 1973), discuss Jones' contributions to the masque, with copious illustrations.

Melodrama. "Melos" is Greek for song, and the term "melodrama" was originally applied to all musical plays, including opera. In early-nineteenth-century London, many plays were produced with a musical accompaniment that (as in modern motion pictures) served simply to fortify the emotional tone of the various scenes; the procedure was developed in part to circumvent the Licensing Act, which allowed "legitimate" plays only as a monopoly of the Drury Lane and Covent Garden theaters, but permitted musical entertainments elsewhere. The term "melodrama" is now often applied to some of the typical plays that were written to be produced to musical accompaniment.

The Victorian melodrama can be said to bear the relation to tragedy that *farce* does to comedy. Typically, the protagonists are *flat* types: the hero is great-hearted, the heroine as pure as the driven snow, and the villain a monster of malignity (the good guys and bad guys of the movie western and some television dramas are modern derivatives from types of characters in the old melodramas). The plot revolves around malevolent intrigue and violent action, while the credibility both of character and plot is sacrificed for violent effect and emotional opportunism. Nineteenth-century melodramas such as *Under the Gaslight* (1867) and the temperance play *Ten Nights in a Barroom* (1858) are still sometimes produced—less for thrills, however, than for laughs.

The terms "melodrama" and "melodramatic" are also, in an extended sense, applied to any literary work or episode, whether in drama or prose fiction, that relies on implausible events and sensational action.

See M. W. Disher, *Blood and Thunder: Mid-Victorian Melodrama and Its Origins* (1949), and *Plots That Thrilled* (1954); Frank Rahill, *The World of Melodrama* (1967); R. B. Heilman, *Tragedy and Melodrama* (1968); David Thorburn, "Television Melodrama," *Television as a Cultural Force,* ed. Douglass Cater (1976).

Metaphysical Poets. John Dryden said in his *Discourse of Satire* (1693) that John Donne in his poetry "affects the metaphysics," meaning that Donne employs the terminology and abstruse arguments of the medieval Scholastic philosophers. In 1779 Samuel Johnson extended the term "metaphysical" from Donne to a school of poets, in the acute and balanced critique which he incorporated in his "Life of Cowley." The name is now applied to a group of seventeenth-century poets who, whether or not directly influenced by Donne, employ similar poetic procedures and imagery, both in secular poetry (Cleveland, Marvell, Cowley) and in religious poetry (Herbert, Vaughan, Crashaw).

Attempts have been made to demonstrate that these poets had in common a philosophical worldview. The term "metaphysical," however, fits these very diverse writers only if it is used, as Johnson used it, to indicate a common poetic style and way of organizing the meditative process or the poetic argument. Donne set the metaphysical mode by writing poems which are sharply opposed to the rich mellifluousness and the idealized view of human nature and of sexual love which had constituted a central tradition in Elizabethan poetry, especially in Spenser and the writers of *Petrarchan sonnets.* Instead, Donne wrote in a diction and meter modeled on the rough give-and-take of actual speech, and often organized his poems in the form of an urgent or heated argument—with a reluctant mistress, or an intruding friend, or God, or death, or with himself. He employed a subtle and often deliberately outrageous logic; he was realistic, ironic, and sometimes cynical in his treatment of the complexity of human motives, especially in the sexual relation; and whether playful or serious, and whether writing the poetry of love or of intense religious experience, he was above all "witty," making ingenious use of *paradox, pun,* and startling parallels in simile and metaphor (see *metaphysical conceit*). The beginnings of four of Donne's poems will illustrate the shock tactic, the dramatic form of direct address, the rough idiom, and the rhythms of the living voice which are characteristic of his metaphysical style:

> Go and catch a falling star,
> Get with child a mandrake root . . .

> For God's sake hold your tongue, and let me love.

> Busy old fool, unruly sun . . .

> Batter my heart, three-personed God . . .

Some, not all, of Donne's poetic procedures have recognizable parallels in each of his contemporaries and successors whom literary historians usually group as metaphysical poets.

These poets have had some admirers in every age, but beginning with the *Neoclassic Period* of the later seventeenth century, they were by most critics and readers regarded as interesting but perversely ingenious and obscure eccentrics, until a drastic revaluation after World War I elevated Donne, together with Herbert and Marvell, high in the hierarchy of English poets (see *canon of literature*). This reversal owed much to H. J. C. Grierson's Introduction to *Metaphysical Lyrics and Poems of the Seventeenth Century* (1912), was given strong impetus by T. S. Eliot's essays "The Metaphysical Poets" and "Andrew Marvell" (1921), and was continued by a great number of commentators, including F. R. Leavis in England, and especially the American *New Critics,* who tended to elevate the metaphysical style into the model of their ideal poetry of "unified sensibility," irony, and paradox. See *dissociation of sensibility.*

See George Williamson, *The Donne Tradition* (1930); F. R. Leavis, *Revaluation* (1936); Cleanth Brooks, *Modern Poetry and the Tradition* (1939); Rosemund Tuve, *Elizabethan and Metaphysical Imagery* (1947); J. E. Duncan, *The Revival of Metaphysical Poetry* (1959); F. J. Warnke, *European Metaphysical Poetry* (1961), which treats the continental vogue of this style; Helen Gardner, ed., *John Donne: A Collection of Critical Essays* (1962); Helen Vendler, *The Poetry of George Herbert* (1975).

Meter. In all sustained spoken English we sense a **rhythm**, that is, a recognizable though variable pattern in the beat of the stresses in the stream of sound. If this rhythm of stresses is structured into a recurrence of regular— that is, approximately equivalent—units of stress pattern, we call it **meter.** Compositions written in meter are known as **verse.**

There is considerable dispute about the best way to analyze and classify English meters. This article will present a traditional stress-and-syllable analysis which has the virtues of being simple, widely accepted, and applicable to by far the greater part of English versification from Chaucer to the present day. Some major departures from this stress-and-syllable meter will be described at the end.

We attend, in reading verse, to the individual **line**, which is a sequence of words printed as a separate entity on the page. The meter is determined by the pattern of stronger and weaker stresses in the syllables composing the words in the verse-line; often, the stronger is called the "stressed" syllable and the weaker one the "unstressed" syllable. (What the ear perceives as a strong stress is not an absolute quantity, but is relative to the degree of stress in the adjacent syllables.) There are three major factors that determine where the **stresses** (in the sense of the relatively stronger stresses, or "accents") will fall in a line of verse: (1) Most important is the "word accent" in words of more than one syllable; in the noun "áccent" itself, for example, the stress falls on the first syllable. (2) There are also many monosyllabic words in the language, and on which of these—in a sentence or a phrase—the stress will fall depends on the grammatical function of the word (we normally put stronger stress on nouns, verbs, and adjectives, for example, than on articles or prepositions), and depends also on the "rhetorical accent," or the emphasis we give a word because we want to enhance its importance in a particular utterance. (3) Another determinant of stress is the prevailing "metrical accent," which is the beat that we expect, in accordance with the stress pattern which was established earlier in the metrical line or passage.

If the prevailing stress pattern enforces a drastic alteration of the normal word accent, we get a **wrenched accent.** Wrenching may be the result of a lack of metrical skill; it was, however, conventional in the *folk ballad* (for example, "fair ladíe," "far countrée"), and is sometimes deliberately used for comic effects, as in Lord Byron's *Don Juan* (1819–24) and in the recent verses of Ogden Nash.

It is possible to distinguish a number of degrees of relative syllabic stress in English speech, but the most common and generally useful fashion of analyzing and classifying the standard English meters is to distinguish only two categories—weak stress and strong stress—and to group the syllables into metric feet according to the patterning of these two stresses. A **foot** is the combination of a strong stress and the associated weak stress or stresses which make up the recurrent metric unit of a line. The relatively stronger-stressed syllable is called, for short, "stressed"; the relatively weaker-stressed syllables are called "light," or "slack," or simply "unstressed."

The four standard feet distinguished in English are:

1) **Iambic** (the noun is "iamb"): a light syllable followed by a stressed syllable.

    Thĕ cúr|fĕw tólls|thĕ knéll|ŏf pár|tĭng dáy.|

    (Thomas Gray, "Elegy Written in a Country Churchyard")

2) **Anapestic** (the noun is "anapest"): two light syllables followed by a stressed syllable.

    Thĕ Ăs sýr|iăn căme dówn|lĭke ă wólf|ŏn thĕ fóld.|

    (Lord Byron, "The Destruction of Sennacherib")

3) **Trochaic** (the noun is "trochee"): a stressed followed by a light syllable.

    Thére thĕy|áre, mў|fíf tў|mén ănd|wó mĕn.|

    (Robert Browning, "One Word More")

Most trochaic lines lack the final unstressed syllable—in the technical term, such lines are **catalectic.** So in Blake's "The Tiger":

    Tí gĕr|! tí gĕr|! búrn ĭng|bríght|
    Ín thĕ|fó rĕst|óf thĕ|níght.|

4) **Dactylic** (the noun is "dactyl"): a stressed syllable followed by two light syllables.

    Éve, wĭth hĕr|bás kĕt, wăs|
    Déep ĭn thĕ|bélls ănd grăss.|

    (Ralph Hodgson, "Eve")

Iambs and anapests, since the strong stress is at the end, are called "rising meter"; trochees and dactyls, with the strong stress at the beginning, "falling meter." Iambs and trochees, having two syllables, are called "duple meter";

anapests and dactyls, having three syllables, are called "triple meter." It should be noted that the iamb is by far the commonest English foot.

Two other feet, distinguished by special titles, occur only as occasional variants from standard feet:

5) **Spondaic** (the noun is "spondee"): two successive syllables with approximately equal strong stresses, as in each of the first two feet of this line:

Góod stróng| thíck stú|pĕ fý|ĭng ín|cĕnse smóke.|

(Browning, "The Bishop Orders His Tomb")

6) **Pyrrhic** (the noun is also "pyrrhic"): a foot composed of two successive syllables with approximately equal light stresses, as in the second and fourth feet in this line:

Mý wăy|is tŏ|bĕ gín|with thĕ|bĕ gín nĭng|

(Byron, *Don Juan*)

(Some traditional metrists do not admit the existence of a true pyrrhic, on the grounds that the prevailing metrical accent—in the above instance, iambic—always imposes a slightly stronger stress on one of the two syllables.)

A metric line is named according to the number of feet composing it:

monometer:	one foot
dimeter:	two feet
trimeter:	three feet
tetrameter:	four feet
pentameter:	five feet
hexameter:	six feet (an **Alexandrine** is a line of six iambic feet)
heptameter:	seven feet (a **fourteener** is another term for a line of seven iambic feet—hence, of fourteen syllables; it tends to break into a unit of four feet followed by a unit of three feet)
octameter:	eight feet

To describe the meter of a line we name (a) the predominant foot and (b) the number of feet it contains. In the illustrations above, for example, the line from Gray's "Elegy" is "iambic pentameter," and the line from Byron's "The Destruction of Sennacherib" is "anapestic tetrameter."

To **scan** a passage of verse is to go through it line by line, analyzing the component feet, and also indicating where any major pauses in the phrasing fall within a line. Here is a **scansion**, signified by conventional symbols, of the first five lines from John Keats' *Endymion* (1818); the passage was chosen because it exemplifies a flexible and variable rather than a highly regular metrical pattern.

1) Ă thíng| ŏf béau|tў ís|ă jóy|fŏr é vĕr:|

2) Ĭts lóve|lĭ néss|ĭn créas|ĕs; // ít|wĭll név ĕr|

3) Páss ĭn|tŏ nóth|ĭng nĕss,|// bŭt stíll|wĭll kéep|

4) Ă bów|ĕr quí|ĕt fŏr|ŭs, // ánd|ă sléep|

5) Fúll ŏf|swĕet dréams,|ănd héalth,|ănd quí|ĕt bréath ĭng.|

The prevailing meter is clearly iambic, and the lines are iambic pentameter. As in all fluent verse, however, there are variations upon the basic iambic foot, and these are sometimes called "substitutions." Thus:

1) The closing feet of lines 1, 2, and 5 end with an extra light syllable, and are said to have a **feminine ending.** In lines 3 and 4, the closing feet, because they are standard iambs, end with a stressed syllable and are said to have **masculine endings.**

2) In lines 3 and 5, the opening iambic feet have been "inverted" to form trochees. (Such initial positions are the most common place for inversions in iambic verse.)

3) I have marked the second foot in line 2, and the third foot of line 3 and line 4, as pyrrhics (two light stresses); these help to give Keats' verses their rapid movement. This is a procedure in scansion about which competent readers disagree: some will feel enough of a metric beat to mark all these feet as iambs; others will mark still other feet (for example, the third foot of line 1) as pyrrhics also. And some metric analysts prefer to use symbols measuring two degrees of strong stress, and will indicate a difference in the feet, as follows:

Ĭts lŏve|lĭ néss|ĭn créas|ĕs.

Notice, however, that these are differences only in nuance; the analysts agree that the prevailing pulse of Keats' versification is iambic throughout.

Two other elements are important in the metric movement of Keats' passage: (1) In lines 1 and 5, the pause in the reading—which occurs naturally at the end of a sentence, clause, or other syntactic unit—coincides with the end of the line; such lines are called **end-stopped.** Lines 2 through 4, on the other hand, are called **run-on lines** (or in a French term, they exhibit **enjambement**—"a striding-over"), because the pressure of the incompleted syntactic unit toward closure carries on over the end of the verse-line. (2) When a strong phrasal pause falls within a line, as in lines 2, 3, and 4, it is called a **caesura**—indicated in the quoted passage by the conventional symbol, //. The management of these internal pauses is important for giving variety and for providing expressive emphases in the long pentameter line.

To understand the function of such an analysis, we must realize that scansion is an abstract scheme which deliberately omits notation of many aspects of the actual reading of a poem that contribute to its movement, rhythm, and total impression. It does not specify, for example, whether the component words in a metric line are short words or long words, or whether the strong stresses fall on short vowels or long vowels; it does not give any indication of the *intonation*—the overall rise and fall in the pitch and loudness of the voice—which we use to bring out the meaning and rhetorical effect of these poetic lines; nor does it indicate the rhythms of the varied phrasal structures within a sustained poetic passage. Such details are omitted in order to lay bare the essential metric skeleton; that is, the fall of the stronger stresses in the syllabic sequence of a verse-line. Moreover, an actual reading of a poem, if it is a skillful reading, will not accord mechanically with the scansion. That is, there is a difference between the scansion, as an abstract metrical norm, and a skilled and expressive oral reading, or **performance**, of a poem; and in fact, no two competent readers will perform the same lines in precisely the same way. But in a performance the metric norm indicated by the scansion is sensed as an implicit understructure of pulses; in fact, the interplay of an expressive performance, sometimes with and sometimes against this underlying structural pattern, gives tension and vitality to our experience of verse.

We should note, finally, that some kinds of versification that occur in English poetry differ from the syllable-and-stress type already described:

1) **Strong-stress meters.** In this meter, native to English and other Germanic languages, only the beat of the strong stresses counts in the scanning, while the number of intervening light syllables is highly variable. Usually there are four strong-stressed syllables in a line, whose beat is emphasized by *alliteration*. This was the meter of Old English poetry and of many Middle English poems, until Chaucer and others popularized the syllable-and-stress meter. In the opening passage, for example, of *Piers Plowman* (later fourteenth century) the four strong stresses (always divided by a medial caesura) are for the most part reinforced by alliteration (see *alliterative meter*); the light syllables, which vary in number, are recessive and do not assert their individual presence:

> In a sómer séson, // whan sóft was the sónne,
> I shópe me in shróudes, // as Í a shépe were,
> In hábits like an héremite, // unhóly of wórkes,
> Went wýde in this wórld, // wónders to hére.

Strong-stress meter still survives in traditional children's rhymes such as "Hickory, dickory, dock," and was revived as an artful literary meter by Samuel Taylor Coleridge in *Christabel* (1816), in which each line has four strong stresses but the number of syllables within a line varies from four to twelve.

What G. M. Hopkins in the later nineteenth century called his **sprung rhythm** is a variant of strong-stress meter: each foot, as he describes it, begins with a stressed syllable, which may either stand alone or be associated with from one to three (occasionally even more) light syllables. Two six-stress lines from Hopkins' "The Wreck of the *Deutschland*" indicate the variety of the rhythms in this meter, and also exemplify its most striking feature: the great weight of the strong stresses, and the frequent juxtaposition of strong stresses (spondees) at any point in the line. The stresses in the second line were marked in a manuscript by Hopkins himself; they indicate that in complex instances, his metric decisions may seem arbitrary:

> The|sóur|scýthe|crínge, and the|bléar|sháre|cóme.|
> Our|héarts' chárity's|héarth's|fíre, our|thóughts' chivalry's|
>   thróng's|Lórd.|

(See Elisabeth Schneider, "Sprung Rhythm," *PMLA*, Vol. 80, 1965.) A number of modern metrists, including T. S. Eliot and Ezra Pound, skillfully interweave both strong-stress and syllable-and-stress meters in some of their versification.

2) **Quantitative meters** in English are written in imitation of Greek and Latin versification, in which the metrical pattern is not determined by the stress but by the "quantity" (duration of pronunciation) of a syllable, and the foot consists of a combination of "long" and "short" syllables. Sir Philip Sidney, Edmund Spenser, and other Elizabethan poets experimented with this meter in English, as did Coleridge, Tennyson, Henry Wadsworth Longfellow, and Robert Bridges later on. The strong accentual character of English, however, as well as the indeterminateness of the duration of a syllable, makes it impossible to sustain a purely quantitative meter for any length. See Derek Attridge, *Well-weighted Syllables: Elizabethan Verse in Classical Meters* (1974).

3) In *free verse* (discussed in a separate essay), the component lines have no (or at least only occasional) metric feet, or uniform stress-patterns.

George Saintsbury, *Historical Manual of English Prosody* (1910), and R. M. Alden, *English Verse* (1930), are well-illustrated treatments of traditional syllable-and-stress metrics. For later discussions of this and alternative metric theories see George R. Stewart, *The Technique of English Verse* (1930); Seymour Chatman, *A Theory of Meter* (1965); and W. K. Wimsatt and Monroe C. Beardsley, "The Concept of Meter" (1959). This last essay is reprinted in W. K. Wimsatt, *Hateful Contraries* (1965), and in Harvey Gross, ed., *The Structure of Verse* (1966)—an anthology which reprints other useful essays, including Northrop Frye, "The Rhythm of Recurrence," and Yvor Winters, "The Audible Reading of Poetry." See also W. K. Wimsatt, ed., *Versification: Major Language Types* (1972); Paul Fussell, *Poetic Meter and Poetic Form* (rev., 1979); John Hollander, *Rhyme's Reason: A Guide to English Verse* (1981).

Miracle Plays, Morality Plays, and Interludes are types of late-medieval drama, written in a variety of verse forms.

The **miracle play** had as its subject either a story from the Bible, or else the life and martyrdom of a saint. In the usage of some historians, however, "Miracle play" denotes only dramas based on saints' lives, and the term **mystery play**—"mystery" in the archaic sense of the "trade" conducted by each of the medieval guilds who sponsored these plays—is applied to dramas based on the Old and New Testaments.

The plays based on biblical narratives originated within the church in about the tenth century, in dramatizations of brief parts of the Latin liturgical service, called "tropes," especially the "Quem quaeritis" ("Whom are you seeking") trope representing the visit of the three Marys to the tomb of Christ. Gradually these evolved into complete plays which were written in English instead of in Latin, produced under the auspices of the various trade guilds, and acted on stages set outside the church. The miracle plays written in England are of unknown authorship. In the fourteenth century there developed in cities such as York and Chester the practice, on the feast of Corpus Christi (sixty days after Easter), of putting on great "cycles" of such plays, representing crucial events in the biblical history of mankind from the Creation and Fall of man, through the Nativity, Crucifixion, and Resurrection of Christ, to the Last Judgment. The precise way that the plays were staged is a matter of scholarly debate, but it is widely agreed that each scene was played on a separate "pageant wagon" which was drawn, in sequence, to one after another fixed "station" in a city, at each of which some parts of the cycle were enacted. The biblical texts were greatly expanded in these plays, and the unknown authors added scenes, comic as well as serious, of their own invention. For examples of the variety, vitality, and power of these dramas, see the Wakefield "Noah" and "Second Shepherd's Play," and the Brome "Abraham and Isaac."

Morality plays were dramatized *allegories* of the representative Christian life in the plot form of a quest for salvation, in which the crucial events are temptations, sinning, and the climactic confrontation with death. The usual protagonist represents Mankind, or Everyman; among the other characters are personifications of virtues, vices, and Death, as well as angels and demons who contest for the prize of the soul of Mankind. A character known as the **Vice** often played the role of the tempter in a fashion both sinister and comic; he is regarded by some literary historians as a precursor both of the cynical, ironic villain and of some of the comic figures in Elizabethan drama, including Shakespeare's Falstaff. The best-known morality play is the fifteenth-century *Everyman*; another fine example, written early in the same century, is *The Castle of Perseverance*.

Interlude (Latin, "between the play") is a term applied to a variety of short stage entertainments, such as secular farces and witty dialogues with a religious or political point. In the late fifteenth and early sixteenth centuries, these little dramas were performed by bands of professional actors; it is believed that they were often put on between the courses of a feast or between the acts of a longer play. Among the better-known interludes are John Heywood's farces of the first half of the sixteenth century, especially *The Four PP* (that is, the Palmer, the Pardoner, the 'Pothecary, and the Peddler, who engage in a lying contest), and *Johan Johan the Husband, Tyb His Wife, and Sir John the Priest*.

Until the middle of the present century, concern with medieval drama was scholarly rather than critical. Since that time a number of studies have dealt with the relations of the texts to the religious and secular culture of medieval Europe, and have stressed the artistic excellence and power of the plays themselves. See Karl Young, *The Drama of the Medieval Church* (2 vols.; 1933); A. P. Rossiter, *English Drama from Early Times to the Elizabethans* (1950); Hardin Craig, *English Religious Drama of the Middle Ages* (1955); Arnold Williams, *The Drama of Medieval England* (1961); T. W. Craik, *The Tudor Interlude* (1962); V. A. Kolve, *The Play Called Corpus Christi* (1966); Rosemary Woolf, *The English Mystery Plays* (1972); Jerome Taylor and Alan Nelson, eds., *Medieval English Drama: Essays Critical and Contextual* (1972); Robert Potter, *The English Morality Play* (1975).

Modernism and Postmodernism. The term **modernism** is widely used to identify new and distinctive features in the subjects, forms, concepts, and styles of literature and the other arts in the early decades of the present century, but especially after World War I (1914–1918). The specific features signified by "modernism" vary with the user, but many critics agree that it involves a deliberate and radical break with some of the traditional bases not only of Western art, but of Western culture in general. Important intellectual precursors of modernism, in this sense, are thinkers who had questioned the certainties that had supported traditional modes of social organization, religion, and morality, and also traditional ways of conceiving the human self—thinkers such as Friedrich Nietzsche (1844–1900), Karl Marx, Sigmund Freud, and James G. Frazer, whose *The Golden Bough* (1890–1915) stressed the correspondence between central Christian tenets and pagan, often barbaric myths and rituals.

Some literary historians locate the beginning of the modernist revolt as far back as the 1890s, but most agree that "high modernism," marked by an unexampled range and rapidity of change, came after the first World War. The year 1922 alone was signalized by the simultaneous appearance of such monuments of modernist innovation as James Joyce's *Ulysses*, T. S. Eliot's *The Waste Land*, and Virginia Woolf's *Jacob's Room*, as well as many other experimental works of literature. The catastrophe of the war had shaken faith in the continuity of Western civilization and raised doubts about the adequacy of traditional literary modes to represent the harsh and dissonant realities of the postwar world. T. S. Eliot wrote in a review of Joyce's *Ulysses* in 1923 that the inherited mode of ordering a literary work, which assumed a relatively coherent and stable social order, could not accord with "the immense panorama of futility and anarchy which is contemporary history." Like Joyce and Ezra Pound in his *Cantos,* Eliot experimented with new forms and a new style that would render contemporary disorder, often contrasting it to a lost order and integration that had been based on the religion and myths of the cultural past. In *The Waste Land* (1922), for example, Eliot replaced the standard flow of poetic language by fragmented utterances, and substituted for the traditional coherence of poetic structure a deliberate dislocation of parts, in which very diverse components are related by connections that are left to the reader to discover, or invent. Major works of modernist fiction, following Joyce's *Ulysses* (1922) and his even more radical *Finnegans Wake* (1939), subvert the basic conventions of earlier prose fiction by breaking up the narrative continuity, departing from the standard ways of representing characters, and violating the traditional syntax and coherence of narrative language by the use of *stream of consciousness* and other innovative modes of narration. Gertrude Stein—often linked with Joyce, Pound, Eliot, and Woolf as a trail-blazing modernist—experimented with writing that achieved its effects by violating the norms of standard English syntax and sentence structure. These new forms of construction in verse, prose, and narrative were emulated and carried further by many poets and novelists; they have obvious parallels in the violation of representational conventions in *expressionism* and *surrealism,* in the modernist paintings and sculpture of Cubism, Futurism, and Abstract Expressionism, and in the violations of standard conventions of melody, harmony, and rhythm by the modernist musical composers Stravinsky and Schoenberg, and their radical followers.

A prominent feature of modernism is the phenomenon called the **avant-garde** (a military metaphor: "advance-guard"); that is, a small, self-conscious group of artists and authors who deliberately undertake, in Ezra Pound's phrase, to "make it new." By violating the accepted conventions and proprieties, not only of art but of social discourse, they set out to create ever-new artistic forms and styles and to introduce hitherto neglected, and sometimes forbidden, subject matters. Frequently avant-garde artists represent themselves as "alienated" from the established order, against which they assert their own autonomy; a prominent aim is to shock the sensibilities of the conventional reader and to challenge the norms and pieties of the dominant bourgeois culture. See Renato Poggioli, *The Theory of the Avant-Garde* (1968). Peter Bürger's *Theory of the Avant-Garde* (1984) is a neo-Marxist analysis of modernism and of its distinctive cultural formation, the avant-garde.

The term **postmodernism** is sometimes applied to the literature and art after World War II (1939–45), when the effects on Western morale of the first war were greatly exacerbated by the experience of Nazi totalitarianism and mass extermination, the threat of total destruction by the atomic bomb, the progressive devastation of the natural environment, and the ominous fact of overpopulation. Postmodernism involves not only a continuation, sometimes carried to an extreme, of the countertraditional experiments of modernism, but also diverse attempts to break away from modernist forms which had, inevitably, become in their turn conventional, as well as to overthrow the élitism of modernist "high art" by recourse to the models of "mass culture" in film, television, newspaper cartoons, and popular music. Many of the works of postmodern literature—by Jorge Luis Borges, Thomas Pynchon, Roland Barthes, and many others—so blend literary genres, cultural and stylistic levels, the serious and the playful, that they resist classification according to traditional literary rubrics. And these literary anomalies are paralleled in other arts by phenomena like pop art, op art, the musical compositions of John Cage, and the films of Jean-Luc Godard and other directors.

An undertaking in some postmodernist writings is to subvert the foundations of our accepted modes of thought and experience so as to reveal the "meaninglessness" of existence and the underlying "abyss," or "void," or "nothingness" on which any supposed security is conceived to be precariously suspended. Postmodernism in literature and the arts has parallels with the movement known as poststructuralism in linguistic and literary theory; poststructuralists undertake to subvert the foundations of language in order to show that its seeming meaningfulness dissipates, for a rigorous inquirer, into a play of conflicting indeterminacies, or else to show that all forms of cultural discourse are manifestations of the ideology, or of the relations and constructions of power, in contemporary society. (See *poststructuralism*.)

For some postmodernist developments in literature, see literature of the *absurd*, *antihero*, *antinovel*, *Beat writers*, *concrete poetry*, *metafiction*, *new novel*. On modernism and postmodernism refer to Richard Ellmann and Charles Feidelson, eds., *The Modern Tradition: Backgrounds of Modern Literature* (1965); Robert M. Adams, *Nil: Episodes in the Literary Conquest of Void during the Nineteenth Century* (1966); Irving Howe, ed., *The Idea of the Modern in*

Literature and the Arts (1967); Lionel Trilling, *Beyond Culture* (1968); Walter Benjamin, "The Work of Art in the Age of Mechanical Reproduction," in *Illuminations* (1969); Paul de Man, "Literary History and Literary Modernity," in *Blindness and Insight* (1971); Hugh Kenner, *The Pound Era* (1971); David Perkins, *A History of Modern Poetry: From the 1890s to the High Modernist Mode* (1976); Gerald Graff, *Literature Against Itself: Literary Ideas in Modern Society* (1979); Clement Greenberg, *The Notion of Post-Modern* (1980); Sanford Schwartz, *The Matrix of Modernism* (1985); Andreas Huyssen, *After the Great Divide: Modernism, Mass Culture, Postmodernism* (1986).

Motif and Theme. A motif is a conspicuous element, such as a type of incident, device, reference, or formula, which occurs frequently in works of literature. The "loathly lady" who turns out to be a beautiful princess is a common motif in *folklore,* and the man fatally bewitched by a fairy lady is a motif adopted from folklore in Keats' "La Belle Dame sans Merci" (1820). Common in lyric poems is the **ubi sunt motif**, the "where-are" formula for lamenting the vanished past ("Where are the snows of yesteryear?"), and also the *carpe diem* motif, whose nature is sufficiently indicated by Robert Herrick's title "To the Virgins, to Make Much of Time." An **aubade**—from the Old French "alba," meaning dawn—is an early-morning song whose usual motif is an urgent request to a beloved to wake up. A familiar example is Shakespeare's "Hark, hark, the lark at heaven's gate sings."

An older term for recurrent poetic concepts or formulas is the **topos** (Greek for "a commonplace"); Ernst R. Curtius, *European Literature and the Latin Middle Ages* (1953), treats many of the ancient literary topoi. The term "motif," or else the German **leitmotif** (a guiding motif), is also applied to the frequent repetition within a single work of a significant verbal or musical phrase, or set description, or complex of images, as in the operas of Richard Wagner or in novels by Thomas Mann, James Joyce, Virginia Woolf, and William Faulkner. See *imagery;* and for a *deconstructive* treatment of recurrent elements or motifs in prose fiction, J. Hillis Miller, *Repetition and Fiction* (1982).

Theme is sometimes used interchangeably with "motif," but the term is more usefully applied to a general concept or doctrine, whether implicit or asserted, which an imaginative work is designed to incorporate and make persuasive to the reader. John Milton states as the explicit theme of *Paradise Lost* to "assert Eternal Providence, / And justify the ways of God to men"; see *didactic literature* and *fiction and truth.* Some critics have claimed that all nontrivial works of literature, including lyric poems, involve an implicit theme which is embodied and dramatized in the evolving meanings and imagery; see, for example, Cleanth Brooks, *The Well Wrought Urn* (1947). For a discussion of the overlapping applications of the critical terms "subject," "theme," and "thesis" see Monroe C. Beardsley, *Aesthetics* (1958), pp. 401–11.

Myth. In classical Greek, "mythos" signified any story or plot, whether true or invented. In its central modern significance, however, a myth is one story in a **mythology**—a system of hereditary stories which were once believed to be true by a particular cultural group, and which served to explain (in terms of the intentions and actions of deities and other supernatural beings) why the world is as it is and things happen as they do, to provide a rationale for social customs and observances, and to establish the sanctions for the rules by which people conduct their lives. Most myths are related to social **rituals**—set forms and procedures in sacred ceremonies—but anthropologists disagree as to whether rituals generated myths or myths generated rituals. If the protagonist is a person rather than a supernatural being, the traditional story is usually not called a myth but a **legend**. If the story concerns supernatural beings who are not gods, and the story is not part of a systematic mythology, it is usually classified as a *folktale*.

Recently the French structuralist Claude Lévi-Strauss departed from the traditional views just described, to treat the myths of a particular culture as signifying systems whose true meanings are unknown to their proponents. He analyzes myths as composed of signs which are to be identified and interpreted on the model of the linguistic theory of Ferdinand de Saussure. See Lévi-Strauss, "The Structural Study of Myth," in *Structural Anthropology* (1968), and refer to *structuralist criticism* and *semiotics*.

It can be said that a mythology is a religion in which we no longer believe. Poets, however, long after having ceased to believe in them, have persisted in using the myths of Jupiter, Venus, Prometheus, Wotan, Adam and Eve, and Jonah for their plots, episodes, or allusions; as Coleridge said, "still doth the old instinct bring back the old names." The term "myth" has also been extended to denote supernatural tales which are deliberately invented by their authors. Plato in the fourth century B.C. used such invented myths in order to project philosophical speculation beyond the point at which certain knowledge is possible; see, for example, his "Myth of Er" in Book X of *The Republic*. The German romantic authors F. W. J. Schelling and Friedrich Schlegel proposed that to write great literature, modern poets must develop a new unifying mythology which will synthesize the insights of the myths of the Western past with the new discoveries of philosophy and the physical science. In the same period in England, William Blake, who felt "I must create a system or be enslaved by another man's," incorporated in his poems a system of mythology he had himself created by fusing hereditary myths, biblical history and prophecy, and his own intuitions, visions, and intellection. A number of modern writers have also asserted that an integrative mythology, whether inherited or invented, is essential to literature. James Joyce in *Ulysses* and *Finnegans Wake*, T. S. Eliot in *The Waste Land*, Eugene O'Neill in *Mourning Becomes Electra*, and many other writers have deliberately woven their modern materials on the pattern of ancient myths, while W. B. Yeats, like his admired predecessor Blake, undertook to construct his own systematic mythology, which he expounded in *A Vision* (1926) and embodied in a number of remarkable lyric poems such as "The Second Coming" and "Byzantium."

Myth has become a prominent term in literary analysis. A large group of writers, the **myth critics**—including Robert Graves, Francis Fergusson, Maud Bodkin, Richard Chase, and (the most influential) Northrop Frye—view the genres and individual plot-patterns of many works of literature, including what on the surface are highly sophisticated and realistic works, as recurrences of basic mythic formulas. As Northrop Frye puts it, "the typical forms of myth become the conventions and genres of literature." According to Frye's theory, there are four main narrative genres—comedy, romance, tragedy, and irony (satire)—and these are "displaced" modes of the four elemental forms of myth that are associated with the seasonal cycle of spring, summer, autumn, and winter. (See *archetypal criticism* and *genre*.)

A reader needs to be alert to the bewildering variety of applications of the term "myth" in contemporary criticism. In addition to those already described, its uses range all the way from signifying any widely held fallacy ("the myth of progress," "the American success myth") to denoting the solidly imagined realm in which a work of fiction is enacted ("Faulkner's myth of Yoknapatawpha County," "the mythical world of *Moby-Dick*").

On classical mythology see H. J. Rose, *A Handbook of Greek Mythology* (1939), and G. M. Kirkwood, *A Short Guide to Classical Mythology* (1959). Among studies of myths especially influential for modern literature and criticism are James G. Frazer, *The Golden Bough* (rev., 1911); Jessie L. Weston, *From Ritual to Romance* (1920); Jane E. Harrison, *Themis* (2d ed., 1927); F. R. R. S. Raglan, *The Hero* (1936). On myth criticism, see William Righter, *Myth and Literature* (1975); and for instances of the theory and practice of myth criticism, Francis Fergusson, *The Idea of a Theater* (1949); Richard Chase, *Quest for Myth* (1949); Philip Wheelwright, *The Burning Fountain* (1954); Leslie Fiedler, *Love and Death in the American Novel* (1960); John B. Vickery, ed., *Myth and Literature* (1966); Northrop Frye, *Anatomy of Criticism* (1957), and "Literature and Myth" in *Relations of Literary Study,* ed. James Thorpe (1967). This last essay has a useful bibliography of the theory and history of myths, as well as of major exponents of myth criticism.

Narrative and Narratology. A **narrative** is a story, whether in prose or verse, involving events, characters, and what the characters say and do. Some literary forms such as the novel and short story in prose, and the epic and romance in verse, are explicit narratives that are told by a narrator. In drama, the narrative is not told, but evolves in terms of the direct presentation on stage of the actions and speeches of the characters. It should be noted that there is an implicit narrative element even in many *lyric* poems. In William Wordsworth's "The Solitary Reaper," for example, we infer from what the lyric speaker says that, coming unexpectedly in the Scottish Highlands upon a girl reaping and singing, he stops, attends, meditates, and then continues his climb up the hill.

Narratology denotes a recent concern with narrative in general. It deals especially with the identification of structural elements and their diverse modes of combination, with recurrent narrative devices, and with the analysis of the kinds of discourse by which a narrative gets told. This theory picks up and elaborates upon many topics in traditional treatments of fictional narratives, from Aristotle's *Poetics* to Wayne Booth's *The Rhetoric of Fiction* (1961), but applies to them concepts and analytic procedures which derive from recent developments in Russian *formalism* and especially in French *structuralism*. Narratologists treat a narrative not in the traditional way, as a fictional representation of life, but as a systematic formal construction. A primary interest of structural narratologists is in the way that narrative discourse fashions a "story"—the mere sequence of events in time—into the organized structure of a literary *plot*. (The Russian formalists had made a parallel distinction between the **fabula**—the elemental materials of a story—and the **syuzhet**, the concrete representation used to convey the story.) The general undertaking is to determine the rules, or codes of composition, that are manifested by the diverse forms of plot, and also to formulate the "grammar" of narrative in terms of structures and narrative formulae that recur in many stories, whatever the differences in the narrated subject matters. In *Narrative Discourse* (1980), followed by *Figures of Literary Discourse* (1982), the French structuralist critic Gerard Genette presented influential analyses of the complex interrelations between a story and the types of discourse in which the story is narrated, and greatly subtilized the treatment of *point of view* in narrative fiction.

Hayden White is a historian who sets out to demonstrate that the narratives written by historians are not simple representations of a sequence of facts, nor the revelation of a design inherent in events. Instead, White analyzes historical narratives as shaped by the imposition of cultural patterns similar to the narratological, *archetypal,* and other structural concepts that had been developed for the criticism of literature; see his *Metahistory* (1973) and *The Content of the Form: Narrative Discourse and Historical Representation* (1987). The philosopher W. B. Gallie has written an influential book on the kind of explanation and of understanding that, in the writing of history, is achieved by narration rather than by propositional statements and logical arguments; see W. B. Gallie, *Philosophy and the Historical Understanding* (1964); also Arthur C. Danto, *Narration and Knowledge* (1985).

A book which did much to inaugurate modern narratology was *The Morphology of the Folktale* by the Russian formalist Vladimir Propp (trans., 1970). For later developments in narrative theory see, in addition to Genette (above): Tzvetan Todorov, *The Poetics of Prose* (trans., 1977); Seymour Chatman, *Story and Discourse: Narrative Structure in Fiction and Film* (1978); and Wallace Martin, *Recent Theories of Narrative* (1986). For recent narratological contributions to older analyses of how a story gets told, see under *point of view.*

Negative Capability. The poet John Keats introduced this term in a letter written in December 1817 to define a literary quality "which Shakespeare possessed so enormously—I mean *Negative Capability,* that is, when man is capable of being in uncertainties, mysteries, doubts, without any irritable reaching after fact and reason." Keats contrasted to this quality the writings of Coleridge, who "would let go by a fine isolated verisimilitude . . . from being incapable of remaining content with half knowledge," and went on to express the general principle "that with a great poet the sense of beauty overcomes every other consideration, or rather obliterates all consideration."

The elusive term has entered critical circulation and has accumulated a large body of commentary. When conjoined to observations in other letters of Keats, "negative capability" can be taken (1) to characterize an impersonal, or objective, author who maintains *aesthetic distance,* as opposed to a subjective author who is personally involved in a work of literature, and as opposed also to an author who writes in order to make persuasive his or her personal beliefs; and (2) to suggest that, when embodied in a beautiful artistic form, the literary subject matter, concepts, and characters are not subject to the ordinary standards of evidence, truth, and morality, as we apply these standards in the course of our practical experience.

Refer to *distance and involvement* and *objective and subjective;* on the diverse interpretations of Keats' "negative capability," see W. J. Bate, *John Keats* (1963).

Neoclassic and Romantic. The simplest use of these extremely variable terms is as noncommittal names for periods of literature. In this application, the "Neoclassic Period" in England spans the 140 years or so after the Restoration (1660), and the "Romantic Period" is usually taken to extend approximately from the outbreak of the French Revolution in 1789—or alternatively, from the publication of *Lyrical Ballads* in 1798—through the first three decades of the nineteenth century. With reference to American literature, the term "neoclassic" is rarely applied to eighteenth-century writers; on the other hand, 1830–65, the era of Emerson, Thoreau, Poe, Melville, and Hawthorne, is sometimes called "the American Romantic Period." (See *periods of English literature* and *periods of American literature*.) The same terms are frequently applied to periods of German, French, and other Continental literatures, but with differences in the historical spans they identify.

Historians have often tried to "define" neoclassicism or romanticism, as though each term denoted a single essential feature which was shared, to varying degrees, by all the major writings of an age. But the course of literary events has not formed itself around such simple entities, and the numerous and conflicting single definitions of neoclassicism and romanticism are either so vague as to be next to meaningless or so specific as to fall far short of equating with the great range and variety of the literary phenomena. A more useful undertaking is simply to specify salient attributes of literary theory and practice, common to a number of the important writers of the Neoclassic Period in England, which serve to distinguish them from many outstanding writers of the Romantic Period. The following list of ideas and characteristics that were widely shared, between 1660 and the late 1700s, by authors such as John Dryden, Alexander Pope, Joseph Addison, Jonathan Swift, Samuel Johnson, Oliver Goldsmith, and Edmund Burke, may serve as an introductory sketch of some prominent features of **neoclassic** literature:

1) These authors exhibited a strong traditionalism, which was often joined to a distrust of radical innovation and was evidenced above all in their immense respect for **classical** writers—that is, the writers of ancient Greece and Rome—who were thought to have achieved excellence, and established the enduring models, in all the major literary *genres*. Hence the term "neoclassic." (It is from this high estimate of the literary achievements of classical antiquity that the term "a **classic**" has come to be applied to any later literary work which is considered to have achieved excellence and to have set a standard in its kind. See the entry *canon of literature.*)

2) Literature was conceived to be primarily an "art"; that is, a set of skills which, though it requires innate talents, must be perfected by long study and practice and consists mainly in the deliberate adaptation of known and tested means to the achievement of foreseen ends upon the audience of readers. The neoclassic ideal, founded especially on Horace's Roman *Ars Poetica* (first century B.C.), is the craftsman's ideal, demanding finish, correction, and attention to detail. Special allowances were often made for the unerring freedom of "natural geniuses," and also for happy strokes, available even to some less gifted poets, which occur without premeditation and achieve, as Alexander Pope said (in his great statement of neoclassic principles *An Essay on Criticism*, 1711), "a grace beyond the reach of art." But the prevailing view was that a natural genius such as Homer or Shakespeare is a rarity, and probably a thing of the past, and that to even the best of artful poets, literary "graces" come only occasionally. The neoclassic writer commonly strove, therefore, for "correctness," was careful to observe the complex demands of stylistic *decorum,* and for the most part respected the established "rules" of his art. The neoclassic **rules of poetry** were, in theory, the essential properties of the various genres (such as epic, tragedy, comedy, pastoral) that have been abstracted from classical works whose long survival has proved their excellence. These properties, many critics believed, must be embodied in modern works if these too are to be excellent and to survive. In England, however, more than in Continental countries, many critics opposed the strict application of rules such as the *three unities* in drama.

3) Human beings, and especially human beings as an integral part of a social organization, were regarded as the primary subject matter of literature. Poetry was held to be an *imitation* of human life—in a common phrase, "a mirror held up to nature." And by the human actions it imitates, and the artistic form it gives to the imitation, poetry is designed to yield both instruction and aesthetic pleasure to the people who read it. Not art for art's sake, but art for humanity's sake, was a central ideal of neoclassic *humanism.*

4) Both in the subject matter and the appeal of art, emphasis was placed on what human beings possess in common—representative characteristics and widely shared experiences, thoughts, feelings, and tastes. "True wit," Pope said in a much-quoted passage of his *Essay on Criticism,* is "what oft was thought but ne'er so well expressed." That is, a primary aim of poetry is to give new and consummate expression to the great commonplaces of human wisdom, whose prevalence and durability are the best warrant of their importance and truth. There was also insistence, it should be noted, on the need to balance or enhance the general, typical, and familiar with the opposing qualities of novelty, particularity, and invention. Samuel Johnson substituted for Pope's definition of true wit the statement that wit "is at once natural and *new,*" and praised Shakespeare because, while his characters are species, they are all "discriminated" and "distinct." But there was wide agreement that the general nature and shared values of humanity are the basic source and test of art, and also that the fact of universal human agreement, everywhere and always, is the best test of moral and religious truths, as well as of aesthetic values. (Compare *deism.*)

5) Neoclassic writers, like the major philosophers of the time, viewed human beings as limited agents who ought to set themselves only accessible goals. Many of the great works of the period, satiric and didactic, attack human "pride," or presumption beyond the natural limits of the species, and enforce the lesson of the golden mean (the avoidance of extremes) and of humanity's need to submit to its restricted position in the cosmic order—an order sometimes envisioned as a natural hierarchy, or *Great Chain of Being.* In art, as in life, what was for the most part praised was the law of measure and the acceptance of limits upon one's freedom. The poets admired extremely the great genres of epic and tragedy, but wrote their own masterpieces in admittedly lesser and less demanding forms such as the essay in verse and prose, the comedy of manners, and especially satire, in which they felt they had more chance to equal or surpass their classical and English predecessors. They submitted to at least some "rules" and other limiting conventions in literary subjects, structure, and diction. Typical was their choice, in many poems, to write within the extremely tight limits of the *closed couplet.* But a distinctive quality of the urbane poetry of the Neoclassic Period was, in the phrase often quoted from Horace, "the art that hides art"; that is, the seeming freedom and ease with which, at its best, it meets the challenge set by traditional and highly restrictive patterns.

Here are some aspects in which **romantic** aims and achievements, in the most prominent and innovative writers during the late eighteenth and early nineteenth centuries, differ most conspicuously from their neoclassic precursors:

1) The prevailing attitude favored innovation as against traditionalism in the materials, forms, and style of literature. Wordsworth's Preface to the second edition of *Lyrical Ballads* in 1800 was written as a poetic "manifesto," or statement of revolutionary aims, in which he denounced the *poetic diction* of the preceding century and proposed to deal with materials from "common life" in "a selection of language really used by men." Wordsworth's serious or tragic treatment of lowly subjects in common language violated the basic neoclassic rule of *decorum,* which asserted that the serious genres should deal only with high subjects in an appropriately elevated style. Other innovations in the period were the exploitation by Samuel Taylor Coleridge, John Keats, and others of the realm of the supernatural and of "the far away and the long ago"; the assumption by William Blake, William Wordsworth, and Percy Bysshe Shelley of the persona of a poet-prophet who writes a visionary mode of poetry; and the use of poetic *symbolism* (especially by Blake and Shelley) deriving from a world-view in which objects are charged with a significance beyond their physical qualities. "I always seek in what I see," as Shelley said, "the likeness of something beyond the present and tangible object."

2) In his Preface to *Lyrical Ballads* Wordsworth repeatedly declared that good poetry is "the spontaneous overflow of powerful feelings." According to this point of view poetry is not primarily a mirror of men in action; on the contrary, its essential element is the poet's own feelings, while the process of composition, since it is "spontaneous," is the opposite of the artful manipulation of means to foreseen ends stressed by the neoclassic critics. (See *expressive criticism.*) Wordsworth carefully qualified this radical doctrine by describing his poetry as "emotion recollected in tranquillity," and by specifying that a poet's spontaneity is the result of a prior process of deep reflection and may be followed by second thoughts and revisions. But the immediate act of composition, if a poem is to be geniune, must be spontaneous—that is, unforced, and free of what Wordsworth decried as the "artificial" rules and conventions of his neoclassic predecessors. "If poetry comes not as naturally as the leaves to a tree," Keats wrote, "it had better not come at all." The philosophical-minded Coleridge substituted for neoclassic "rules," which he describes as imposed by the poet from without, the concept of the inherent organic "laws" of the poet's *imagination;* that is, he conceives that each poetic work, like a growing plant, evolves according to its internal principles into its final organic form.

3) To a remarkable degree external nature—the landscape, together with its flora and fauna—became a persistent subject of poetry, and was described with an accuracy and sensuous nuance unprecedented in earlier writers. It is a mistake, however, to describe the romantic poets as simply "nature poets." While many major poems by Wordsworth and Coleridge—and to a great extent by Shelley and Keats—set out from and return to an aspect or change of aspect in the landscape, the outer scene is not presented for its own sake but only as a stimulus for the poet to engage in the most characteristic human activity, that of thinking. Representative romantic poems are in fact poems of feelingful meditation which, though often stimulated by a natural phenomenon, are concerned with central human experiences and problems. Wordsworth asserted that it is "the Mind of Man" which is "my haunt, and the main region of my song."

4) Neoclassic poetry was about other people, but much of romantic poetry invited the reader to identify the protagonists with the poets themselves, either directly, as in Wordsworth's *Prelude* (1805; revised 1850) and a number of romantic lyric poems (see *lyric*), or in altered but recognizable form, as in Lord Byron's *Childe Harold* (1812–18). In prose we find a parallel vogue in the revealingly personal essays of Charles Lamb and William Hazlitt and in a number of spiritual and intellectual autobiographies: Thomas De Quincey's *Confessions of an English Opium Eater* (1822), Coleridge's *Biographia Literaria* (1817), and Thomas Carlyle's fictionalized *Sartor Resartus* (1833–34). And whether romantic subjects were the poets themselves or other people, they were no longer represented as part of an organized society but, typically, as solitary figures engaged in a long, and sometimes infinitely elusive, quest; often they were also social nonconformists or outcasts. Many important romantic works had as protagonist the isolated rebel, whether for good or ill: Prometheus, Cain, the Wandering Jew, the Satanic hero-villain, or the great outlaw.

5) What seemed the infinite social promise of the French Revolution in the early 1790s, fostered the sense in writers of the early Romantic Period that theirs was a great age of new beginnings and high possibilities. Many writers viewed a human being as endowed with limitless aspiration toward the infinite good envisioned by the faculty of imagination. "Our destiny," Wordsworth says in a visionary moment in *The Prelude,* "our being's heart and home,/Is with infinitude, and only there," and our desire is for "something evermore about to be." "Less than everything," Blake announced, "cannot satisfy man." Humanity's undaunted aspirations beyond its assigned limits, which to the neoclassic moralist had been its tragic error of generic "pride," now became humanity's glory and a mode of triumph, even in failure, over the pettiness of circumstance. In a parallel way, the typical neoclassic judgment that the highest art is the perfect achievement of limited aims gave way to a dissatisfaction with rules and inherited restrictions. According to a number of romantic writers, the highest art consists in an endeavor beyond finite human possibility; as a result, neoclassical satisfaction in the perfectly accomplished, because limited, enterprise was replaced by a preference for the glory of the imperfect, in which the artist's very failure attests the grandeur of his aim. Also, Romantic writers once more entered into competition with their greatest predecessors in audacious long poems in the most exacting genres: Wordsworth's *Prelude* (a rerendering, at epic length and in the form of a spiritual autobiography, of the central themes of John Milton's *Paradise Lost*); Blake's visionary and prophetic epics; Shelley's *Prometheus Unbound* (emulating Greek drama); Keats' Miltonic epic *Hyperion;* and Byron's ironic conspectus of all modern European civilization, *Don Juan.*

See *Enlightenment,* and refer to R. S. Crane, "Neoclassical Criticism," in *Dictionary of World Literature,* ed. Joseph T. Shipley (rev., 1970); A. O. Lovejoy, *Essays in the History of Ideas* (1948); James Sutherland, *A Preface to Eighteenth Century Poetry* (1948); W. J. Bate, *From Classic to Romantic* (1948); Harold Bloom, *The Visionary Company: A Reading of English Romantic Poetry* (1961); René Wellek, "The Concept of Romanticism in Literary History" and "Romanticism Re-examined," in *Concepts of Criticism* (1963); Northrop Frye, ed., *Romanticism Reconsidered* (1963), and *A Study of English Romanticism* (1968); M. H. Abrams, *The Mirror and the Lamp: Romantic Theory and the Critical Tradition* (1953), and *Natural Supernaturalism: Tradition and Revolution in Romantic Literature* (1971); Thomas McFarland, *Romanticism and the Forms of Ruin* (1981); Marilyn Butler, *Romantics, Rebels and Reactionaries: English Literature and Its Background 1760–1830* (1982); Jerome McGann, *The Romantic Ideology* (1983); Marilyn Gaull, *English Romanticism: The Human Context* (1988); Isaiah Berlin, *The Crooked Timber of Humanity: Chapters in the History of Ideas* (1990). Hugh Honour, in his books on *Neo-classicism* (1969) and on *Romanticism* (1979), stresses the visual arts. A collection of essays that define or discuss romanticism is Robert F. Gleckner and Gerald E. Enscoe, eds., *Romanticism: Points of View* (rev., 1975). In *Poetic Form and British Romanticism* (1986), Stuart Curran stresses the continuity within the innovation in romantic uses of traditional poetic genres.

Novel. The term "novel" is now applied to a great variety of writings that have in common only the attribute of being extended works of *fiction* written in prose. As an extended narrative, the novel is distinguished from the *short story* and from the work of middle length called the *novelette;* its magnitude permits a greater variety of characters, greater complication of plot (or plots), ampler development of milieu, and more sustained exploration of character and motives than do the shorter, more concentrated modes. As a narrative written in prose, the novel is distinguished from the long narratives in verse of Geoffrey Chaucer, Edmund Spenser, and John Milton which, beginning with the eighteenth century, the novel has increasingly supplanted. Within these limits the novel includes such diverse works as Samuel Richardson's *Pamela* and Laurence Sterne's *Tristram Shandy;* Charles Dickens' *Pickwick Papers* and Henry James' *The Wings of the Dove;* Leo Tolstoy's *War and Peace* and Franz Kafka's *The Trial;* Ernest Hemingway's *The Sun Also Rises* and James Joyce's *Ulysses* and *Finnegans Wake;* C. P. Snow's *Strangers and Brothers* and Vladimir Nabokov's *Ada or Ardor.*

The term for the novel in most European languages is **roman**, which is derived from the medieval term, the *romance.* The English name for the form, on the other hand, is derived from the Italian **novella** (literally, "a little new thing"), which was a short tale in prose. In fourteenth-century Italy there was a vogue for collections of such tales, some serious and some scandalous; the best-known of these collections is Boccaccio's *Decameron,* which is still available in English translation at any well-stocked bookstore. Currently the term "novella" (or in the German form, **Novelle**) is often used as an equivalent for novelette: a prose fiction of middle length, such as Joseph Conrad's *Heart of Darkness* or Thomas Mann's *Death in Venice.* (See under *short story.*)

Long narrative romances in prose were written by Greek writers as early as the second and third centuries A.D. Typically they dealt with separated lovers who, after perilous adventures and hairbreadth escapes, are happily reunited at the end. The best known of these Greek romances, influential in later European literature, were the *Aethiopica* by Heliodorus and the charming pastoral narrative *Daphnis and Chloe* by Longus. Thomas Lodge's *Rosalynde* (the model for Shakespeare's *As You Like It*) and Sir Philip Sidney's *Arcadia* were Elizabethan continuations of the pastoral romance of the ancient Greeks. (See *pastoral.*)

Another important predecessor of the later novel was the **picaresque narrative**, which emerged in sixteenth-century Spain, although the most popular instance, *Gil Blas* (1715), was written by the Frenchman Le Sage. "Picaro" is Spanish for "rogue," and a typical story concerns the escapades of an insouciant rascal who lives by his wits and shows little if any alteration of character through the long succession of his adventures; picaresque fiction is realistic in manner, **episodic** in structure (as opposed to the sustained development of a single *plot*), and often satiric in aim. The first, and very lively, English example was Thomas Nashe's *The Unfortunate Traveller* (1594). We recognize the survival of the picaresque type in many later novels such as

Mark Twain's *The Adventures of Tom Sawyer* (1876), Thomas Mann's *Felix Krull* (1954), and Saul Bellow's *The Adventures of Augie March* (1953). The development of the novel owes much to prose works which, like the picaresque story, were written to deflate romantic or idealized fictional forms. Cervantes' great quasi-picaresque narrative *Don Quixote* (1605) was the single most important progenitor of the modern novel; in it, an engaging madman who tries to live by the ideals of chivalric romance in the everyday world is used to explore the general relations of illusion and reality in human life.

After these precedents and many others—including the seventeenth-century *character* (a brief sketch of a typical personality or way of life) and French courtly romances such as Madame de La Fayette's *La Princesse de Clèves* (1678)—what is recognizably the novel as we now think of it appeared in England in the early eighteenth century. In 1719 Daniel Defoe wrote *Robinson Crusoe* and in 1722 *Moll Flanders*. Both of these are still picaresque in type, in the sense that they are a sequence of episodes held together largely because they happened to one person; and Moll is herself a colorful female version of the old picaro—"twelve Year a Whore, five times a Wife (whereof once to her own Brother), Twelve Year a Thief, Eight Year a Transported Felon in Virginia," as the title page resoundingly informs us. But *Robinson Crusoe* is given an enforced unity of action by its focus on the problem of surviving on an uninhabited island, while both stories present so convincing a central character, set in so solid and detailedly realized a world, that Defoe is often credited with writing the first "novel of incident."

The credit for having written the first English "novel of character," or "psychological novel," is almost unanimously given to Samuel Richardson for his *Pamela; or, Virtue Rewarded* (1740). *Pamela* is the story of a sentimental but shrewd young woman who, by prudently safeguarding her beleaguered chastity, succeeds in becoming the wife of a wild young gentleman instead of his debauched servant girl. The distinction between the novel of incident and the novel of character cannot be drawn sharply; but in the novel of incident the greater interest is in what the *protagonist* will do next and on how the story will turn out; in the novel of character, it is on the protagonist's motives for what he or she does, and on how the protagonist as a person will turn out. On twentieth-century developments in the novel of character see Leon Edel, *The Modern Psychological Novel* (rev., 1965).

Pamela, like its greater and tragic successor, Richardson's *Clarissa* (1747–48), is an **epistolary novel**; that is, the narrative is conveyed entirely by an exchange of letters. Later novelists have preferred alternative devices for limiting the narrative *point of view* to one or another single character, but the epistolary technique is still occasionally revived—for example, in Mark Harris' hilarious novel *Wake Up, Stupid* (1959).

Novels may have any kind of plot form—tragic, comic, satiric, or romantic. A common distinction—which was employed by Hawthorne, in his Preface to *The House of the Seven Gables* (1851) and elsewhere, and has been adopted and expanded by a number of recent critics—is that between two basic types of prose fiction: the realistic novel (which is the novel proper) and the "romance." The **realistic novel** is characterized as the fictional attempt to give the effect of *realism,* by representing complex characters with mixed motives who are rooted in a social class, operate in a highly developed social structure, interact with many other characters, and undergo plausible and everyday modes of experience. This novelistic mode, rooted in such eighteenth-century writers as Defoe and Fielding, achieved a high development in the master-novelists of the nineteenth century, including Jane Austen, George Eliot, Anthony Trollope, and William Dean Howells in England and America; Stendhal, Balzac, and Flaubert in France; and Turgenev and Tolstoy in Russia. The **prose romance**, on the other hand, has as precursors the *chivalric romance* of the Middle Ages and the *Gothic novel* of the later eighteenth century. It usually deploys characters who are sharply discriminated as heroes or villains, masters or victims; its protagonist is often solitary, and relatively isolated from a social context; it tends to be set in the historical past, and the *atmosphere* is such as to suspend the reader's expectations based on everyday experience. The plot of the prose romance emphasizes adventure, and is frequently cast in the form of the quest for an ideal, or the pursuit of an enemy; and the nonrealistic and occasionally melodramatic events are claimed by some critics to project in symbolic form the primal desires, hopes, and terrors in the depths of the human mind, and to be therefore analogous to the materials of dream, myth, ritual, and folklore. Examples of romance novels are Walter Scott's *Rob Roy* (1817), Alexandre Dumas' *The Three Musketeers* (1844–45), Emily Brontë's *Wuthering Heights* (1847), and an important mode of American fiction which extends from Edgar Allan Poe, James Fenimore Cooper, Nathaniel Hawthorne, and Herman Melville to recent writings of William Faulkner and Saul Bellow. On the realistic novel in the nineteenth century see Harry Levin, *The Gates of Horn: A Study of Five French Realists* (1963); Ivan Williams, *The Realist Novel in England* (1975); G. J. Becker, *Master European Realists* (1982). On the prose romance in America, see Richard Chase, *The American Novel and Its Tradition* (1957); Northrop Frye, "The Mythos of Summer: Romance," in *Anatomy of Criticism* (1957); Joel Porte, *The Romance in America* (1969); Michael D. Bell, *The Development of American Romance* (1980); and for a skeptical view of the usual division between novel and romance, Nina Baym, *Novels, Readers, and Reviewers: Responses to Fiction in Antebellum America* (1984).

Other common subclasses of the novel are based on differences in subject matter, emphasis, and artistic purpose:

Bildungsroman and **Erziehungsroman** are German terms signifying "novel of formation" or "novel of education." The subject of these novels is the development of the protagonist's mind and character, in the passage from childhood through varied experiences—and often through a spiritual crisis—into maturity and the recognition of his or her identity and role in the world. The mode was begun by K. P. Moritz's *Anton Reiser* (1785–90) and Goethe's *Wilhelm Meister's Apprenticeship* (1795–96) and includes George Eliot's *The Mill on the Floss* (1860), Charles Dickens' *Great Expectations* (1861), Somerset Maugham's *Of Human Bondage* (1915), and Thomas Mann's *The*

Magic Mountain (1924). An important subtype of the Bildungsroman is the **Künstlerroman** ("artist-novel"), which represents the growth of a novelist or other artist into the stage of maturity that signalizes the recognition of the protagonist's artistic destiny and mastery of an artistic craft. Instances of this type include some of the major twentieth-century novels: Marcel Proust's *Remembrance of Things Past* (1913–27), James Joyce's *A Portrait of the Artist as a Young Man* (1914–15), Thomas Mann's *Tonio Kröger* (1903) and *Dr. Faustus* (1947), and Andre Gide's *The Counterfeiters* (1926). See Susanne Howe, *Wilhelm Meister and His English Kinsmen* (1930); Lionel Trilling, "The Princess Casamassima," in *The Liberal Imagination* (1950); Maurice Beebe, *Ivory Towers and Sacred Founts: The Artist as Hero in Fiction* (1964); Jerome H. Buckley, *Season of Youth: The Bildungsroman from Dickens to Golding* (1974); Martin Swales, *The German Bildungsroman from Wieland to Hesse* (1978).

The **social novel** emphasizes the influence of the social and economic conditions of an era on characters and events; often it also embodies an implicit or explicit thesis recommending political and social reform. Examples of social novels are Harriet Beecher Stowe's *Uncle Tom's Cabin* (1852), Upton Sinclair's *The Jungle* (1906), John Steinbeck's *The Grapes of Wrath* (1939).

Some realistic novels make use of events and personages from the historical past to add interest and picturesqueness to the narrative. What we usually specify as the **historical novel**, however, began in the nineteenth century with Sir Walter Scott. The historical novel not only takes its setting and some characters and events from history, but makes the historical events and issues crucial for the central characters and narrative. Some of the greatest historical novels also use the protagonists and actions to reveal what the author regards as the deep forces that impel the historical process. Examples of historical novels are Scott's *Ivanhoe* (1819), set in the period of Norman domination of the Saxons at the time of Richard I; Dickens' *A Tale of Two Cities* (1859), in Paris and London during the French Revolution; Tolstoy's *War and Peace* (1869), during Napoleon's invasion of Russia; and Margaret Mitchell's *Gone with the Wind* (1936), in Georgia during the Civil War and Reconstruction. A highly influential treatment of the form was by the Marxist scholar and critic Georg Lukács, *The Historical Novel* (1937; trans. 1962); a comprehensive later commentary is Harry E. Shaw, *The Forms of Historical Fiction: Sir Walter Scott and His Successors* (1983).

One twentieth-century variant of the historical novel is known as **documentary fiction**, which incorporates into a novel not only historical characters and events, but also contemporary journalistic reports: John Dos Passos, *USA* (1938); E. L. Doctorow, *Ragtime* (1975) and *Billy Bathgate* (1989). Another recent offshoot is the form that one of its innovators, Truman Capote, named the **nonfiction novel**. This uses a variety of novelistic techniques to give a graphic rendering of recent characters and happenings, and is based not only on historical records but often on personal interviews with the chief agents. Truman Capote's *In Cold Blood* (1965) and Norman Mailer's *The Executioner's Song* (1979) are instances of this mode; both these books offer a detailed rendering of the life, personality, and actions of murderers, based on a sustained series of prison interviews with the protagonists themselves. A third variant is the *fabulative* historical novel that interweaves history with fantasized, even fantastic events: John Barth, *The Sot-Weed Factor* (1960, rev. 1967); Thomas Pynchon, *Gravity's Rainbow* (1973). See John Hollowell, *Fact and Fiction: The New Journalism and the Nonfiction Novel* (1977); and Barbara Foley, *Telling the Truth: The Theory and Practice of Documentary Fiction* (1986). Cushing Strout, in *The Veracious Imagination* (1981), studies other recent developments in novels, as well as the theater form called **documentary drama**, which combines fiction with history, journalistic reports, and biography.

The **regional novel** emphasizes the setting, speech, and social structure and customs of a particular locality, not merely as local color, but as important conditions affecting the temperament of the characters and their ways of thinking, feeling, and interacting. Instances of such localities are "Wessex" in Thomas Hardy's novels, and "Yoknapatawpha County," Mississippi, in Faulkner's.

Beginning with the second half of the nineteenth century the novel has displaced all other literary forms in popularity. The novelistic art has received the devoted attention of some of the greatest masters of modern literature—Flaubert, Henry James, Proust, Mann, Joyce, and Virginia Woolf. (Henry James' prefaces, gathered into one volume as The *Art of the Novel*, 1934, exemplify the care and subtlety that have been lavished on this craft.) There has been constant experimentation with new fictional methods, such as management of the *point of view* to minimize or eliminate the apparent role of the author-narrator, the use of *symbolist* and *expressionist* techniques and of devices adopted from the art of the cinema, the dislocation of time sequence, the adaptation of forms and motifs from myths and dreams, and the exploitation of *stream of consciousness* narration in a way that converts the story of outer action and events into a drama of the life of the mind.

In recent decades such experimentation has reached a radical extreme (see *postmodernism*). Vladimir Nabokov is a supreme technician who writes **involuted novels** (a work whose subject incorporates an account of its own genesis and development—for example, his *Pale Fire*), employs multilingual puns and jokes, incorporates esoteric data about butterflies (a subject in which he was an accomplished scientist) and strategies from chess, crossword puzzles, and other games, parodies other novels (and his own as well), and sets elaborate traps for the unwary reader. This is also the era of what is sometimes called the **antinovel**—that is, a work which is deliberately constructed in a negative fashion, relying for its effects on the deletion of standard elements, on violating traditional norms, and on playing against the expectations established in the reader by the novelistic methods and conventions of the past. Thus Alain Robbe-Grillet, a leader among the exponents of the **nouveau roman** (the **new novel**) in France has written *Jealousy* (1957), in which he leaves out such standard elements as plot, characterization, descriptions of states of mind, normal settings in time and space, and a frame of reference to the world in which the work is set. We are simply presented in this novel with a sequence of perceptions, mainly visual, which we may *naturalize* (that is, make intelligible on the model of standard narrative procedures) by postulating that we are occupying the physical space and sharing the hyperacute observations of a jealous husband, from which we may infer also the tortured state of his disintegrating mind. Other new novelists are Natalie Sarraute and Philippe Sollers. See Roland Barthes, *Writing Degree Zero* (trans., 1967), and Stephen Heath, *The Nouveau Roman: A Study in the Practice of Writing* (1972).

The term **magic realism**, originally applied in the 1920s to a school of painters, is used to describe the prose fiction of Jorge Luis Borges in Argentina, as well as the work of writers such as Gabriel García Márquez in Colombia, Günter Grass in Germany, and John Fowles in England. These writers interweave, in an ever-shifting pattern, a sharply etched *realism* in representing ordinary events and descriptive details together with fantastic and dreamlike elements, as well as with materials derived from myth and fairy tales. Robert Scholes has popularized **metafiction** as an overall term for the large and growing class of novels which depart drastically from the traditional categories either of realism or romance, and also the term **fabulation** for the current mode of free-wheeling narrative invention. These novels violate, in various ways, standard novelistic expectations by drastic—and sometimes highly effective—experiments with subject matter, form, style, temporal sequence, and fusions of the everyday, the fantastic, the mythical, and the nightmarish, in renderings that blur traditional distinctions between what is serious or trivial, horrible or ludicrous, tragic or comic. Recent fabulators include Thomas Pynchon, John Barth, Donald Barthelme, William Gass, Robert Coover, and Ishmael Reed. See Robert Scholes, *Fabulation and Metafiction* (1979)—an expansion of his *The Fabulators* (1967); James M. Mellard, *The Exploded Form: The Modernist Novel in America* (1980); and Patricia Waugh, *Metafiction* (1984). Refer also to the essays in this *Glossary* on the literature of the *absurd* and *black humor.*

See *fiction* and *narratology,* and in addition to the books already mentioned, refer to the following. Histories of the novel: E. A. Baker, *History of the English Novel* (12 vols.; 1924 ff.); Arnold Kettle's Marxist survey, *An Introduction to the English Novel* (2 vols.; 1951); Dorothy Van Ghent, *The English Novel: Form and Function* (1953); Walter Allen, *The English Novel* (1954); Ian Watt, *The Rise of the Novel* (1957); and J. Hillis Miller's deconstructive mode of criticism of the novel, *Fiction and Repetition* (1982). On the art of the novel: Percy Lubbock, *The Craft of Fiction* (1921); E. M. Forster, *Aspects of the Novel* (1927); and two later influential books, Wayne C. Booth, *The Rhetoric of Fiction* (1961), and Frank Kermode, *The Sense of an Ending* (1968). Philip Stevick, ed., *The Theory of the Novel* (1967) is a collection of important essays by various critics, and Daniel Schwarz, *The Humanistic Heritage* (1986), reviews theories of prose fiction from 1900 to the present.

Objective and Subjective. The social critic John Ruskin complained in 1856 that "German dullness and English affectation have of late much multiplied among us the use of two of the most objectionable words that were ever coined by the troublesomeness of metaphysicians—namely, 'objective' and 'subjective.'" Ruskin was at least in part right. The words were imported into English criticism from the post-Kantian German critics of the late-eighteenth and early-nineteenth centuries, and they have certainly been troublesome. Amid the great variety of ways in which the opposition has been applied to literature, one is sufficiently widespread to be worth specifying. A **subjective** work is one in which the author incorporates personal experiences, or projects into the narrative his or her personal disposition, judgments, values, and feelings. An **objective** work is one in which the author presents the invented situation or the fictional characters and their thoughts, feelings, and actions and undertakes to remain detached and noncommittal. Thus a subjective *lyric* is one in which we are invited to associate the "I," or lyric speaker, with the poet (Coleridge's "Frost at Midnight," Wordsworth's "Tintern Abbey," Shelley's "Ode to the West Wind," Sylvia Plath's "Daddy"); in an objective lyric the speaker is obviously an invented character (Robert Browning's "My Last Duchess," T. S. Eliot's "Love Song of J. Alfred Prufrock," Wallace Stevens' "Sunday Morning"). A subjective novel is one in which the author (or at any rate the narrator) intervenes to comment and deliver judgments about the characters and actions represented; an objective novel is one in which the author is self-effacing and tries to create the effect that the story tells itself. Many critics claim, however, that the difference between a subjective and objective literary work is not absolute, but a matter of degree. See *confessional poetry, distance and involvement, negative capability, persona,* and *point of view.*

On the introduction of the terms "objective" and "subjective" into English criticism and the variousness of their application, see M. H. Abrams, *The Mirror and the Lamp* (1953), pp. 235–44. For their application to modern criticism of the novel, see Wayne C. Booth, *The Rhetoric of Fiction* (1961), Chapter 3.

Objective Correlative. This term, which had been coined by the American painter and poet Washington Allston (1779–1843), was introduced by T. S. Eliot, rather casually, into his essay "Hamlet and His Problems" (1919); its subsequent vogue in literary criticism, Eliot has said, astonished him. "The only way of expressing emotion," Eliot wrote, "is by finding an 'objective correlative'; in other words, a set of objects, a situation, a chain of events which shall be the formula of that *particular* emotion," and which will evoke the same emotion from the reader. Eliot's formulation has been often criticized for falsifying the way a poet actually composes, since no object or situation is in itself a "formula" for an emotion, but depends for its emotional significance and effect on the way it is rendered and used by a particular poet. The vogue of Eliot's concept of an outer correlative of inner feelings was due in part to its accord with the reaction of the *New Criticism* against vagueness of description and the direct statement of feelings in poetry—an oft-cited example was Shelley's "Indian Serenade": "I die, I faint, I fail"—and in favor of definiteness, impersonality, and descriptive concreteness.

See Eliseo Vivas, "The Objective Correlative of T. S. Eliot," reprinted in *Critiques and Essays in Criticism,* ed. Robert W. Stallman (1949).

Occasional Poems are written to celebrate or memorialize a specific occasion, such as a birthday, a marriage, a death, a military engagement or victory, the dedication of a public building, or the opening performance of a play. Edmund Spenser's "Epithalamion," John Milton's "Lycidas," Andrew Marvell's "An Horatian Ode upon Cromwell's Return from Ireland," and Alfred, Lord Tennyson's "The Charge of the Light Brigade" are all poems that have long survived their original occasions, and W. B. Yeats' "Easter, 1916" and W. H. Auden's "September 1, 1939" are notable modern examples. England's poet laureate is often called on to meet the emergency of royal anniversaries and important public events with an appropriate literary effort.

Ode. A long lyric poem that is serious in subject and treatment, elevated in style, and elaborate in its stanzaic structure. As Norman Maclean has said, the term now calls to mind a *lyric* which is "massive, public in its proclamations, and Pindaric in its classical prototype" ("From Action to Image," in *Critics and Criticism,* ed. R. S. Crane, 1952). The prototype was established by the Greek poet Pindar, whose odes were modeled on the songs by the *chorus* in Greek drama. His complex stanzas were patterned in sets of three: moving in a dance rhythm to the left, the chorus chanted the **strophe;** moving to the right, the **antistrophe;** then, standing still, the **epode.**

The **regular** or **Pindaric ode** in English is a close imitation of Pindar's form, with all the strophes and antistrophes written in one *stanza* pattern, and all the epodes in another; the typical construction can be conveniently studied in Thomas Gray's "The Progress of Poesy" (1757). The **irregular ode** was introduced in 1656 by Abraham Cowley, who imitated the Pindaric style and matter but disregarded the recurrent stanzaic pattern in each strophic triad; instead, he allowed each stanza to establish its own pattern of variable line lengths, number of lines, and rhyme scheme. This type of irregular stanzaic structure, which is free to alter in accordance with shifts in subject and mood, has been the most common for the English ode ever since; Wordsworth's great "Ode: Intimations of Immortality" (1807) is representative.

Pindar's odes were **encomiastic;** that is, they were written to praise and glorify someone—in the instance of Pindar, the ode celebrated a victorious athlete in the Olympic games. The earlier English odes, and many later ones, were also written to eulogize something: either a person (John Dryden's "Anne Killigrew"), or the arts of music or poetry (Dryden's "Alexander's Feast"), or a time of day (Collins' "Ode to Evening"), or abstract concepts (Gray's "Hymn to Adversity" and Wordsworth's "Ode to Duty"). Romantic poets perfected the personal ode of description and passionate meditation, which is stimulated by (and sometimes at its close reverts to) an aspect of the outer scene and turns on the attempt to solve either a personal emotional problem or a generally human one (Wordsworth's "Intimations" ode, Coleridge's "Dejection: An Ode," Shelley's "Ode to the West Wind"). Recent examples of this latter type are Allen Tate's "Ode to the Confederate Dead" and Wallace Stevens' "The Idea of Order at Key West." See M. H. Abrams, "Structure and Style in the Greater Romantic Lyric," in *The Correspondent Breeze,* 1984.

The **Horatian ode** was originally modeled on the matter, tone, and form of the odes of the Roman Horace. In contrast to the passion, visionary boldness, and formal language of Pindar's odes, Horatian odes are calm, meditative, and colloquial; they are also usually **homostrophic** (that is, written in a single repeated stanza form), and shorter than the Pindaric ode. Examples are Marvell's "An Horatian Ode upon Cromwell's Return from Ireland" (1650) and Keats' ode "To Autumn" (1820).

See Robert Shafer, *The English Ode to 1660* (1918); G. N. Shuster, *The English Ode from Milton to Keats* (1940); Carol Maddison, *Apollo and the Nine: A History of the Ode* (1960)—this book includes a discussion of the odes of Pindar and Horace (Chapter 2); Paul H. Fry, *The Poet's Calling in the English Ode* (1980).

Onomatopoeia, sometimes called **echoism**, is used both in a narrow and in a broad sense.

1) In the narrow and more common use, onomatopoeia designates a word, or a combination of words, whose sound seems to resemble closely the sound it denotes: "hiss," "buzz," "rattle," "bang." There is no exact duplication, however, of nonverbal by verbal sounds; the seeming similarity is due as much to the meaning, and to the feel of articulating the words, as to their sounds. Two lines of Alfred, Lord Tennyson's "Come Down, O Maid" (1847) are often cited as a skillful instance of onomatopoeia:

> The moan of doves in immemorial elms,
> And murmuring of innumerable bees.

The American critic John Crowe Ransom has remarked that by making only two changes in the consonants of the last line, we lose the echoic effect because we change the meaning drastically: "And murdering of innumerable beeves."

The sounds seemingly mimicked by onomatopoeic words need not be pleasant ones. Robert Browning liked squishy and scratchy effects, as in "Meeting at Night" (1845):

> As I gain the cove with pushing prow,
> And quench its speed i' the slushy sand.

> A tap at the pane, the quick sharp scratch
> And blue spurt of a lighted match. . . .

Compare *euphony and cacophony.*

2) In the broad sense, "onomatopoeia" is applied to words or passages which seem to correspond to, or to strongly suggest, what they denote in any way whatever—in size, movement, or force, as well as sound (see *sound-symbolism*). Alexander Pope recommends such extended verbal mimicry in his *Essay on Criticism* (1711) when he says that "the sound should seem an echo of the sense," and goes on to illustrate his maxim by mimicking two different kinds of action or motion by the meanings, the metrical movement, and the difficulty or ease of utterance of the poetic lines that describe them:

When Ajax strives some rock's vast weight to throw,
The line too labors, and the words move slow;
Not so when swift Camilla scours the plain,
Flies o'er th' unbending corn, and skims along the main.

Oral Formulaic Poetry. Poetry that is composed and transmitted by singers or reciters. Its origins are prehistoric, yet it continues to flourish even now among populations which for the most part cannot read or write. Oral poetry includes both narrative forms (see *epic* and *ballad*) and lyric forms (see *folk songs*). There is no fixed version of an oral composition, since each performer tends to render it differently, and sometimes introduces differences between one performance and the next. Such poems, however, typically incorporate verbal formulas, or set words or word patterns, which help a performer to improvise a narrative or song on a given theme, and also to recall and repeat, although often with variations, a poem that has been learned from someone else.

Some oral ballads and songs have been collected and published ever since the eighteenth century. The systematic analysis of oral formulaic poetry in its origins and early renderings, however, was begun in the 1930s by the American scholar Milman Parry on field trips to Yugoslavia, the last place in Europe where the custom of composing and transmitting oral poetry, especially heroic narratives of warfare, still survived. Albert B. Lord and other successors continued Parry's work, and also applied the principles of this contemporary oral poetry retrospectively to an analysis of the constitution of the Homeric epics, the Anglo-Saxon *Beowulf,* the Old French *Chanson de Roland,* and other epic poems which, although they survive only in a written form, had originated and evolved as oral formulaic poetry. Research in oral literary performances is also being carried on in Africa, Asia, and other parts of the world where the ancient tradition maintains its vitality. Walter J. Ong, *Orality and Literacy: The Technologizing of the Word* (1982) analyzes the effects on literary compositions of the shift from an oral to a print culture.

A description of Milman Parry's work is in *Serbocroatian Heroic Songs,* ed. Albert B. Lord, Vol. 1; see also Albert B. Lord, *The Singer of Tales* (1960); Adam Parry, ed., *The Making of Homeric Verse: The Collected Papers of Milman Parry* (1971); Ruth Finnegan, *Oral Poetry: Its Nature, Significance and Social Context* (1977); and J. M. Foley, *Oral Traditional Literature* (1980, reprinted 1983).

Palinode. A poem or poetic passage in which the poet disavows or retracts an earlier poem or type of subject matter. An elaborate and charming example is the Prologue to *The Legend of Good Women* in which Geoffrey Chaucer, contrite after being charged by the God of Love with having slandered women lovers in *Troilus and Criseyde* and his translation of the *Romance of the Rose,* undertakes by way of penance this poem on women who were saints in their fidelity to the creed of love. (Refer to *courtly love.*) Palinodes are especially common in love poetry. The Elizabethan sonnet by Sir Philip Sidney, "Leave me, O love which reachest but to dust," is a palinode renouncing the poetry of sexual love for that of heavenly love.

Pantomime and Dumb Show.   Pantomime is acting on the stage without speech, using only posture, gesture, bodily movement, and exaggerated facial expression to **mime** ("mimic") a character's actions and to express a character's feelings. Elaborate pantomimes, halfway between drama and dance, were put on in ancient Greece and Rome, and the form was revived, often for comic purposes, in Renaissance Europe. Mimed dramas enjoyed a vogue in eighteenth-century England, and in the present century the silent movies encouraged a brief revival of the art and produced a superlative pantomimist in Charlie Chaplin. Miming survived into the present in French masters such as Marcel Marceau in the theater and Jacques Tati in the cinema, and England still retains the institution of the Christmas pantomime. In America and many other countries, circus clowns are expert pantomimists, and miming has recently been revived in the theater for the deaf.

A **dumb show** is an episode of pantomime introduced into a spoken play. It was a common device in Elizabethan drama, in imitation of its use by Seneca, the Roman writer of tragedies. Two well-known dumb shows are the preliminary episode, summarizing the action to come, of the play-within-a-play in *Hamlet* (III. ii), and the miming of the banishment of the Duchess and her family in John Webster's *The Duchess of Malfi* (III. iv).

See R. J. Broadbent, *A History of Pantomime* (1901).

Paradox.   A paradox is a statement which seems on its face to be self-contradictory or absurd yet turns out to make good sense. An instance is the conclusion to John Donne's sonnet "Death, Be Not Proud":

> One short sleep past, we wake eternally
> And death shall be no more; *Death, thou shalt die.*

The paradox is used occasionally by almost all poets, but was a persistent and central device in seventeenth-century *metaphysical poetry,* both in its religious and secular forms. Donne, who wrote a prose collection titled *Problems and Paradoxes,* exploited the figure in his poetry. "The Canonization," for example, is organized as an extended proof, full of local paradoxes, of the paradoxical thesis that sexual lovers are saints.

If the paradoxical utterance conjoins two terms that in ordinary usage are contraries, it is called an **oxymoron**; an example is Alfred, Lord Tennyson's "*O Death in life,* the days that are no more." The oxymoron was a familiar type of *Petrarchan conceit* in Elizabethan love poetry, in phrases like "pleasing pains," "I burn and freeze," "loving hate." It is also a frequent figure in devotional prose and religious poetry as a way of expressing the Christian mysteries, which transcend human sense and logic. So John Milton describes the appearance of God, in *Paradise Lost* (III, 380):

> Dark with excessive bright thy skirts appear.

Paradox was a prominent concern of many *New Critics,* who, however, extended the term from its limited application to a type of *figurative language* so as to make it encompass all surprising deviations from, or qualifications of, common perceptions or commonplace opinions. It is only in this greatly expanded sense of the term that Cleanth Brooks is able to claim, with some plausibility, that "the language of poetry is the language of paradox," in *The Well Wrought Urn* (1947). See also the recent theory called *deconstruction* for the claim that all uses of language disseminate themselves into the unresolvable paradox called an *aporia*.

Pastoral. The originator of the pastoral was the Greek poet Theocritus, who in the third century B.C. wrote poems representing the life of Sicilian shepherds. ("Pastor" is Latin for "shepherd.") Virgil later imitated Theocritus in his Latin *Eclogues,* and in doing so established the enduring model for the traditional **pastoral**: a deliberately conventional poem expressing an urban poet's nostalgic image of the peace and simplicity of the life of shepherds and other rural folk in an idealized natural setting. The *conventions* that hundreds of later poets imitated from Virgil's imitations of Theocritus include a shepherd reclining under a spreading beech tree and meditating the rural muse, or piping as though he would ne'er grow old, or engaging in a friendly singing contest, or expressing his good or bad fortune in a love affair, or grieving over the death of a fellow shepherd. From this last type developed the *pastoral elegy,* which persisted long after the other traditional types had lost their popularity. Other terms often used synonymously with pastoral are **idyll**, from the title of Theocritus' pastorals; **ecologue** (literally, "a selection"), from the title of Virgil's pastorals; and **bucolic poetry**, from the Greek word for "herdsman."

Classical poets often described the pastoral life as possessing features of the mythical **golden age**. This term derives from the chronological *primitivism* that was propounded in the Greek Hesiod's *Work and Days* (eighth century B.C.) and by many later Greek and Roman writers. The earliest period of humanity, regarded as a time of total felicity, was described figuratively as an age of gold; the continuous decline through time was expressed by the sequence "the age of silver" and "the brazen age" to the present sad condition of humanity, "the iron age." Christian pastoralists combined the golden age of pagan fable with the Garden of Eden in the Bible, and also exploited the religious symbolism of "shepherd" (in the ecclesiastical or parish "pastor," and the figure of Christ as the Good Shepherd) to give many pastoral poems a Christian range of reference. (See Harry Levin, *The Myth of the Golden Age in the Renaissance,* 1969.) In the Renaissance the traditional pastoral was also adapted to diverse satirical and allegorical uses. Edmund Spenser's *Shepherd's Calendar* (1579), which popularized the mode in English poetry, included most of the varieties of pastoral poems current in that period.

Such was the attraction of the pastoral dream that Renaissance writers incorporated it into various other literary forms. Sir Philip Sidney's *Arcadia* (1581–84) was a long pastoral *romance* written in an elaborately artful prose. (**Arcadia** was a mountainous region of Greece which Virgil substituted for Theocritus' Sicily as his idealized pastoral milieu.) There was also the pastoral lyric (Christopher Marlowe's "The Passionate Shepherd to His Love"), and the pastoral drama. John Fletcher's *The Faithful Shepherdess* is an example of this last type, and Shakespeare's *As You Like It*, based on the contemporary pastoral romance *Rosalynde* by Thomas Lodge, is set in the forest of Arden, a green refuge from the troubles and complications of ordinary life where all enmities are reconciled, all problems resolved, and the course of true love made to run smooth.

The last important series of traditional pastorals, and an extreme instance of their calculated and graceful display of high artifice, was Alexander Pope's *Pastorals* (1709). Five years later John Gay, in his *Shepherd's Week*, wrote a *burlesque* of the type by applying its elegant formulas to the crudity of actual rustic manners and language, inadvertently showing later poets the way to the seriously realistic treatment of rural life. In 1783 George Crabbe published *The Village* specifically in order to

> paint the cot
> As Truth will paint it and as bards will not.

How far the term then lost its traditional application to a poetry of aristocratic artifice is indicated by Wordsworth's title for his realistic rendering of a rural tragedy in 1800: "Michael, A Pastoral Poem."

In recent decades the term "pastoral" has been expanded in various ways. William Empson, for example, identified as pastoral any work which contrasts simple and complicated life, to the advantage of the former: the simple life may be that of the shepherd, the child, or the working man; in Empson's view this mode of life serves as an oblique way to criticize the class structure of society. Empson thus applies the term to works ranging from Andrew Marvell's seventeenth-century poem "The Garden" to Lewis Carroll's *Alice in Wonderland* and the modern proletarian novel. Other critics apply the term "pastoral" to any work which represents a withdrawal from ordinary life to a place apart that is close to the elemental rhythms of nature, where the protagonist achieves a new perspective on a former mode of life amid the complexities and conflicts of the social world.

W. W. Gregg, *Pastoral Poetry and Pastoral Drama* (1906); the Introduction to *English Pastoral Poetry from the Beginnings to Marvell*, ed. Frank Kermode (1952); Thomas G. Rosenmeyer, *The Green Cabinet: Theocritus and the European Pastoral Lyric* (1969); Andrew V. Ettin, *Literature and the Pastoral* (1985). For modern expansions of the concept see William Empson, *Some Versions of Pastoral* (1950), and Eleanor T. Lincoln, ed., *Pastoral and Romance: Modern Essays in Criticism* (1969).

Pathetic Fallacy. A phrase invented by John Ruskin in 1856 to signify any description of inanimate natural objects that ascribes to them human capabilities, sensations, and emotions (*Modern Painters*, Vol. 3, Chapter 12). As used by Ruskin—for whom "truth" was a primary criterion of art—the term was derogatory; for, he claimed, such descriptions do not represent the "true appearances of things to us" but "the extraordinary, or false appearances, when we are under the influence of emotion, or contemplative fancy." Two of Ruskin's examples are the lines

> The spendthrift crocus, bursting through the mould
> Naked and shivering, with his cup of gold,

and Coleridge's description in "Christabel" of

> The one red leaf, the last of its clan,
> That dances as often as dance it can.

These passages, Ruskin says, however beautiful, are false and "morbid." Only in the greatest poets is the use of the pathetic fallacy valid, and then only at those rare times when it would be inhuman to resist the pressure of powerful feelings to humanize the perceived fact.

Ruskin's contention would make not only his *romantic* predecessors but just about all poets, including Shakespeare, "morbid." "Pathetic fallacy" is now used, for the most part, as a neutral name for a very common phenomenon in descriptive poetry, in which the ascription of human traits to inanimate nature is less formal and more indirect than in the figure called *personification.*

See Josephine Miles, *Pathetic Fallacy in the Nineteenth Century* (1942); Harold Bloom, ed., *The Literary Criticism of John Ruskin* (1965), Introduction and pp. 62–78.

Pathos in Greek meant the passions, or suffering, or deep feeling generally, as distinguished from **ethos**, a person's overall disposition or character. In modern criticism, however, pathos, in a more limited sense, is attributed to a scene or passage that is designed to evoke the feelings of tenderness, pity, or sympathetic sorrow from the audience. In the Victorian era a number of prominent writers exploited pathos beyond the endurance of most readers today—examples are the rendering of the death of Little Nell in Charles Dickens' *The Old Curiosity Shop* and of the death of Little Eva in Harriet Beecher Stowe's *Uncle Tom's Cabin.* (See *sentimentalism.*) To many modern readers, the greatest passages of literary pathos do not dwell on the details of suffering but achieve the effect by understatement and suggestion. Examples are the speech of King Lear when he is briefly reunited with Cordelia (IV. vii. 59 ff.), beginning

> Pray, do not mock me.
> I am a very foolish fond old man,

and William Wordsworth's terse revelation of the grief of the old father for the loss of his son in *Michael* (1800), ll. 465–66:

> Many and many a day he thither went,
> And never lifted up a single stone.

Periods of American Literature. The division of American literature into convenient historical segments, or "periods," lacks the fairly clear consensus among literary scholars that we find with reference to English literature; see *periods of English literature.* The many syllabi of college surveys reprinted in *Reconstructing American Literature* (ed. Paul Lauter, 1983) demonstrate how variable are the temporal divisions and their names, especially since the recent efforts to do greater justice to literature written by women and by ethnic minorities. A number of recent historians, anthologists, and teachers of American literature simply divide their survey into dated sections, without affixing period names. A prominent tendency, however, is to recognize the importance of major wars in marking significant changes in literature. This tendency, as the American scholar Cushing Strout has remarked, "suggests that there is an order in American political history more visible and compelling than that indicated by specifically literary or intellectual categories."

The following divisions of American literary history recognize the importance assigned by many literary historians to the Revolutionary War (1775–81), the Civil War (1861–65), World War I (1914–18), and World War II (1939–45). Under these broad divisions are listed some of the more widely used terms to distinguish periods and subperiods of American literature. These terms, it will be noted, are diverse in kind; they may signify a span of time, or else a form of political organization, or a prominent intellectual or imaginative mode, or a predominant literary form.

1607–1775. This overall era, from the founding of the first settlement at Jamestown to the outbreak of the American Revolution, is often called the **Colonial Period.** Writings were for the most part religious, practical, or historical. Notable among the seventeenth-century writers of journals and narratives concerning the founding and early history of some of the colonies were William Bradford, John Winthrop, and the theologian Cotton Mather. In the following century Jonathan Edwards was a major philosopher as well as theologian, and Benjamin Franklin an early American master of lucid and cogent prose. Not until 1937, when Edward Taylor's writings were first published from manuscript, was he discovered to have been an able religious poet in the *metaphysical* style of the English devotional poets Herbert and Crashaw. Anne Bradstreet was the chief Colonial poet of secular and domestic as well as religious subjects.

The publication in 1773 of *Poems on Various Subjects* by Phillis Wheatley, then a nineteen-year-old slave who had been born in Africa, inaugurated the long and distinguished, but until recently neglected, line of **Black writers** (or by what has recently come to be a preferred name, **African-American** writers) in America. The unique complexity and diversity of the African-American cultural heritage—both Western and African, oral and written, slave and free, Judeo-Christian and pagan, plantation and urban, integrationist and Black nationalist—have effected tensions and fusions that, over the course of time, have produced a highly innovative and distinctive literature, as well as musical forms that have come to be considered America's unique contribution to the Western musical tradition. See J. Saunders Redding, *To Make a Poet Black* (1939; reissued 1986); Houston A. Baker, Jr., *Black Literature in America* (1971); Bernard W. Bell, *The Afro-American Novel and Its Tradition* (1987); Henry L. Gates, Jr., *Figures in Black* (1987).

The period between the Stamp Act of 1765 and 1790 is sometimes distinguished as the **Revolutionary Age.** It was the time of Thomas Paine's influential revolutionary tracts; of Thomas Jefferson's "Statute of Virginia for Religious Freedom," "Declaration of Independence," and many other writings; of *The Federalist Papers* in support of the Constitution, most notably those by Alexander Hamilton and James Madison; and of the patriotic and satiric poems by Philip Freneau and Joel Barlow.

1775–1865. The years 1775–1828, the **Early National Period** ending with the triumph of Jacksonian democracy in 1828, signalized the emergence of a national imaginative literature, including the first American comedy (Royall Tyler's *The Contrast,* 1787), the earliest American novel (William Hill Brown's *The Power of Sympathy,* 1789), and the establishment in 1815 of the first enduring American magazine, *The North American Review.* Washington Irving achieved international fame with his essays and stories; Charles Brockden Brown wrote authentic American versions of the *Gothic novel* of mystery and terror; the career of James Fenimore Cooper, the first major American novelist, was well launched; and William Cullen Bryant and Edgar Allan Poe wrote poetry that was relatively independent of English precursors. In the year 1760 was published the first of a long series of **slave narratives** and autobiographies written by Black slaves who had escaped or been freed. Most of these were published between 1830 and 1865, including Frederick Douglass' *Narrative of the Life of Frederick Douglass* (1845) and Harriet Jacobs' *Incidents in the Life of a Slave Girl* (1861).

The span 1828–1865 from the Jacksonian era to the Civil War, often identified as the **Romantic Period in America** (see *neoclassic and romantic*), marks the full coming of age of a native American literature. This period is sometimes known also as the **American Renaissance,** the title of F. O. Matthiessen's influential book (1941) about its outstanding writers, Ralph Waldo Emerson, Henry David Thoreau, Edgar Allan Poe, Herman Melville, and Nathaniel Hawthorne (see also *symbolism*), or else as the **Age of Transcendentalism,** after the philosophical and literary movement, centered on Emerson, that was dominant in New England (see *Transcendentalism*). In all the major literary genres except drama, writers produced works of an originality and excellence not exceeded in later American history. Emerson, Thoreau, and the early feminist Margaret Fuller shaped the ideas, ideals, and literary aims of many contemporary and later American writers. It was the age not only of continuing writings by William Cullen Bryant, Washington Irving, and James Fenimore Cooper, but also of the novels and short stories of Poe, Hawthorne, Melville, Harriet Beecher Stowe, and the southern novelist William Gilmore Simms; of the poetry of Poe, John Greenleaf Whittier, Emerson, Henry Wadsworth Longfellow, and the most innovative and influential of all American poets, Walt Whitman; and of the beginning of distinguished American criticism in the essays of Poe, Simms, and James Russell Lowell. The tradition of African-American publications of poetry by women was continued by Francis Ellen Watkins Harper, and the African-American novel was inaugurated by William Wells Brown's *Clotel* (1853) and by Harriet E. Wilson's *Our Nig* (1859).

1865–1914. The cataclysm of the bloody Civil War and of the Reconstruction, followed by a burgeoning industrialism and urbanization in the North, profoundly altered the American sense of itself, and also American literary modes. 1865–1900 is often known as the **Realistic Period,** by reference to the novels by Mark Twain, William Dean Howells, and Henry James, as well as by John W. DeForest, Harold Frederic, and the Black novelist Charles W. Chesnutt. These works, though diverse, are often labeled "realistic" in contrast to the "romances" of their predecessors in prose fiction, Poe,

Hawthorne, and Melville (see *prose romance* and *realism*). Other authors wrote regional, or *local color,* forms of realistic fiction; these include (in addition to Mark Twain's novels on the Mississippi region) Bret Harte in California, Sarah Orne Jewett in Maine, Mary Wilkins Freeman in Massachusetts, and George W. Cable and Kate Chopin in Louisiana. Chopin is now viewed as an early and major *feminist* novelist. Whitman continued writing poetry up to the last decade of the century, and (unknown to him and almost everyone else) was joined by Emily Dickinson; although only seven of Dickinson's more than a thousand short poems were published in her lifetime, she is now recognized to be one of the most distinctive and eminent of American poets. Sidney Lanier published his experiments in versification based on the meters of music; the Black author Paul Laurence Dunbar published both poems and novels between 1893 and 1905; and in the 1890s Stephen Crane, although he was only twenty-nine when he died, published short poems in free verse that anticipate the experiments of Ezra Pound and the *Imagists,* and wrote also the brilliantly innovative short stories and short novels that look forward to two later narrative modes, naturalism and impressionism. The years 1900–1914, although James, Howells, and Mark Twain were still writing, are discriminated as the **Naturalistic Period**, in recognition of the powerful though sometimes crudely wrought novels by Frank Norris, Jack London, and Theodore Dreiser, which typically represent characters who are joint victims of their instinctual drives and of external sociological forces; see *naturalism.*

1914–1939. The era between the two world wars, marked also by the trauma of the great economic depression beginning in 1929, was that of the emergence of what is still known as "modern literature," which in America reached an eminence rivaling that of the American Renaissance of the mid-nineteenth century; unlike most of the authors of that earlier period, however, the American modernists also achieved great international recognition and influence. (See *modernism.*) *Poetry* magazine, founded in Chicago by Harriet Monroe in 1912, published many of the experimental authors. Among the notable poets were Edgar Lee Masters, Edwin Arlington Robinson, Robert Frost, Carl Sandburg, Wallace Stevens, William Carlos Williams, Ezra Pound, Robinson Jeffers, Marianne Moore, T. S. Eliot, Edna St. Vincent Millay, and E. E. Cummings—authors who wrote in an unexampled variety of poetic modes. These included the *Imagism* of Amy Lowell, H. D. (Hilda Doolittle), and others, the metric poems by Frost and the free-verse poems by Williams in the American vernacular, the formal and typographic experiments of Cummings, the poetic naturalism of Jeffers, and the assimilation to their own distinctive uses by Pound and Eliot of the forms and procedures of French *symbolism,* merged with the intellectual and figurative methods of the English *metaphysical poets.* Among the major writers of prose fiction were Edith Wharton, Sinclair Lewis, Ellen Glasgow, Willa Cather, Gertrude Stein, Sherwood Anderson, John Dos Passos, F. Scott Fitzgerald, William Faulkner, Ernest Hemingway, Thomas Wolfe, and John Steinbeck. America produced in this period its first great dramatist in Eugene O'Neill, as well as a group of distinguished literary critics that included Van Wyck

Brooks, Malcolm Cowley, T. S. Eliot, Edmund Wilson, and the irreverent and caustic H. L. Mencken.

The writers of this era are often subclassified in a variety of ways. The flamboyant and pleasure-seeking 1920s are called the **Jazz Age,** a title popularized by F. Scott Fitzgerald's *Tales of the Jazz Age* (1922). The same decade was also the early period of the **Harlem Renaissance.** After World War I, the population of the area of upper Manhattan known as Harlem was almost exclusively Black, and became the national center of African-American culture, including the arts of theater, music, and dance. Distinguished writers—poets, novelists, playwrights, and essayists—who lived in Harlem or wrote about Harlem include James Weldon Johnson, Claude McKay, Jean Toomer, Langston Hughes, Countee Cullen, W. E. B. DuBois, and (in later decades) James Baldwin. (See Nathan Irvin Huggins, *Harlem Renaissance,* 1971.)

Many prominent American writers of the decade following the end of World War I, disillusioned by their war experiences and alienated by what they perceived as the crassness of American culture and its "puritanical" repressions, are often tagged (in a term first applied by Gertrude Stein to young Frenchmen of the time) as the **Lost Generation.** A number of these writers became "expatriates," moving either to London or to Paris in their quest for a richer literary and artistic milieu and a freer way of life. Ezra Pound, Gertrude Stein, and T. S. Eliot lived out their lives abroad, but most of the younger "exiles," as Malcolm Cowley called them (*Exile's Return,* 1934), came back to America in the 1930s. Hemingway's *The Sun Also Rises* and Fitzgerald's *Tender Is the Night* are novels that represent the mood and way of life of two groups of American expatriates. In "the radical '30s," the period of the great depression and of the economic and social reforms in the New Deal inaugurated by President Franklin Delano Roosevelt, some authors joined radical political movements, and many others dealt in their literary works with pressing social issues of the time—including, in the novel, William Faulkner, John Dos Passos, James T. Farrell, Thomas Wolfe, and John Steinbeck, and in the drama, Eugene O'Neill, Clifford Odets, and Maxwell Anderson.

1939 to the Present, the **contemporary period.** World War II, and especially the disillusionment with Soviet Communism consequent upon the Moscow trials for alleged treason and Stalin's signing of the Russo-German pact with Hitler in 1939, largely ended the literary radicalism of the 1930s. For several decades the *New Criticism*—dominated by conservative southern writers, the **Agrarians,** who in the 1930s had championed a return from an industrial to an agricultural economy—typified the prevailing critical tendency to isolate literature from the life of the author and from society and to conceive a work of literature, in formal terms, as an organic and autonomous entity (see John L. Stewart, *The Burden of Time: The Fugitives and Agrarians,* 1965). The eminent and influential critics Edmund Wilson and Lionel Trilling, however—as well as other critics grouped with them as "the New York Intellectuals," including Philip Rahv, Alfred Kazin, and Irving Howe—continued through the 1960s to deal with a work of literature humanistically and historically, in the context of its author's life, temperament, and social milieu, and in terms of the work's moral and imaginative qualities and its consequences for society. Since the latter 1970s, a number of American critics have adopted various forms of poststructural theories and practice, derived in large part from French and European thinkers. (See *poststructuralism.*)

The 1950s, while often regarded in retrospect as a period of cultural conformity and complacency, was marked by the emergence of vigorous anti-establishment and anti-traditional literary movements: the *Beat writers* such as Allen Ginsberg and Jack Kerouac; the American exemplars of the literature of the *absurd;* the "Black Mountain Poets," Charles Olson and Robert Creeley; and the "New York Poets," John Ashbery, Kenneth Koch, and Frank O'Hara. It was also a time of *confessional poetry* and the literature of extreme sexual candor, marked by the emergence of Henry Miller as a notable author (his autobiographical and fictional works, begun in the 1930s, had earlier been available only under the counter) and the writings of Norman Mailer, William Burroughs, and Vladimir Nabokov (*Lolita* was published in 1955). The **counterculture** of the 1960s and early '70s continued some of these modes, but in a fashion made extreme and fevered by the rebellious youth movement and the vehement and sometimes violent opposition to the war in Vietnam; for an approving treatment of this movement, see Theodore Roszak, *The Making of a Counter Culture* (1969), and for a later retrospect, Morris Dickstein, *Gates of Eden: American Culture in the Sixties* (1978).

Important American writers after World War II include, in prose fiction, Vladimir Nabokov (who emigrated to America in 1940), Eudora Welty, Robert Penn Warren, Bernard Malamud, James Gould Cozzens, Saul Bellow, Mary McCarthy, Norman Mailer, John Updike, Kurt Vonnegut, Jr., Thomas Pynchon, John Barth, and E. L. Doctorow; in poetry, Marianne Moore, Robert Penn Warren, Theodore Roethke, Elizabeth Bishop, Robert Lowell, Allen Ginsberg, Adrienne Rich, Sylvia Plath, A. R. Ammons, and John Ashbery; and in drama, Thornton Wilder, Arthur Miller, Tennessee Williams, and Edward Albee. African-American writers such as Ralph Ellison, James Baldwin, Richard Wright, Gwendolyn Brooks, Zora Neale Hurston, Imamu Amiri Baraka (LeRoi Jones), Lorraine Hansberry, and Nikki Giovanni achieved prominence in a variety of literary forms; many African-American women, including Alice Walker and Toni Morrison, are notable novelists; and in the 1990s there is an increasing number of Black directors of notable cinemas. (See *Modern Black Writers,* ed. Michael Popkin, 1978; Barbara Christian, *Black Women Novelists,* 1980.)

The contemporary literary scene in America is crowded and varied, and these lists could readily be expanded; we must await the passage of time to determine which writers now active will emerge as enduringly major figures in the *canon* of American literature.

Periods of English Literature. For convenience of discussion, historians divide the continuity of English literature into segments of time which are called "periods." The exact number, dates, and names of these periods vary, but the list below conforms to widespread practice. The list is followed by a brief comment on each period, in chronological order.

450–1066	Old English (or Anglo-Saxon) Period	
1066–1500	Middle English Period	
1500–1660	The Renaissance	
	1558–1603	Elizabethan Age
	1603–1625	Jacobean Age
	1625–1649	Caroline Age
	1649–1660	Commonwealth Period (or Puritan Interregnum)
1660–1785	The Neoclassical Period	
	1660–1700	The Restoration
	1700–1745	The Augustan Age (or Age of Pope)
	1745–1785	The Age of Sensibility (or Age of Johnson)
1785–1830	The Romantic Period	
1832–1901	The Victorian Period	
	1848–1860	The Pre-Raphaelites
	1880–1901	Aestheticism and Decadence
1901–1914	The Edwardian Period	
1910–1936	The Georgian Period	
1914–	The Modern Period	
	1945–	Postmodernism

Old English Period, or the **Anglo-Saxon Period**, extended from the invasion of Celtic England by Germanic tribes (the Angles, Saxons, and Jutes) in the first half of the fifth century to the conquest of England in 1066 by the Norman French under the leadership of William the Conqueror. Only after they had been converted to Christianity in the seventh century did the Anglo-Saxons, whose earlier literature had been oral, begin to develop a written literature. (See *oral formulaic poetry*.) A high level of culture and learning was soon achieved in various monasteries; the eighth-century churchmen Bede and Alcuin were major scholars who wrote in Latin, the standard language of international scholarship. The poetry written in the vernacular Anglo-Saxon, known also as Old English, included *Beowulf* (eighth century), the greatest of Germanic epic poems, and such lyric laments as "The Wanderer," "The Seafarer," and "Deor," all of which, though composed by Christian writers, reflect the conditions of life in the pagan past. Caedmon and Cynewulf were poets who wrote on biblical and religious themes, and there survive a number of Old English lives of saints, sermons, and paraphrases of books of the Bible. Alfred the Great, a West Saxon king (871–99) who for a time united all the kingdoms of southern England against a new wave of Germanic invaders, the Vikings, was no less important as a patron of literature than as a warrior. He himself translated into Old English various books of Latin prose, supervised translations by other hands, and instituted the Anglo-Saxon Chronicle, a continuous record, year by year, of important events in England.

See H. M. Chadwick, *The Heroic Age* (1912); S. B. Greenfield, *A Critical History of Old English Literature* (1965); C. L. Wrenn, *A Study of Old English Literature* (1966).

Middle English Period. The four and a half centuries between the Norman Conquest in 1066, which effected radical changes in the language, life, and culture of England, and about 1500, when the standard literary language (deriving from the dialect of the London area) had become recognizably "modern English"—that is, similar to the language we speak and write today.

The span from 1100 to 1350 is sometimes discriminated as the **Anglo-Norman Period,** because the non-Latin literature of that time was written mainly in Anglo-Norman, the French dialect spoken by the invaders who had established themselves as the ruling class of England. When the native vernacular, descended from Anglo-Saxon and known as "middle English," came into general literary use, it was at first mainly the vehicle for religious and homiletic writings. The first great age of primarily secular literature was the second half of the fourteenth century—the age of Chaucer and John Gower, of William Langland's great religious and satirical poem *Piers Plowman,* and of the anonymous master who wrote four major poems in complex *alliterative meter,* including the elegy *Pearl,* and *Sir Gawain and the Green Knight.* This last work is the most accomplished of the English *chivalric romances;* the best prose romance was Thomas Malory's *Morte d'Arthur,* written a century later. The outstanding poets of the fifteenth century were the "Scottish Chaucerians," who included King James I of Scotland and Robert Henryson. The fifteenth century was more important for popular literature than for the artful literature addressed to the upper classes: it was the age of many excellent songs, secular and religious, and of *folk ballads,* as well as the flowering time of the medieval drama, the *miracle* and *morality plays,* which were written and produced for the general public.

See W. L. Renwick and H. Orton, *The Beginnings of English Literature to Skelton* (rev., 1952); H. S. Bennett, *Chaucer and the Fifteenth Century* (1947); Edward Vasta, ed., *Middle English Survey: Critical Essays* (1965).

The **Renaissance,** 1500–1660; see the essay *Renaissance,* below.

Elizabethan Age. The period of the reign of Elizabeth I, 1558–1603. This was a time of rapid development in English commerce, maritime power, and nationalist feeling—the defeat of the Spanish Armada occurred in 1588. It was a great (in drama the greatest) age of English Literature—the age of Sir Philip Sidney, Christopher Marlowe, Edmund Spenser, Shakespeare, Sir Walter Raleigh, Francis Bacon, Ben Jonson, and many other extraordinary writers of prose and of dramatic, lyric, and narrative poetry.

Jacobean Age. The reign of James I (in Latin, "Jacobus"), 1603–25, which followed that of Queen Elizabeth. This was the period in prose writings of Bacon, John Donne's sermons, Robert Burton's *Anatomy of Melancholy,* and the King James translation of the Bible. It was also the period of Shakespeare's greatest tragedies and tragicomedies, and of major writings by other notable poets and playwrights including Donne, Ben Jonson, Michael Drayton, Sir Francis Beaumont and John Fletcher, John Webster, George Chapman, Thomas Middleton, and Philip Massinger.

See Basil Willey, *The Seventeenth Century Background* (1934); Douglas Bush, *English Literature in the Earlier Seventeenth Century* (1945); C. V. Wedgewood, *Seventeenth Century English Literature* (1950).

Caroline Age. The reign of Charles I, 1625–49; the name is derived from "Carolus," the Latin version of "Charles." This was the time of the English Civil War fought between the supporters of the king (known as "Cavaliers") and the supporters of Parliament (known as "Roundheads," from their custom of wearing their hair cut short). John Milton began his writing during this period; it was the age also of the religious poet George Herbert and of the prose writers Robert Burton and Sir Thomas Browne.

Associated with the court were the **Cavalier poets**, writers of witty and polished lyrics of courtship and gallantry. The group included Richard Lovelace, Sir John Suckling, and Thomas Carew. Robert Herrick, although a country parson, is often classified with the Cavalier poets because, like them, he was a **Son of Ben**—that is, an admirer and follower of Ben Jonson—in many of his lyrics of love and gallant compliment.

See Robin Skelton, *Cavalier Poets* (1960).

Commonwealth Period, also known as the **Puritan Interregnum,** extends from the end of the Civil War and the execution of Charles I in 1649 to the restoration of the Stuart monarchy under Charles II in 1660. In this period England was ruled by Parliament under the Puritan leader Oliver Cromwell; his death in 1658 marked the dissolution of the Commonwealth. Drama almost disappeared for eighteen years after the Puritans, on moral and religious grounds, closed the public theaters in September 1642. It was the age of Milton's political pamphlets, of Hobbes' political treatise *Leviathan* (1651), of the prose writers Sir Thomas Browne, Thomas Fuller, Jeremy Taylor, and Izaak Walton, and of the poets Henry Vaughan, Edmund Waller, Abraham Cowley, Sir William Davenant, and Andrew Marvell.

The **Neoclassical Period,** 1660–1785; see *neoclassic and romantic,* above.

Restoration. This period takes its name from the restoration of the Stuart line (Charles II) to the English throne in 1660, at the end of the *Commonwealth;* it is specified as lasting until 1700. The urbanity, wit, and licentiousness of the life centering on the court, in sharp contrast to the seriousness and sobriety of the earlier Puritan regime, is reflected in much of the literature of this age. The theaters came back to vigorous life after the revocation of the ban placed on them by the Puritans in 1642; Sir George Etherege, William Wycherley, William Congreve, and John Dryden developed the distinctive comedy of manners called *Restoration comedy,* and Dryden, Thomas Otway, and other playwrights developed the even more distinctive form of tragedy called *heroic drama.* Dryden was the major poet and critic, as well as one of the major dramatists. Other poets were the satirists Samuel Butler and the Earl of Rochester; notable writers in prose, in addition to the masterly Dryden, were Samuel Pepys, Sir William Temple, the religious writer John Bunyan, and the philosopher John Locke.

See Basil Willey, *The Seventeenth Century Background* (1934); L. I. Bredvold, *The Intellectual Milieu of John Dryden* (1932).

Augustan Age. The original Augustan Age was the brilliant literary period of Virgil, Horace, and Ovid under the Roman emperor Augustus (27 B.C.–A.D. 14). In the eighteenth century and later, however, the term was frequently applied also to the literary period in England from approximately

1700 to 1745. The leading writers of the time (such as Alexander Pope, Jonathan Swift, and Joseph Addison) themselves drew the parallel to the Roman Augustans, and deliberately imitated their literary forms and subjects, their emphasis on social concerns, and their ideals of moderation, decorum, and urbanity. (See *neoclassicism.*) A major representative of popular, rather than classical, writing in this period was the novelist, journalist, and pamphleteer Daniel Defoe.

Age of Sensibility. The period between the death of Alexander Pope (1744) and 1785, which was one year after the death of Samuel Johnson and one year before Robert Burns' *Poems, Chiefly in Scottish Dialect.* (Alternative dates frequently proposed for the end of this period are 1789 and 1798; see *Romantic Period.*) An older name for this half-century, the **Age of Johnson**, stresses the dominant position of Samuel Johnson (1709–84) and his literary and intellectual circle, which included Oliver Goldsmith, Edmund Burke, James Boswell, Edward Gibbon, and Hester Lynch Thrale. These authors on the whole represented a culmination of the literary and critical modes of *neoclassicism* and the worldview of the *Enlightenment.* The more recent name, "Age of Sensibility," puts its stress on the emergence, in other writers of the 1740s and later, of new cultural attitudes, theories of literature, and types of poetry; we find in this period, for example, a growing sympathy for the Middle Ages, *cultural primitivism,* an awakening interest in ballads and other folk literature, a turn from neoclassic "correctness" and its emphasis on judgment and restraint to an emphasis on instinct and feeling, the development of a *literature of sensibility,* and above all the exaltation by some critics of "original genius" and a "bardic" poetry of the sublime and visionary imagination. Thomas Gray expressed this anti-neoclassic sensibility and set of values in his "Stanzas to Mr. Bentley" (1752):

> But not to one in this benighted age
> Is that diviner inspiration given,
> That burns in Shakespeare's or in Milton's page,
> The pomp and prodigality of Heaven.

Other poets manifesting similar shifts in thought and taste were William Collins and Joseph and Thomas Warton (poets who, together with Gray, began in the 1740s the vogue for what Johnson slightingly referred to as "ode, and elegy, and sonnet"), Christopher Smart, and William Cowper. Thomas Percy published his influential *Reliques of Ancient English Poetry* (1765), which included many *folk ballads* and a few medieval metrical romances, and James Macpherson in the same decade published his greatly doctored (and in considerable part fabricated) versions of the poems of the Gaelic bard Ossian (Oisin), which were immensely popular throughout Europe. This was also the period of the great novelists, some realistic and satiric and some "sentimental": Samuel Richardson, Henry Fielding, Tobias Smollett, and Laurence Sterne.

See W. J. Bate, *From Classic to Romantic* (1946); Northrop Frye, "Towards Defining an Age of Sensibility," in *Fables of Identity* (1963), and ed., *Romanticism Reconsidered* (1965); F. W. Hilles and Harold Bloom, eds., *From Sensibility to Romanticism* (1965).

Romantic Period. The Romantic Period in English literature is dated as beginning in 1785 (see *Age of Sensibility*)—or alternatively in 1789 (the outbreak of the French Revolution), or in 1798 (the publication of William Wordsworth's and Samuel Taylor Coleridge's *Lyrical Ballads*)—and as ending either in 1830 or else in 1832, the year in which Sir Walter Scott died and the passage of the Reform Bill signaled the political preoccupations of the Victorian era. For some characteristics of the thought and writings of this great literary period, as well as for a list of suggested readings, see *neoclassic and romantic*. The term is often applied also to literary movements in European countries and America; see *periods of American literature*. Romantic characteristics are usually said to have been manifested first in Germany and England in the 1790s, and not to have appeared in France and America until two or three decades after that time. Major English writers of the period, in addition to Wordsworth and Coleridge, were the poets Robert Burns, William Blake, Lord Byron, Percy Bysshe Shelley, John Keats, and Walter Savage Landor, the prose writers Charles Lamb, William Hazlitt, Thomas De Quincey, Mary Wollstonecraft, and Leigh Hunt, and the novelists Jane Austen, Sir Walter Scott, and Mary Shelley. The span between 1787 and the close of the eighteenth century was that of the *Gothic romances* by William Beckford, Matthew Gregory Lewis, William Godwin, and above all, Anne Radcliffe.

Victorian Period. The beginning of the Victorian Period is frequently dated 1830, or alternatively 1832 (the passage of the first Reform Bill), and sometimes 1837 (the accession of Queen Victoria); it extends to the death of Victoria in 1901. The year 1870 is often used to distinguish between what is called "early Victorian" and "late Victorian." Much writing of the period, whether imaginative or didactic, in verse or in prose, dealt with or reflected contemporary social, economic, religious, and intellectual issues and problems. Among these were the industrial revolution and its effects on the economic and social structure; rapid urbanization and the deterioration of rural England; massive poverty, growing class tensions, and pressures toward political and social reform; what was often called "the woman question" (that is, the early *feminist* movement for equal status and rights); and the impact on philosophy and religious fundamentalism of Charles Darwin's theory of evolution, and also of the general extension of **positivism** (the method of empirical investigation and proof developed in the physical sciences) into all areas of speculation and inquiry. It was an age of immense, variegated, and often self-critical literary activity. The frequently derogatory connotations of the term "Victorian" in our time—sexual priggishness, narrow-mindedness, complacency, the stress on respectability—are indeed based on attitudes and values expressed by many members of the rapidly expanding Victorian middle class; but current attacks on such Victorian attributes merely echo the attacks voiced by a number of writers within the age itself. Among the notable poets were Alfred, Lord Tennyson, Robert Browning, Elizabeth Barrett Browning, Matthew Arnold, and Gerard Manley Hopkins. The most prominent essayists were Thomas Carlyle, John Ruskin, Arnold, and Walter Pater; the most distinguished of many excellent novelists (this was a great age of English prose fiction) were Charles Dickens, William

Makepeace Thackeray, Charlotte and Emily Brontë, Elizabeth Gaskell, George Eliot, George Meredith, Anthony Trollope, Thomas Hardy, and Samuel Butler.

See G. M. Young, *Victorian England: Portrait of an Age* (2d ed., 1953); Jerome Buckley, *The Victorian Temper* (1951); W. E. Houghton, *The Victorian Frame of Mind* (1957). On aspects of love and sexuality in that age, see Steven Marcus, *The Other Victorians* (1966), and Peter Gay, *The Bourgeois Experience, Victoria to Freud,* Vol. 1, *Education of the Senses* (1984), and Vol. 2, *The Tender Passion* (1986).

Two prominent literary movements within the Victorian era are distinguished as follows:

Pre-Raphaelites. In 1848 a group of English artists, including Dante Gabriel Rossetti, William Holman Hunt, and John Millais, organized the "Pre-Raphaelite Brotherhood." Their aim was to replace the reigning academic style of painting by a return to the truthfulness, simplicity, and spirit of devotion which these artists attributed to the Italian painting before the time of Raphael (1483–1520) and the high Italian *Renaissance.* The ideals of this group of painters were taken over by a literary movement which included Dante Gabriel Rossetti himself (who was a poet as well as a painter), his sister Christina Rossetti, William Morris, and Algernon Swinburne. Rossetti's poem "The Blessed Damozel" typifies the medievalism, the pictorial realism with symbolic overtones, and the union of flesh and spirit, sensuousness and religiousness, associated with the earlier writings of this school. See also Christina Rossetti's "Goblin Market" (1862) and William Morris' narrative in verse *The Earthly Paradise* (1868–70).

See William Gaunt, *The Pre-Raphaelite Tragedy* (1942); Graham Hough, *The Last Romantics* (1949).

Aestheticism and Decadence, 1880–1900. See the entries above on *Aestheticism,* and on *Decadence.*

Edwardian Period. The span between the death of Victoria (1901) and the beginning of World War I (1914) is named for King Edward VII, who reigned from 1901 to 1910. Poets writing at the time included Thomas Hardy, Alfred Noyes, William Butler Yeats, and Rudyard Kipling; dramatists included James Barrie, John Galsworthy, George Bernard Shaw, and the playwrights of the *Celtic Revival* such as Lady Gregory, Yeats, and John M. Synge. Many of the major achievements were in prose fiction—works by Thomas Hardy, Joseph Conrad, Ford Madox Ford, John Galsworthy, H. G. Wells, Rudyard Kipling, and Henry James, who published his three great final novels, *The Wings of the Dove, The Ambassadors,* and *The Golden Bowl,* between 1902 and 1904.

Georgian Period is a term applied both to the reigns in England of the four successive Georges (1714–1830) and (more frequently) to the reign of George V (1910–36). **Georgian poets** usually designates a group of writers in the latter era who loomed large in four anthologies entitled *Georgian Poetry,* which were published by Edward Marsh between 1912 and 1922. Marsh favored writers we now tend to regard as relatively minor poets such as Rupert Brooke, Walter de la Mare, Ralph Hodgson, W. H. Davies, and John Masefield. The term "Georgian poetry" has come to connote verse which is mainly rural in subject matter, deft and delicate rather than bold and passionate in manner, and traditional rather than experimental in technique and form.

Modern Period. The application of the term "modern," of course, varies with the passage of time, but it is frequently applied specifically to the literature written since the beginning of World War I in 1914. This period has been marked by persistent and multidimensioned experiments in subject matter, form, and style, and has produced major achievements in all the literary genres. Among the notable writers are the poets W. B. Yeats, Wilfred Owen, T. S. Eliot, W. H. Auden, Robert Graves, Dylan Thomas, and Seamus Heaney; the novelists Joseph Conrad, James Joyce, D. H. Lawrence, Virginia Woolf, E. M. Forster, Graham Greene, Doris Lessing, and Nadine Gordimer; the dramatists G. B. Shaw, Sean O'Casey, Noel Coward, Samuel Beckett, and Tom Stoppard; and the critics T. S. Eliot, I. A. Richards, F. R. Leavis, and William Empson. **Postmodern Period** is a name sometimes applied to the era after World War II (1939–45); see *modernism and postmodernism.*

Persona, Tone, and Voice. These terms, frequent in recent criticism, reflect the tendency to think of all narrative and lyric works of literature as a mode of speech, or in what is now a favored term, as *discourse.* To conceive a work as an utterance suggests that there is a speaker who has determinate personal qualities, and who expresses attitudes both toward the characters and materials within the work and toward the audience to whom the work is addressed. In his *Rhetoric* (fourth century B.C.), Aristotle, followed by other Greek and Roman rhetoricians, pointed out that an orator establishes in the course of his oration an *ethos,* that is, a personal character, which itself functions as a means of persuasion. For example, if the impression a speaker projects is that of a person of rectitude, intelligence, and goodwill, the audience is instinctively inclined to give credence to such a speaker's arguments. The current concern with the nature and function of the author's presence in a work of imaginative literature is related to this traditional concept, and is part of the strong rhetorical emphasis in modern criticism. (See *rhetoric, rhetorical criticism,* and *speech-act theory.*)

Applications of the terms "persona," "tone," and "voice" vary greatly and involve difficult concepts in modern philosophy and social psychology—concepts such as "the self," "personal identity," "role-playing," and "sincerity." This essay will merely sketch some central uses of these terms that have proved useful in analyzing our experience of diverse works of literature.

Persona was the Latin word for the mask worn by actors in the classical theater, from which was derived the term **dramatis personae** for the list of characters who play a role in a drama, and ultimately the English word "person," a particular individual. In recent literary discussion "persona" is often applied to the first-person narrator, whether this is the "I" of a narrative poem or novel or of the speaker whose voice we hear in a lyric poem. Examples of personae, in this broad application, are the visionary first-person narrator of John Milton's *Paradise Lost* (who in the opening passages of various books of that epic discourses at some length about himself); the Gulliver who tells us about his misadventures in *Gulliver's Travels;* the "I" who carries on most of the conversation in Alexander Pope's satiric dialogue *Epistle to Dr. Arbuthnot;* the genial narrator of Henry Fielding's *Tom Jones,* who pauses frequently for leisurely discourse with his reader; the speaker who talks first to himself, then to his sister, in William Wordsworth's "Tintern Abbey"; the speaker who utters all of John Keats' "Ode to a Nightingale," from "My heart aches" at the beginning to the ending, "Fled is that music:—Do I wake or sleep?"; and the Duke who tells the emissary about his former wife in Robert Browning's "My Last Duchess." Calling all of these speakers "personae" serves to indicate that they are all, to some degree, adapted to the generic and formal requirements and the artistic aims of a particular literary work. We need, however, to go on to make distinctions between such speakers as Jonathan Swift's Gulliver and Browning's Duke, who are entirely fictional characters very different from their authors; the narrators in Pope's *Epistle* and Fielding's *Tom Jones,* who are presented as closer to their authors, although clearly adapted to the roles they are designed to play in those works; and the speakers in the autobiographical passages in *Paradise Lost,* in "Tintern Abbey," and in "Ode to a Nightingale," where we are invited to attribute the voice we hear, and the sentiments it utters, to the poet in his own person.

In an influential discussion, I. A. Richards defined **tone** as the expression of a literary speaker's "attitude to his listener." "The tone of his utterance reflects . . . his sense of how he stands toward those he is addressing" (*Practical Criticism,* 1929, Chapters 1 and 3). In a more complex definition, the Soviet critic Mikhail Bakhtin said that tone, or "intonation," is "oriented *in two directions:* with respect to the listener as ally or witness and with respect to the object of the utterance as the third, living participant whom the intonation scolds or caresses, denigrates or magnifies." ("Discourse in Life and Discourse in Art," in Bakhtin's *Freudianism: A Marxist Critique,* trans. 1976.) The sense in which the term is used in recent criticism is suggested by the phrase "tone of voice," as applied to nonliterary speech. The way we speak reveals, by subtle clues, our conception of, and attitude to, the things we are talking about, our personal relation to our auditor, as well as our assumptions about the social level, intelligence, and sensitivity of that auditor. The tone of a speech can be described as critical or approving, formal or intimate, outspoken or reticent, solemn or playful, arrogant or prayerful, angry or loving, serious or ironic, condescending or obsequious, and so on through numberless possible nuances of relationship and attitude both to object and auditor. Some current critical uses of "tone," however, are broader, and coincide in reference with what other critics prefer to call "voice."

Voice, in a recently evolved usage, signifies the equivalent in imaginative literature to Aristotle's "ethos" in a speech of persuasive rhetoric, and suggests also the traditional rhetorician's concern with the importance of the physical voice in an oration. The term in criticism points to the fact that we are aware of a voice beyond the fictitious voices that speak in a work, and a person behind all the dramatis personae, and behind even the first-person narrator. We have the sense of a pervasive authorial presence, a determinate intelligence and moral sensibility, which has invented, ordered, rendered, and expressed all these literary characters and materials in just this way. The particular qualities of the author's ethos, or voice, in Henry Fielding's novel *Tom Jones* (1749) manifest themselves, among other things, in the fact that he has chosen to create the wise, ironic, and worldly persona who ostensibly tells the story and talks to the reader about it. The sense of a distinctive authorial presence is no less evident in the work of recent writers who, unlike Fielding, pursue a strict policy of authorial noninterference and by effacing themselves, try to give the impression that the story tells itself (see *point of view*). There is great diversity in the quality of the authorial mind, temperament, and sensibility which, by inventing, controlling, and rendering the particular fiction, pervades works—all of them "objective" or impersonal in narrative technique—such as James Joyce's *Ulysses,* Virginia Woolf's *Mrs. Dalloway,* Ernest Hemingway's "The Killers," and William Faulkner's *The Sound and the Fury.* For a particular emphasis on the importance of the author's implicit presence in a work, see *critics of consciousness.*

Of the critics listed below who deal with this concept, Wayne C. Booth prefers the term **implied author** over "voice," in order better to indicate that the reader of a work of fiction has the sense not only of the timbre and tone of a speaking voice, but of a total human presence. Booth's view is that this implied author is "an ideal, literary, created version of the real man"—that is, the implied author, although related to the actual author, is nonetheless part of the total fiction, whom the author gradually brings into being in the course of his composition, and who plays an important role in the total effect of a work on the reader. Critics such as Walter J. Ong, on the other hand, distinguish between the author's "false voice" and his "true voice,' and regard the latter as the expression of the author's genuine self or identity; as they see it, for a writer to discover his true "voice" is to discover himself. All of these critics agree, however, that the sense of a convincing authorial voice and presence, whose values, beliefs, and moral vision serve implicitly as controlling forces throughout a work, helps to sway the reader to yield that unstinting imaginative consent without which a poem or novel would remain an elaborate verbal game.

Refer to Bakhtin's view of the multiplex voices in narrative fiction, in *dialogic criticism.* See: Richard Ellmann, *Yeats: The Man and the Masks* (1948)—which discusses Yeats' theory of a poet's "masks" or "personae," both in his life and his art; Reuben Brower, "The Speaking Voice," in *Fields of Light* (1951); Wayne C. Booth, *The Rhetoric of Fiction* (1961), Chapter 3; W. J. Ong, *The Barbarian Within* (1962); J. O. Perry, ed., *Approaches to the Poem* (1965)—Sec. 3, "Tone, Voice, Sensibility," includes selections from I. A. Richards, Reuben Brower, and W. J. Ong; Walter J. Slatoff, *With Respect to Readers* (1970); Lionel Trilling, *Sincerity and Authenticity* (1972); and Robert C. Elliott, *The Literary Persona* (1982).

Platonic Love. In Plato's *Symposium* 210–212, Socrates recounts the doctrine about Eros (love) that, he modestly says, has been imparted to him by the wise woman Diotima. She bids us not to linger in the love evoked by the beauty in a single human body, but to mount up as by a stair, "from one going on to two, and from two to all fair forms," then up from the beauty of the body to the beauty of the mind, until we arrive at final contemplation of the Idea, or Form, of "beauty absolute, separate, simple, and everlasting." From this Ideal Beauty the human soul is in exile, and of it the beauties of the body and in the entire world of sense-perception are only distant, distorted, and impermanent reflections. Plotinus and other **Neoplatonists** (the "new Platonists," a school of Platonic philosophers of the third to the fifth century) developed the view that all beauty in the sensible world—as well as all goodness and truth—is an "emanation" (radiation) from the One or Absolute, which is the source of all being and all value. From both Platonic and Neoplatonic sources, Christian thinkers of the Italian Renaissance, merging this concept of the Absolute with the biblical God, developed the theory that genuine beauty of the body is only the outer manifestation of a moral and spiritual beauty of the soul, which in turn is rayed out from the absolute beauty of the one God Himself. The Platonic lover is irresistibly attracted to the bodily beauty of a beloved person, but reveres it as a sign of the spiritual beauty that it shares with all other beautiful bodies, and at the same time regards it as the lowest rung on a ladder that leads up from sensual desire to the pure contemplation of Heavenly Beauty in God.

Highly developed versions of this conception of Platonic love are to be found in Dante, Petrarch, and other writers of the thirteenth and fourteenth centuries, and in many Italian, French, and English authors of sonnets and other love poems during the Renaissance. See, for example, the exposition in Book IV of Castiglione's *The Courtier* (1528), and in Edmund Spenser's "An Hymn in Honor of Beauty." As Spenser wrote in one of the sonnets he called *Amoretti* (1595):

> Men call you fayre, and you doe credit it. . . .
> But only that is permanent and free
> From frayle corruption, that doth flesh ensew.
> That is true beautie: that doth argue you
> To be divine and borne of heavenly seed:
>
> Derived from that fayre spirit, from whom al true
> And perfect beauty did at first proceed.

From this complex religious and philosophical doctrine, the modern notion that Platonic love is simply love that stops short of sexual gratification is a crude reduction.

The concept of Platonic love has fascinated some later poets, especially Shelley; see his "Epipsychidion" (1821). But his friend Byron took a skeptical view of such lofty claims for the human Eros-impulse. "Oh Plato! Plato!" Byron sighed,

> you have paved the way,
> With your confounded fantasies, to more
> Immoral conduct by the fancied sway
> Your system feigns o'er the controlless core
> Of human hearts, than all the long array
> Of poets and romancers. . . .
>
> (*Don Juan,* I. cxvi)

See Plato's *Symposium* and *Phaedrus,* and the exposition of Plato's doctrine of Eros, which Plato applied to homosexual as well as heterosexual love, in G. M. A. Grube, *Plato's Thought* (1935), Chapter 3. Refer to J. S. Harrison, *Platonism in English Poetry of the Sixteenth and Seventeenth Centuries* (1903); Paul Shorey, *Platonism Ancient and Modern* (1938); George Santayana, "Platonic Love in Some Italian Poets," in *Selected Critical Writings,* ed. Norman Henfrey (2 vols.; 1968), I, 41–59.

Plot. The plot in a dramatic or narrative work is constituted by its events and actions, as these are rendered and ordered toward achieving particular emotional and artistic effects. This description is deceptively simple, because the actions (including verbal discourse as well as physical actions) are performed by particular characters in a work, and are the means by which they exhibit their moral and dispositional qualities. Plot and *character* are therefore interdependent critical concepts—as Henry James has said, "What is character but the determination of incident? What is incident but the illustration of character?" Notice also that a plot is distinguishable from the "story"—that is, a bare synopsis of the temporal order of what happens in a work of literature. When we summarize the story in a literary work, we say that first this happens, then that, then that. . . . It is only when we specify how this is related to that, and in what ways all these matters are rendered, ordered, and organized so as to achieve their particular effects, that a synopsis begins to be adequate to the plot. (On the distinction between story and plot see also *narratology.*)

There are a great variety of plot forms. For example, some plots are designed to achieve tragic effects, and others to achieve the effects of comedy, romance, satire, or of some other *genre.* Each of these types in turn exhibits diverse plot-patterns, and may be represented in the mode either of drama or of narrative, and either in verse or in prose. The following terms, widely current in traditional criticism, are useful in distinguishing the component elements of plots and in helping to discriminate types of plots in both narrative and dramatic literature.

The chief character in a work, on whom our interest centers, is called the **protagonist** (or alternatively, the **hero** or **heroine**), and if he or she is pitted against an important opponent, that character is called the **antagonist.** Elizabeth Bennett is the protagonist, or heroine, of Jane Austen's *Pride and Prejudice* (1813); Hamlet is the protagonist and King Claudius the antagonist in Shakespeare's play, and the relation between them is one of **conflict.** If the antagonist is evil, or capable of cruel and criminal actions, he or she is called the **villain.** Many, but far from all, plots deal with a conflict; Thornton Wilder's play *Our Town* (1938), for example, does not. In addition to the conflict between individuals, there may be the conflict of a protagonist against fate, or against the circumstances that stand between him and a goal he has set himself; and in some works, the chief conflict is between opposing desires or values in the protagonist's own temperament.

A character in a work who, by sharp contrast, serves to stress and highlight the distinctive temperament of the protagonist is termed a **foil.** Thus Laertes the man of action is a foil to the dilatory Hamlet; the firebrand

Hotspur is a foil to the cool and calculating Prince Hal in Shakespeare's *Henry IV, 1;* and in *Pride and Prejudice,* the gentle and compliant Jane Bennett serves as a foil to her strong-willed sister Elizabeth. ("Foil" originally signified "leaf," and came to be applied to the thin sheet of bright metal placed under a jewel to enhance its brilliance.)

If a character initiates a scheme which depends for its success on the ignorance or gullibility of the person or persons against whom it is directed, it is called an **intrigue.** Iago is a villain who intrigues against Othello and Cassio in Shakespeare's tragedy *Othello.* A number of comedies, including Ben Jonson's *Volpone* (1607) and many *Restoration* plays (for example, William Congreve's *The Way of the World* and William Wycherley's *The Country Wife*), have plots which turn largely on the success or failure of an intrigue.

As a plot progresses it arouses expectations in the audience or reader about the future course of events and actions and how characters will respond to them. A lack of certainty, on the part of a concerned reader, about what is going to happen, especially to characters with whom the reader has established a bond of sympathy, is known as **suspense.** If what in fact happens violates any expectations we have formed, it is known as **surprise.** The interplay of suspense and surprise is a prime source of vitality in a traditional plot. The most effective surprise, especially in realistic narratives, is one which turns out, in retrospect, to have been grounded in what has gone before, even though we have hitherto made the wrong inference from the given facts of circumstance and character. As E. M. Forster put it, the shock of the unexpected, "followed by the feeling, 'oh, that's all right,' is a sign that all is well with the plot." A "surprise ending," in the pejorative sense, is one in which the author resolves the plot without adequate earlier grounds in characterization or events, often by the use of highly unlikely coincidence; there are numerous examples in the short stories of O. Henry. (For one type of manipulated ending, see *deus ex machina.*) *Dramatic irony* is a special kind of suspenseful expectation, when the audience or readers foresee the oncoming disaster or triumph but the character does not.

A plot is commonly said to have **unity of action** (or to be "an artistic whole") if it is apprehended by the reader or auditor as a complete and ordered structure of actions, directed toward the intended effect, in which none of the important component parts, or **incidents**, is nonfunctional; as Aristotle put this concept (*Poetics,* Sec. 8), all the parts are "so closely connected that the transposal or withdrawal of any one of them will disjoint and dislocate the whole." Aristotle claimed that it does not constitute a unified plot to present a series of episodes which are strung together simply because they happen to a single character. Many *picaresque narratives,* nevertheless, such as Daniel Defoe's *Moll Flanders* (1722), have held the interest of readers for centuries with such an *episodic* plot structure; while even so tightly integrated a plot as that of Henry Fielding's *Tom Jones* (1749) introduces, for variety's sake, a long digressive story by the Man of the Hill.

A successful later development which Aristotle did not foresee is the type of structural unity that can be achieved with **double plots**, familiar in *Elizabethan* drama. In this form, a **subplot**—a second story that is complete and interesting in its own right—is introduced into the play; when skillfully invented and managed, the subplot serves to broaden our perspective on the main plot and to enhance rather than diffuse the overall effect. The integral subplot may have the relation of analogy to the main plot (the Gloucester story in *King Lear*), or else of counterpoint against it (the comic subplot involving Falstaff in *Henry IV, 1*). Edmund Spenser's *The Faerie Queene* (1590–96) is an instance of a narrative romance which interweaves main plot and a multiplicity of subplots into an intricately interrelated structure, in a way that the critic C. S. Lewis compares to the **polyphonic** art of contemporary Elizabethan music, in which two or more diverse melodies are carried on simultaneously.

The order of a unified plot, Aristotle pointed out, is a continuous sequence of beginning, middle, and end. The **beginning** initiates the main action in a way which makes us look forward to something more; the **middle** presumes what has gone before and requires something to follow; and the **end** follows from what has gone before but requires nothing more; we are satisfied that the plot is complete. The structural beginning (sometimes also called the "initiating action," or "point of attack") need not be the initial stage of the action that is brought to a climax in the narrative or play. The epic, for example, plunges *in medias res* (see *epic*), many short stories begin at the point of the climax itself, and the writer of a drama often captures our attention in the opening scene with a representative incident, related to and closely preceding, the event which precipitates the central situation or conflict. Thus Shakespeare's *Romeo and Juliet* opens with a street fight between the servants of two great houses, and his *Hamlet* with the apparition of a ghost; the **exposition** of essential prior matters—the feud between the Capulets and Montagues, or the posture of affairs in the Royal House of Denmark—Shakespeare weaves rapidly and skillfully into the dialogue of these startling initial scenes. In the novel, the modern drama, and especially the motion picture, such exposition is sometimes managed by **flashbacks**: interpolated narratives or scenes (often justified, or *naturalized,* as a memory, a reverie, or a confession by one of the characters) which represent events that happened before the time at which the work opened. Arthur Miller's play *Death of a Salesman* (1949) and Ingmar Bergman's film *Wild Strawberries* make persistent and skillful use of this device.

The German critic Gustav Freytag, in *Technique of the Drama* (1863), introduced an analysis of plot that is known as **Freytag's Pyramid**. He described the typical plot of a five-act play as a pyramidal shape, consisting of a rising action, climax, and falling action. Although the total pattern that Freytag described applies only to a limited number of plays, various of his terms are frequently echoed by critics of prose fiction as well as drama. As applied to *Hamlet,* for example, the **rising action** (a section that Aristotle had called the **complication**) begins, after the opening scene and exposition, with the ghost's telling Hamlet that he has been murdered by his brother Claudius; it continues with the developing conflict between Hamlet and Claudius, in which Hamlet, despite setbacks, succeeds in controlling the course of events. The rising action reaches the **climax** of the hero's fortunes with his proof of the King's guilt by the device of the play within a play (III. ii). Then comes the **crisis**, the reversal or "turning point" of the fortunes of the protagonist, in his failure to kill the King while he is at prayer. This inaugurates the **falling action**; from now on the antagonist, Claudius, largely controls the course of events, until the **catastrophe**, or outcome, which is decided by the death of the hero, as well as of Claudius, the Queen, and Laertes. "Catastrophe" is usually applied to tragedy only; a more general term for this precipitating final scene, which is applied to both comedy and tragedy, is the **denouement** (French for "unknotting"): the action or intrigue ends in success or failure for the protagonist, the mystery is solved, or the misunderstanding cleared away. A frequently used alternative term for the outcome of a plot is the **resolution**.

In many plots the denouement involves a **reversal**, or in Aristotle's Greek term, **peripety**, in the protagonist's fortunes, whether to the protagonist's failure or destruction, as in tragedy, or success, as in comic plots. The reversal frequently depends on a **discovery** (in Aristotle's term, **anagnorisis**). This is the recognition by the protagonist of something of great importance hitherto unknown to him or to her: Cesario reveals to the Duke at the end of Shakespeare's *Twelfth Night* that he is really Viola; the fact of Iago's lying treachery dawns upon Othello; Fielding's Joseph Andrews, in his comic novel by that name (1742), discovers on the evidence of a birthmark—"as fine a strawberry as ever grew in a garden"—that he is in reality the son of Mr. and Mrs. Wilson.

Since the 1920s, a number of writers of prose fiction and drama have deliberately designed their works to frustrate the expectations that the reader or auditor has formed by habituation to traditional plots; some writers have even attempted to dispense altogether with a recognizable plot. (See, for example, literature of the *absurd, modernism and postmodernism, antinovel,* the *new novel.*) Also, various recent types of critical theory have altered radically many traditional concepts in the classification and analysis of plots. The *archetypal critic* Northrop Frye reduced all plots to four types that reflect the myths corresponding to the four seasons of the year. Structuralist critics, who conceive diverse plots as sets of alternative conventions and codes for constructing a fictional narrative, analyze and classify these conventional plot forms on the model of linguistic theory. (See *structuralist criticism* and *narratology,* and the discussion of plots in Jonathan Culler, *Structuralist Poetics,* 1975, pp. 205–24.) And some of the most recent critical theorists have undertaken to explode entirely the traditional treatments of plots, on the ground that any notion of the "unity" of a plot and of its "teleological" progress toward a resolution are illusory, or else that the resolution itself is only a facade to mask the irreconcilable conflicts and contradictions (whether psychological or social) that are the true components of any literary text. (See *poststructuralism.*)

See Aristotle, *Poetics;* E. M. Forster, *Aspects of the Novel* (1927); R. S. Crane, "The Concept of Plot and the Plot of *Tom Jones,*" in *Critics and Criticism* (1952); Wayne C. Booth, *The Rhetoric of Fiction* (1961); Elder Olson, *Tragedy and the Theory of Drama* (1966); Robert Scholes and Robert Kellogg, *The Nature of Narrative* (1966); Frank Kermode, *The Sense of an Ending: Studies in the Theory of Fiction* (1967); Eric S. Rabkin, *Narrative Suspense* (1974); Seymour Chatman, *Story and Discourse: Narrative Structure in Fiction and Film* (1980).

Poetic Diction. The term **diction** signifies the kinds of words, phrases, sentence structures, and figurative language that constitute any work of literature. A writer's diction can be analyzed under a great variety of categories, such as the degree to which the vocabulary and phrasing is abstract or concrete, Latin or Anglo-Saxon in origin, colloquial or formal, technical or common, literal or figurative.

The poetry of almost all ages has been written in a distinctive language, a "poetic diction," which includes words, phrasing, and figures not current in the ordinary discourse of the time. In modern discussion, however, the term **poetic diction** is applied especially to poets who, like Edmund Spenser in the Elizabethan age or G. M. Hopkins in the Victorian age, deliberately employed a diction which deviated markedly not only from common speech, but even from the writings of other poets of their era. And in a frequent use, "poetic diction" is applied to the poetry of a specific literary period, to denote the special style developed by *neoclassic* writers of the eighteenth century who, like Thomas Gray, believed that "the language of the age is never the language of poetry" (letter to West, 1742). This neoclassic poetic diction was in large part derived from the characteristic usage of admired earlier poets such as the Roman Virgil, Edmund Spenser, and John Milton, and was based on the reigning principle of *decorum,* according to which a poet must adapt the "level" and type of his diction to the mode and status of a particular genre (see *style*). Formal satire, such as Alexander Pope's *Epistle to Dr. Arbuthnot* (1735), because it represented a poet's direct commentary on everyday matters, permitted—indeed required—the use of language really spoken by urbane and cultivated people of the time. But the higher genres, such as epic, tragedy, and ode, required a refined and elevated poetic diction to raise the style to the level of the form, while pastoral and descriptive poems required the use of a special diction to make possible reference to what was considered their lowly materials, by investing these materials with a dignity and elegance appropriate to poetry.

Prominent characteristics of eighteenth-century poetic diction were its *archaism* and its use of recurrent *epithets;* its preference for resounding words derived from Latin ("refulgent," "irriguous," "umbrageous"); the frequent *invocations* to, and *personifications* of, abstractions and inanimate objects; and the persistent use of circumlocution, or **periphrasis,** to avoid what were perceived as low, technical, or commonplace terms through a roundabout substitute that was thought to be of higher dignity and decorum. Among the many periphrases in James Thomson's *The Seasons* (1726–30) are "the finny tribe" for "fish," "the bleating kind" for "sheep," and "from the snowy leg . . . the inverted silk she drew" instead of "she took off her silk stocking."

The following stanza from Thomas Gray's excellent period piece, "Ode on a Distant Prospect of Eton College" (1747), manifests all these devices of poetic diction. Contemporary readers took special pleasure in the ingenious periphrases by which Gray, to achieve the stylistic elevation appropriate to an ode, managed to describe schoolboys at play, but to evade the use of common, hence unpoetic, words such as "swim," "cage," "boys," "hoop," and "bat":

> Say, Father Thames, for thou hast seen
> Full many a sprightly race
> Disporting on thy margent green
> The paths of pleasure trace;
> Who foremost now delight to cleave
> With pliant arm thy glassy wave?
> The captive linnet which enthrall?
> What idle progeny succeed
> To chase the rolling circle's speed,
> Or urge the flying ball?

In William Wordsworth's famed attack on the neoclassic doctrine of a special language for poetry, in his Preface of 1800 to *Lyrical Ballads,* he claimed that there is no *"essential* difference between the language of prose and metrical composition"; decried the poetic diction of eighteenth-century writers as "artificial," "vicious," and "unnatural"; set up as the criterion for a valid poetic language that it be, not a matter of artful contrivance, but the "spontaneous overflow of powerful feelings"; and, by a drastic reversal of the class-hierarchy of linguistic decorum, claimed that the best model for the natural expression of feeling is not upper-class speech, but the speech of "humble and rustic life."

See Thomas Quayle, *Poetic Diction: A Study of Eighteenth-Century Verse* (1924); Geoffrey Tillotson, "Eighteenth-Century Poetic Diction" (1942), reprinted in *Eighteenth-Century English Literature,* ed. James L. Clifford (1959); J. Arthos, *The Language of Natural Description in Eighteenth-Century Poetry* (1949); M. H. Abrams, "Wordsworth and Coleridge on Diction and Figures," in *The Correspondent Breeze* (1984); and for a more general treatment of the diverse vocabularies of poets, Owen Barfield, *Poetic Diction* (rev., 1973).

Poetic Justice was a term coined by Thomas Rymer, an English critic of the later seventeenth century, to signify the distribution, at the end of a literary work, of earthly rewards and punishments in proportion to the virtue or vice of the various characters. Rymer's view was that a poem (in a sense that includes dramatic tragedy) is an ideal realm of its own, and should be governed by ideal principles of *decorum* and morality and not by the random way things often work out in the real world. No important critics or literary writers since Rymer's day have acceded, in any but a highly qualified way, to his recommendation of poetic justice; it would, for example, destroy the possibility of tragic suffering, which exceeds what the protagonist has deserved because of his *tragic flaw.*

See Introduction to *The Critical Works of Thomas Rymer,* ed. Curt A. Zimansky (1956); M. A. Quinlan, *Poetic Justice in the Drama* (1912).

Poetic License. John Dryden in the late seventeenth century defined poetic license as "the liberty which poets have assumed to themselves, in all ages, of speaking things in verse which are beyond the severity of prose." In its most common use the term is confined to *diction* alone, to justify the poet's departure from the rules and conventions of standard spoken and written prose in matters such as syntax, word order, the use of archaic or newly coined words, and the conventional use of *eye-rhymes* (wind-bind, daughter-laughter). The degree and kinds of linguistic freedom assumed by poets have varied according to the conventions of each age, but in every case the justification of the freedom lies in the success of the effect. The great opening sentence of Milton's *Paradise Lost* (1667), for example, departs radically, but with eminent success, from the colloquial language of his time in the choice and order of words, in idiom and figurative construction, and in syntax, to achieve a distinction of language and grandeur of announcement commensurate with Milton's high subject and the tradition of the epic form.

In a broader sense "poetic license" is applied not only to language, but to all the ways in which poets and other literary authors are held to be free to violate the ordinary norms both of common discourse and of literal truth, including the devices of meter and rhyme, the recourse to literary *conventions,* and the representation of fictional characters and events. A special case is **anachronism**—the placing of an event or person or thing outside of its historical era. Shakespeare described his Cleopatra as wearing Elizabethan corsets; and in *Julius Caesar,* which is set in ancient Rome, he introduced a clock that strikes the hour. Another instance is the poet's departure from geographical or historical fact, whether from ignorance or design. It need not diminish our enjoyment of the work that Shakespeare attributed a seacoast to landlocked Bohemia in *The Winter's Tale,* or that Keats, in writing "On First Looking into Chapman's Homer" (1816), mistakenly made Cortez instead of Balboa the discoverer of the Pacific Ocean.

See Geoffrey N. Leech, *A Linguistic Guide to English Poetry* (1969), Chapter 3, "Varieties of Poetic License."

Point of View signifies the way a story gets told—the mode (or modes) established by an author by means of which the reader is presented with the characters, dialogue, actions, setting, and events which constitute the *narrative* in a work of fiction. The question of point of view has always been a practical concern of the novelist, and there have been scattered observations on the matter in critical writings since the emergence of the modern novel in the eighteenth century. Henry James' Prefaces to his various novels, however—collected as *The Art of the Novel* in 1934—and Percy Lubbock's *The Craft of Fiction* (1926), which codified and expanded upon James' comments, made point of view one of the most prominent and persistent concerns in modern treatments of the art of prose fiction.

Authors have developed many different ways to present a story, and many single works exhibit a diversity of methods. The simplified classification below, however, is widely recognized and can serve as a preliminary frame of reference for analyzing traditional types of narration and for determining the predominant type in mixed narrative modes. It establishes a broad division between third-person and first-person narratives, then divides third-person narratives into subclasses according to the degree and kind of freedom or limitation which the author assumes in getting the story across to the reader. In a **third-person narrative**, the **narrator** is someone outside the story proper who refers to all the characters in the story by name, or as "he," "she," "they." Thus Henry Fielding's narrator begins *Tom Jones* (1749): "In that part of the western division of this kingdom which is commonly called Somersetshire, there lately lived, and perhaps still lives, a gentleman whose name was Allworthy. . . ." In a **first-person narrative**, the narrator speaks as "I," and is himself to a greater or lesser degree a participant in the story. J. D. Salinger's *The Catcher in the Rye* (1951) begins: "If you really want to hear about it, the first thing you'll really want to know is where I was born, and what my lousy childhood was like, and how my parents were occupied and all before they had me, and all that David Copperfield kind of crap. . . ."

I   Third-person points of view:

1)   The **omniscient point of view.** This is a common term for the large and varied works of fiction written in accord with the *convention* that the narrator knows everything that needs to be known about the agents, actions, and events, and also has privileged access to the characters' thoughts, feelings, and motives; and that the narrator is free to move at will in time and place, to shift from character to character, and to report (or conceal) their speech, doings, and states of consciousness.

Within this mode, the **intrusive narrator** is one who not only reports, but also comments on and evaluates the actions and motives of the characters, and sometimes expresses personal views about human life in general. Most works are written in the convention that the omniscient narrator's reports and judgments are to be taken as authoritative by the reader, and so serve to establish what counts as the facts and values within the fictional world. This is the fashion in which many of the greatest novelists have written, including Fielding, Jane Austen, Charles Dickens, William Makepeace Thackeray, George Eliot, Thomas Hardy, Fyodor Dostoevsky, and Leo Tolstoy. (In Fielding's *Tom Jones* and Tolstoy's *War and Peace,* 1863–69, the intrusive narrator goes so far as to interpolate essays suggested by the subject matter of the novels.) On the other hand, the omniscient narrator may choose to be **unintrusive** (alternative terms are **impersonal** or **objective**). Flaubert in *Madame Bovary* (1857), for example, for the most part describes, reports, or "shows" the action in dramatic scenes without introducing his own comments or judgments. More radical instances of the unintrusive narrator, who gives up even the privilege of access to inner feelings and motives, are to be found in a number of Ernest Hemingway's short stories; for example, "The Killers," and "A Clean, Well-Lighted Place." (See *showing and telling,* under *character.*) For an extreme use of impersonal representation, see the comment on Robbe-Grillet's *Jealousy,* under *novel.*

Gérard Genette subtilized in various ways the analysis of third-person point of view. For example, he distinguishes between **focus of narration** (the teller of the story) and **focus of character** (who perceives what is told us in any part of the story). Both the focus of narration and the focus of character (that is, of perception) in a single story may shift rapidly from the narrator to a character in the story, and from one character to another. Hemingway's "The Short and Happy Life of Francis Macomber," for example, is a third-person narrative in which the focus of perception is, in various passages, the narrator, the hunter Wilson, Mrs. Macomber, Mr. Macomber, and even, briefly, the hunted lion. See Gérard Genette, *Narrative Discourse: An Essay in Method* (1972, trans. 1980).

2) The **limited point of view.** The narrator tells the story in the third person, but stays inside the confines of what is experienced, thought, and felt by a single character (or at most by very few characters) within the story. Henry James, who refined this narrative mode, described such a selected character as his "focus," or "mirror," or "center of consciousness." In a number of James' later works all the events and actions are represented as they unfold before, and filter to the reader through, the particular perceptions and awareness of one of his characters; for example, Strether in *The Ambassadors* (1903) or Maisie in *What Maisie Knew* (1897). A short and artfully sustained example of this limited narration is Katherine Mansfield's story "Bliss" (1920).

Later writers developed this technique into *stream-of-consciousness* narration, in which we are presented with outer observations only as they impinge on the continuous current of thought, memory, feelings, and associations which constitute an observer's total awareness. The limitation of point of view represented both by James' "center of consciousness" narration and by the "stream-of-consciousness" narration sometimes used by James Joyce, Virginia Woolf, William Faulkner, and others, is often said to exemplify the "self-effacing author," or "objective narration," more effectively than does the use of an unintrusive but omniscient narrator. In the latter instance, it is said, the reader remains aware that someone, or some outside voice, is telling us about what is going on; the alternative mode, in which the point of view is limited to the consciousness of a character within the story itself, gives readers the illusion of experiencing events that evolve before their own eyes. For a revealing analysis, however, of the way even an author who restricts the narrative center of consciousness to a single character nonetheless communicates authorial judgments on people and events, and also controls the judgments of the reader, see Ian Watt, "The First Paragraph of *The Ambassadors;* An Explication," reprinted in James' *The Ambassadors,* ed. S. P. Rosenbaum (1964). See also *persona, tone, and voice,* above.

II   **First-person points of view:**

This mode, insofar as it is consistently carried out, limits the matter of the narrative to what the first-person narrator knows, experiences, infers, or can find out by talking to other characters. We distinguish between the narrative "I" who is only a fortuitous witness and auditor of the matters he relates (Marlow in *Heart of Darkness* and other works by Joseph Conrad); or who is a participant, but only a minor or peripheral one, in the story (Ishmael in Herman Melville's *Moby-Dick,* Nick in F. Scott Fitzgerald's *The*

Great Gatsby); or who is himself or herself the central character in the story (Daniel Defoe's *Moll Flanders,* Charles Dickens' *Great Expectations,* Mark Twain's *The Adventures of Huckleberry Finn,* J. D. Salinger's *The Catcher in the Rye*). For a special type of first-person narrative, see *epistolary novel.*

Two other frequently discussed narrative tactics, relevant to a consideration of points of view, need to be mentioned:

The **self-conscious narrator** shatters any illusion that he or she is telling something that has actually happened by revealing to the reader that the narration is a work of fictional art, or by flaunting the discrepancies between its patent fictionality and the reality it seems to represent. This can be done either seriously (Henry Fielding's narrator in *Tom Jones* and Marcel in Marcel Proust's *Remembrance of Things Past,* 1913–27) or for primarily comic purposes (Tristram in Laurence Sterne's *Tristram Shandy,* 1759–67, and the narrator of Lord Byron's versified *Don Juan,* 1819–24), or for purposes which are both serious and comic (Thomas Carlyle's *Sartor Resartus,* 1833–34). See Robert Alter, *Partial Magic: The Novel as a Self-Conscious Genre* (1975), and refer to *romantic irony.*

One variety of self-conscious narrative exploited in recent prose fiction is called the **self-reflexive novel,** or the *involuted novel,* which incorporates into its narration reference to the process of composing the fictional story itself. An early modern version, André Gide's *The Counterfeiters* (1926), is also one of the most intricate. As Harry Levin summarized its self-involution: it is "the diary of a novelist who is writing a novel [to be called *The Counterfeiters*] about a novelist who is keeping a diary about the novel he is writing"; the nest of Chinese boxes was further multiplied by Gide's publication, also in 1926, of his own *Journal of The Counterfeiters,* kept while he was composing the novel. Vladimir Nabokov is an ingenious exploiter of involuted fiction; for example, in *Pale Fire* (1962). See *metafiction.*

The **fallible** or **unreliable narrator** is one whose perception, interpretation, and evaluation of the matters he or she narrates do not coincide with the implicit opinions and norms manifested by the author, which the author expects the alert reader to share. Henry James made repeated use of the narrator whose excessive innocence, or oversophistication, or moral obtuseness, makes him a flawed and distorting "center of consciousness" in the work; the result is an elaborate structure of ironies. (See *irony.*) Examples of James' use of a fallible narrator are his short stories "The Aspern Papers" and "The Liar." *The Sacred Fount* and *The Turn of the Screw* are works by James in which, according to some critics, the clues for correcting the views of the fallible narrator are inadequate, so that what we are meant to take as factual within the story, and the evaluations intended by the author, remain problematic. See, for example, the remarkably diverse critical interpretations collected in *A Casebook on Henry James' "The Turn of the Screw,"* ed. Gerald Willen (1960), and in *The Turn of the Screw,* ed. Robert Kimbrough (1966). The critic Tzvetan Todorov, on the other hand, has classified *The Turn of the Screw* as an instance of **fantastic literature,** which he defines as deliberately designed by the author to leave the reader in a state of uncertainty whether the events are to be explained by reference to natural or to supernatural causes. (*The Fantastic: A Structural Approach to a Literary Genre,* trans. Richard Howard, 1973.)

A recently developed "grammar of narration"—that is, the analysis of grammatical usages that deviate from those in ordinary discourse but are characteristic of fictional narratives—impinges on critical treatments of point of view, but from a different analytic perspective. The systematic study of such phenomena was begun by Kate Hamburger in *The Logic of Literature* (1957, trans. 1973). One focus of grammatical analysis is the special play of **deictics**—that is, of words such as "now," "then," "here," "there," "today," "last month," personal pronouns and certain tenses of verbs—whose reference depends on the particular speaker and his or her position in place and time. In many narratives, usually in a way not noticed by the reader, the references of such terms constantly shift or merge, as the narration moves from the narrator, by whom the events are told in the past tense (e.g., then and there), to a character in the narration, for whom the action is present (e.g., here and now). Another notable grammatical usage has been called **free indirect discourse** (equivalent to the French "style indirect libre"), or "represented speech and thought." These terms refer to the way, in many narratives, that the reports of what a character says and thinks shift in pronouns, adverbs, tense, and grammatical mode, as we move—or sometimes hover—between the direct narrated reproductions of these events as they occur to the character and the indirect representation of such events by the narrator. Thus, a direct representation, "He thought, 'I will see her home now, and may then stop at my mother's,'" might shift, in an indirect representation, to: "He would see her home then, and might afterward stop at his mother's." Refer to *narrative and narratology,* above; and see Roy Pascal, *The Dual Voice: Free Indirect Speech and Its Functioning in the Nineteenth-Century European Novel* (1977); Dorrit Cohn, *Transparent Minds: Narrative Modes for Presenting Consciousness in Fiction* (1978); Ann Banfield, *Unspeakable Sentences: Narration and Representation in the Language of Fiction* (1982).

Drastic experimentation in recent prose fiction has complicated in many ways traditional renderings of point of view; see *fiction* and *persona, tone, and voice.* On point of view, in addition to the writings mentioned above, refer to Norman Friedman, "Point of View in Fiction," *PMLA* 70 (1955); Leon Edel, *The Modern Psychological Novel* (rev., 1964), Chapters 3–4; Wayne C. Booth, *The Rhetoric of Fiction* (1961); Franz Stanzel, *A Theory of Narrative* (1979, trans. 1984); Susan Lanser, *The Narrative Act: Point of View in Fiction* (1982); Wallace Martin, *Recent Theories of Narrative* (1986).

Primitivism and Progress. A **primitivist** is someone who prefers what is "natural" (in the sense of that which exists prior to or independently of human culture, reasoning, and contrivance) to what is "artificial" (in the sense of what human beings achieve by thought, activities, laws and conventions, and the complex arrangements of a civilized society). A useful, although not mutually exclusive, distinction has been made between two manifestations of primitivism:

1) **Cultural primitivism** is the preference of what is conceived to be "nature" and "the natural" over "art" and "the artificial" in any area of human culture and values. For example, in ethics a primitivist lauds the "natural" (that is, the innate) instincts and passions over the dictates of reason and prudential forethought; in social philosophy, the ideal is the simple and "natural" forms of social and political order in place of the anxieties and frustrations engendered by a complex and highly developed social organization; in milieu, a primitivist prefers outdoor "nature," unmodified by human intervention, to cities or artful gardens; and in literature and the other arts, the primitivist lauds spontaneity, the free expression of emotion, and the intuitive products of "natural genius," as against a reasoned adaptation of artistic means to foreseen ends and a conformity to "artificial" forms, rules, and conventions. Typically, the cultural primitivist asserts that in the modern world, the life, activities, and products of "primitive" people—who are considered to live in a way more accordant to "nature" because they are isolated from civilization—are at least in some ways preferable to the life, activities, and products of people living in a highly developed society, especially in cities. The eighteenth-century cult of the **Noble Savage**—who is conceived to be "naturally" intelligent, moral, and possessed of high dignity in thought and deed—and the concurrent vogue of "natural" poetry written by supposedly uneducated peasants or working folk, were both aspects of primitivism. Cultural primitivism has played a prominent and persistent role in American thought and literature, where the "new world" was early interpreted in terms both of the *golden age* of the distant past and the Christian millennium of the future, the American Indian was sometimes identified with the legendary Noble Savage, and the American pioneer was often represented as a new Adam who had cut free from the artifice and corruptions of European civilization in order to reassume a "natural" life of freedom, innocence, and simplicity. See Henry Nash Smith, *Virgin Land* (1950), and R. W. B. Lewis, *The American Adam* (1955).

2) **Chronological primitivism** signifies the belief that the ideal era of humanity's way of life lies in the very distant past, when men and women lived naturally, simply, and freely, and that the process of history has been a gradual "decline" from that happy stage into an increasing degree of artifice, complexity, inhibitions, prohibitions, and consequent anxieties and discontents in the psychological, social, and cultural order. In its extreme form, this ideal era is postulated as having existed in "the state of nature," before society and civilization had even begun; more commonly, it is placed at some later stage of development, and sometimes as late as the era of classical Greece. Many, but not all, cultural primitivists are also chronological primitivists.

A historical concept that is antithetic to chronological primitivism emerged in the seventeenth century and reached its height in the nineteenth century. This is the idea of **progress**: the doctrine that, by virtue of the development and exploitation of art, science and technology, and wisdom, the course of history represents an overall improvement in the life, morality, and happiness of human beings from early barbarity to the present stage of civilization; sometimes it is also claimed that this historical progress of humanity will continue indefinitely—possibly to end in a final stage of social, rational, and moral perfection. (See *Enlightenment.*)

Primitivism is as old as humanity's recorded thought and imaginings, and is reflected in the myths of a vanished age of gold and a lost Garden of Eden. It achieved a special vogue, however, in the eighteenth century, by way of reaction to the prevailing stress on artfulness and high civilization during the *Neoclassic Period,* in a European movement in which Jean-Jacques Rousseau (1712–78) was a central figure. D. H. Lawrence (1885–1930) is a recent example of a broadly primitivistic thinker, in his laudation of the spontaneous instinctual life, his belief in an ancient, vanished condition of humanity's personal and social wholeness, his resort to "primitive" modes of life that survive outside the bounds of sophisticated societies, and his attacks on the disintegrative effects of modern science and technology and the economy and culture these developments have generated. There are obvious strains of primitivism in the outlook and life-style of "hippie" and related subcultures in our time, and in the establishment of communes whose ideal is a radically simplified individual and social life close to the soil. But most men and women, and many writers of literature, are primitivists in some moods, longing to escape from the complexities, fever, anxieties, and "alienation" of modern civilization into the elemental simplicities of a lost natural life. That imagined life may be identified with the individual's own childhood, or with the prehistoric or classical or medieval past, or be conceived as existing still in some primitive, carefree, faraway place on earth.

See H. N. Fairchild, *The Noble Savage* (1928); J. B. Bury, *The Idea of Progress* (1932); Lois Whitney, *Primitivism and Ideas of Progress* (1934); A. O. Lovejoy and George Boas, *Primitivism and Related Ideas in Antiquity* (1948); A. O. Lovejoy, *Essays in the History of Ideas* (1948). Friedrich Nietzsche's *The Genealogy of Morals* (1887) and Sigmund Freud's *Civilization and Its Discontents* (1949—see *psychoanalysis*) involve aspects of cultural primitivism, in their stress on the compelling needs of the body and of the elemental human instincts, especially sexuality, which require a complex and perhaps impossible reconciliation with the repressions and inhibitions that are inescapable in a civilized society. A recent work of radical cultural primitivism is Norman O. Brown's *Life Against Death* (1959).

Problem Play. A type of drama which was popularized by the great Norwegian playwright Henrik Ibsen. In problem plays, the situation faced by the protagonist is presented by the author as a representative instance of a contemporary social problem; often the dramatist manages—by the use of a character who speaks for the author, or by the evolution of the plot, or both—to propose a solution to the problem which is at odds with prevailing opinion. The problematic issue may be the inadequate autonomy, scope, and dignity allotted to women in the middle-class nineteenth-century family (Henrik Ibsen's *A Doll's House,* 1879); or the morality of prostitution, regarded as a typical product of the economic arrangements in a capitalist society (George Bernard Shaw's *Mrs. Warren's Profession,* 1898); or the crisis in racial and ethnic relations in present-day America (in numerous current dramas and films). Compare *social novel*.

In a specialized application, the term **problem plays** is sometimes applied to a group of Shakespeare's plays, also called "bitter comedies"— especially *Troilus and Cressida, Measure for Measure,* and *All's Well That Ends Well*—which explore dark and ignoble aspects of human nature, and in which the resolution of the plot seems to many readers to be problematic, in that it does not settle or solve, except superficially, the moral problems raised in the play. See A. P. Rossiter, "The Problem Plays," in *Shakespeare: Modern Essays in Criticism,* ed. Leonard F. Dean (rev., 1967); and Robert M. Adams, *Shakespeare—The Four Romances* (1989).

A subtype of the modern problem play is the **discussion play**, in which the social issue is not incorporated into a plot but expounded in the give and take of a sustained debate among the characters. See Shaw's *Getting Married,* and Act III of his *Man and Superman;* also his book on Ibsen's plays, *The Quintessence of Ibsenism* (1891).

Prose is an inclusive term for all discourse, spoken or written, which is not patterned into the lines and rhythms either of metric verse or of free verse. (See *meter.*) It is possible, however, to discriminate a great variety of non-metric types of language, which can be placed along a spectrum according to the degree to which they exploit, and make prominent, modes of formal organization. At one end is the irregular, and only occasionally formal, prose of ordinary discourse. Distinguished written discourse, in what John Dryden called "that other harmony of prose," is no less an art than distinguished verse; in all literatures, in fact, artfully written prose seems to have developed later than written verse. As written prose gets more "literary"—whether its function is descriptive, expository, narrative, or expressive—it exhibits more patent, though highly diverse, modes of rhythm and other formal features. The prose translations of the poetic books of the Old Testament in the King James Bible, for example, have a repetition, balance, and contrast of clauses which approximate the form that in the nineteenth century was named the **prose poem**: densely compact, pronouncedly rhythmic, and highly sonorous compositions which are written as a continuous sequence of sentences without line breaks. Examples of prose poems are, in French, Charles Baudelaire's *Little Poems in Prose* (1869) and Arthur Rimbaud's *Illuminations* (1886), and in English, excerptible passages in Walter Pater's prose essays, such as his famous meditation on Leonardo da Vinci's painting the *Mona Lisa,* in *The Renaissance* (1873). Farther along the formal spectrum comes the interruption of the continuity of prose by line breaks and the controlled rhythms, pauses, syntactical suspensions, and cadences in *free verse*. At the far end of the spectrum we get the regular, recurrent units of weaker and stronger stressed syllables that constitute the meters of English verse.

See *style,* and for a special form of elaborately formal prose, *euphuism.* Refer to George Saintsbury, *A History of English Prose Rhythm* (1912); M. Boulton, *Anatomy of Prose* (1954); George L. Trager and Henry Lee Smith, Jr., *An Outline of English Structure* (1951). E. D. Hirsch discusses the development of English prose in *The Philosophy of Composition* (1977), pp. 51–72. Refer also to the list of readings under *style*. On the prose poem, see Jonathan Monroe, *A Poverty of Objects: The Prose Poem and the Politics of Genre* (1987).

Prosody signifies the systematic study of **versification** in poetry; that is, a study of the principles and practice of *meter, rhyme,* and *stanza* forms. Sometimes the term "prosody" is extended to include also the study of sound patterns and effects such as *alliteration, assonance, euphony,* and *onomatopoeia.*

Pun. A play on words that are either identical in sound (**homonyms**) or very similar in sound, but are sharply diverse in meaning. Puns have had serious literary uses. The authority of the Pope in Roman Catholicism goes back to the Greek pun uttered by Christ in Matthew 16:18, "Thou art Peter [Petros] and upon this rock [petra] I will build my church." Shakespeare and other writers used puns seriously, as well as for comic purposes. In *Romeo and Juliet* (III. i. 101) Mercutio, bleeding to death, says grimly, "Ask for me tomorrow and you shall find me a grave man"; and John Donne's solemn "Hymn to God the Father" (1633) puns throughout on his own name and the verb "done." In the eighteenth century and thereafter, however, the literary use of the pun has been almost exclusively comic. A great exception is James Joyce's *Finnegans Wake* (1939), which exploits puns throughout in order to help sustain its complex effect, at once serious and comic, of multiple levels of meaning; see *portmanteau word.*

A special type of pun, known as the **equivoque**, is the use of a single word or phrase which has two disparate meanings, in a context which makes both meanings equally relevant. An example is the epitaph suggested for a bank teller:

> He checked his cash, cashed in his checks,
> And left his window. Who is next?

Purple Patch. A translation of Horace's Latin phrase "purpureus . . . pannus" in his versified *Ars Poetica* (first century B.C.). It signifies a marked heightening of style in rhythm, diction, and figurative language that makes a section of verse or prose—especially a descriptive passage—stand out from its context. The term is sometimes applied without derogation to a set piece, separable and quotable, in which an author rises to an occasion. An example is the eulogy of England by the dying John of Gaunt in Shakespeare's *Richard II* (II. i. 40 ff.), beginning

> This royal throne of kings, this scept'red isle,
> This earth of majesty, this seat of Mars,
> This other Eden, demi-paradise. . . .

Other well-known examples are Lord Byron's depiction of the Duchess of Richmond's ball on the eve of Waterloo in *Childe Harold's Pilgrimage,* Canto III, xxi–xxviii (1816), and Walter Pater's prose description of the *Mona Lisa* in his essay on Leonardo da Vinci in *The Renaissance* (1873). Usually, however, "purple passage" connotes disparagement, implying that an author has self-consciously girded himself to perform a piece of fine writing.

Realism and Naturalism. Realism is applied by literary critics in two diverse ways: (1) to identify a nineteenth-century movement in the writing of novels that included Honoré de Balzac in France, George Eliot in England, and William Dean Howells in America (see *realistic novel*), and (2) to designate a recurrent mode, in various eras and literary forms, of representing human life and experience in literature.

Realistic fiction is often opposed to romantic fiction. The *romance* is said to present life as we would have it be—more picturesque, fantastic, adventurous, or heroic than actuality; realism, on the other hand, is said to represent life as it really is. This distinction in terms of subject matter, while relevant, is clearly inadequate. Casanova, T. E. Lawrence, and Winston Churchill were people in real life, but their biographies demonstrate that truth can be stranger than literary realism. It is more useful to identify realism in terms of the effect on the reader: realistic fiction is written so as to give the effect that it represents life and the social world as it seems to the common reader, evoking the sense that its characters might in fact exist, and that such things might well happen. To achieve such effects, the novelists we identify as realists may or may not be selective in subject matter—although most of them prefer the commonplace and the everyday over rarer aspects of life—but they must render their materials in ways that make them seem to their readers the very stuff of ordinary experience. For example, Daniel Defoe in the early eighteenth century dealt with the extraordinary adventures of a shipwrecked mariner named Robinson Crusoe and with the extraordinary misadventures of a woman named Moll Flanders; but he made his novels seem to readers a mirror held up to reality by his reportorial manner of rendering all the events, whether ordinary or extraordinary, in the same circumstantial, matter-of-fact, and seemingly unselective way. Both the fictions of Franz Kafka and the present-day novels of *magic realism* achieve their effects in large part by exploiting a realistic manner in rendering events that are in themselves fantastic, absurd, or impossible.

Russian *formalists,* followed more systematically by *structuralist critics,* proposed that both the selection of subject matter and the techniques of rendering in a realistic novel depend on their accordance with literary *conventions* and codes which the reader has learned to interpret, or *naturalize,* in a way that makes the text seem a reflection of everyday reality. (See Roland Barthes, "The Reality Effect," in *French Literary Theory Today,* ed. Tzvetan Todorov, 1982, and Jonathan Culler, *Structuralist Poetics,* 1975, Chapter 7, "Convention and Naturalization.") Some theorists draw the conclusion that, since all literary representations are constituted by arbitrary conventions, there is no valid ground for holding any one kind of fiction to be more realistic than any other. It is, however, a matter of common experience that some novels indeed have the effect of representing the ordinary course of events. Skepticism about the possibility of fictional realism is not an empirical doctrine which is based on widespread experience in reading literature, but a metaphysical doctrine that denies the existence of any reality that is independent of altering human conventions and cultural formations. (For philosophical discussions of conventionality and reality, see the essays by Hilary Putnam, Nelson Goodman, and Menachem Brinker in *New Literary History,* Vol. 13, 1981, and Vol. 14, 1983.)

Naturalism is sometimes claimed to give an even more accurate depiction of life than is realism. But naturalism is not only, like realism, a special selection of subject matter and a special way of rendering those materials; it is distinctively a mode of fiction that was developed by a school of writers in accordance with a particular philosophical thesis. This thesis, a product of post-Darwinian biology in the nineteenth century, held that a human being exists entirely in the order of nature and does not have a soul nor any mode of participating in a religious or spiritual world beyond nature; and therefore, that such a being is merely a higher-order animal whose character and behavior are entirely determined by two kinds of forces, heredity and environment. A person inherits compulsive instincts—especially hunger, the accumulative drive, and sexuality—and is then subject to the social and economic forces in the family, the class, and the milieu into which that person is born. The French novelist Émile Zola, beginning in the 1870s, did much to develop this theory in what he called "le roman expérimental" (that is, the novel organized in the mode of a scientific experiment on the behavior of the characters it depicts). Zola and later naturalistic writers, such as the Americans Frank Norris, Stephen Crane, and Theodore Dreiser, try to present their subjects with scientific objectivity and with elaborate documentation, sometimes including an almost medical frankness about activities and bodily functions usually unmentioned in earlier literature. They tend to choose characters who exhibit strong animal drives such as greed and sexual desire, and who are victims both of glandular secretions within and of sociological pressures without. The end of the naturalistic novel is usually "tragic," but not, as in classical and Elizabethan *tragedy,* because of a heroic but losing struggle of the individual mind and will against gods, enemies, and circumstances. Instead the protagonist of the naturalistic plot, a pawn to multiple compulsions, usually disintegrates, or is wiped out.

Aspects of the naturalistic selection and management of subject matter and its austere or harsh manner of rendering its materials are apparent in many modern novels and dramas, such as Hardy's *Jude the Obscure,* 1895 (although Hardy largely substituted a cosmic determinism for biological and environmental determinism), various plays by Eugene O'Neill in the 1920s, and Norman Mailer's novel of World War II, *The Naked and the Dead.* An enlightening exercise is to distinguish how the relation between the sexes is represented in a romance (Richard Blackmore's *Lorna Doone,* 1869), an ironic comedy of manners (Jane Austen's *Pride and Prejudice,* 1813), a realistic novel (William Dean Howells' *A Modern Instance,* 1882), and a naturalistic novel (Émile Zola's *Nana,* 1880, or Theodore Dreiser's *An American Tragedy,* 1925). Movements originally opposed both to nineteenth-century realism and naturalism (though some modern works, such as Joyce's *Ulysses,* 1922, combine aspects of all these novelistic modes) are *expressionism* and *symbolism* (see *Symbolist Movement*).

Socialist Realism was a term used by Marxist critics for novels which they held to embody or "reflect" characters and events that accord with the Marxist view that the struggle between economic classes is the essential dynamic of society. After the 1930s, and until the recent past, "Socialist Realism" was the official doctrine governing the literary writings of authors in the former Soviet Union. In its crude version, it was a term of approbation applied mainly to novels which adhere to the Communist party line and emphasize the oppressions by bourgeois capitalists, the virtues of the proletariat, and the felicities of life under Soviet Socialism. A flexible Marxist such as Georg Lukács, however, employed complex criteria of narrative realism to laud the traditional classics of European realistic fiction. See *Marxist criticism,* and refer to Georg Lukács, *Studies in European Realism* (trans. 1964); Marc Slonim, *Soviet Russian Literature* (1967), and George Bisztray, *Marxist Models of Literary Realism* (1978).

On realism: Erich Auerbach, *Mimesis: The Representation of Reality in Western Literature* (1953); Ernst Gombrich, *Art and Illusion* (1960); Harry Levin, *The Gates of Horn: A Study of Five French Realists* (1963); René Wellek, "The Concept of Realism in Literary Scholarship," in *Concepts of Criticism* (1963); J. P. Stern, *On Realism* (1973); Ivan Williams, *The Realist Novel in England* (1975); George Levine, *The Realistic Imagination* (1981).

Refrain. A line, or part of a line, or a group of lines, which is repeated in the course of a poem, sometimes with slight changes, and usually at the end of each stanza. The refrain occurs in many ballads and work poems, and is a frequent element in Elizabethan songs, where it may be merely a non-verbal carrier of the melodic line, as in Shakespeare's "It Was a Lover and His Lass": "With a hey, and a ho, and a hey nonino." A famous refrain is that which closes each stanza in Edmund Spenser's "Epithalamion" (1594)—"The woods shall to me answer, and my echo ring"—in which sequential changes indicate the altering sounds during the successive hours of the poet's wedding day. The refrain in Spenser's "Prothalamion"—"Sweet Thames, run softly, till I end my song"—is echoed ironically in Part III of T. S. Eliot's *The Waste Land* (1922), where it is applied to the Thames in the modern age of polluted rivers.

A refrain may consist only of a single word—"Nevermore" as in Poe's "The Raven" (1845)—or of an entire stanza. If the stanza-refrain occurs in a song, as a section to be sung by all the auditors, it is called the **chorus;** for example, in "Auld Lang Syne" and many other songs by Robert Burns in the late eighteenth century.

Renaissance ("rebirth") is the name commonly applied to the period of European history following the Middle Ages; it is usually said to have begun in Italy in the late fourteenth century and to have continued, both in Italy and other countries of western Europe, through the fifteenth and sixteenth centuries. In this period the European arts of painting, sculpture, architecture, and literature reached an eminence not exceeded in any age. The development came late to England in the sixteenth century, and did not have its flowering until the *Elizabethan* and *Jacobean* periods; sometimes, in fact, John Milton (1608–74) is described as the last great Renaissance poet.

Many attempts have been made to define "the Renaissance" in a brief assertion, as though a single essence underlay the complex features of the intellectual and cultural life of numerous countries over several hundred years. It has, for example, been described as the birth of the modern world out of the ashes of the Dark Ages; as the discovery of the world and the discovery of man; and as the era of untrammeled individualism in life, thought, religion, and art. Recently some historians, finding that attributes similar to these were present in various people and places in the Middle Ages, and also that many elements long held to be medieval survived into the Renaissance, have denied that the Renaissance ever existed. This skeptical opinion serves as a reminder that history is a continuous process, and that "periods" are not given by history but invented by historians. Nonetheless, the division of the temporal continuum into named segments is an all but indispensable convenience in discussing history. Furthermore, during the span of time called "the Renaissance," it is possible to identify a number of events and discoveries which, beginning approximately in the fifteenth century, clearly effected radical and distinctive changes in the beliefs, productions, and manner of life of many people, especially in the upper and the intellectual classes.

All these occurrences may be regarded as putting a strain on the relatively closed and stable world of the great civilization of the later Middle Ages, when most of the essential and permanent truths about God, man, and the universe were considered to be adequately known. The full impact of many developments in the Renaissance did not make itself felt until the Enlightenment in the later seventeenth and the eighteenth centuries, but the fact that they occurred in this period indicates the vitality, the audacity, and the restless curiosity of many men of the era, whether scholars, thinkers, artists, or adventurers. Prominent among these developments were:

1) The new learning. Renaissance scholars of the classics, called *humanists,* revived the knowledge of the Greek language, discovered and disseminated a great number of Greek manuscripts, and added considerably to the number of Roman authors and works which had been known to the Middle Ages. The result was to open out the sense of the vastness of the historical past, as well as to enlarge immensely the stock of ideas, materials, literary forms, and styles available to Renaissance writers. In the mid-fifteenth century the invention of printing on paper from movable type made books for the first time cheap and plentiful, and floods of publications, ancient and modern, poured from the presses of Europe to satisfy the demands of the expanding population who had learned to read. The rapidity of the spread of ideas, discoveries, and types of literature in the Renaissance was made possible by this new technology of printing.

The humanistic revival sometimes resulted in pedantic scholarship, sterile imitations of ancient works and styles, and a rigidly authoritarian rhetoric and literary criticism. It also bred, however, the gracious and tolerant humanity of an Erasmus, and the high concept of a cultivated Renaissance aristocracy expressed in Baldassare Castiglione's *Il Cortegiano* ("The Courtier"), published in 1528. This was the most admired and widely translated of the many Renaissance **courtesy books**, or books on the character, obligations, and training of the man of the court. It sets up the ideal of the completely rounded or "universal" man, developed in all his faculties and skills, physical, intellectual, and artistic. He is especially trained to be a warrior and statesman, but is capable also as athlete, philosopher, artist, conversationist, and man of society. The courtier's relations to women, and of women to men, are represented in accordance with the quasi-religious code of *Platonic love,* and his activities and productions are crowned by the grace of **sprezzatura**—the Italian term for what seems the casual ease with which someone has been schooled to meet the demands of very complex and exacting rules. Leonardo da Vinci in Italy and Sir Philip Sidney in England are often represented as embodying the many aspects of the courtly ideal.

2) The new religion. The **Reformation** led by Martin Luther (1483–1546) was a successful heresy which struck at the very foundations of the institutionalism of the Roman Catholic Church. This early Protestantism was grounded on each individual's inner experience of spiritual struggle and salvation. Faith (based on the word of the Bible) was alone thought competent to save, and salvation itself was regarded as a direct transaction with God in the theater of the individual soul, without the necessity of intermediation by Church, priest, or sacrament. For this reason Protestantism is sometimes said to have been an extreme manifestation of "Renaissance individualism" in northern Europe; it soon, however, developed its own type of institutionalism in the theocracy proposed by John Calvin (1509–64) and his Puritan followers. England in characteristic fashion muddled its way into Protestantism under Henry VIII and Elizabeth I, empirically finding a middle way that minimized violence and hastened a stable new settlement.

3) The new world. In 1492 Christopher Columbus, acting on the persisting and widespread belief in the old Greek idea that the world is a globe, sailed west to find a new commercial route to the East, only to be frustrated by the unexpected barrier of a new continent. The succeeding explorations of this continent and its native populations, and its settlement by Europeans, gave new materials to the literary imagination; the magic world of Shakespeare's *The Tempest,* for example, as well as the treatment of its native inhabitants by Prospero and others, is based on a contemporary account of a shipwreck on Bermuda and other writings about voyages to the New World. More important for English literature, however, was the fact that economic exploitation of the new world—often cruel, and devastating to the native peoples—put England at the center, rather than as heretofore at the edge, of the chief trade routes, and so helped establish the commercial prosperity that in England, as in Italy earlier, was a necessary though not sufficient condition for the development of a vigorous intellectual and artistic life.

4) The new cosmos. The cosmos of medieval astronomy and theology was **Ptolemaic** (that is, based on the astronomy of Ptolemy, second century) and pictured a stationary earth around which rotated the successive spheres of the moon, the various planets, and then the fixed stars. Heaven, or the Empyrean, was thought to be situated above the spheres, and Hell to be situated either at the center of the earth (as in Dante's *Inferno*) or else below the system of the spheres (as in John Milton's *Paradise Lost*). In 1543 Copernicus published his new hypothesis concerning the system of the universe; this gave a much simpler and more coherent explanation of accumulating observations of the actual movements of the heavenly bodies, which had led to ever greater complications of the Ptolemaic world picture. The **Copernican theory** proposed a system in which the center is the sun, not the earth, and in which the earth is not stationary, but only one planet among many planets, all of which revolve around the sun.

Investigations have not borne out the earlier assumption by historians that the world picture of Copernicus and his followers delivered an immediate and profound shock to the theological and secular beliefs of thinking men. For example in 1611, when Donne wrote in "The First Anniversary" that "new Philosophy calls all in doubt," for "the Sun is lost, and th' earth," he did so only to support the ancient theme, or literary *topos,* of the world's decay, and to enforce a standard Christian "contemptus mundi" (contempt for the worldly). Still later, Milton in *Paradise Lost* (1667) expressed a suspension of judgment between the Ptolemaic and Copernican theories; he adopted, however, the older Ptolemaic scheme as the cosmic setting for his poem, because it was more firmly traditional and better adapted to his narrative purposes.

Much more important, in the long run, was the effect on men's opinions of the general principles and methods of the **new science** developed by the great successors of Copernicus in the late sixteenth and early seventeenth centuries, such as the physicists Johannes Kepler and Galileo and the English physician and physiologist William Harvey. Even after Copernicus, the cosmos of many writers in the Elizabethan era remained not only Ptolemaic; it remained also an animate cosmos that was invested with occult powers and inhabited by demons and spirits, and was widely believed to control men's lives by stellar influences and to be itself subject to control by the powers of witchcraft and of magic. The cosmos that emerged in the course of the seventeenth century, as a product of the scientific procedure of constructing hypotheses capable of being tested by precisely measured sense-observations, was the physical cosmos of René Descartes (1596–1650). "Give me extension and motion," Descartes wrote, "and I will construct the universe." This universe of Descartes and the new science consisted of extended particles of matter which moved in space according to fixed mathematical laws, free from interference by angels, demons, human prayer, or occult magical powers. This universe was, however, subject to the limited manipulations of experimental scientists who set out in this way to discover the laws of nature, and who, in Francis Bacon's phrase, had learned to obey nature in order to be her master. In Descartes and other thinkers, the working hypotheses of the scientists about the physical world were converted into a philosophical worldview, which was made current by popular expositions, and—together with the methodological principle that controlled observation is the criterion of truth in many areas of knowledge—helped constitute the climate of eighteenth-century opinion known as the *Enlightenment.*

Refer to J. Burckhardt, *Civilization of the Renaissance in Italy* (first published in 1860); H. O. Taylor, *Thought and Expression in the 16th Century* (1920); E. A. Burtt, *The Metaphysical Foundations of Modern Science* (rev., 1932); W. K. Ferguson, *The Renaissance in Historical Thought* (1948); C. S. Lewis, *English Literature in the 16th Century* (1954); Marjorie Nicolson, *Science and Imagination* (1956); Thomas S. Kuhn, *The Copernican Revolution* (1957); Paul O. Kristeller, *Renaissance Thought: The Classic, Scholastic, and Humanistic Strains* (rev., 1961); John R. Hale, *Renaissance* (1965).

Rhetoric. In his *Poetics* the Greek philosopher Aristotle defined poetry as a mode of *imitation*—a fictional representation in a verbal medium of human beings thinking, feeling, acting, and interacting—and focused his discussion on elements such as plot, character, thought, and diction within the work itself. In his *Rhetoric,* on the other hand, Aristotle defined rhetorical discourse as the art of "discovering all the available means of persuasion in any given case," and focused his discussion on the means and devices that an orator uses in order to achieve the intellectual and emotional effects on an audience that will persuade them to accede to his point of view. Most of the later rhetoricians of the classical era concurred in the view that rhetoric concerns the principles of that type of discourse whose chief aim is to persuade an audience to think or act in a particular way. (A notable exception is the major Roman rhetorician Quintilian who, in the first century, gave rhetoric a moral basis by defining it as the art "of a good man skilled in speaking.") In a general sense, then, rhetoric can be described as the study of language in its practical uses, focusing on the effects of language, especially persuasion, and on the means by which one can achieve these effects on auditors or readers.

Following Aristotle's lead, classical theorists analyzed an effective rhetorical discourse as consisting of three components: *invention* (the finding of arguments or proofs), **disposition** (the arrangement of such materials), and *style* (the choice of words, verbal patterns, and rhythms that will most effectively express and convey these materials). This last topic of "style" came to include extensive classifications and analyses of figurative language. Rhetoricians also discriminated three main classes of oratory, each of which uses characteristic devices to achieve its aims:

1) **Deliberative**—to persuade an audience (such as a legislative assembly) to approve or disapprove of a matter of public policy, and to act accordingly.

2) **Forensic**—to achieve (for example, in a judicial trial) either the condemnation or approval of some person's actions.

3) **Epideictic**—"display rhetoric," used on appropriate, usually ceremonial, occasions to enlarge upon the praiseworthiness (or sometimes, the blameworthiness) of a person or group of persons, and in so doing, to display the orator's own talents and skill at rising to the rhetorical demands of the occasion. Abraham Lincoln's "Gettysburg Address" is a famed instance of epideictic oratory. In America, it remains traditional for a chosen speaker to meet the challenge of the

Fourth of July or other dates of national significance by appropriately ceremonious oratory. The *ode* is a poetic form often used for epideictic purposes.

Figurative language, although extensively dealt with in classical and later traditional rhetorics, had been considered as only one element of style, and often, as subordinated to the overall aim of persuasion. In the present century, however (and especially in the last fifty years), the analysis of the types and functions of figurative language has been increasingly excerpted from this rhetorical context and made an independent and central concern, not only by critics of literature but also by language theorists and by philosophers. Some recent theorists regard all modes of discourse as comprising "rhetorical" and figurative elements which are inherently nonreferential and counterlogical, and therefore defeat all attempts to speak or write in ways that have determinate meanings, or that refer to a world beyond language. (See *deconstruction.*)

Refer to *ethos* (the rhetorical concept of a speaker's projected character that functions as a means of persuasion) under *persona, tone, and voice;* also *rhetorical criticism.* See Aristotle's *Rhetoric,* ed. Lane Cooper (1932); Quintilian, *Institutes of Oratory* (4 vols.; Loeb Classical Library, 1920–22); M. L. Clarke, *Rhetoric at Rome: A Historical Survey* (1953); George Kennedy, *The Art of Persuasion in Greece* (1963); Edward P. J. Corbett, *Classical Rhetoric for the Modern Student* (3d ed., 1990).

Rhetorical Criticism. The Roman Horace in his versified *Art of Poetry* (first century B.C.) declared that the aim of a poet is either to instruct or delight a reader, and preferably to do both. This view, by making poetry a means to achieve effects on its audience, breaks down Aristotle's distinction between imitative poetry and persuasive rhetoric (see *rhetoric*). Such *pragmatic criticism* became the dominant type of literary theory from late classical times through the eighteenth century. Discussions of poetry in that long span of time absorbed and expanded upon the analytic terms that had been developed in traditional rhetoric, and represented a poem mainly as a deployment of established artistic means for achieving foreseen effects upon its readers. The triumph in the early nineteenth century of *expressive* theories of literature (which conceive a work primarily as the expression of the feelings, temperament, and mental powers of the author), followed by the dominance, beginning in the 1920s, of *objective* theories of literature (which maintain that a work must be considered as an object in itself, independently of the attributes and intentions of the author and the responses of a reader), served to diminish, and sometimes to eliminate, rhetorical considerations in literary criticism.

Since the late 1950s, however, there has been a revival of interest in literature as a mode of communication between author and reader, and this has led to the development of a **rhetorical criticism** which, without departing from a primary focus on the literary work itself, undertakes to identify and analyze those elements within a poem or a prose narrative which are there primarily in order to effect certain responses in a reader. As Wayne

Booth said in the Preface to his influential book *The Rhetoric of Fiction* (1961), his subject is "the rhetorical resources available to the writer of epic, novel, or short story as he tries, consciously or unconsciously, to impose his fictional world upon the reader." A number of recent critics of prose fiction and of narrative and nonnarrative poems have focused attention on the author's use of a variety of means—including the authorial presence or *voice* that he or she projects—in order to inform, to achieve imaginative consent, and to engage the interest and guide the emotional responses of the readers to whom, whether consciously or not, the literary work is addressed. (See *persona, tone, and voice.*) Since the 1960s there has also emerged a prominent mode of reader-response criticism which focuses upon a reader's complex interpretive responses to the sequence of words in a literary text; most of its spokesmen, however, either ignore or reject the rhetorical view that such responses are effected by devices that are contrived for that purpose by the author. (See *reader-response criticism.*)

For recent examples of the rhetorical criticism of poetry and fiction see (in addition to Wayne Booth) Kenneth Burke, *A Rhetoric of Motives* (1955); M. H. Nichols, *Rhetoric and Criticism* (1963); Donald C. Bryant, ed., *Papers in Rhetoric and Poetic* (1965); Edward P. J. Corbett, ed., *Rhetorical Analyses of Literary Works* (1969); Brian Vickers, *Classical Rhetoric in English Poetry* (2d ed., 1989).

Rhetorical Figures. It is convenient to list under this heading some common "figures of speech" which depart from what is experienced by users as standard, or *literal,* language mainly by the arrangement of their words to achieve special effects, and not, like metaphors and other *tropes,* by a radical change in the meaning of the words themselves. See this distinction under *figurative language.*

An **apostrophe** is a direct and explicit address either to an absent person or to an abstract or nonhuman entity. Often the effect is of high formality, or else of a sudden emotional impetus. Many *odes* are constituted throughout in the mode of such an address. So John Keats begins his "Ode on a Grecian Urn" (1820) by apostrophizing the Urn—"Thou still unravished bride of quietness"—and directs the entirety of the poem to the Urn and the figures represented on it. Samuel Taylor Coleridge's fine lyric "Recollections of Love" (1817) is addressed to an absent woman; at the end of the poem, Coleridge, while speaking still to his beloved, turns by a sudden impulse to apostrophize also the River Greta:

> But when those meek eyes first did seem
> To tell me, Love within you wrought—
> O Greta, dear domestic stream!
>
> Has not, since then, Love's prompture deep,
> Has not Love's whisper evermore
> Been ceaseless, as thy gentle roar?
> Sole voice, when other voices sleep,
> Dear under-song in clamor's hour.

Many apostrophes, as in these examples from Keats and Coleridge, imply a *personification* of the nonhuman object that is addressed. (See Jonathan Culler, "Apostrophe," in *The Pursuit of Signs,* 1981.)

If such an address is to a god or muse or some other being to assist the poet in his composition, it is called an **invocation;** so John Milton invokes divine guidance at the opening of *Paradise Lost:*

> And chiefly Thou, O Spirit, that dost prefer
> Before all temples th' upright heart and pure,
> Instruct me. . . .

A **rhetorical question** is a sentence in the grammatical form of a question which is not asked in order to request information or to invite a reply, but to achieve an expressive force different from, and usually more effective than, a direct assertion. In everyday discourse, for example, if we utter the rhetorical question "Isn't it a shame?" it functions as a forceful alternative to the assertion "It's a shame." (In terms of modern *speech-act theory,* its "illocutionary force" is not to question but to assert.) The figure is often used in persuasive discourse, and tends to impart an oratorical tone to discourse utterance, whether in prose or verse. When "fierce Thalestris" in Alexander Pope's *The Rape of the Lock* (1714) asks Belinda,

> Gods! Shall the ravisher display your hair,
> While the fops envy, and the ladies stare?

she does not stay for an answer, which she obviously thinks should be "No!" (A common form of rhetorical question is one that won't take "Yes" for an answer.) Shelley's "Ode to the West Wind" (1820) closes with the most famous rhetorical question in English:

> O, Wind,
> If Winter comes, can Spring be far behind?

This figure was a favorite of W. B. Yeats. A well-known instance is "Among School Children," which ends with the rhetorical question, "How can we know the dancer from the dance?" In this instance the poetic context probably indicates that the question is left hanging because it is unanswerable, posing a problem for which there is no certain resolution.

Chiasmus (derived from the Greek term for the letter X, or for a cross-over) is a sequence of two phrases or clauses which are parallel in syntax, but reverse the order of the corresponding words. So in this line from Pope, the verb first precedes, then follows, the adverbial phrase:

> *Works* without show, and without pomp *presides.*

The cross-over is sometimes reinforced by alliteration and other similarities in the length and component sounds of words, as in Pope's summary of the common fate of coquettes after marriage:

> A *fop* their *passion*, but their *prize* a *sot.*

In Yeats' "An Irish Airman Foresees His Death" (1919), the chiasmus consists in a reversal of the position of an entire phrase:

> The years to come seemed *waste of breath,*
> A *waste of breath* the years behind.*

And as a reminder that all figures of speech are used in prose as well as in verse, here is an instance of chiasmus from Shelley's *Defence of Poetry* (1821): "Poetry is the record of the best and happiest moments of the happiest and best minds."

Zeugma in Greek means "yoking"; in the most common present usage, it is applied to expressions in which a single word stands in the same grammatical relation to two or more other words, but with an obvious shift in its significance. Sometimes the word is literal in one relation and metaphorical in the other. Here are examples of zeugma in Pope:

> Or *stain* her honour, or her new brocade.

> *Obliged* by hunger, and request of friends.

Byron uses zeugma for grimly comic effects in his description of a shipwreck in *Don Juan* (1819–24):

> And the waves oozing through the port-hole *made*
> His berth a little damp, and him afraid.

> The loud tempests *raise*
> The waters, and repentance for past sinning.

To achieve the maximum of concentrated verbal effects within the tight limits of the *closed couplet,* Pope in the early eighteenth century exploited all the language patterns described in this essay with supreme virtuosity. He is the foremost English master of the rhetorical figures, as Shakespeare is of tropes.

Other linguistic patterns or "schemes" that are sometimes classified as rhetorical figures are treated elsewhere in this book; see *antithesis, alliteration, assonance,* rhetorical *climax* (under *bathos*), and *parallelism.* For concise definitions and examples of additional figures of speech which are less commonly referred to in literary analyses, see Edward P. J. Corbett, *Classical Rhetoric for the Modern Student* (3d ed., 1990).

Rhyme. In English versification, standard rhyme consists of the repetition, in the rhyming words, of the last stressed vowel and of all the speech sounds following that vowel: láte-fáte; fóllow-hóllow.

End rhymes, by far the most frequent type, occur at the end of a verse-line. **Internal rhymes** occur within a verse-line, as in the Victorian poet Algernon Swinburne's

> Sister, my sister, O *fleet sweet* swallow.

---

* Lines from "An Irish Airman Foresees His Death" reprinted with permission of Macmillan Publishing Company from *The Poems of W. B. Yeats: A New Edition,* edited by Richard J. Finneran. Copyright 1919 by Macmillan Publishing Company, renewed 1947 by Bertha Georgie Yeats.

A stanza from Coleridge's "The Rime of the Ancient Mariner" illustrates the patterned use both of internal rhymes (within lines 1 and 3) and of an end rhyme (lines 2 and 4):

> In mist or *cloud,* on mast or *shroud,*
> It perched for vespers *nine;*
> Whiles all the *night,* through fog-smoke *white,*
> Glimmered the white moon-*shine.*

The numbered lines in the following stanza of Wordsworth's "The Solitary Reaper" (1807) are followed by a column which, in the conventional way, marks the terminal rhyme elements by a corresponding sequence and repetition of the letters of the alphabet:

> *1)* Whate'er her theme, the maiden sang   *a*
> *2)* As if her song could have no *ending;*   *b*
> *3)* I saw her singing at her work   *c*
> *4)* And o'er the sickle *bending*—   *b*
> *5)* I listened, motionless and *still;*   *d*
> *6)* And as I mounted up the *hill,*   *d*
> *7)* The music in my heart I *bore,*   *e*
> *8)* Long after it was heard no *more.*   *e*

Lines 1 and 3 do not rhyme with any other line. Both in lines 5 and 6 and lines 7 and 8 the rhyme consists of a single stressed syllable, and is called a **masculine rhyme:** stíll–híll, bóre–móre. In lines 2 and 4, the rhyme consists of a stressed syllable followed by an unstressed syllable, and is called a **feminine rhyme:** énding–bénding. (On syllabic stress-patterns, see *meter.*)

A feminine rhyme, since it involves the repetition of two syllables, is also known as a **double rhyme.** A rhyme involving three syllables is called a **triple rhyme;** such rhymes, since they coincide with surprising patness, usually have a comic quality. In *Don Juan* (1819–24) Byron often uses triple rhymes such as compárison–gárrison, and sometimes intensifies the comic effect by permitting the pressure of the rhyme to force a distortion of the pronunciation; thus he addresses the husbands of pedantic wives:

> But—Oh! ye lords of ladies intelléctual
> Inform us truly, have they not hen-*pécked you all?*

This maltreatment of words, called **forced rhyme,** in which the poet gives the effect of seeming to surrender helplessly to the exigencies of a difficult rhyme, has been comically exploited by the recent poet Ogden Nash:

> Farewell, farewell, you old rhinocerous,
> I'll stare at something less prepocerous.*

If the correspondence of the rhymed sounds is exact, it is called **perfect rhyme,** or else "full" or "true rhyme." Until recently almost all English writers

---

* Lines from "The Rhinoceros" by Ogden Nash, from *Verses from 1929 On* by Ogden Nash. Copyright 1933 by Ogden Nash. By permission of Little, Brown and Company. Also reprinted by permission of Curtis Brown, Ltd., copyright © 1933.

of serious poems have limited themselves to perfect rhymes, except for an occasional *poetic license* such as **eye-rhymes**: words whose endings are spelled alike, and in most instances were once pronounced alike, but have in the course of time acquired a different pronunciation: prove–love, daughter–laughter. Many modern poets, however, deliberately supplement perfect rhyme with **imperfect rhyme** (also known as "partial," or "near," or "slant" rhyme, or else as "pararhyme"). This effect is fairly common in *folk poetry* such as children's verses, and it was employed occasionally by various writers of art lyrics such as Thomas Vaughan in the seventeenth, William Blake in the late eighteenth, and very frequently by Emily Dickinson in the nineteenth century. More recently, Gerard Manley Hopkins, W. B. Yeats, Wilfred Owen, and other poets have systematically exploited partial rhymes, in which the vowels are only approximate or else quite different, and occasionally even the rhymed consonants are similar rather than identical. Wilfred Owen, in 1917–18, constructed the following six-line stanza using only two sets of partial rhymes, established at the ends of the first two lines:

> The centuries will burn rich loads
>   With which we groaned,
> Whose warmth shall lull their dreamy lids,
>   While songs are crooned.
> But they will not dream of us poor lads,
>   Lost in the ground.*

In his poem "The Force That Through the Green Fuse Drives the Flower" (1933), Dylan Thomas uses, very effectively, such distantly approximate rhymes as (with masculine endings) trees–rose, rocks–wax, tomb–worm, and (with feminine endings) flower–destroyer–fever.

The passages quoted will illustrate some of the many effects that can be achieved by the device that has been called "making ends meet in verse"—the pleasure of the expected yet varying chime; the reinforcement of syntax and rhetorical emphasis when a strong masculine rhyme concurs with the end of a clause, sentence, or stanza; the sudden grace of movement which may be lent by a feminine rhyme; the broadening of the comic by a pat coincidence of sound; the haunting effect of the limited *consonance* in partial rhymes. Cunning artificers in verse make rhyme more than an auxiliary sound effect; they use it to enhance or contribute to the significance of the words. When Pope in the earlier eighteenth century satirized two contemporary pedants in the lines

> Yet ne'er one sprig of laurel graced these ribalds,
> From slashing Bentley down to piddling Tibalds,

the rhyme of "Tibalds," as W. K. Wimsatt has said, demonstrates "what it means to have a name like that," with its implication that the scholar is as graceless as his appellation. And in one of its important functions, rhyme ties individual lines into the larger pattern of a *stanza*.

---

* Lines from "Miners" by Wilfred Owen, from *The Collected Poems of Wilfred Owen*. Copyright © 1963 Chatto & Windus, Ltd. Reprinted by permission of New Directions Publishing Corporation.

See George Saintsbury, *History of English Prosody* (3 vols.; 1906–10); H. C. K. Wyld, *Studies in English Rhymes* (1923); W. K. Wimsatt, "One Relation of Rhyme to Reason," in *The Verbal Icon* (1954); Donald Wesling, *The Chances of Rhyme: Device and Modernity* (1980). For an analysis of the complex interrelations between sound-repetitions and meaning, see Roman Jakobson, "Linguistics and Poetics," in *Style and Language,* ed. Thomas A. Sebeok (1960).

Roman à Clef (French for "novel with a key") is a work of prose fiction in which the author expects the knowing reader to identify, despite alterations in their names, actual people of the time. One example is Thomas Love Peacock's *Nightmare Abbey* (1818), whose characters are entertaining *caricatures* of such contemporary literary figures as Coleridge, Byron, and Shelley. A later instance is Aldous Huxley's *Point Counter Point* (1928), in which we find, under fictional names, well-known English people of the 1920s such as the novelist D. H. Lawrence, the critic Middleton Murry, and the right-wing political extremist Oswald Mosely.

Satire can be described as the literary art of diminishing or derogating a subject by making it ridiculous and evoking toward it attitudes of amusement, contempt, scorn, or indignation. It differs from the *comic* in that comedy evokes laughter mainly as an end in itself, while satire "derides"; that is, it uses laughter as a weapon, and against a butt that exists outside the work itself. That butt may be an individual (in "personal satire"), or a type of person, a class, an institution, a nation, or even (as in the Earl of Rochester's "A Satyr against Mankind," 1675, and much of Jonathan Swift's *Gulliver's Travels,* 1726, especially Book IV) the whole human race. The distinction between the comic and the satiric, however, is sharp only at its extremes. Shakespeare's Falstaff is a comic creation, presented primarily for our enjoyment; the puritanical Malvolio in Shakespeare's *Twelfth Night* is for the most part comic but has aspects of satire directed against the type of the fatuous and hypocritical Puritan; Ben Jonson's *Volpone* (1607) clearly satirizes the type of person whose cleverness—or stupidity—is put at the service of his cupidity; and John Dryden's *MacFlecknoe* (1682), while representing a permanent type of the pretentious *poetaster,* satirized specifically the living author Thomas Shadwell.

Satire has usually been justified by those who practice it as a corrective of human vice and folly; Alexander Pope, for example, remarked that "those who are ashamed of nothing else are so of being ridiculous." Its frequent claim (not always borne out in the practice) has been to ridicule the failing rather than the individual, and to limit its ridicule to corrigible faults, excluding those for which a person is not responsible. As Swift said, speaking of himself in his ironic "Verses on the Death of Dr. Swift" (1739):

> Yet malice never was his aim;
> He lashed the vice, but spared the name. . . .
> His satire points at no defect,
> But what all mortals may correct. . . .
> He spared a hump, or crooked nose,
> Whose owners set not up for beaux.

Satire occurs as an incidental element within numerous works whose overall mode is not satiric—in a certain character or situation, or in an interpolated passage of ironic commentary on some aspect of the human condition or of contemporary society. But for many literary achievements, verse or prose, the attempt to diminish a subject by ridicule is the primary organizing principle, and these works constitute the formal *genre* labeled "satires." In discussing such writings the following distinctions are useful.

1) Critics make a broad division between formal (or "direct") satire and indirect satire. In **formal satire** the satiric voice speaks out in the first person. This "I" may address either the reader (as in Pope's *Moral Essays*, 1731–35; see for example Epistle II, "Of the Characters of Women"), or else a character within the work itself, who is called the **adversarius** and whose major artistic function is to elicit and add credibility to the satiric speaker's comments. (In Pope's "Epistle to Dr. Arbuthnot," 1735, Arbuthnot serves as adversarius.) Two types of formal satire are commonly distinguished, taking their names from the great Roman satirists Horace and Juvenal. The types are defined by the character of the *persona* whom the author presents as the first-person satiric speaker, and also by the attitude and *tone* that such a persona manifests toward both the subject matter and the readers of the work.

In **Horatian satire** the character that the speaker manifests is that of an urbane, witty, and tolerant man of the world, who is moved more often to wry amusement than to indignation at the spectacle of human folly, pretentiousness, and hypocrisy, and who uses a relaxed and informal language to evoke from readers a wry smile at human failings and absurdities— sometimes including his own. Horace himself described his aim as "to laugh people out of their vices and follies." Pope's *Moral Essays* and other formal satires for the most part sustain an Horatian stance.

In **Juvenalian satire** the character of the speaker is that of a serious moralist who uses a dignified and public style of utterance to decry modes of vice and error which are no less dangerous because they are ridiculous, and who undertakes to evoke from readers contempt, moral indignation, or an unillusioned sadness at the aberrations of humanity. Samuel Johnson's "London" (1738) and "The Vanity of Human Wishes" (1749) are distinguished instances of Juvenalian satire. In its most denunciatory modes, it resembles the *jeremiad,* whose model is not Roman but Hebraic.

2) **Indirect satire** is cast in some other literary form than that of direct address to the reader. The most common indirect form is that of a fictional narrative, in which the objects of the satire are characters who make themselves and their opinions ridiculous or obnoxious by what they think, say, and do, and are sometimes made even more ridiculous by the author's comments and narrative style.

One type of indirect satire is **Menippean satire**, modeled on a Greek form developed by the Cynic philosopher Menippus. It is sometimes called **Varronian satire**, after a Roman imitator, Varro; while Northrop Frye, in *Anatomy of Criticism,* pp. 308–12, suggests an alternative name, the **anatomy**, after a major English instance of the type, Burton's *Anatomy of Melancholy* (1621). Such satires are written in prose, usually with interpolations of verse, and constitute a miscellaneous form often held together by a loosely constructed narrative. A major feature is a series of extended dialogues and debates (often conducted at a banquet or party) in which a group of loquacious eccentrics, pedants, literary people, and representatives of various professions or philosophical points of view serve to make ludicrous the attitudes and viewpoints they typify by the arguments they urge in their support. Examples are Rabelais' *Gargantua and Pantagruel* (1564), Voltaire's *Candide* (1759), Thomas Love Peacock's *Nightmare Abbey* (1818) and other satiric fiction, and Huxley's *Point Counter Point* (1928); in this last novel, as in those of Peacock, the central satiric scenes are discussions and disputes during a weekend at a country manor. Frye also classifies Lewis Carroll's two books about Alice in Wonderland as "perfect Menippean satires."

It should be noted that any narrative or other literary vehicle can be adapted to the purposes of indirect satire. John Dryden's *Absalom and Achitophel* turns Old Testament history into a satiric allegory on *Restoration* political maneuverings. In *Gulliver's Travels* Swift converts to satiric use the early-eighteenth-century accounts of voyage and discovery, and his *Modest Proposal* is written in the form of a project in political economy. Many of Joseph Addison's *Spectator* papers are satiric essays; Byron's *Don Juan* is a versified satiric form of the old episodic *picaresque* fiction; Ben Jonson's *The Alchemist,* Molière's *The Misanthrope,* Wycherley's *The Country Wife,* and Shaw's *Arms and the Man* are satiric plays; and Gilbert and Sullivan's *Patience,* and other works such as John Gay's eighteenth-century *Beggar's Opera* and its modern adaptation by Bertolt Brecht *The Threepenny Opera* (1928), are satiric operettas. T. S. Eliot's *The Waste Land* (1922) employs motifs from myth in a work which can be considered as by and large a verse satire directed against what Eliot perceives as the spiritual dearth in twentieth-century life. The greatest number of recent satires, however, are written in prose, and especially in novelistic form; for example Evelyn Waugh's *The Loved One,* Joseph Heller's *Catch-22,* and Kurt Vonnegut, Jr.'s, *Player Piano* and *Cat's Cradle.* Much of the current vogue of *black humor* occurs in satiric works whose butt is what the author conceives as the widespread contemporary condition of social chaos, cruelty, or inanity.

Good English satire has been written in every period beginning with the Middle Ages. Pieces in the English *Punch* and the American *New Yorker* demonstrate that formal essayistic satire, like satiric novels and plays, still commands a wide audience; and W. H. Auden is a recent author who wrote excellent satiric poems. The proportioning of the examples in this article, however, indicates how large the Restoration and eighteenth century loom in satiric achievement: the greatest age of English, and probably of world, satire is the century and a half that included Dryden, the Earl of Rochester, Samuel Butler, Wycherley, Addison, Pope, Swift, Gay, Fielding, Johnson, Oliver Goldsmith, and late in the period (it should not be overlooked) the Robert Burns of "The Holy Fair" and "Holy Willie's Prayer" and the William Blake of *The Marriage of Heaven and Hell.* This same span of time was also in France the period of such excellent satirists as Boileau, La Fontaine, and Voltaire, as well as Molière, the most eminent of all satirists in drama.

The articles on *burlesque,* on *irony,* and on *wit, humor, and the comic* describe some of the derogatory modes and devices available to satirists. Consult Ian Jack, *Augustan Satire* (1952); James Sutherland, *English Satire* (1958); R. C. Elliott, *The Power of Satire* (1960); Gilbert Highet, *The Anatomy of Satire* (1962); Alvin B. Kernan, *The Plot of Satire* (1965); Matthew Hodgart, *Satire* (1969); Charles Sanders, *The Scope of Satire* (1971); Raman Selden, *English Verse Satire, 1590–1765* (1978). Anthologies: Ronald Paulson, ed., *Satire: Modern Essays in Criticism* (1971); Ashley Brown and John L. Kimmey, eds., *Satire: An Anthology* (1977), which includes both satiric writings and critical essays on satire.

Sensibility, Literature of. When a modern critic talks of a poet's **sensibility,** the reference is to a characteristic way of responding, in sensation, thought, and feeling, to experience; and when T. S. Eliot claimed that a *dissociation of sensibility* set in with the poetry of John Milton and John Dryden, he signified that there occurred at that time a division between a poet's sensuous, intellectual, and emotional modes of experience. When a literary historian, however, talks of the **literature of sensibility,** the reference is to a particular cultural phenomenon of the eighteenth century. This type of literature was fostered by the moral philosophy that had developed as a reaction against seventeenth-century Stoicism (which emphasized reason and the unemotional will as the sole motives to virtue), and even more importantly, as a reaction against Thomas Hobbes' claims, in *Leviathan* (1651), that a human being is innately selfish and that the mainsprings of human behavior are self-interest and the drive for power and status. In opposition to such views, many sermons, philosophical writings, and popular tracts and essays proclaimed that "benevolence"—wishing other persons well—is an innate human sentiment and motive, and that central aspects of moral experience are the feelings of sympathy and "sensibility"—that is, a hair-trigger responsiveness to another person's distresses and joys. (See *sympathy.*) "Sensibility" also connoted an intense emotional responsiveness to beauty and sublimity, whether in nature or in art, and such responsiveness was often represented as an index to a person's gentility—that is, to one's upper-class status.

Emphasis on the human capacities of sympathy and wishing others well were important in developing social consciousness and a sense of communal responsibility in an era of expanding commercialism and of an economics based on self interest. But highly exaggerated forms of sympathy and benevolence became a prominent aspect of eighteenth-century culture and literature. It was a commonplace in popular morality that readiness to shed a sympathetic tear is the sign both of polite breeding and a virtuous heart, and such a view was often accompanied by the observation that sympathy with another's grief, unlike personal grief, is a pleasurable emotion, hence to be sought as a value in itself. Common phrases in the cult of sensibility were the *oxymorons* "the luxury of grief," "pleasurable sorrows," and "the sadly pleasing tear." A late-eighteenth-century mortuary inscription in Dorchester Abbey reads:

Reader! If thou hast a Heart fam'd for Tenderness and Pity, Contemplate this Spot. In which are deposited the Remains of a Young Lady. . . . When Nerves were too delicately spun to bear the rude Shakes and Jostlings which we meet with in this transitory world, Nature gave way; She sunk and died a Martyr to Excessive Sensibility.

It is clear that much of what in that age was called, with approval, "sensibility" we now call, with disapproval, *sentimentalism*.

In literature these ideas and tendencies were reflected in the **drama of sensibility,** or **sentimental comedy,** which were representations of middle-class life that replaced in the theater the tough amorality and the comic or satiric representation of aristocratic sexual license in *Restoration comedy.* In the contemporary plays of sensibility, Oliver Goldsmith remarked in his "Comparison between Sentimental and Laughing Comedy" (1773), "the virtues of private life are exhibited rather than the vices exposed, and the distresses rather than the faults of mankind make our interest in the piece;" the characters, "though they want humor, have abundance of sentiment and feeling;" with the result, he added, that the audience "sit at a play as gloomy as at the tabernacle." Plays such as Richard Steele's *The Conscious Lovers* (1722) and Richard Cumberland's *The West Indian* (1771) present monumentally benevolent heroes and heroines of the middle class, whose dialogue abounds with elevating moral sentiments and who, prior to the manipulated happy ending, suffer tribulations designed to evoke the maximum in pleasurable tears from the audience.

The **novel of sensibility,** or **sentimental novel,** of the latter part of the eighteenth century similarly emphasized the tearful distresses of the virtuous, either at their own sorrows or at those of their friends; some of them represented in addition a sensitivity to beauty or sublimity which also expressed itself in tears. Samuel Richardson's *Pamela; or, Virtue Rewarded* (1740) exploits sensibility in some of its scenes; and Laurence Sterne, in *Tristram Shandy* and *A Sentimental Journey,* published in the 1760s, gives us his own inimitable compound of sensibility, self irony, and innuendo. The vogue of sensibility was international. Jean-Jacques Rousseau's novel *Julie, or the New Héloise* (1761) dealt with lovers of sensibility, and in his great autobiography, *The Confessions* (written 1764–70), Rousseau represented himself, in some circumstances and moods, as a man of extravagant sensibility. Goethe's novel *The Sorrows of Young Werther* (1774) is a famed presentation of the aesthetic sensitivities and finespun emotional tribulations of a young man who, frustrated in his love for a woman betrothed to another, and in general unable to adapt his sensibility to the demands of ordinary life, finally shoots himself.

An extreme English instance of the sentimental novel is Henry MacKenzie's *The Man of Feeling* (1771), which represents a hero of such exquisite sensibility that he goes into a decline from excess of pent-up tenderness toward a young lady, and dies in the perturbation of finally declaring to her his emotion. "If all his tears had been tears of blood," declares an editor of the novel, Hamish Miles, "the poor man could hardly have been more debile." Jane Austen's gently satiric treatment of a young woman of sensibility in *Sense and Sensibility* (begun 1797, published 1811) marks the decline of the fashion; but the exploitation of the mode of literary sensibility survives in such later novelistic episodes as the death of Little Nell in Charles Dickens' *Old Curiosity Shop* (1841) and the death of Little Eva in Harriet Beecher Stowe's *Uncle Tom's Cabin* (1852), in some Victorian *melodramas,* as well as in many movies that Hollywood labeled "tearjerkers."

Herbert Ross Brown, *The Sentimental Novel in America* (1940); C. A. Moore, *Backgrounds of English Literature, 1700–1760* (1953); Arthur Sherbo, *English Sentimental Drama* (1957); L. I. Bredvold, *The Natural History of Sensibility* (1962); R. P. Utter and G. B. Needham, *Pamela's Daughters* (1963); R. S. Crane, "Suggestions toward a Genealogy of the 'Man of Feeling,'" in *The Idea of the Humanities* (2 vols.; 1967); Janet Todd, *Sensibility: An Introduction* (1986); John Dwyer, *Virtuous Discourse: Sensibility and Community in Late Eighteenth-Century Scotland* (1987).

Sentimentalism is now a pejorative term applied to what is perceived to be an excess of emotion to an occasion, and especially to an overindulgence in the "tender" emotions of pathos and sympathy. Since what constitutes emotional excess or overindulgence is relative both to the judgment of the individual and to large-scale historical changes in culture and in literary fashion, what to the common reader of one age is a normal expression of humane feeling may seem sentimental to many later readers. The emotional responses of a lover that Shelley expresses and tries to evoke from the reader in his "Epipsychidion" (1821) seemed sentimental to the *New Critics* of the 1930s and later, who insisted on the need for an ironic counterpoise to intense feeling in poetry. Most readers now find both the *drama* and *novel of sensibility* of the eighteenth century ludicrously sentimental, and respond with jeers instead of tears to once celebrated episodes of pathos, such as many of the death scenes, especially those of children, in various Victorian novels and dramas. A staple in current anthologies of bad poetry are sentimental poems which were no doubt written, and by some people read, with deep and sincere feeling. A useful distinction between sentimental and non-sentimental is one which does not depend on the intensity or type of the feeling expressed or evoked, but labels as sentimental a work or passage in which the feeling is rendered in commonplaces and *clichés,* instead of being freshly verbalized and sharply realized in the details of the representation.

See *pathos;* and refer to I. A. Richards, *Practical Criticism* (1929), Chapter 6; Laurence Lerner, "A Note on Sentimentality," *The Truest Poetry* (1960); and the discussion of sentimentality by Monroe C. Beardsley, "Bad Poetry," in *The Possibility of Criticism* (1970).

Setting. The overall setting of a narrative or dramatic work is the general locale, historical time, and social circumstances in which its action occurs; the setting of a single episode or scene within a work is the particular physical location in which it takes place. The general setting of *Macbeth,* for example, is medieval Scotland, and the setting for the particular scene in which

Macbeth comes upon the witches is a blasted heath. The setting of James Joyce's *Ulysses* is Dublin on June 16, 1904, and its opening episode is set in the Martello Tower overlooking Dublin Bay. In works by writers such as Edgar Allan Poe, Thomas Hardy, and William Faulkner, the general and individual settings are important elements in generating the *atmosphere* of their works. The Greek term **opsis** ("scene," or "spectacle") is now occasionally used to denote a particular visible or picturable setting in any work of literature, including a lyric poem.

When applied to a theatrical production, "setting" is synonymous with **décor** and **mise en scène**, which are French terms denoting both the scenery and the **properties**, or movable pieces of furniture, on the stage. The term "mise en scène" sometimes includes also the positioning of the actors in a particular scene.

Seven Deadly Sins. In medieval and later Christian theology these sins were usually identified as Pride, Covetousness, Lust, Envy, Gluttony, Anger, and Sloth. They were called "deadly" because they were considered to put the soul of anyone manifesting them in peril of eternal perdition; such sins could be expiated only by absolute penitence. Among them, Pride was often considered primary, since it was believed to have motivated the original fall of Satan in heaven. Sloth was accounted a deadly sin because it was a torpid spiritual condition that threatened to make a person despair of any chance of achieving divine Grace. Alternative names for sloth were "accidie," "dejection," and "spiritual dryness"; it was a condition close to that which present-day psychiatrists diagnose as acute depression.

The seven deadly (or "cardinal") sins were defined and discussed by such major theologians as Gregory the Great and Thomas Aquinas, and served as the topic of countless moral sermons. They also played an important role in many works of medieval and Renaissance literature—sometimes in elaborately personified forms—including William Langland's *Piers Plowman* (B, Passus 5), Geoffrey Chaucer's "Parson's Tale," William Dunbar's "The Dance of the Sevin Deidly Synnis," and Edmund Spenser's *Faerie Queene* (Book I, Canto 4). Refer to Morton W. Bloomfield, *The Seven Deadly Sins* (1952).

The Seven Deadly Sins were balanced by the **Seven Cardinal Virtues.** Three of these, called the "theological virtues" because they were stressed in the New Testament, were Faith, Hope, and Charity (that is, Love)—see St. Paul's *I Corinthians* 13:13: "And now abideth faith, hope, and charity, these three." The other four, the "natural virtues," were derived from the moral philosophy of the ancient Greeks: Justice, Prudence, Temperance, and Fortitude.

Short Story. A short story is a brief work of prose fiction, and most of the terms for analyzing the component elements, the types, and the various narrative techniques of the *novel* are applicable to the short story as well. The short story differs from the **anecdote**—the unelaborated narration of a single incident—in that, like the novel, it organizes the action, thought, and interactions of its characters into the artful pattern of a plot. (See *narratology*.) And as in the novel, the plot form may be comic, tragic, romantic, or satiric;

the story is presented to us from one of many available *points of view;* and it may be written in the mode of fantasy, realism, or naturalism.

In the **tale,** or "story of incident," the focus of interest is on the course and outcome of the events, as in Edgar Allan Poe's *The Gold Bug* (1843) and in other tales of detection, in many of the stories of O. Henry (1862–1910), and in the stock but sometimes well-contrived western and adventure stories in the popular magazines. "Stories of character" focus instead on the state of mind and motivation, or on the psychological and moral qualities, of the protagonists. In some of the stories of character by Anton Chekhov (1860–1904), the Russian master of the form, nothing more happens than an encounter and conversation between two people. Ernest Hemingway's classic "A Clean, Well-Lighted Place" consists only of a curt conversation between two waiters about an old man who each day gets drunk and stays on in the café until it closes, followed by a brief meditation on the part of one of the waiters. In some stories there is a balance of interest between external action and character. Hemingway's "The Short Happy Life of Francis Macomber" is as violent in its packed events as any sensational adventure-tale, but every particular of the action and dialogue is contrived to test and reveal, with a surprising set of *reversals,* the moral quality of all three protagonists.

The short story, however, differs from the novel in the dimension that Aristotle called "magnitude," and this limitation of length imposes differ-ences both in the effects that can be achieved and in the choice, elaboration, and management of the elements to achieve those effects. Edgar Allan Poe, who is sometimes called the originator of the short story as an established genre, was at any rate its first critical theorist. He defined what he called "the prose tale" as a narrative which can be read at one sitting of from half an hour to two hours, and is limited to "a certain unique or single effect" to which every detail is subordinate (Review of Nathaniel Hawthorne's *Twice-Told Tales,* 1842). Poe's comment applies to many short stories, and points to the economy of management which the tightness of the form always imposes in some degree. We can say that, by and large, the short story writer intro-duces a very limited number of persons, cannot afford the space for the leisurely analysis and sustained development of character, and cannot under-take to develop as dense and detailed a social milieu as does the novelist. The author often begins the story close to, or even on the verge of, the climax, minimizes both prior exposition and the details of the *setting,* keeps the com-plications down, and clears up the denouement quickly—sometimes in a few sentences. (See *plot.*) The central incident is often selected to manifest as much as possible of the protagonist's life and character, and the details are devised to carry maximum import for the development of the plot. This spareness in the narrative often gives the artistry in a good short story higher visibility than the artistry in the more capacious and loosely structured novel.

Many distinguished short stories depart from this paradigm in various ways. It must be remembered that the name covers a great diversity of prose fiction, all the way from the **short short story,** which is a slightly elaborated anecdote of perhaps five hundred words, to such long and complex forms as Herman Melville's *Billy Budd* (c. 1890), Henry James' *The Turn of the Screw*

(1898), Joseph Conrad's *Heart of Darkness* (1902), and Thomas Mann's *Mario and the Magician* (1930). In such works, the status of middle length between the tautness of the short story and the expansiveness of the novel is sometimes indicated by the name **novelette,** or *novella.* This form has been especially exploited in Germany (where it is called the *Novelle*) after it was introduced by Goethe in 1795 and carried on by Heinrich von Kleist and many other writers; the genre has also been the subject of special critical attention by German theorists (see the list of readings below).

The short narrative, in both verse and prose, is one of the oldest and most widespread of literary forms; the Hebrew Bible, for example, includes the stories of Jonah, Ruth, and Esther. Some of the narrative types which preceded the short story, treated elsewhere in this *Glossary,* are the *fable,* the *exemplum,* the *folktale,* the *fabliau,* and the *parable.* Early in its history, there developed the device of the **frame-story**: a preliminary narrative within which one or more of the characters proceeds to tell a series of short stories. This device was widespread in the oral and written literature of the East, as in the collection of stories called *The Arabian Nights,* and was used by Boccaccio for his prose *Decameron* (1353) and by Chaucer for his versified *Canterbury Tales* (c. 1387). In the latter instance, Chaucer developed the frame-story of the journey, dialogue, and interactions of the Canterbury pilgrims to such a degree that the frame itself approximated the form of a plot. Within this frame-plot, each story constitutes a complete and rounded narrative, yet functions also both as a means of characterizing the teller and as a vehicle for the quarrels and topics of argument en route. In its more recent forms, the frame-story may enclose either a single narrative (Henry James' *The Turn of the Screw*) or a sequence of narratives (Joel Chandler Harris' stories as told by Uncle Remus, 1881 and later; see under *beast fable*).

The form of prose narrative which approximates the contemporary concept of the short story was developed in the nineteenth century by Washington Irving, Hawthorne, and Poe in America, Sir Walter Scott in England, E. T. A. Hoffmann in Germany, Balzac in France, and Gogol and Turgenev in Russia. The short story in English has flourished in America more than in England; Frank O'Connor has called it "the national art form," and its American masters include (in addition to the writers mentioned above) William Faulkner, Katherine Anne Porter, Eudora Welty, Flannery O'Connor, John O'Hara, J. F. Powers, John Cheever, and J. D. Salinger.

See H. S. Canby, *The Short Story in English* (1909); Sean O'Faolain, *The Short Story* (1948); Frank O'Connor, *The Lonely Voice: A Study of the Short Story* (1962); R. L. Pattee, *The Development of the American Short Story* (rev., 1966). On the novella: Ronald Paulson, *The Novelette Before 1900* (1968); Mary Doyle Springer, *Forms of the Modern Novella* (1976); Martin Swales, *The German Novelle* (1977). On the frame-story and tales in the ancient collection of Arabic stories, see the Introduction to *The Arabian Nights,* trans. Husain Haddawy (1990).

Sociology of Literature. Most literary historians and critics have taken some account of the relation of individual authors to the circumstances of the social and cultural era in which they live and write, as well as of the relation of a literary work to the segment of society that its fiction represents or to which the work is addressed. (For major exceptions in recent types of criticism see *Russian formalism, New Criticism, structuralism, deconstruction.*) The term "sociology of literature," however, is applied only to the writings of those historians and critics whose primary, and sometimes exclusive, interest is in the ways that the constitution of a literary work is affected by such circumstances as its author's class status, gender, and individual interests; the ways of thinking and feeling characteristic of its era; the economic conditions of the writer's profession and of the publication and distribution of books; and the social class, conceptions, and values of the audience to which an author addresses the literary product, or to which it is made available. Sociological critics treat a work of literature as inescapably conditioned—in the choice and development of its subject matter, the ways of thinking it incorporates, its evaluations of the modes of life it renders, and even in its form—by the social, political, and economic organization and forces of its age; they also tend to view the interpretation and assessment of a literary work by any reading public as shaped by the circumstances specific to that public's time and place. The French historian Hippolyte Taine is sometimes considered the first modern sociologist of literature in his *History of English Literature* (1863), which analyzed a work as largely explicable by reference to three factors: its author's "race," geographical and social "milieu," and historical "moment."

For prominent sociological emphases in recent critical writings, see *feminist criticism*—which focuses on the role of "patriarchal" assumptions as determinants of literary content, form, values, and interpretations—and also *Marxist criticism*. It should be noted that Marx's view of the economic basis of social organization, class ideologies, and class conflict have influenced the work of many critics who, although not committed to Marxist doctrine, stress the sociological context and content of works of literature. The most thoroughgoing treatments of literature as a cultural product that is totally embedded in the circumstances of a time and place are by adherents of the current modes of criticism classified as the *new historicism*.

In addition to the readings listed under *feminist criticism, Marxist criticism,* and *new historicism,* see the pioneering study by Alexandre Beljame, *Men of Letters and the English Public*—i.e., in the eighteenth century (1883, trans. 1948); Levin Schücking, *The Sociology of Literary Taste* (rev., 1941); Harry Levin, "Literature as an Institution," in *The Gates of Horn* (1963); Hugh Dalziel Duncan, *Language and Literature in Society, with a Bibliographical Guide to the Sociology of Literature* (1953). Collections of essays in sociological criticism include Joseph P. Strelka, ed., *Literary Criticism and Sociology* (1973); Elizabeth and Tom Burns, eds., *Sociology of Literature and Drama: Selected Readings* (1973); and the issue of *Critical Inquiry* devoted to the sociology of literature, Vol. 14 (Spring, 1988).

Soliloquy is the act of talking to oneself, whether silently or aloud. In drama it denotes the *convention* by which a character, alone on the stage, utters his thoughts aloud; playwrights use this device as a convenient way to convey information about a character's motives and state of mind, or for purposes of general exposition, and sometimes in order to guide the judgments and responses of the audience. Christopher Marlowe's *Dr. Faustus* (first performed in 1594) opens with a long expository soliloquy, and concludes with another which expresses Faustus' frantic mental and emotional condition during his belated attempts to escape damnation. The best-known of all dramatic soliloquies is Hamlet's speech which begins "To be or not to be." (Compare *monologue.*)

A related stage device is the **aside,** in which a character expresses to the audience his or her thought or intention in a short speech which, by convention, is inaudible to the other characters on the stage. Both devices, common in Elizabethan and later drama, fell into disuse in the later nineteenth century, when increasing demands that plays convey the illusion of real life impelled the dramatists to exploit indirect means for conveying information and guidance to the audience. Eugene O'Neill, however, revived and extended the aside and made it a central device throughout his play *Strange Interlude* (1928).

Sonnet. A lyric poem consisting of a single *stanza* of fourteen iambic pentameter lines linked by an intricate rhyme scheme. There are two major patterns of rhyme in the English sonnet:

1) The **Italian** or **Petrarchan sonnet** (named after the fourteenth-century Italian poet Petrarch) falls into two main parts: an **octave** (eight lines) rhyming *abbaabba* followed by a **sestet** (six lines) rhyming *cdecde* or some variant, such as *cdccdc.* Petrarch's sonnets were first imitated in England, both in their stanza form and their subject, the hopes and pains of an adoring male lover, by Sir Thomas Wyatt in the early sixteenth century. (See *Petrarchan conceit.*) The Petrarchan form was later used, and for a variety of subjects, by Milton, Wordsworth, D. G. Rossetti, and other sonneteers, who sometimes made it technically easier in English (which does not have as many rhyming possibilities as Italian) by introducing a new pair of rhymes in the second four lines of the octave.

2) The Earl of Surrey and other English experimenters in the sixteenth century also developed a stanza form called the **English sonnet,** or else the **Shakespearean sonnet,** after the greatest practitioner. This sonnet falls into three *quatrains* and a concluding *couplet: abab cdcd efef gg.* There was one notable variant, the **Spenserian sonnet,** in which Spenser links each quatrain to the next by a continuing rhyme: *abab bcbc cdcd ee.*

John Donne shifted from the hitherto standard subject, sexual love, to a variety of religious themes in his *Holy Sonnets,* written early in the seventeenth century; and Milton, in the latter part of that century, expanded the range of the sonnet to other matters of serious concern. Except for a lapse in the English *Neoclassic Period,* the sonnet has remained a popular form to the present day and includes among its distinguished practitioners, in the nineteenth century, Wordsworth, Keats, Elizabeth Barrett Browning, and Dante

Gabriel Rossetti, and more recently Edwin Arlington Robinson, Edna St. Vincent Millay, W. B. Yeats, Robert Frost, W. H. Auden, and Dylan Thomas. The stanza is just long enough to permit a fairly complex lyric development, yet so short and so exigent in its rhymes as to pose a standing challenge to the artistry of the poet. The rhyme pattern of the Petrarchan sonnet has on the whole favored a statement of problem, situation, or incident in the octave, with a resolution in the sestet. The English form sometimes uses a similar division of material, but often presents a repetition-with-variation of a statement in each of the three quatrains; in either case, the final couplet usually imposes an *epigrammatic* turn at the end. In Drayton's fine Elizabethan sonnet in the English form "Since there's no help, come let us kiss and part," the lover brusquely declares in the first quatrain, then reiterates in the second, that he is glad that the affair is cleanly ended, but in the concluding couplet suddenly drops his swagger to make one last plea. Here are the last quatrain and couplet:

> Now at the last gasp of love's latest breath,
> When, his pulse failing, passion speechless lies,
> When faith is kneeling by his bed of death,
> And innocence is closing up his eyes;
>> Now if thou wouldst, when all have given him over,
>> From death to life thou mightst him yet recover.

Following Petrarch's early example, a number of Elizabethan poets wrote **sonnet sequences**, or **sonnet cycles**, in which a series of sonnets are linked together by exploring the varied aspects of a relationship between lovers, or else by indicating a development in the relationship that constitutes a kind of implicit plot. Shakespeare wrote his sonnets in a sequence, as did Sidney in *Astrophel and Stella* (1580) and Spenser in *Amoretti* (1595). Later examples of the sonnet sequence on various subjects are Wordsworth's *The River Duddon,* D. G. Rossetti's *House of Life,* Elizabeth Barrett Browning's *Sonnets from the Portuguese,* and the American poet William Ellery Leonard's *Two Lives.* Dylan Thomas' *Altarwise by Owl-light* (1936) is a sequence of ten sonnets which are meditations on the poet's own life. George Meredith's *Modern Love* (1862), which concerns a bitterly unhappy marriage, is sometimes called a sonnet sequence, even though its poems consist not of fourteen but of sixteen lines.

See T. W. H. Crosland, *The English Sonnet* (1917); L. G. Sterner, *The Sonnet in American Literature* (1930); L. C. John, *The Elizabethan Sonnet Sequences* (1938); J. W. Lever, *The Elizabethan Love Sonnet* (1956); J. B. Leishman, *Themes and Variations in Shakespeare's Sonnets* (1963).

Stanza. A stanza (Italian for "stopping place") is a grouping of the verse-lines in a poem, set off by a space in the printed text. Usually the stanzas of a given poem are marked by a recurrent pattern of rhyme, and are also uniform in the number and lengths of the component lines. Some unrhymed poems, however, are divided into stanzaic units (for example, William Collins' "Ode to Evening," 1747), and some rhymed poems are composed of stanzas that vary in their component lines (for example, the *irregular ode*).

Of the great diversity of English stanza forms, many have no special names and must be described by specifying the number of lines, the type and number of metric *feet* in each line, and the pattern of the *rhyme*. Some stanzas, however, recur so frequently that they have been given the convenience of a name, as follows:

A **couplet** is a pair of rhymed lines. The **octosyllabic couplet** has lines of eight syllables, usually consisting of four iambic feet. So in Andrew Marvell's "To His Coy Mistress" (1681):

> The grave's a fine and private place,
> But none, I think, do there embrace.

Iambic pentameter lines rhyming in pairs are called **decasyllabic** ("ten-syllable") **couplets**, and also *heroic couplets*.

The **tercet**, or **triplet**, is a stanza of three lines, usually with a single rhyme. The lines may be the same length (as in Robert Herrick's "Upon Julia's Clothes," 1648, written in tercets of iambic tetrameter), or else of varying lengths. In Richard Crashaw's "Wishes to His Supposed Mistress" (1646), the lines of each tercet are successively in *iambic dimeter, trimeter,* and *tetrameter:*

> Who e'er she be
> That not impossible she
> That shall command my heart and me.

Terza rima is composed of tercets which are interlinked, in that each is joined to the one following by a common rhyme: *aba, bcb, cdc,* and so on. Dante composed his *Divine Comedy* (early fourteenth century) in terza rima; but although Sir Thomas Wyatt introduced the form early in the sixteenth century, it has not been a common meter in English, in which rhymes are much harder to find than in Italian. Shelley, however, used it brilliantly in "Ode to the West Wind" (1820), and it occurs also in the poetry of Milton, Browning, and T. S. Eliot.

The **quatrain**, or four-line stanza, is the most common in English versification, and is employed with various meters and rhyme schemes. The *ballad stanza* (in alternating four- and three-foot lines rhyming *abcb,* or less frequently *abab*) is one common quatrain; when this same stanza occurs in *hymns,* it is called **common measure**. The **heroic quatrain**, in iambic pentameter rhyming *abab,* is the stanza of Gray's "Elegy Written in a Country Churchyard" (1751).

Rime royal was introduced by Chaucer in *Troilus and Criseyde* (the latter 1380s) and other narrative poems; it is believed to take its name, however, from its later use by "the Scottish Chaucerian," King James I of Scotland, in his poem *The Kingis Quair* ("The King's Book"), written about 1424. It is a seven-line, iambic pentameter stanza rhyming *ababbcc.*

Ottava rima, as the Italian name indicates, has eight lines; it rhymes *abababcc.* Like terza rima and the sonnet, it was brought from Italian into English by Sir Thomas Wyatt in the first half of the sixteenth century. Although employed by a number of earlier poets, it is notable especially as the stanza which helped Byron discover what he was born to write, the satiric poem *Don Juan* (1819–24). Note the comic effect of the *forced rhyme* in the concluding couplet:

> Juan was taught from out the best edition,
> Expurgated by learned men, who place,
> Judiciously, from out the schoolboy's vision,
> The grosser parts; but, fearful to deface
> Too much their modest bard by this omission,
> And pitying sore his mutilated case,
> They only add them all in an appendix,
> Which saves, in fact, the trouble of an index.

Spenserian stanza is a still longer form devised by Edmund Spenser for *The Faerie Queene* (1590–96)—nine lines, in which the first eight lines are iambic pentameter and the last iambic hexameter (an *Alexandrine*), rhyming *ababbcbcc*. Enchanted by Spenser's gracious movement and music, many poets have attempted the form in spite of its difficulties. Its greatest successes have been in poems which, like *The Faerie Queene*, evolve in a leisurely way, with ample time for unrolling the richly textured stanzas; for example, James Thomson's "The Castle of Indolence" (1748), John Keats' "The Eve of St. Agnes" (1820), Percy Bysshe Shelley's "Adonais" (1821), and the narrative section of Alfred, Lord Tennyson's "The Lotus Eaters" (1832).

There are also various elaborate stanza forms imported from France, such as the rondeau, the villanelle, and the triolet, containing intricate repetitions of rhymes and lines, which have been used mainly, but not exclusively, for *light verse*. Their revival by W. H. Auden, William Empson, and other mid-twentieth-century poets was a sign of renewed interest in high metrical artifice. Dylan Thomas' "Do not go gentle into that good night" is a **villanelle;** that is, it consists of five *tercets* and a *quatrain,* all on two rhymes, and with systematic later repetitions of lines 1 and 3 of the first tercet. One of the most intricate of these French forms is the **sestina:** a poem of six six-line stanzas in which the end-words in the lines of the first stanza are repeated, in a set order of variation, as the end-words of the stanzas that follow. The sestina concludes with a three-line envoy which incorporates, in the middle and at the end of the lines, all six of these end words. (An **envoy,** or "send-off," is a short formal stanza which is appended to a poem by way of conclusion.) Despite its extreme difficulty, the sestina has been managed with success by the Elizabethan Sir Philip Sidney, the Victorian Algernon Swinburne, and the modern poets W. H. Auden and John Ashbery.

See *meter.* Stanzas discussed elsewhere in the *Glossary* are *ballad stanza, blank verse, heroic couplet,* and *sonnet.* The nature and history of the various stanzas are briefly described and exemplified in R. M. Alden, *English Verse* (1903), and in Paul Fussell, *Poetic Meter and Poetic Form* (rev., 1979).

Stock Characters are character types that occur repeatedly in a particular literary genre, and so are recognizable as part of the *conventions* of the form. The *Old Comedy* of the Greeks had three stock characters whose interactions constituted the standard plot: the **alazon,** or impostor and self-deceiving braggart; the **eiron,** or self-derogatory and understating character, whose contest with the alazon is central to the comic plot; and the **bomolochos,** buffoon, whose antics add an extra comic element. (See Lane Cooper, *An Aristotelian Theory of Comedy,* 1922.) In his *Anatomy of Criticism* (1957), Northrop Frye revived these old terms, added a fourth, the **agroikos**—the rustic or easily deceived character—and identified the persistence of these types (very broadly defined) in comic plots up to our own time.

The plot of an Elizabethan *romantic comedy,* such as Shakespeare's *As You Like It* and *Twelfth Night,* often turned on a heroine disguised as a handsome young man; and a stock figure in the Elizabethan comedy of intrigue was the clever servant who, like Mosca in Ben Jonson's *Volpone,* connives with his master to fleece another stock character, the stupid **gull.** Nineteenth-century comedy, on stage and in fiction, exploited the stock Englishman with a monocle, an exaggerated Oxford accent, and a defective sense of humor. Western stories and films generated the tight-lipped sheriff who lets his gun do the talking; while a familiar figure in the fiction of the recent past was the stoical Hemingway hero, unillusioned but faithful to his primal code of honor and loyalty in a civilization grown effete and corrupt. The *Beat* or hipster or alienated intellectual who, with or without the help of drugs, has opted out of the Establishment is an even more recent stock character.

The artistic success of a character in literature does not depend on whether or not an author incorporates an established type, but on how well the type is recreated as a convincing individual who fulfills his or her function in the overall plot. Two of Shakespeare's greatest characters are patently conventional. Falstaff is in part a re-rendering of the *Vice,* the comic tempter of the medieval morality play, and in part of the familiar braggart soldier, or **miles gloriosus** of Roman and Renaissance comedy, whose ancestry goes back to the Greek alazon; and Hamlet combines some stock attributes of the hero of Elizabethan *revenge tragedies* with those of the Elizabethan melancholic man. Jane Austen's delightful character Elizabeth Bennet in *Pride and Prejudice* (1813) can be traced back through Restoration comedy to the intelligent, witty, and dauntless heroines of Shakespeare's romantic comedies.

Stock Response. A derogatory term for a reaction thought to be habitual and stereotyped, in place of one which is genuinely and aptly responsive to a given object, situation, or text. The term is sometimes applied to the response of authors themselves to characters, situations, or topics that they set forth in a work; usually, however, it is used to describe standard and inadequate responses of readers to a passage within a work. I. A. Richards, in his *Practical Criticism* (1929), Chapter 5, gave currency to this term by citing and analyzing stock responses by students who wrote critiques on unidentified poems presented for their interpretation and evaluation.

Stock Situations are the counterparts to *stock characters;* that is, they are often-used types of incidents or of sequences of actions in a drama or narrative. Instances range from single situations—the eavesdropper who is hidden behind a bush or in a closet, or the suddenly discovered will or birthmark—to the overall pattern of a plot. The Horatio Alger books for boys, in mid-nineteenth-century America, were all variations on the stock plot of rags-to-riches-by-pluck-and-luck, and we recognize the stock boy-meets-girl incident in the opening episode of much popular fiction and in many motion pictures.

Some recent critics distinguish certain recurrent character types and elements of plot, such as the sexually irresistible but fatal enchantress, the sacrificial scapegoat, and the underground journey, as "archetypal" components which are held to recur, not simply because they are functional literary conventions, but because, like dreams and myths, they express elemental and universal human impulses, anxieties, and needs. See *archetype.*

Stream of Consciousness was a phrase used by William James in his *Principles of Psychology* (1890) to describe the unbroken flow of perceptions, thoughts, and feelings in the waking mind; it has since been adopted to describe a narrative method in modern fiction. Long passages of **introspection,** describing in detail what passes through a character's awareness, are found in novelists from Samuel Richardson to Henry James; the long chapter 42 of James' *Portrait of a Lady,* for example, is entirely given over to the narrator's description of the process of Isabel's memories, thoughts, and feelings. As early as 1888 a minor French writer, Edouard Dujardin, wrote a short novel *Les Lauriers sont coupés* ("The Laurels Have Been Cut") which is a rather crude but sustained attempt to represent the scenes and events of the story solely as they impinge upon the consciousness of the central character. As it has been refined since the 1920s, **stream of consciousness** is the name for a special mode of narration that undertakes to reproduce, without a narrator's intervention, the full spectrum and the continuous flow of a character's mental process, in which sense perceptions mingle with conscious and half-conscious thoughts, memories, expectations, feelings, and random associations.

Some critics use "stream of consciousness" interchangeably with the term **interior monologue.** It is useful, however, to follow the usage of critics who use the former as the inclusive term, denoting all the diverse means employed by authors to describe or to represent the overall state and process of consciousness in a character. "Interior monologue" is then reserved for that species of stream of consciousness which undertakes to present to the reader the course and rhythm of consciousness precisely as it occurs in a character's mind. In interior monologue the author does not intervene, or at any rate intervenes minimally, as describer, guide, or commentator, and does not tidy the vagaries of the mental process into grammatical sentences or into a logical order. The interior monologue, in its radical form, is sometimes described as the exact presentation of the process of consciousness; but because sense perceptions, mental images, feelings, and some aspects of thought itself are nonverbal, it is clear that the author can present these elements only by converting them into some kind of verbal equivalent. Much of this conversion is a matter of narrative *conventions* rather than of unedited, point-for-point reproduction. (For the linguistic techniques for rendering the states and flow of consciousness, see Dorrit Cohn, *Transparent Minds: Narrative Modes for Presenting Consciousness in Fiction,* 1978.)

James Joyce developed a variety of devices for stream-of-consciousness narrative in *Ulysses* (1922). Here is a passage of interior monologue from the "Lestrygonian" episode, in which Leopold Bloom saunters through Dublin, observing and musing:

> Pineapple rock, lemon platt, butter scotch. A sugar-sticky girl shoveling scoopfuls of creams for a christian brother. Some school great. Bad for their tummies. Lozenge and comfit manufacturer to His Majesty the King. God. Save. Our. Sitting on his throne, sucking red jujubes white.

Dorothy Richardson sustains a stream-of-consciousness mode of narrative, focused exclusively on the mind and perceptions of her heroine, throughout the twelve volumes of her novel *Pilgrimage* (1915–38); Virginia Woolf employs the procedure as a primary, although not exclusive narrative mode in several novels, including *Mrs. Dalloway* (1925) and *To the Lighthouse* (1927); and William Faulkner exploits it brilliantly in the first three of the four parts of *The Sound and the Fury* (1929).

Refer to *narratology* and *point of view,* and see: Leon Edel, *The Modern Psychological Novel* (1955); Robert Humphrey, *Stream of Consciousness in the Modern Novel* (1954); Melvin Friedman, *Stream of Consciousness: A Study in Literary Method* (1955).

Style is traditionally defined as the manner of linguistic expression in prose or verse—it is *how* speakers or writers say whatever it is that they say. The style of a particular work or writer has been analyzed in terms of the characteristic modes of its *diction,* or choice of words; its sentence structure and syntax; the density and types of its figurative language; the patterns of its rhythm, component sounds, and other formal features; and its rhetorical aims and devices.

In standard theories of *rhetoric,* styles were usually classified into three main levels: the **high** (or grand), the **middle** (or mean), and the **low** (or base, or plain) **style**. The doctrine of *decorum,* which was influential through the eighteenth century, required that the level of style in a work be appropriate to the social class of the speaker, to the occasion on which it is spoken, and to the dignity of its literary genre (see *poetic diction*). The modern critic Northrop Frye has introduced a variant of this long-persisting analysis of stylistic levels in literature. He makes a primary differentiation between the **demotic style** (which is modeled on the language, rhythms, and associations of ordinary speech) and the **hieratic style** (which employs a variety of formal elaborations that separate the literary language from ordinary speech). Frye then proceeds to distinguish a high, middle, and low level in each of these classes. See *The Well-Tempered Critic* (1963), Chapter 2.

In analyzing style, two types of sentence structure are often distinguished:

The **periodic sentence** is one in which the component parts, or "members," are so composed that the closure of its syntactic structure remains suspended until the end of the sentence; the effect tends to be formal or oratorical. An example is the eloquent opening sentence of James Boswell's *Life of*

Samuel Johnson (1791), in which the structure of the *syntax* is not concluded until we reach the final noun, "task":

> To write the life of him who excelled all mankind in writing the lives of others, and who, whether we consider his extraordinary endowments, or his various works, has been equalled by few in any age, is an arduous, and may be reckoned in me a presumptuous task.

In the **nonperiodic** (or **loose**) **sentence**—which is more relaxed and conversational in effect—the component members are continuous, but so loosely joined that the sentence would have been syntactically complete if a period had been inserted at one or more places before the actual close. So Joseph Addison's two sentences in *Spectator 105,* describing the limited topics in the conversation of a "man-about-town," or dilettante, could each have closed at several points in the sequence of their component clauses:

> He will tell you the names of the principal favourites, repeat the shrewd sayings of a man of quality, whisper an intrigue that is not yet blown upon by common fame; or, if the sphere of his observations is a little larger than ordinary, will perhaps enter into all the incidents, turns, and revolutions in a game of ombre. When he has gone thus far he has shown you the whole circle of his accomplishments, his parts are drained, and he is disabled from any farther conversation.

Another distinction often made in discussing prose style is that between parataxis and hypotaxis:

A **paratactic style** is one in which the members within a sentence, or else a sequence of complete sentences, are put one after the other without any expression of their connection or relations except (at most) the noncommittal connective "and." Ernest Hemingway's style is characteristically paratactic. The members in this sentence from his novel *The Sun Also Rises* (1926) are joined merely by "ands": "It was dim and dark and the pillars went high up, and there were people praying, and it smelt of incense, and there were some wonderful big buildings." The curt paratactic sentences in his short story "Indian Camp" omit all connectives: "The sun was coming over the hills. A bass jumped, making a circle in the water. Nick trailed his hand in the water. It felt warm in the sharp chill of the morning."

A **hypotactic style** is one in which the temporal, logical, and syntactic relations between members and sentences are expressed by words (such as "when," "then," "because," "therefore") or by phrases (such as "in order to," "as a result") or by the use of subordinate phrases and clauses. The style in this *Glossary* is mainly hypotactic.

A very large number of loosely descriptive terms are used to characterize kinds of style, such as "pure," "ornate," "florid," "gay," "sober," "simple," "elaborate," and so on. Styles are also classified according to a literary period or tradition ("the *metaphysical* style," "Restoration prose style"); according to an influential text ("biblical style," *euphuism*); according to a type of use ("a scientific style," "journalese"); or according to the distinctive practice of an individual author (the "Shakespearean" or "Miltonic style"; "Johnsonese"). Historians of English prose style, especially in the seventeenth and eighteenth centuries, have distinguished between the vogue of the "Ciceronian style" (named after the characteristic practice of the Roman writer Cicero), which is elaborately constructed, highly periodic, and typically builds to a climax, and the opposing vogue of the clipped, concise, pointed, and uniformly-stressed sentences in the "Attic" or "Senecan" styles (named after the practice of the Roman Seneca). See J. M. Patrick and others, eds., *Style, Rhetoric, and Rhythm: Essays by Morris W. Croll* (1966), and George Williamson, *The Senecan Amble: A Study in Prose Form from Bacon to Collier* (1951).

See *prose*, and for some recent developments in the treatment of style, *stylistics* and *discourse analysis*. Among the more traditional theorists and analysts of style are Herbert Read, *English Prose Style* (1928); Bonamy Dobree, *Modern Prose Style* (1934); W. K. Wimsatt, *The Prose Style of Samuel Johnson* (1941); P. F. Baum, *The Other Harmony of Prose* (1952); Erich Auerbach, *Mimesis: The Representation of Reality in Western Literature* (1953); Josephine Miles, *Eras and Modes in English Poetry* (1957). For attempts to distinguish and analyze "mannerist," "baroque," and "rococo" styles in seventeenth-century and later poetry and prose, see Wylie Sypher, *Four Stages of Renaissance Style* (1955), and *Rococo to Cubism in Art and Literature* (1960).

Surrealism ("superrealism") was launched as a concerted artistic movement in France by André Breton's *Manifesto on Surrealism* (1924). The expressed aim was a revolt against all restraints on free creativity; included among the restraints to be violated were logical reason, standard morality, social and artistic conventions and norms, and any control over the artistic process by forethought and intention. To ensure the unhampered operation of the "deep mind," which they regarded as the only source of valid knowledge as well as art, surrealists turned to **automatic writing** (writing delivered over entirely to the promptings of the unconscious mind), and to exploiting the material of dreams, of states of mind between sleep and waking, and of natural or artificially induced hallucinations.

Surrealism was a revolutionary movement in painting, sculpture, and the other arts, as well as literature; and it often joined forces, although briefly, with one or another revolutionary movement in the political and social realm. The effects of surrealism extended far beyond the small group of its professed adherents such as André Breton, Louis Aragon, and the painter Salvador Dali. The influence, direct or indirect, of surrealist innovations can be found in many modern writers of prose and verse who have broken with conventional modes of artistic organization to experiment with free association, a broken syntax, nonlogical and nonchronological order, dreamlike and nightmarish sequences, and the juxtaposition of bizarre, shocking, or seemingly unrelated images. In England and America such effects can be found in a wide range of writings, from the poetry of Dylan Thomas to the flights of fantasy, hallucinative writing, startling inconsequences, and *black humor* in the novels of Henry Miller, William Burroughs, and Thomas Pynchon.

For a precursor of some aspects of surrealism, see *decadence;* for later developments that continued some of the surrealist innovations, see literature of the *absurd, antinovel, magic realism,* and *postmodernism.* Refer to David Gascoyne, *A Short Survey of Surrealism* (1935); A. E. Balakian, *Literary Origins of Surrealism* (1947); Herbert Read, *The Philosophy of Modern Art* (1955); M. Nadeau, *History of Surrealism* (1967); Paul C. Ray, *The Surrealist Movement in England* (1971).

Symbol. In the broadest sense a symbol is anything which signifies something; in this sense all words are symbols. In discussing literature, however, the term **symbol** is applied only to a word or phrase that signifies an object or event which in its turn signifies something, or has a range of reference, beyond itself. Some symbols are "conventional" or "public": thus "the Cross," "the Red, White, and Blue," and "the Good Shepherd" are terms that refer to symbolic objects of which the further significance is determinate within a particular culture. Poets, like all of us, use such conventional symbols; many poets, however, also use "private" or "personal symbols." Often they do so by exploiting widely shared associations between an object or event or action and a particular concept; for example, the general association of a peacock with pride and of an eagle with heroic endeavor, or the rising sun with birth and the setting sun with death, or climbing with effort or progress and descent with surrender or failure. Some poets, however, repeatedly use symbols whose significance they largely generate themselves, and these pose a more difficult problem in interpretation.

Take as an example the word "rose," which in its literal use signifies a kind of flower. In Robert Burns' line "O my love's like a red, red rose," the word "rose" is used as a *simile;* and in the lines by Winthrop Mackworth Praed,

> She was our queen, our rose, our star;
> And then she danced—O Heaven, her dancing!

the word "rose" is used as a *metaphor.* In *The Romance of the Rose,* a long medieval *dream vision,* we read about a half-opened rose to which the dreamer's access is aided by a character called "Fair Welcome," but impeded or forbidden by other characters called "Reason," "Shame," and "Jealousy." We readily recognize that the whole narrative is a sustained *allegory* about an elaborate courtship, in which most of the agents are personified abstractions and the rose itself functions as an allegorical **emblem** (that is, an object whose significance is made determinate by its particular qualities and by the role it plays in the narrative) which represents both the lady's love and her lovely body. Then we read William Blake's poem "The Sick Rose."

> O Rose, thou art sick.
> The invisible worm
> That flies in the night
> In the howling storm
>
> Has found out thy bed
> Of crimson joy,
> And his dark secret love
> Does thy life destroy.

This rose is not the vehicle for a simile or metaphor, because it lacks the paired subject—"my love," or the girl referred to as "she," in the examples just cited—which is an identifying feature of these figures. And it is not an allegorical rose, since, unlike the flower in *The Romance of the Rose,* it is not part of an obvious double order of correlated references, one literal and the second allegorical, in which the allegorical or emblematic reference of the rose is made determinate by its role within the literal narrative. Blake's rose *is* a rose—yet it is patently also something more than a rose: words such as "bed," "joy," "love," which do not comport literally with an actual flower, together with the sinister tone and the intensity of the lyric speaker's feeling, press the reader to infer that the described object has a further range of suggested but unspecified reference which makes it a symbol. But Blake's rose is a personal symbol and not—like the symbolic rose in the closing cantos of Dante's fourteenth-century *Paradiso* and other Christian poems—an element in a set of conventional and widely known religious symbols, in which concrete objects of this passing world are used to signify, in a relatively determinate way, the objects and truths of a higher eternal realm. (See Barbara Seward, *The Symbolic Rose,* 1960.) Only from the implicit suggestions in the poem itself—the sexual connotations of "bed" and "love," especially in conjunction with "joy" and "worm"—supplemented by our knowledge both of similar elements and topics in Blake's other poems and of widespread associations in our culture with the objects described in this poem, are we led to infer that Blake's lament for a crimson rose which has been entered and sickened unto death by a dark and secret worm symbolizes the destruction wrought by furtiveness, deceit, and hypocrisy in what should be a frank and joyous relationship of physical love. Various critics of the poem, however, have proposed alternative interpretations of its symbolic significance. It is an attribute of many private symbols—the White Whale in Melville's *Moby-Dick* (1851) is another famed example—as well as a reason why they are an irreplaceable literary device, that they suggest a direction or a broad area of significance rather than, like an emblem in an allegorical narrative, a relatively determinate reference.

In the copious modern literature on the nature of the literary symbol, reference is often made to two seminal passages, written early in the nineteenth century by Coleridge in England and Goethe in Germany, concerning the difference between an allegory and a symbol. Coleridge is in fact describing what he believes to be the uniquely symbolic nature of the Bible as a sacred text, but later commentators have assumed (probably mistakenly) that he intended his comment to define the general nature of a symbol as used also in secular literature:

> Now an allegory is but a translation of abstract notions into a picture-language, which is itself nothing but an abstraction from objects of the senses. . . . On the other hand a symbol . . . is characterized by a translucence of the special [i.e., of the species] in the individual, or of the general [i.e., of the genus] in the special, or of the universal in the general; above all by the translucence of the eternal through and in the temporal. It always partakes of the reality which it renders intelligible; and while it

> enunciates the whole, abides itself as a living part in that unity of which it is the representative. [Allegories] are but empty echoes which the fancy arbitrarily associates with apparitions of matter. . . .
>
> (Coleridge, *The Statesman's Manual,* 1816)

Goethe had been meditating about the nature of the literary symbol in secular writings since the 1790s, but gave his concept its clearest formulation in 1824:

> There is a great difference, whether the poet seeks the particular for the sake of the general or sees the general in the particular. From the former procedure there ensues allegory, in which the particular serves only as illustration, as example of the general. The latter procedure, however, is genuinely the nature of poetry; it expresses something particular, without thinking of the general or pointing to it.
>
> Allegory transforms the phenomenon into a concept, the concept into an image, but in such a way that the concept always remains bounded in the image, and is entirely to be kept and held in it, and to be expressed by it.
>
> Symbolism [however] transforms the phenomenon into idea, the idea into an image, and in such a way that the idea remains always infinitely active and unapproachable in the image, and even if expressed in all languages, still would remain inexpressible.
>
> (Goethe, *Maxims and Reflections,* Nos. 279, 1112, 1113)

It will be noted that, whatever the differences between these cryptic passages, both Coleridge and Goethe stress that an allegory presents a pair of subjects (an image and a concept) and a symbol only one (the image alone); that the allegory is specific in its reference, while the symbol remains indefinite, but richly—even infinitely—suggestive in its significance; and also that for this very reason, a symbol is the higher mode of literary expression. To these claims, characteristic in the Romantic Period, critics until the recent past have for the most part agreed. In express opposition to romantic theory, however, Paul de Man has elevated allegory over symbol because, he claims, it is less "mystified" about its own status as a fiction and a rhetorical device. See de Man, "The Rhetoric of Temporality," in *Interpretation: Theory and Practice,* ed. C. S. Singleton (1969), and *Allegories of Reading* (1979).

See W. B. Yeats, "The Symbolism of Poetry" (1900), in *Essays and Introductions* (1961); H. Flanders Dunbar, *Symbolism in Medieval Thought* (1929); C. S. Lewis, *The Allegory of Love: A Study in Medieval Tradition* (1936); Elder Olson, "A Dialogue on Symbolism," in R. S. Crane, ed., *Critics and Criticism* (1952); W. Y. Tindall, *The Literary Symbol* (1955); Harry Levin, "Symbolism and Fiction," in *Contexts of Criticism* (1957); Isabel C. Hungerland, *Poetic Discourse* (1958), Chapter 5; Maurice Beebe, ed., *Literary Symbolism* (1960).

Symbolist Movement. Various poets of the *Romantic Period,* including Novalis and Hölderlin in Germany and Shelley in England, often used private *symbols* in their poetry; Shelley, for example, repeatedly made symbolic use of objects such as the morning and evening star, a boat moving upstream, winding caves, and the conflict between a serpent and an eagle. William Blake, however, exceeded all his romantic contemporaries in his recourse to a persistent and sustained **symbolism**—that is, a system of symbolic elements—both in his lyric poems and his long prophetic, or epic poems. In the *Romantic Period in America,* a symbolist procedure was prominent in the novels of Nathaniel Hawthorne and Herman Melville, the prose of Emerson and Thoreau, and the poetic theory and practice of Poe. (See Charles Feidelson, Jr., *Symbolism and American Literature,* 1953.) These writers derived the mode in large part from the native Puritan tradition of typology (see *interpretation: typological and allegorical*), and also from the theory of correspondences of the Swedish theologian Emanuel Swedenborg (1688–1772).

In the usage of literary historians, however, the expression **Symbolist Movement** designates specifically a group of French writers beginning with Charles Baudelaire (*Fleurs du mal,* 1857) and including such later poets as Arthur Rimbaud, Paul Verlaine, Stéphane Mallarmé, and Paul Valéry. Baudelaire based the symbolic mode of his poems in part on the example of the American Edgar Allan Poe, but especially on the ancient belief in **correspondences**—the doctrine that there exist inherent and systematic analogies between the human mind and the outer world, and also between the natural and the spiritual worlds. As Baudelaire put this doctrine: "Everything, form, movement, number, color, perfume, in the *spiritual* as in the *natural* world, is significative, reciprocal, converse, *correspondent*." The techniques of the French **Symbolists**, who exploited an order of private symbols in a poetry of rich suggestiveness rather than explicit signification, had an immense influence throughout Europe, and (especially in the 1890s and later) in England and America on poets such as Arthur Symons and Ernest Dowson (see *Decadence*) as well as W. B. Yeats, Ezra Pound, Dylan Thomas, Hart Crane, E. E. Cummings, and Wallace Stevens. Major symbolist poets in Germany are Stefan George and Rainer Maria Rilke.

The *Modern Period,* in the decades after World War I, was a notable era of symbolism in literature. Many of the major writers of the period exploit symbols which are in part drawn from religious and esoteric traditions and in part from their own invention. Some of the works of the age are symbolist in their settings, their agents, and their actions, as well as in the objects they refer to. Instances of a persistently symbolic procedure occur in lyrics (Yeats' "Byzantium" poems, Dylan Thomas' series of sonnets *Altarwise by Owl-light*), in longer poems (Hart Crane's *The Bridge,* T. S. Eliot's *The Waste Land,* Wallace Stevens' "The Comedian as the Letter C"), and in novels (James Joyce's *Finnegans Wake,* William Faulkner's *The Sound and the Fury*).

See Arthur Symons, *The Symbolist Movement in Literature* (rev., 1919); Edmund Wilson, *Axel's Castle* (1936); C. M. Bowra, *The Heritage of Symbolism* (1943); Kenneth Cornell, *The Symbolist Movement* (1951); Edward Engelberg, ed., *The Symbolist Poem* (1967); and Anna Balakian, ed., *The Symbolist Movement in the Literature of European Languages* (1982). For an attempt to decode William Blake's complex symbolism, see S. Foster Damon, *A Blake Dictionary: The Ideas and Symbols of William Blake* (1965).

Synesthesia is the psychological term for experiencing two or more kinds of sensation when only one sense is being stimulated. In literature the term is applied to descriptions of one kind of sensation in terms of another; color is attributed to sounds, odor to colors, sound to odors, and so on. A complex example of synesthesia (which is sometimes also called "sense transference" or "sense analogy") is this passage from Shelley's "The Sensitive Plant" (1820):

> And the hyacinth purple, and white, and blue,
> Which flung from its bells a sweet peal anew
> Of music so delicate, soft, and intense,
> It was felt like an odor within the sense.

The varicolored, bell-shaped hyacinths send out a peal of music which affects the sense as though it were (what in fact it is) the scent of the flowers. Keats, in the "Ode to a Nightingale" (1819), calls for a draught of wine

> Tasting of Flora and the country green,
> Dance, and Provençal song, and sunburnt mirth;

that is, he calls for a drink tasting of sight, color, motion, sound, and heat. Occasional uses of synesthetic imagery have been made by poets ever since Homer. Such imagery became much more frequent in the Romantic period, and was especially exploited by the French *Symbolists* of the middle and later nineteenth century; see Baudelaire's sonnet "Correspondances," and Rimbaud's sonnet on the color of vowel sounds "A black, E white, I red, U green, O blue."

Refer to June Downey, *Creative Imagination* (1929), and to the general discussion and detailed analyses of synesthesia in Richard H. Fogel, *The Imagery of Keats and Shelley* (1949), Chapter 3.

Tension became a common descriptive and evaluative word in the criticism of the 1930s and later, especially after Allen Tate, one of the *New Critics,* proposed it as a term to be made by "lopping the prefixes off the logical terms *extension* and *intension.*" In technical logic the "intension" of a word is the set of abstract attributes which must be possessed by any object to which the word can be literally applied, and the "extension" of a word is the class of concrete objects to which the word applies. The meaning of good poetry, according to Tate, "is its 'tension,' the full organized body of all the extension and intension that we can find in it." ("Tension in Poetry," 1938, in *On the Limits of Poetry,* 1948.) It would seem that by this statement Tate meant that a good poem incorporates both the abstract and the concrete, the general idea and the particular image, in an integral whole. (See *concrete and abstract,* above.)

Other critics use "tension" to characterize poetry that manifests an equilibrium of the serious and the ironic, or "a pattern of resolved stresses," or a harmony of opponent tendencies, or any other mode of that stability-in-opposition which was the favorite way in the *New Criticism* for conceiving the organization of a good poem. And some critics, dubious perhaps about the validity of Tate's logical derivation of the term, simply apply "tension" to any poem in which the elements seem tightly rather than loosely interrelated.

Three Unities. In the sixteenth and seventeenth centuries, critics of the drama in Italy and France added to Aristotle's *unity of action* two other unities, to constitute one of the *rules* of drama known as "the three unities." On the assumption that **verisimilitude**—the achievement of an illusion of reality in the audience—requires that the action represented by a play approximate the actual conditions of the staging of the play, they imposed the requirement of the "unity of place" (that the action represented be limited to a single location) and the requirement of the "unity of time" (that the time represented be limited to the two or three hours it takes to act the play, or at most to a single day of either twelve or twenty-four hours). In large part because of the potent example of Shakespeare, many of whose plays represent frequent changes of place and the passage of many years, the unities of place and time never dominated English *neoclassicism* as they did criticism in Italy and France; a final blow was the famous attack against them, and against the principle of dramatic verisimilitude on which they were based, in Samuel Johnson's "Preface to Shakespeare" (1765). Since then in England, the unities of place and time (as distinguished from the unity of action) have been regarded as optional devices, available to the playwright to achieve special effects of dramatic concentration.

See Joel Spingarn, *Literary Criticism in the Renaissance* (rev., 1924); J. W. H. Atkins, *English Literary Criticism: Seventeenth and Eighteenth Centuries* (1957); René Wellek, *A History of Modern Criticism*, Vol. 1, "The Later Eighteenth Century" (1955); Bernard Weinberg, *A History of Literary Criticism in the Italian Renaissance* (1961).

Touchstone is a hard stone used to determine, by the streak left on it when rubbed by a piece of gold, whether the metal is pure gold, and if not, the degree to which it contains an alloy. The word was introduced into literary criticism by Matthew Arnold in "The Study of Poetry" (1880) to denote short but distinctive passages, selected from the writings of the greatest poets, which he used to determine the excellence of passages or poems which are compared to them. Arnold proposed this method of evaluation as a corrective for what he called the "fallacious" estimates of poems according to their "historic" importance in the development of literature, or else according to their "personal" appeal to an individual critic. As Arnold put it:

> There can be no more useful help for discovering what poetry belongs to the class of the truly excellent . . . than to have always in one's mind lines and expressions of the great masters, and to apply them as a touchstone to other poetry. . . . If we have any tact we shall find them . . . an infallible touchstone for detecting the presence or absence of high poetic quality, and also the degree of this quality, in all other poetry which we may place beside them.

The touchstones he proposed are passages from Homer, Dante, Shakespeare, and Milton, ranging in length from one to four lines. Two of his best-known touchstones are also the shortest: Dante's "In la sua volontade è nostra pace" ("In His will is our peace"; *Paradiso*, III.85), and the close of Milton's description in *Paradise Lost,* IV, 271–2, of the loss to Ceres of her daughter Proserpine, ". . . which cost Ceres all that pain / To seek her through the world."

Tragedy. The term is broadly applied to literary, and especially to dramatic, representations of serious and important actions which eventuate in a disastrous conclusion for the *protagonist,* or chief character. More precise and detailed discussions of the tragic form properly begin—although they should not end—with Aristotle's classic analysis in the *Poetics* (fourth century B.C.). Aristotle based his theory on induction from the only examples available to him, the tragedies of Greek dramatists such as Aeschylus, Sophocles, and Euripides. In the subsequent two thousand years and more, many new and artistically effective types of serious plots ending in a catastrophe have been developed—types that Aristotle had no way of foreseeing. The many attempts to stretch Aristotle's analysis to apply to later tragic forms serve merely to blur his critical categories and to obscure important differences among diverse types of plays. When flexibly managed, however, Aristotle's descriptions apply in some part to many tragic plots, and his analytic concepts serve as a suggestive starting point for identifying the differentiae of various non-Aristotelian modes of tragic construction.

Aristotle defined tragedy as "the imitation of an action that is serious and also, as having magnitude, complete in itself," in the medium of poetic language and in the manner of dramatic rather than of narrative presentation, which incorporates "incidents arousing pity and fear, wherewith to accomplish the catharsis of such emotions." (See *imitation.*) Precisely how to interpret Aristotle's **catharsis**—which in Greek signifies "purgation," or "purification," or both—is much disputed. On two matters, however, a number of commentators agree. Aristotle in the first place sets out to account for the undeniable, though remarkable, fact that many tragic representations of suffering and defeat leave an audience feeling not depressed, but relieved, or even exalted. In the second place, Aristotle uses this distinctive effect on the reader, "the pleasure of pity and fear," as the basic way to distinguish the tragic from comic or other forms, and he regards the dramatist's aim to produce this effect in the highest degree as the principle which determines both the choice of the tragic protagonist and the organization of the tragic plot.

Accordingly, Aristotle says that the **tragic hero** will most effectively evoke both our pity and terror if he is neither thoroughly good nor thoroughly evil but a mixture of both; and also that the tragic effect will be stronger if the hero is "better than we are," in the sense that he is of higher than ordinary moral worth. Such a man is exhibited as suffering a change in fortune from happiness to misery because of a mistaken act, to which he is led by his **hamartia**—his "error of judgment" or, as it is often though less literally translated, his **tragic flaw.** (One common form of hamartia in Greek tragedies was **hubris,** that "pride" or overweening self-confidence which leads a protagonist to disregard a divine warning or to violate an important moral law.) The tragic hero moves us to pity because, since he is not an evil man, his misfortune is greater than he deserves; but he moves us also to fear, because we recognize similar possibilities of error in our own lesser and fallible selves. Aristotle grounds his analysis of "the very structure and incidents of the play" on the same principle; the plot, he says, which will most effectively evoke "tragic pity and fear" is one in which the events develop through complication to a *catastrophe* in which there occurs (often by an *anagnorisis*, or discovery of facts hitherto unknown to the hero) a sudden *peripeteia*, or reversal in his fortune from happiness to disaster. See *plot*.

Authors in the Middle Ages lacked direct knowledge either of classical tragedies or of Aristotle's theory. **Medieval tragedies** are simply the story of a person of high status who, whether deservedly or not, is brought from prosperity to wretchedness by an unpredictable turn of the wheel of fortune. The short narratives in "The Monk's Tale" of *The Canterbury Tales* (late fourteenth century) are all, in Chaucer's own term, "tragedies" of this kind. With the Elizabethan era came both the beginning and the acme of dramatic tragedy in England. The tragedies of this period owed much to the native religious drama, the *miracle* and *morality plays*, which had developed independently of classical influence, but with a crucial contribution from the Roman writer Seneca (first century), whose dramas got to be widely known earlier than those of the Greek tragedians.

Senecan tragedy was written to be recited rather than acted; but to English playwrights, who thought that these tragedies had been intended for the stage, they provided the model for an organized five-act play with a complex plot and an elaborately formal style of dialogue. Senecan drama, in the Elizabethan Age, had two main lines of development. One of these consisted of academic tragedies written in close imitation of the Senecan model, including the use of a *chorus*, and usually constructed according to the rules of the *three unities*, which had been elaborated by Italian critics of the sixteenth century; the earliest English example was Thomas Sackville and Thomas Norton's *Gorboduc* (1562). The other and much more important development was written for the popular stage, and is called the **revenge tragedy**, or (in its most sensational form) the **tragedy of blood**. This type of play derived from Seneca's favorite materials of murder, revenge, ghosts, mutilation, and carnage, but while Seneca had relegated such matters to long reports of offstage actions by messengers, the Elizabethan writers usually represented them on stage to satisfy the appetite of the contemporary audience for violence and horror. Thomas Kyd's *The Spanish Tragedy* (1586) established this popular form; its subject is a murder and the quest for vengeance, and it includes a ghost, insanity, suicide, a play-within-a-play, sensational incidents, and a gruesomely bloody ending. Christopher Marlowe's *The Jew of Malta* (c. 1592) and Shakespeare's *Titus Andronicus* (c. 1590) are in this mode; and from this lively but unlikely prototype came one of the greatest of tragedies, *Hamlet,* as well as John Webster's fine horror plays of 1612–13, *The Duchess of Malfi* and *The White Devil*.

Many major tragedies in the brief flowering time between 1585 and 1625, by Marlowe, Shakespeare, George Chapman, Webster, Sir Francis Beaumont and John Fletcher, and Philip Massinger, deviate radically from the Aristotelian norm. Shakespeare's *Othello* is one of the few plays which accords closely with Aristotle's basic concepts of the tragic hero and plot.

The hero of *Macbeth*, however, is not a good man who commits a tragic error, but an ambitious man who knowingly turns great gifts to evil purposes and therefore, although he retains something of our sympathy by his courage and self-insight, deserves his destruction at the hands of his morally superior antagonists. Shakespeare's *Richard III* presents first the success, then the ruin, of a malign protagonist who nonetheless arouses in us a reluctant admiration by his intelligence and imaginative power and by the shameless candor by which he glories in his ambition and malice. Most Shakespearean tragedies, like Elizabethan tragedies generally, also depart from Aristotle's paradigm by introducing humorous characters, incidents, or scenes, called *comic relief,* which were in various degrees made relevant to the tragic plot. There developed also in this age the mixed mode called *tragicomedy,* a popular non-Aristotelian form which produced a number of artistic successes. And later in the seventeenth century the Restoration Period produced the curious genre, a cross between epic and tragedy, called *heroic tragedy.*

Until the close of the seventeenth century almost all tragedies were written in verse and had as protagonists men of high rank whose fate affected the fortunes of a state. A few minor Elizabethan tragedies, such as *A Yorkshire Tragedy* (of uncertain authorship), had as the chief character a man of the lower class, but it remained for eighteenth-century writers to popularize the **bourgeois** or **domestic tragedy,** which was written in prose and presented a protagonist from the middle or lower social ranks who suffers a commonplace or domestic disaster. George Lillo's *The London Merchant: or, The History of George Barnwell* (1731), about a merchant's apprentice who succumbs to a heartless courtesan and comes to a bad end by robbing his employer and murdering his uncle, is still read, at least in college courses.

Since that time most successful tragedies have been in prose, and represent middle-class, or occasionally even working-class, heroes and heroines. One of the more notable modern tragedies, Arthur Miller's *The Death of a Salesman* (1949), relies for its tragic seriousness on the degree to which Willy Loman, in his bewildered defeat by life, is representative of the ordinary man whose aspirations reflect the false values of a commercial society; the effect on the audience is one of compassionate understanding rather than of tragic pity and terror. A term sometimes applied to a recurrent protagonist in modern serious plays and prose fiction, to signify his discrepancy from the heroes of traditional tragedies, is the **antihero**: a person who, instead of manifesting largeness, dignity, power, and heroism in the face of fate, is petty, ignominious, ineffectual, or passive. Extreme instances are the characters who people the world stripped of certainties, values, or even meaning, in Samuel Beckett's dramas—the tramps Vladimir and Estragon in *Waiting for Godot,* or the blind and paralyzed old man, Hamm, who is the protagonist in *Endgame.* In some recent works, tragic effects involve elements that traditionally belonged to the genre of farce; see literature of the *absurd* and *black comedy.*

Tragedy since World War I has also been innovative in other ways, including experimentation with new versions of ancient types. Eugene O'Neill's *Mourning Becomes Electra* (1931), for example, is an adaptation of Aeschylus' *Oresteia,* with the locale shifted from Greece to New England, the poetry altered to rather flat prose, and the tragedy of fate converted into a tragedy of the psychological compulsions of a family trapped in a tangle of Freudian complexes (see *psychoanalysis*). T. S. Eliot's *Murder in the Cathedral* (1935) is a tragic drama which, like Greek tragedy, is written in verse and has a chorus, but also incorporates elements of two early Christian forms, the medieval *miracle play* (dealing with the martyrdom of a saint) and the medieval *morality play*.

See *genre*, and refer to A. C. Bradley, *Shakespearean Tragedy* (1904); H. D. F. Kitto, *Greek Tragedy* (rev., 1954); Elder Olson, *Tragedy and the Theory of Drama* (1961); George Steiner, *The Death of Tragedy* (1961); R. B. Sewall, ed., *Tragedy: Modern Essays in Criticism* (1963).

Tragicomedy. A type of Elizabethan and Jacobean drama which intermingled both the standard characters and subject matter and the standard plot-forms of tragedy and comedy. Thus, the important agents in tragicomedy included both people of high degree and people of low degree, even though, according to the reigning critical theory, only upper-class characters were appropriate to tragedy, while members of the middle and lower classes were the proper subject of comedy; see *decorum*. Also, tragicomedy represented a serious action which threatened a tragic disaster to the protagonist, yet, by an abrupt reversal of circumstance, turned out happily. As John Fletcher wrote in his Preface to *The Faithful Shepherdess* (c. 1610), tragicomedy "wants [i.e., lacks] deaths, which is enough to make it no tragedy, yet brings some near it, which is enough to make it no comedy, which must be a representation of familiar people. . . . A god is as lawful in [tragicomedy] as in a tragedy, and mean people as in a comedy."

Shakespeare's *Merchant of Venice* is by these criteria a tragicomedy, because it mingles people of the aristocracy with lower-class characters (such as the Jewish merchant Shylock and the clown Launcelot Gobbo), and also because the developing threat of death to Antonio is suddenly reversed at the end by Portia's ingenious casuistry in the trial scene. Francis Beaumont and John Fletcher in *Philaster* and numerous other plays on which they collaborated from about 1606 to 1613, inaugurated a mode of tragicomedy that employs a romantic and fast-moving plot of love, jealousy, treachery, intrigue, and disguises, and ends in a melodramatic reversal of fortune for the protagonists, who had hitherto seemed headed for disaster. Shakespeare wrote his late plays *Cymbeline* and *The Winter's Tale*, between 1609 and 1611, in this very popular mode of the tragicomic *romance*. The name "tragicomedy" is sometimes applied also to plays with *double plots*, one serious and the other comic.

See E. M. Waith, *The Pattern of Tragicomedy in Beaumont and Fletcher* (1952); M. T. Herrick, *Tragicomedy* (1955).

Transcendentalism in America. A philosophical and literary movement, centered in Concord and Boston, which was prominent in the intellectual and cultural life of New England from 1836 until just before the Civil War. It was inaugurated in 1836 by a Unitarian discussion group that came to be called the Transcendental Club; in the seven years or so that the group met at various houses, it included at one time or another Ralph Waldo Emerson, Bronson Alcott, Frederick Henry Hedge, W. E. Channing and W. H. Channing, Theodore Parker, Margaret Fuller, Elizabeth Peabody, George Ripley, Nathaniel Hawthorne, Henry Thoreau, and Jones Very. A quarterly periodical *The Dial* (1840–44) printed many of the early essays, poems, and reviews by the Transcendentalists.

Transcendentalism was neither a systematic nor a sharply definable philosophy, but rather an intellectual mode and emotional mood that was expressed by very diverse, and in some instances rather eccentric, voices. Modern historians of the movement tend to take as its central exponents Emerson (especially in *Nature,* "The American Scholar," the Divinity School Address, "The Over-Soul," and "Self Reliance") and Thoreau (especially in *Walden* and his journals). The term "transcendental," as Emerson pointed out in his lecture "The Transcendentalist" (1841), was taken from Immanuel Kant the German philosopher (1724–1804). Kant had confined the expression "transcendental knowledge" to the cognizance of those forms and categories—such as space, time, quantity, causality—which, in his view, are imposed on perception by the constitution of all human minds; he regarded these aspects as the universal conditions of sense-experience. Emerson and others, however, extended the concept of transcendental knowledge, in a way whose validity Kant had specifically denied, to include an intuitive cognizance of moral and other truths that transcend the limits of human sense-experience. The intellectual antecedents of American Transcendentalism, in addition to Kant, were many and diverse, and included post-Kantian German Idealists, the English thinkers Samuel Taylor Coleridge and Thomas Carlyle (themselves exponents of forms of German Idealism), Plato and Neoplatonists, the occult Swedish theologian Emanuel Swedenborg, and some varieties of Oriental philosophy.

What the various Transcendentalists had in common was less what they proposed than what they were reacting against. By and large, they were opposed to rigid rationalism; to eighteenth-century empirical philosophy of the school of John Locke, which derived all knowledge from sense impressions; to highly formalized religion, and especially the Calvinist orthodoxy of New England; and to the social conformity, materialism, and commercialism that they found increasingly dominant in American life. Among the counter-views that were affirmed by Transcendentalists, especially Emerson, were confidence in the validity of knowledge that is grounded in feeling and intuition, and a consequent tendency to accept what, to logical reasoning, might seem contradictions; an ethics of individualism that stressed self-trust, self-reliance, and self-sufficiency; a turn away from modern society, with its getting and spending, to the scenes and objects of the natural world, which were regarded both as physical facts and as correspondences to the human spirit (see *correspondences*); and, in place of a formal or doctrinal religion, a general faith in a divine "Principle," or "Spirit," or "Soul" (Emerson's "Over-Soul") in which both humanity and the cosmos participate. This omnipresent Spirit, Emerson said, constitutes the "Unity within which every man's particular being is contained and made one with all other"; it manifests itself to human consciousness as influxes of inspired insights, and is the source of the profoundest truths and the necessary condition of all moral and spiritual development.

Walden (1854) records how Thoreau tested his distinctive and radically individualist version of Transcendental values by withdrawing from societal complexities and distractions to a life of solitude and complete self-reliance in a natural setting at Walden Pond. He simplified his material wants to those he could satisfy by the bounty of the woods and lake or could provide by his own labor, attended minutely to natural objects in the material world both for their inherent interest and as correlatives to the mind of the observer, and devoted his leisure to reading, meditation, and writing. In his nonconformity to social and legal requirements that violated his moral sense, he chose a day in jail rather than pay his poll tax to a government that supported the Mexican War and slavery. Brook Farm, on the other hand, was a short-lived experiment (1841–47) by more socially oriented Transcendentalists who established a commune on the professed principle of the equal sharing of work, pay, and cultural benefits. Hawthorne, who lived there for a while, later wrote about Brook Farm, with considerable skepticism about both its goals and practices, in *The Blithedale Romance* (1852).

The Transcendental movement, with its optimism about the indwelling divinity, self-sufficiency, and high potentialities of human nature, did not survive the crisis of the Civil War and its aftermath; and Melville, like Hawthorne, satirized aspects of Transcendentalism in his fiction. Some of its basic concepts and values, however, were assimilated by Walt Whitman, were later echoed in writings by Henry James and other major American authors, and continue to re-emerge, in both liberal and radical modes, in latter-day America. The voice of Thoreau, for example, however distorted, can be recognized still in some doctrines of the *counterculture* of the 1960s and later.

See *periods of American literature*, and refer to: Octavius B. Frothingham, *Transcendentalism in New England* (1876); Harold C. Goddard, *Studies in New England Transcendentalism* (1908); F. O. Matthiessen, *American Renaissance* (1941); the anthology edited, together with commentary, by Perry Miller, *The Transcendentalists* (1950); Joel Porte, *Emerson and Thoreau: Transcendentalists in Conflict* (1966); Lawrence Buell, *Literary Transcendentalism: Style and Vision in the American Renaissance* (1973).

Utopias and Dystopias. *Utopia* was the title of a book about an imaginary commonwealth, written in Latin (1515–16) by the Renaissance *humanist* Sir Thomas More. The title plays on two Greek words, "eutopia" (good place) and "outopia" (no place); and the term **utopia** has come to signify the entire class of fictional writings which represents an ideal but nonexistent political state and way of life. The first and greatest instance of the type was Plato's *Republic* (later fourth century B.C.), which sets forth, in dialogue form, the eternal Idea or Form of a commonwealth as a model that can at best be merely approximated by political organizations in the actual world. Most utopias, like that of Sir Thomas More, represent their ideal state in the fiction of a distant country reached by a venturesome traveler. There have been many utopias written since More gave impetus to the genre, some as mere Arcadian dreams, others intended as blueprints for social and technological improvements in the actual world. They include Tommaso Campanella's *City of the Sun* (1623), Francis Bacon's *New Atlantis* (1627), Edward Bellamy's *Looking Backward* (1888), William Morris' *News from Nowhere* (1891), and James Hilton's *Lost Horizon* (1934).

The utopia can be distinguished from literary representations of imaginary places which, either because they are inordinately superior to the present world or manifest exaggerated versions of some of its unsavory aspects, serve primarily as vehicles for *satire* on human life and society; notable examples are the fourth book of Swift's *Gulliver's Travels* (1726) and Samuel Butler's *Erewhon* (1872). Samuel Johnson's *Rasselas* (1759) presents the "Happy Valley," which functions as a gentle satire on humanity's stubborn but hopeless dream of a utopia. Not only does Rasselas discover that no mode of life in this world guarantees happiness; he also realizes that the utopian satisfaction of all human wishes in the Happy Valley merely replaces the unhappiness of frustrated desires with the unhappiness of boredom; see Chapters 1–3.

Another related but distinctive form is that of **science fiction**, represented by the works of H. G. Wells, Jules Verne, and many current writers, which explores the marvels of discovery and production that may result from future developments in science and technology. There are also forms of science fiction that are related to the satiric mode of utopian fiction; for example, an aspect or tendency of current scientific research is attacked by imagining its disastrous conclusion, as in Kurt Vonnegut, Jr.'s, *Cat's Cradle* (1963) and the motion picture *Dr. Strangelove, or: How I Learned to Stop Worrying and Love the Bomb.*

The term **dystopia** ("bad place") has recently come to be applied to works of fiction, including science fiction, which represent a very unpleasant imaginary world in which ominous tendencies of our present social, political, and technological order are projected in some disastrous future culmination. Examples are Aldous Huxley's *Brave New World* (1932), George Orwell's *1984* (1949), Ursula K. Le Guin's *The Dispossessed: An Ambiguous Utopia* (1974), and Margaret Atwood's *The Handmaid's Tale* (1986).

See J. O. Hertzler, *The History of Utopian Thought* (1923); Lewis Mumford, *The Story of Utopias* (1922); Karl Mannheim, *Ideology and Utopia* (1934); Chad Walsh, *From Utopia to Nightmare* (1962); Nell Eurich, *Science in Utopia* (1967); Robert Scholes and Eric S. Rabkin, *Science Fiction: History, Science, Vision* (1977); and the anthology *Utopian Literature: A Selection*, ed. J. W. Johnson (1960).

Wit, Humor, and the Comic. At present both "wit" and "humor" designate species of the general class of the **comic**: any element in a work of literature, whether a character, event, or utterance, which is designed to amuse or to excite mirth in the reader or audience. Wit and humor, however, had a variety of meanings in earlier literary criticism, and a brief comment on their history will help to clarify the difference between the terms in present usage.

Wit once signified the human faculty of intelligence, inventiveness, and mental acuity, a sense it still retains in the term "half-wit." In the sixteenth and seventeenth centuries it came to be used also for ingenuity in literary invention, and especially for the ability to develop brilliant, surprising, and paradoxical figures of speech; hence "wit" was often applied to the mode of literature we now call *metaphysical poetry.* And in the eighteenth century there were frequent attempts to distinguish the "false wit" of Abraham Cowley and other metaphysical stylists, who were said to aim at a merely superficial dazzlement, and "true wit," regarded as the apt rephrasing of truths whose enduring validity is attested by the fact that they are commonplaces. So Alexander Pope defined "true wit" in his *Essay on Criticism* (1711) as "What oft was thought, but ne'er so well expressed." (See under *neoclassic.*)

The most common present use of the term derives from its seventeenth-century application to a brilliant and paradoxical style. "Wit," that is, now denotes a kind of verbal expression which is brief, deft, and intentionally contrived to produce a shock of comic surprise; its typical form is that of the epigram. (See *epigram.*) The surprise is usually the result of an unforeseen connection or distinction between words or concepts which frustrates the listener's expectation, but only to satisfy it in a different way. Philip Guedalla wittily said: "History repeats itself. Historians repeat each other." Thus the trite comment about history by writers of history turns out to be unexpectedly appropriate, but with an unlooked-for turn of meaning, to the writers of history as well. "The only sure way to double your money," remarked the American comedian Abe Martin, "is to fold it and put it in your hip pocket." The resulting laughter, in a famous phrase of the German philosopher Immanuel Kant, arises "from the sudden transformation of a strained expectation into nothing"; it might be more accurate to say, however, "from the sudden satisfaction of an expectation, but in a way we did not expect."

Abe Martin's remark is what the *psychoanalyst* Sigmund Freud called "harmless wit," which evokes a laugh or smile that is without malice. What Freud distinguished as "tendency wit," on the other hand, is aggressive: it is a derisive and derogatory turn of phrase, directing the laugh at a particular person or butt. "Mr. James Payn," in Oscar Wilde's barbed comment on a contemporary novelist of the 1890s, "hunts down the obvious with the enthusiasm of a short-sighted detective. As one turns over the pages, the suspense of the author becomes almost unbearable."

The witty prose epigram, whether harmless or derogatory in its comic intent, is to be distinguished from the **aphorism**: the pithy and pointed statement of a serious maxim, opinion, or general truth. One of the best known of aphorisms is also one of the shortest: *Ars longa, vita brevis*—"art is long, life is short." It first occurs in a work attributed to the great Greek physician Hippocrates which, under the title *Aphorisms,* consisted of tersely worded precepts on the practice of medicine. (See John Gross, ed., *The Oxford Book of Aphorisms,* 1983.)

Repartee is a term aptly taken from fencing to signify a contest of wit, in which each person tries to cap the remark of the other, or to turn it to his or her own advantage. Attacking Disraeli in Parliament, Gladstone remarked that "the honorable gentleman will either end on the gallows or die of some loathsome disease." To which Disraeli rejoined: "That depends on whether I embrace the honorable gentleman's principles or his mistresses." *Restoration comedies* often included episodes of sustained repartee; a classic example is the give and take in the discussion of their coming marriage by the witty lovers Mirabel and Millamant in William Congreve's *The Way of the World* (1700), Act IV.

Humor is a term that goes back to the ancient theory that the particular mixture of the *four humours* determines each type of personality, and from the derivative application of the term "humorous" to one of the comically eccentric characters in the Elizabethan *comedy of humours*. As we now use the word, "humor" may be ascribed either to a comic utterance or to a comic appearance or mode of behavior. A humorous utterance differs from a witty utterance in one or both of two ways: (1) wit, as we saw, is always intended by the speaker to be comic, but many speeches that we find comically humorous are intended by the speakers themselves to be serious; and (2) a humorous saying is not cast in the neatly epigrammatic form of a witty saying. For example, the verbose chatter of the old Nurse in Shakespeare's *Romeo and Juliet* is humorous only to the audience, not to the speaker; similarly, the discussion of the mode of life of the goldfish in Central Park by the inarticulate and irascible taxi driver in J. D. Salinger's *The Catcher in the Rye* (1951) is unintentionally but superbly humorous, and is not cast in the form of a witty turn of phrase.

More important still is the difference that wit refers only to the spoken or written word, but humor has a much broader range of reference. We find humor, for example, in the way Charlie Chaplin looks, dresses, and acts, and also in the sometimes wordless cartoons in *The New Yorker*. In a thoroughly humorous situation, the sources of the fun are very complex. In Act III, Scene iv of Shakespeare's *Twelfth Night*, Malvolio's appearance and actions, and his utterances as well, are humorous, but all despite his own very solemn intentions; and our comic enjoyment is increased by our knowledge of the suppressed hilarity of the plotters who are hidden auditors onstage. The greatness of a comic creation like Shakespeare's Falstaff is that he exploits the full gamut of comic possibilities. Falstaff is humorous in the way he looks and in what he does; what he says is sometimes witty, and at almost all other times humorous; while his actions and speech are sometimes unintentionally humorous, sometimes intentionally humorous, and not infrequently—as in his whimsical account to his skeptical auditors of how he bore himself in the highway robbery, in the second act of *Henry IV, Part 1*—they are humorous even beyond his intention.

One other point should be made about humor and the comic. In the normal use, the term "humor" refers to what is purely comic: it evokes, as it is sometimes said, sympathetic laughter, or else laughter which is an end in itself. If we extend Freud's distinction between harmless and tendency wit, we can say that humor is a "harmless" form of the comic. There is, however, another mode of the comic that might be called "tendency comedy," in which we are made to laugh at a person not merely because he is ridiculous, but because he is being ridiculed—the laughter is derisive, with some element of contempt or malice, and serves as a weapon against its subject. Tendency comedy and tendency wit, but not humor, are among the devices that a writer most exploits in *satire,* the literary art of derogating by deriding a subject.

On the alternative use of the term "comic" to define the formal features of a type of dramatic or narrative plot, see *comedy;* on the widespread form of humor-in-horror in present-day literature, see *black humor.* For diverse theories of wit, humor, and the comic, together with copious examples, refer to Sigmund Freud, *Wit and Its Relation to the Unconscious* (1916); Max Eastman, *Enjoyment of Laughter* (1936); D. H. Monro, *The Argument of Laughter* (1951); Louis Kronenberger, *The Thread of Laughter* (1952); Stuart M. Tave, *The Amiable Humorist* (1960); George Williamson, *The Proper Wit of Poetry* (1961).

The essay on *criticism* in the preceding section of the *Glossary* describes the diverse types of literary theory and practice from Aristotle to the recent past. The following section contains essays on the numerous innovative literary theories and methods of critical analysis that have appeared in the "modern period" since World War I, including radically revised and amplified versions of earlier *Marxist criticism* and *psychological and psychoanalytic criticism*. The arrangement of the essays is in the alphabetic order of their titles. The chronological order in which the major new forms of criticism came into prominence is approximately as follows:

1920s and 1930s:	*Russian formalism.*
1930s and 1940s:	*archetypal criticism.*
1940s and 1950s:	*New Criticism; phenomenology* (as applied to literary criticism); *stylistics.*
1960s:	*structuralist criticism;* modern forms of *feminist criticism.*
1970s:	theory of the *anxiety of influence; deconstruction; discourse analysis;* forms of *reader-response criticism; reception-theory; semiotics; speech-act theory.*
1980s:	*dialogic criticism; new historicism; cultural studies.*

A number (but not all) of the critical perspectives and practices since the 1970s, because they share distinctive features, are often grouped together as "poststructural criticism"; see the entry below, *poststructuralism.*

Archetypal Criticism. An important antecedent of the literary theory of the archetype was the treatment of myth in writings by a group of comparative anthropologists at Cambridge University, especially James G. Frazer's *The Golden Bough* (1890–1915), which identified elemental patterns of myth and ritual that, it claimed, recur in the legends and ceremonials of many diverse and far-flung cultures. Another antecedent was the depth psychology of Carl G. Jung (1875–1961), who applied the term "archetype" to what he called "primordial images," the "psychic residue" of repeated patterns of experience in the lives of our very ancient ancestors which, he maintained, survive in the "collective unconscious" of the human race and are expressed in myths, religion, dreams, and private fantasies, as well as in works of literature. See *Jungian criticism,* under *psychoanalytic criticism.*

Archetypal literary criticism was given great impetus by Maud Bodkin's *Archetypal Patterns in Poetry* (1934), and flourished especially during the

1950s and 1960s. In criticism the term **archetype** denotes recurrent narrative designs, patterns of action, character types, or images which are said to be identifiable in a wide variety of works of literature, as well as in myths, dreams, and even ritualized modes of social behavior. Such archetypes are held to reflect a set of universal, primitive, and elemental mental forms or patterns, whose effective embodiment in a literary work evokes a profound response from the reader. Some archetypal critics have dropped Jung's theory of the collective unconscious as the deep source of these patterns; in the words of Northrop Frye, this theory is "an unnecessary hypothesis," and the recurrent archetypes are simply there, "however they got there."

Among the prominent practitioners of various modes of **archetypal criticism,** in addition to Maud Bodkin, are G. Wilson Knight, Robert Graves, Philip Wheelwright, Richard Chase, and Joseph Campbell. These critics tend to emphasize the occurrence of mythical patterns in literature, on the assumption that myths are closer to the elemental archetype than the artful manipulations of sophisticated writers (see *myth critics*). The death-rebirth theme is often said to be the archetype of archetypes, and is held to be grounded in the cycle of the seasons and the organic cycle of human life; this archetype, it has been claimed, occurs in primitive rituals of the king who is annually sacrificed, myths of gods who die to be reborn, and a multitude of diverse literary writings, including the Bible, Dante's *Divine Comedy* in the early fourteenth century, and Samuel Taylor Coleridge's "Rime of the Ancient Mariner" in 1798. Among the other archetypal themes, images, and characters that have been frequently traced in literature are the journey underground, the heavenly ascent, the search for the father, the Paradise-Hades image, the Promethean rebel-hero, the scapegoat, the earth goddess, and the fatal woman.

In the remarkable and influential book *The Anatomy of Criticism* (1957), Northrop Frye developed the archetypal approach—which he combined with the *typological interpretation* of the Bible and the conception of the imagination in the writings of the poet and painter William Blake (1757–1827)— into a radical and comprehensive revision of traditional grounds both of the theory of literature and the practice of literary criticism. Frye proposes that the totality of literary works constitute a "self-contained literary universe" which has been created over the ages by the human imagination so as to incorporate the alien and indifferent world of nature into persisting archetypal forms that serve to satisfy enduring human desires and needs. In this literary universe, four radical **mythoi** (that is, plot forms, or organizing structural principles), correspondent to the four seasons in the cycle of the natural world, are incorporated in the four major *genres* of comedy (spring), romance (summer), tragedy (autumn), and satire (winter). Within the overarching archetypal mythos of each of these genres, individual works of literature also play variations upon a number of more limited archetypes—that is, conventional patterns and types that literature shares with social rituals as well as with theology, history, law, and, in fact, all "discursive verbal structures." Viewed archetypally, Frye asserts, literature turns out to play an essential role in refashioning the material universe into an alternative verbal universe that is humanly intelligible and viable, because it is adapted to essential human needs and concerns. Frye continued, in a long series of later writings, to expand his archetypal theory, to make a place in its overall scope for various traditional critical concepts and procedures, and to apply it both to social practices and to the elucidation of writings ranging from the Bible to contemporary poets and novelists. See A. C. Hamilton, *Northrop Frye: Anatomy of His Criticism* (1990).

In addition to the works mentioned above, consult: C. G. Jung, "On the Relation of Analytical Psychology to Poetic Art" (1922), in *Contributions to Analytical Psychology* (1928), and "Psychology and Literature," in *Modern Man in Search of a Soul* (1933); G. Wilson Knight, *The Starlit Dome* (1941); Robert Graves, *The White Goddess* (1948); Richard Chase, *Quest for Myth* (1949); Philip Wheelwright, *The Burning Fountain* (1954), and *Metaphor and Reality* (1962); Northrop Frye, "The Archetypes of Literature," in *Fables of Identity* (1963); Joseph Campbell, *The Hero with a Thousand Faces* (2d ed., 1968). *Archetypal Patterns in Women's Fiction* (1981), by Annis Pratt and others, is a feminist application of archetypal criticism. For discussions and critiques of archetypal theory and practice see H. M. Block, "Cultural Anthropology and Contemporary Literary Criticism," *Journal of Aesthetics and Art Criticism* 11 (1952); Murray Krieger, ed., *Northrop Frye in Modern Criticism* (1966); Robert Denham, *Northrop Frye and Critical Method* (1978); Frank Lentricchia, *After the New Criticism* (1980), Chapter 1.

Deconstruction, as applied in the criticism of literature, designates a theory and practice of reading which claims to "subvert" or "undermine" the assumption that the system of language provides grounds that are adequate to establish the boundaries, the coherence or unity, and the determinate meanings of a text. Typically, a deconstructive reading sets out to show that conflicting forces within the text itself inevitably dissipate the seeming definiteness of its structure and meanings into an indefinite array of multiplex, incompatible, and undecidable possibilities.

The originator and namer of deconstruction is the French thinker Jacques Derrida, among whose precursors were Friedrich Nietzsche (1844–1900) and Martin Heidegger (1889–1976)—German philosophers who put to radical question the validity of basic philosophical concepts such as "knowledge," "truth," and "identity"—as well as Sigmund Freud (1856–1939), whose *psychoanalysis* violated traditional concepts of a coherent human consciousness and a unitary self. Derrida presented his basic views in three books, all published in 1967, entitled *Of Grammatology, Writing and Difference,* and *Speech and Phenomena;* since then, he has reiterated, expanded, and applied those views in a rapid sequence of publications.

Derrida's writings are complex and elusive, and the summary here can only indicate some of their main tendencies. His point of vantage is what, in *Of Grammatology,* he calls "the axial proposition that there is nothing outside the text" ("il n'y a rien hors du texte," or alternatively "il n'y a pas de hors-texte"). Like all Derrida's key terms and statements, this has multiple significations, but a primary one is that, in attempting to interpret a text, one cannot get beyond the sequence of verbal signs to anything that stands outside of, and independent of, the language system that constitutes the text—for example, things that it refers to in an extra-textual world, or the intention of its speaker or writer to express a determinate signification. Derrida's reiterated claim is that not only all Western philosophies and theories of language, but all Western uses of language, hence all Western culture, are **logocentric;** that is, they are centered or grounded on a "logos," or, as stated in a phrase he adopts from Heidegger, they rely on "the metaphysics of presence." They are logocentric, according to Derrida, in part because they are **phonocentric;** that is, they grant, implicitly or explicitly, logical "priority," or "privilege," to speech over writing as the model for analyzing all discourse. By logos, or **presence**, Derrida signifies what he alternatively calls an "ultimate referent"—a self-certifying absolute, ground, or foundation, outside the play of language itself, that is directly present to our awareness and suffices to "center" (that is, to anchor and organize) the structure of the linguistic system in such a way as to fix the bounds, coherence, and determinate meanings of any spoken or written utterance within that system. (On Derrida's "decentering" of structuralism, see *poststructuralism.*) Historical instances of claims for such an absolute ground for language are God as the guarantor of its validity, or a Platonic Form of the true reference of a general term, or a "telos" or goal toward which all process strives, or an intention to signify something determinate that is directly known to the person who initiates an utterance. Derrida undertakes to show that these and all other attempts by Western philosophy to establish an absolute ground in presence, and all implicit reliance on such a ground in using language, are illusory. Especially, he directs his skeptical exposition against the phonocentric assumption—which he regards as central in Western theories of language—that at the instant of speaking, the "intention" of a speaker to mean something determinate by an utterance is immediately and fully present in the speaker's consciousness and communicable to an auditor. (See *intention,* under *interpretation and hermeneutics.*)

Derrida expresses his alternative conception of the "undecidable" play of linguistic meanings in terms derived from Saussure's view that in a linguistic sign-system, both the *signifiers* (the material elements of a language, whether spoken or written) and the *signifieds* (their conceptual meanings) owe their seeming identity, not to their own "positive" or inherent features, but to their differences from other speech-sounds, written marks, or conceptual significations. (See Saussure, in *linguistics in modern criticism* and in *semiotics.*) From this view Derrida evolves his own radical claim that the features that, in any particular utterance, would establish the signified meaning of a word—since this significance is nothing other than a network of differences from other significations—are never "present" to us in their own positive identity. On the other hand, neither can these identifying features be said to be strictly "absent"; instead, in any spoken or written utterance, the seeming meaning is the result only of a "self-effacing" **trace**—self-effacing because one is not aware of it—which consists of all the nonpresent meanings whose differences from the present instance are the sole factor which invest the utterance with its "effect" of having a meaning in its own right. The consequence, according to Derrida, is that we can never, in any instance of speech or writing, have a fixed and decidable present meaning. He says that the differential play (*jeu*) of language does produce the "effects" of decidable meanings in an utterance or text, but asserts that these effects are illusory.

In a characteristic move, Derrida coins the *portmanteau* term **différance**, in which, he says, he uses the spelling "-ance" instead of "-ence" to indicate a fusion of two senses of the French verb "différer": to be different, and to defer. This double sense points to the phenomenon that, on the one hand, a text proffers the "effect" of having a significance that is the product of its difference, but that on the other hand, since this proffered significance can never come to rest in an actual presence, or extra-linguistic "transcendental signified," its determinate specification is deferred from one linguistic interpretation to another in a movement or "play," as Derrida puts it, *en abyme*—that is, in an endless regress. To Derrida's view, then, it is différance that makes possible the meaning whose possibility (as a decidable meaning) it necessarily baffles. As Derrida says in another of his coinages, the meaning of any spoken or written utterance, by the operation of internal linguistic forces, is ineluctably **disseminated**—a term which includes, among its deliberately contradictory significations, that of having an effect of meaning (a "semantic" effect), of dispersing meanings among innumerable alternatives, and of negating any specific meaning. There is thus no ground, in the incessant play of différance that constitutes language, for attributing a decidable meaning, or even a finite set of determinately multiple meanings (which he calls "polysemism"), to any utterance that we speak or write. As Derrida puts it in *Writing and Difference*: "The absence of a transcendental signified extends the domain and the play of signification infinitely" (p. 280).

Several of Derrida's skeptical procedures have been especially influential in deconstructive literary criticism. One is to deconstruct the innumerable binary oppositions—such as speech/writing, nature/culture, truth/error, male/female—which are essential structural elements in logocentric language. Derrida shows that such oppositions constitute a tacit hierarchy, in which the first term functions as privileged and superior and the second term as derivative and inferior. Derrida's procedure is to invert the hierarchy, by showing that the secondary term can be made out to be derivative from, or a special case of, the primary term; but instead of stopping at this reversal, he goes on to destabilize both hierarchies, leaving them in a condition of undecidability. (Among deconstructive literary critics, a favorite demonstration is to take the standard hierarchical opposition of literature / criticism, to invert it so as to make criticism primary and literature secondary, and then to represent, as an undecidable set of oppositions, the assertions that criticism is a species of literature, and that literature is a species of criticism.) A second operation influential in literary criticism is Derrida's deconstruction of any attempt to establish a determinate bound, or limit, or margin, to a textual work so as to differentiate what is "inside" from what is "outside" the work. A third operation is his analysis of the inherent nonlogicality, or rhetoricity—that is, the inescapable reliance on *rhetorical figures* and *figurative language*—in all uses of language, including in what philosophers have claimed to be the strictly literal and logical arguments of philosophy. Derrida, for example, emphasizes the indispensable reliance in all modes of discourse on metaphors that are assumed to be merely convenient substitutes for *literal,* or "proper" meanings; then he undertakes to show, on the one hand, that metaphors cannot be reduced to literal meanings, but on the other hand that supposedly literal terms are themselves metaphors whose metaphoric nature has been forgotten.

Derrida's characteristic procedure is not to describe his deconstructive concepts and operations in a systematic exposition, but to allow them to emerge in a sequence of exemplary close readings of passages from writings that range from Plato through Jean-Jacques Rousseau to the present era—writings that, by standard classification, are mainly philosophical, although occasionally literary. He describes his procedure as a "double reading." Initially, that is, he interprets a text as, in the standard fashion, "lisible" (readable or intelligible), since it engenders "effects" of having determinate meanings. But this reading, Derrida says, is only "provisional," as a stage toward a second, or deconstructive, "critical reading," which disseminates the provisional meaning into an indefinite range of significations that, he claims, always involve (in a term taken from logic) an **aporia**—an insuperable deadlock, or "double bind," of incompatible or contradictory meanings which are "undecidable," in that we lack any available and sufficient ground for choosing among them. The result, in Derrida's rendering, is that each text deconstructs itself, by undermining its own supposed grounds and dispersing itself into incoherent meanings in a way, he claims, that the deconstructive reader neither initiates nor produces; deconstruction is something that simply "happens" to a critical reading. Derrida asserts, furthermore, that he has no option except to express and attempt to communicate his own deconstructive readings in the inherited logocentric language, hence that his own interpretive texts deconstruct themselves in the very act of deconstructing the texts to which they are applied. He insists, however, that "deconstruction has nothing to do with destruction," and that all the standard, as well as specialized, uses of language will inevitably go on; what he undertakes, he says, is merely to "situate" or "reinscribe" all such texts in a system of différance which shows the instability and ultimate self-subversion of the effects to which they owe their seeming intelligibility.

Derrida did not propose deconstruction as a mode of literary criticism, but as a way of reading all types of texts so as to reveal and subvert the tacit metaphysical presuppositions of Western thought. His views and procedures, however, have been taken up by literary critics, especially in America, who have adapted Derrida's elaborate mode of "critical reading" to the kind of "close reading" of particular literary texts which had earlier been the familiar procedure of the *New Criticism;* they do so, however, as Paul de Man has said, in a way which shows that new-critical close readings "were not nearly close enough." The end results of the two kinds of close reading are utterly diverse. The new-critical explications of texts had undertaken to show that a great literary work, in the tight internal relations of its figurative and paradoxical meanings, constitutes a freestanding, bounded, and organic entity of multiplex yet determinate meanings. On the contrary, a radically deconstructive close reading undertakes to show that a literary text lacks a "totalized" boundary that makes it an entity, much less an organic unity, and lacks also any adequate ground for its own linguistic procedures. As a consequence the text, by a play of internal counter-forces, disseminates into an indefinite range of self-conflicting significations. The claim is sometimes made by deconstructive critics that a literary text is superior to nonliterary texts, but only because by its self-reference, it shows itself to be more aware of features that all texts inescapably share: its fictionality, its lack of a genuine ground, and especially its patent "rhetoricity," or use of figurative procedures—features that make any "right reading" or "correct reading" of a text impossible.

Paul de Man was an innovative and influential critic who applied deconstruction to the reading of literary texts. In de Man's later writings, he represented the conflicting forces within a text under the headings of "grammar" (the code or rules of language) and "rhetoric" (the unruly play of figures and tropes), and aligned these with other opposed forces, such as the "constative" and "performative" linguistic functions that had been distinguished by John Austin (see *speech-act theory*). In its grammatical aspect, language aspires to determinate, referential, and logically ordered assertions, which are persistently dispersed by its rhetorical aspect into an open set of non-referential and illogical possibilities. A literary text, then, of inner necessity says one thing and performs another, or as de Man alternatively puts the matter, a text "simultaneously asserts and denies the authority of its own rhetorical mode" (*Allegories of Reading*, 1979, p. 17). The inevitable result, for a critical reading, is an aporia of "vertiginous possibilities."

Barbara Johnson, once a student of de Man's, has applied deconstructive readings not only to literary texts, but to the writings of other critics, including Derrida himself. Her succinct statement of the aim and methods of a deconstructive reading is often cited:

> *Deconstruction* is not synonymous with *destruction*. . . . The de-construction of a text does not proceed by random doubt or arbitrary subversion, but by the careful teasing out of warring forces of signification within the text itself. If anything is destroyed in a deconstructive reading, it is not the text, but the claim to unequivocal domination of one mode of signifying over another.
>
> (*The Critical Difference*, 1980, p. 5)

J. Hillis Miller, once the leading American representative of the *Geneva School* of consciousness-criticism, is now one of the most prominent and widely read of deconstructors, known especially for his application of this type of critical reading to prose fiction. Miller's statement of the deconstructive practice indicates the drastic result of applying to works of literature the concepts and procedures that Derrida had developed for deconstructing the foundations of Western metaphysics:

> Deconstruction as a mode of interpretation works by a careful and circumspect entering of each textual labyrinth. . . . The deconstructive critic seeks to find, by this process of retracing, the element in the

system studied which is alogical, the thread in the text in question which will unravel it all, or the loose stone which will pull down the whole building. The deconstruction, rather, annihilates the ground on which the building stands by showing that the text has already annihilated the ground, knowingly or unknowingly. Deconstruction is not a dismantling of the structure of a text but a demonstration that it has already dismantled itself.

Miller's conclusion is that any literary text, as a ceaseless play of "irreconcilable" and "contradictory" meanings, is "indeterminable" and "undecidable"; hence, that "all reading is necessarily misreading." ("Stevens' Rock and Criticism as Cure, II," in Miller's *Theory Then and Now* (1991), p. 126, and "Walter Pater: A Partial Portrait," *Daedalus*, Vol. 105, 1976.)

For other aspects of Derrida's views see *poststructuralism*, below. Some of the central books by Jacques Derrida available in English, with the dates of translation into English, are *Of Grammatology*, translated and introduced by Gayatri C. Spivak, 1976; *Writing and Difference* (1978); and *Dissemination* (1981). A useful anthology of selections from Derrida is *A Derrida Reader: Between the Blinds*, ed. Peggy Kamuf (1991); *Acts of Literature*, ed. Derek Attridge (1992), is a selection of Derrida's discussions of literary texts. An accessible introduction to Derrida's views is the edition by Gerald Graff of Derrida's noted dispute with John R. Searle about the speech-act theory of John Austin, entitled *Limited Inc.* (1988); on this dispute see also Jonathan Culler, "Meaning and Iterability," in *On Deconstruction* (1982). Books exemplifying types of deconstructive literary criticism: Paul de Man, *Blindness and Insight* (1971), and *Allegories of Reading* (1979); Barbara Johnson, *The Critical Difference: Essays in the Contemporary Rhetoric of Reading* (1980), and *A World of Difference* (1987); J. Hillis Miller, *Fiction and Repetition: Seven English Novels* (1982), *The Linguistic Moment: From Wordsworth to Stevens* (1985), and *Theory Then and Now* (1991); Cynthia Chase, *Decomposing Figures: Rhetorical Readings in the Romantic Tradition* (1986). Expositions of Derrida's deconstruction and of its applications to literary criticism: Geoffrey Hartman, *Saving the Text* (1981); Jonathan Culler, *On Deconstruction* (1982); Richard Rorty, "Philosophy as a Kind of Writing," in *Consequences of Pragmatism* (1982); Michael Ryan, *Marxism and Deconstruction* (1982); Mark C. Taylor, ed., *Deconstruction in Context* (1986); Christopher Norris, *Paul de Man* (1988). Among the many critiques of Derrida and of various practitioners of deconstructive literary criticism are Terry Eagleton, *The Function of Criticism* (1984); M. H. Abrams, "The Deconstructive Angel," "How to Do Things with Texts," and "Construing and Deconstructing," in *Doing Things with Texts* (1989); Frank Ellis, *Against Deconstruction* (1989); Frank Kermode, *An Appetite for Poetry* (1989).

Dialogic Criticism is modeled on the theory and critical procedures of the Soviet critic Mikhail Bakhtin who, although he published his major works in the 1920s and 1930s, remained virtually unknown to the West until the 1980s, when translations of his writings gave him a wide and rapidly increasing influence. To Bakhtin a literary work is not (as in various *poststructural* theories) a text whose meanings are produced by the play of impersonal linguistic or economic or cultural forces, but a site for the dialogic interaction of multiple voices, or modes of discourse, each of which is not merely a verbal but a social phenomenon, and as such is the product of manifold determinants of class, social group, and speech community. Each utterance, furthermore, whether in actual life or as represented in literature, owes its precise inflection and meaning to attendant factors—the relation of its speaker to an actual or anticipated listener, and the relation of the utterance to the prior utterances to which it is (explicitly or implicitly) a response, as well as to the specific social situation in which it is both spoken and interpreted.

Bakhtin's prime interest was in the novel, and especially in the ways that the voices that constitute any novel disrupt the authority of the author's single voice. In *Problems of Dostoevsky's Poetics* (1929, trans. by Caryl Emerson, 1984), he contrasts the **monologic** novels of writers such as Leo Tolstoy—which undertake to subordinate the voices of all the characters to the authoritative discourse and controlling purposes of the author—to the **dialogic form** (or "polyphonic form") of Fyodor Dostoevsky's novels, in which the characters are liberated to speak "a plurality of independent and unmerged voices and consciousnesses, a genuine polyphony of fully valid voices." In Bakhtin's view, however, a novel can never be totally monologic, since the narrator's reports of the utterances of another character are inescapably "double-voiced" (in that we can distinguish therein the author's own accent and inflection), and also dialogic (in that the author's discourse continually reinforces, alters, or contests with the speech that it reports). In *Rabelais and His World* (trans., 1984), Bakhtin proposed his widely cited concept of the **carnivalesque** in certain literary works. This literary mode parallels the flouting of authority and inversion of social hierarchies that are licensed to manifest themselves in the carnival season, by introducing a mingling of voices from diverse social levels that are free to mock and subvert authority, and to flout social norms by ribaldry and other modes of profaning what is ordinarily regarded as sacrosanct. Bakhtin traces the occurrence of the carnivalesque in ancient, medieval, and Renaissance writers (especially in Rabelais); he also asserts that the mode recurs later, especially in the play of irreverent, parodic, and subversive voices in the novels of Dostoevsky.

In an essay on "Discourse in the Novel" (1934–35), Bakhtin develops his view that the novel is a literary form that is constituted by a multiplicity of divergent and contending social voices that achieve their full significance only in the sustained process of their dialogic interaction both with each other and with the voice of the narrator. Bakhtin explicitly sets his theory against Aristotle's *Poetics,* which proposed that the primary component in narrative forms is a plot that evolves coherently from a beginning to an end in which all complications are resolved (see *plot*). Instead, Bakhtin elevates *discourse* (equivalent to Aristotle's subordinate element of *diction*) into the primary component of a narrative work; and he describes discourse as a medley of voices, social attitudes, and values that are not only opposed, but irreconcilable, with the result that the work remains unresolved and open-ended. Although he wrote during the Stalinist regime in Russia, Bakhtin's libertarian and open concept of the literary narrative is obviously, although tacitly, opposed to the Soviet version of Marxist criticism, with its emphasis on the way a novel reflects or distorts the true social reality, or expresses a single dominant ideology, or should exemplify a "social realism" that accords with an authoritarian party line (see *Marxist criticism*).

Bakhtin's views have been, in some part and in diverse ways, incorporated by representatives of various types of modern critical theory and practice, whether traditional or poststructural. Among current students of literature, those who are identified specifically as "dialogic critics" follow Bakhtin's example by proposing that the primary component in the constitution of narrative works, or of literature generally—and of general culture as well—is a plurality of contending and mutually qualifying social voices, with no possibility of a decisive resolution into a monologic truth. Self-reflexively, they consider their own criticism to be simply one voice among many in the contention of critical theories and practices, coexisting with its compeers in a sustained tension of opposition and mutual definition. As Don Bialostosky, a chief spokesman for dialogic criticism, has voiced its rationale and ideal:

> As a self-conscious practice, dialogic criticism turns its inescapable involvement with some other voices into a program of articulating itself with all the other voices of the discipline, the culture, or the world of cultures to which it makes itself responsible. . . .
>
> Neither a live-and-let-live relativism nor a settle-it-once-and-for-all authoritarianism but a strenuous and open-ended dialogism would keep them talking to themselves and to one another, discovering their affinities without resting in them and clarifying their differences without resolving them.
>
> ("Dialogic Criticism," in G. Douglas Atkins and
> Laura Morrow, eds., *Contemporary Literary
> Theory,* 1989, pp. 223–24)

Refer to the related critical enterprise called *discourse analysis;* and in addition to the writings mentioned above, see Mikhail Bakhtin's *The Dialogic Imagination,* ed. Michael Holquist (1981). For Bakhtin's life and intellectual views, with attention to the problem of identifying writings that Bakhtin published under the names of colleagues, see Katerina Clark and Michael Holquist, *Mikhail Bakhtin* (1984), and Gary Saul Morson and Caryl Emerson, *Mikhail Bakhtin: Creation of a Poetics* (1990). An influential early exposition that publicized Bakhtin's ideas in the West was Tzvetan Todorov, *Mikhail Bakhtin: The Dialogical Principle* (1984); a recent book describing the wide dissemination of these ideas is David Lodge's *After Bakhtin* (1990). For a critical view of Bakhtin's claims, see René Wellek, *A History of Modern Criticism 1750–1950,* Vol. 7 (1991), pp. 354–71.

Discourse Analysis. Traditional linguists and philosophers of language, as well as literary students of *style* and *stylistics,* have typically focused their analyses on isolated units of language—the sentence, or even single words, phrases, and instances of figurative language. Discourse analysis, on the other hand, as inaugurated in the 1970s, concerns itself with the use of language in a running discourse, continued over a sequence of sentences and involving the interaction of speaker (or writer) and auditor (or reader) in a specific situational context.

Modern discourse analysis was in large part inaugurated by the speech-act philosopher H. P. Grice, who in 1975 coined the term **implicature** to explain how we are able to identify the illocutionary force of an utterance that lacks an explicit indicator of its illocutionary intention. (See *speech-act theory*.) For example, how can we account for the fact that the utterance, "Can you pass the salt?" although it is in the syntactical form of a question, is used by the speaker, and correctly understood by the hearer, to be a polite form of request? (H. P. Grice, "Logic and Conversation," in *Syntax and Semantics*, ed. P. Cole and J. L. Morgan, III, 1975.) Grice proposed that users of a language share a set of implicit expectations which he calls the "communicative presumption"—for example, that an utterance is intended by a speaker to be true, clear, and above all relevant—and that interpretations vary in accordance with the ways that utterances accord with, or seem intentionally to violate, the expectations set up by this shared presumption. Other language theorists have greatly expanded the analysis of the collective assumptions that help to make utterances meaningful and intelligible, and serve also to make a sustained discourse a coherent development of significations instead of a mere collocation of independent sentences. One assumption is that speakers and hearers (or writers and readers) share a large body of non-linguistic knowledge and experience; another is that the speaker is using language in a way that is intentional, purposive, and in accordance with linguistic and cultural conventions; a third is that there is a shared knowledge of the complex ways in which the meaning of a locution varies with the particular situation, as well as the type of discourse, in which it is uttered.

Some proponents of stylistics include discourse analysis within their area of investigation. (See *stylistics*.) And since the late 1970s, a number of critics have increasingly adapted discourse analysis to the examination of the *dialogue* in novels and dramas. A chief aim is to explain how the characters represented in a literary work, and also the readers of that work, are constantly able to infer meanings that are not explicitly asserted or indicated in a discursive interchange. The claim is that such inferences are "rule-governed," in that they depend on sets of assumptions, shared by users and interpreters of discourse, which come into play to establish meanings; furthermore, these meanings vary systematically, in accordance with whether the rule-guided expectations are fulfilled or intentionally violated. Such explorations of conversational discourse in literature often extend to the re-analysis of *point of view* and other traditional topics in the criticism of literary narratives. (Compare the entry on *dialogic criticism*.)

See Malcolm Coulthard, *An Introduction to Discourse Analysis* (1977); Gillian Brown and George Yule, *Discourse Analysis* (1983); Teun A. van Dijk and Walter Kintsch, *Strategies of Discourse Comprehension* (1983); Wendell V. Harris, *Interpretive Acts* (1988), Chapter 2.

Feminist Criticism. As a self-aware and concerted approach to literature, feminist criticism was not inaugurated until late in the 1960s. Behind it, however, lie two centuries of struggle for women's rights, marked by such books as Mary Wollstonecraft's *A Vindication of the Rights of Woman* (1792), John Stuart Mill's *The Subjection of Women* (1869), and the American Margaret Fuller's *Woman in the Nineteenth Century* (1845). Feminist literary criticism continues in our time to be closely interrelated with the movement by political **feminists** for social, economic, and cultural freedom and equality.

An important precursor in feminist criticism was Virginia Woolf, who, in addition to her fiction, wrote *A Room of One's Own* (1929) and numerous other essays on women authors and on the cultural, economic, and educational disabilities within what she called a "patriarchal" society that have hindered or prevented women from realizing their creative possibilities. (See the collection of her essays, *Women and Writing,* ed. M. Barrett, 1979.) A much more radical critical mode was launched in France by Simone de Beauvoir's *The Second Sex* (1949), a wide-ranging critique of the cultural identification of women as merely the negative object, or "Other," to man as the defining and dominating "Subject" who is assumed to represent humanity in general; the book dealt also with "the great collective myths" of women in the works of many male writers. In America, modern feminist criticism began with Mary Ellman's deft and witty discussion, in *Thinking about Women* (1968), about the derogatory stereotypes of women in literature written by men, and also about the alternative and subversive points of view in some writings by women. Even more influential was Kate Millett's polemical and hard-hitting *Sexual Politics,* published the following year. By "politics" Millett refers to the mechanisms that express and enforce the relations of power in society; she represents Western social arrangements and institutions as covert ways of manipulating power so as to establish and perpetuate the dominance of men and the subordination of women. In her book she attacks the male bias in Freud's psychoanalytic theory, and also analyzes selected passages by D. H. Lawrence, Henry Miller, Norman Mailer, and Jean Genet as revealing the ways in which their authors, in fictional fantasy, aggrandize their aggressive phallic selves and degrade women as submissive sexual objects.

Since 1969 there has been an explosion of feminist writings without close parallel in the history of previous critical innovations, in a movement that, as Elaine Showalter has remarked, displays the urgency and excitement of a religious awakening. This current criticism, in America, England, France, and other countries, is not a unitary theory or procedure. It manifests, among those who practice it, a great variety of critical vantage points and procedures, including adaptations of *psychoanalytic, Marxist,* and diverse *poststructuralist* theories, and its vitality is signalized by the vigor (sometimes even rancor) of the debates within the ranks of professed feminists themselves. The various feminisms, however, share some assumptions and concepts that constitute a common ground for the diverse ways that individual critics explore the factor of sexual difference and privilege in the production, the form and content, the reception, and the critical analysis and evaluation of works of literature:

1) The basic view is that Western civilization is pervasively **patriarchal** (ruled by the father)—that is, it is male-centered and controlled, and is organized and conducted in such a way as to subordinate women to men in all cultural domains: familial, religious, political, economic, social, legal, and artistic. From the Hebrew Bible and Greek philosophy to the present, the female tends to be defined by negative reference to the male as the human norm, hence as an Other, or kind of non-man, by her lack of the identifying male organ, of male powers, and of the male character traits that are presumed, in the patriarchal view, to have achieved the most important inventions and works of civilization and culture. Women themselves are taught, in the process of their being socialized, to internalize the reigning patriarchal *ideology* (that is, the conscious and unconscious presuppositions about male superiority), and so are conditioned to derogate their own sex and to cooperate in their own subordination.

2) It is widely held that while one's sex is determined by anatomy, the prevailing concepts of **gender**—of the traits that constitute what is masculine and what is feminine—are largely, if not entirely, cultural constructs that were generated by the omnipresent patriarchal biases of our civilization. As Simone de Beauvoir put it, "One is not born, but rather becomes, a woman. . . . It is civilization as a whole that produces this creature . . . which is described as feminine." In this way the masculine in our culture has come to be identified as active, dominating, adventurous, rational, creative; the feminine, by systematic opposition to such traits, has come to be identified as passive, acquiescent, timid, emotional, and conventional.

3) The further claim is that this patriarchal (or "masculinist," or "androcentric") ideology pervades those writings which have been considered great literature, and which until recently have been written almost entirely by men for men. Typically, the most highly regarded literary works focus on male protagonists—Oedipus, Ulysses, Hamlet, Tom Jones, Captain Ahab, Huck Finn—who embody masculine traits and ways of feeling and pursue masculine interests in masculine fields of action. To these males, the female characters, when they play any role, are marginal and subordinate, and are represented either as complementary to or in opposition to masculine desires and enterprises. Such works, lacking autonomous female role models, and implicitly addressed to male readers, either leave the woman reader an alien outsider or else solicit her to identify against herself by taking up the position of the male subject and so assuming male values and ways of perceiving, feeling, and acting. It is often held, in addition, that the traditional aesthetic categories and criteria for analyzing and appraising literary works, although represented in standard critical theory as objective, disinterested, and universal, are in fact infused with masculine assumptions, interests, and ways of reasoning, so that the standard rankings, and also the critical treatments, of literary works have in fact been tacitly but thoroughly gender-biased.

A major interest of feminist critics in English-speaking countries has been to reconstitute all the ways we deal with literature so as to do justice to female points of view, concerns, and values. One emphasis has been to alter the way a woman reads the literature of the past so as to make her not an acquiescent, but (in the title of Judith Fetterley's book published in 1978)

The Resisting Reader; that is, one who resists the author's intentions and design in order, by a "revisionary rereading," to bring to light and to counter the covert sexual biases written into a literary work. Another prominent procedure has been to identify recurrent "images of women," especially in novels and poems written by men. These are often represented as falling into two antithetic patterns. On the one side we find idealized projections of men's desires (the Madonna, the Muse of the arts, Dante's Beatrice, the pure and innocent virgin, the "Angel in the House" that was represented by the Victorian poet Coventry Patmore); on the other side are demonic projections of men's sexual resentments and terrors (Eve and Pandora as the sources of all evil, destructive sensual temptresses such as Delilah and Circe, the malign witch, the castrating mother). While many feminist critics have decried the literature written by men for its depiction of women as marginal, docile, and subservient to men's interests and emotional needs and fears, some of them have also identified male writers who, in their view, have managed to rise above the sexual prejudices of their time sufficiently to understand and represent the cultural pressures that have shaped the characters of women and forced upon them their negative or subsidiary social roles; the latter class is said to include, in selected works, such authors as Chaucer, Shakespeare, Samuel Richardson, Henrik Ibsen, and George Bernard Shaw.

A number of feminists have concentrated, not on the woman as reader, but on what Elaine Showalter calls **gynocriticism**—that is, a criticism which concerns itself with developing a specifically female framework for dealing with works written by women, in all aspects of their production, motivation, analysis, and interpretation, and in all literary forms, including journals and letters. Notable books in this mode include Patricia Meyer Spacks, *The Female Imagination* (1975), on English and American novels of the past three hundred years; Ellen Moers, *Literary Women* (1976), on major women novelists and poets in England, America, and France; Elaine Showalter, *A Literature of Their Own: British Women Novelists from Brontë to Lessing* (1977); and Sandra Gilbert and Susan Gubar, *The Madwoman in the Attic* (1979). This last book stresses especially the psychodynamics of women writers in the nineteenth century. Its authors propose that the "anxiety of authorship" that resulted from the stereotype that literary creativity is an exclusively male prerogative, effected in women writers a psychological duplicity that projected a monstrous counterfigure to the heroine, typified by Bertha Rochester, the madwoman in Charlotte Brontë's *Jane Eyre;* such a figure is "usually in some sense the *author's* double, an image of her own anxiety and rage."

One concern of gynocritics is to identify what are taken to be the distinctively feminine subject matters in literature written by women—the world of domesticity, for example, or the special experiences of gestation, giving birth, and nurturing, or mother-daughter and woman-woman relations—in which personal and affectional issues, and not external activism, are the primary interest. Another concern is to uncover in literary history a female tradition, expressed by a subcommunity of women writers who were aware of, emulated, and found support in earlier women writers, and who in turn provide models and emotional support to their own readers and successors. A third undertaking is to show that there is a distinctive feminine mode of experience, or "subjectivity," in thinking, feeling, valuing, and perceiving oneself and the outer world. Related to this is the attempt (thus far, without much agreement about details) to specify the traits of a "woman's language," or distinctively feminine *style* of speech and writing, in sentence structure, types of relations between the elements of a discourse, and characteristic figures and imagery. Some feminists have turned their critical attention to the great number of women's domestic and "sentimental" novels, which are noted perfunctorily and in derogatory fashion in standard literary histories, yet which dominated the market for fiction in the nineteenth century and produced most of the best-sellers of the time; instances of this last critical enterprise are Elaine Showalter's *A Literature of Their Own* (1977) on British writers, and Nina Baym's *Woman's Fiction: A Guide to Novels by and about Women in America, 1820–1870* (1978). Sandra Gilbert and Susan Gubar have written the later history of women's writings in *No Man's Land: The Place of the Woman Writer in the Twentieth Century* (2 vols.; 1988–89).

The often-asserted goal of feminist critics has been to enlarge and reorder, or in some instances entirely to displace, the literary canon—that is, the set of works which, by a cumulative consensus have come to be considered "major" and to serve as the chief subjects of literary history, criticism, scholarship, and teaching (see *canon of literature*). Feminist studies have served to raise the status of many female authors hitherto more or less scanted by scholars and critics (including Anne Finch, George Sand, Elizabeth Barrett Browning, Elizabeth Gaskell, Christina Rossetti, Harriet Beecher Stowe, and Sidonie-Gabrielle Colette) and to bring into purview other authors who have been largely overlooked as subjects for serious consideration (among them Margaret Cavendish, Aphra Behn, Lady Mary Wortley Montagu, Joanna Baillie, Kate Chopin, Charlotte Perkins Gilman, and a number of African-American writers such as Zora Neale Hurston). Some feminists have devoted their critical attention especially to the literature written by lesbian writers, or that deals with lesbian relationships in a heterosexual culture.

American and English critics have for the most part engaged in empirical and thematic studies of writings by and about women. The most prominent feminist critics in France, however, have been occupied with the "theory" of the role of gender in writing, conceptualized within various *poststructural* frames of reference, above all Lacan's reworkings of Freudian *psychoanalysis* in terms of Saussure's linguistic theory. English-speaking feminists, for example, have drawn attention to demonstrable and specific evidences that a male bias is encoded in our linguistic conventions; instances include the use of "man" or "mankind" for human beings in general, of "chairman" and "spokesman" for people of either sex, and of the pronouns "he" and "his" to refer back to ostensibly gender-neutral nouns such as "God," "human being," "child," "inventor," "author," "poet" (see Sally McConnell-Ginet, Ruth Borker, and Nelly Furman, eds., *Women and Language in Literature and Society,* 1980). The sweepingly radical claim of French theorists, on the other hand, whatever their differences, is that all Western languages, in all their features, are utterly and irredeemably male-engendered, male-constituted, and male-dominated. Discourse, it is asserted, in a term proposed by Lacan, is "phallogocentric"; that is, it is centered and organized throughout by implicit recourse to the phallus (used in a symbolic rather than a literal sense) both as its supposed "logos," or ground, and as its prime signifier and power-source. Phallogocentrism manifests itself in Western discourse not only in its vocabulary and syntax, but also in its rigorous rules of logic, its proclivity for fixed classifications and oppositions, and its criteria for what we take to be valid evidence and objective knowledge. The basic problem for the French theorists is to establish the very possibility of a woman's language that will not, when a woman writes, automatically be appropriated into this phallogocentric language, for such appropriation forces her into complicity with the linguistic features that impose on females a condition of marginality and subservience, or even of linguistic nonentity.

To evade this dilemma, Hélène Cixous posits the existence of an incipient "feminine writing" (écriture féminine) which has its source in the mother, in that stage of the mother-child relation before the child acquires the male-centered verbal language. Thereafter, in her view, this prelinguistic potentiality in the unconscious manifests itself in those written texts which, abolishing all repressions, undermine and subvert the fixed signification, the logic, and the "closure" of our phallocentric language, and open out into a joyous freeplay of meanings. Alternatively, Luce Irigaray posits a "woman's writing" which evades the male monopoly and the risk of appropriation into the existing system by establishing as its generative principle, in place of the monolithic phallus, the diversity, fluidity, and multiple possibilities inherent in the structure and erotic functioning of the female sexual organs and in the distinctive nature of female sexual experiences. Julia Kristeva posits a "chora," or prelinguistic, pre-Oedipal, and unsystematized signifying process, centered on the mother, that she labels "semiotic." This process is repressed as we acquire the father-controlled, syntactically ordered, and logical language that she calls "symbolic." The semiotic process, however, can break out in a revolutionary way—her prime example is avant-garde poetry, whether written by women or by men—as a "heterogeneous destructive causality" that disrupts and disperses the authoritarian "subject" and strikes free of the oppressive order and rationality of our standard discourse which, as the product of the "law of the Father," consigns women to a negative and marginal status.

In recent years a number of feminists have used *poststructuralist* positions and techniques to question the founding concepts of feminism itself. They point out the existence of differences and adversarial strands within the supposedly monolithic history of patriarchal discourse, and they emphasize the inherent linguistic instability in the basic conceptions of "woman" or "the feminine," as well as the diversities within these supposedly universal and uniform female identities that result from differences in race, class, nationality, and historical situation. See Barbara Johnson, *A World of Difference* (1987); Rita Felski, *Beyond Feminist Aesthetics: Feminist Literature and Social Change* (1989); and the essays in *Feminism/Postmodernism,* ed. Linda J. Nicholson (1990).

Feminist theoretical and critical writings, although recent in origin, expand yearly in volume and range. There exist a number of specialized feminist journals and publishing houses, almost all colleges and universities now have programs in women's studies and courses in women's literature and feminist criticism, and ever-increasing place is given to writings by and about women in literary anthologies, periodicals, and conferences. Of the many critical and theoretical innovations of the last several decades, the concern with the effects of sexual differences in the writing, interpretation, analysis, and assessment of literature seems destined to have the most prominent and enduring effects on literary history, criticism, and academic instruction, as conducted by men as well as by women.

In addition to the books mentioned above, the following works are especially useful. Sandra Gilbert and Susan Gubar, eds., *The Norton Anthology of Literature by Women* (1985)—the editorial materials provide a concise history, as well as biographies and bibliographies, of female authors since the Middle Ages. Jane Gallop, *The Daughter's Seduction: Feminism and Psychoanalysis* (1982). Histories and critiques of feminist criticism: K. K. Ruthven, *Feminist Literary Studies: An Introduction* (1984); and Toril Moi, *Sexual/Textual Politics: Feminist Literary Theory* (1985)—much of this book is devoted to feminist theorists in France. Collections of essays in feminist criticism: Elaine Showalter, ed., *The New Feminist Criticism* (1985); Patrocinio P. Schweickart and Elizabeth A. Flynn, eds., *Gender and Reading: Essays on Readers, Texts, and Contexts* (1986); Robyn R. Warhol and Diane Price Herndl, eds., *Feminisms: An Anthology of Literary Theory and Criticism* (1991). A recent critique of some feminist views by a feminist is Elizabeth Fox-Genovese, *Feminism without Illusions: A Critique of Individualism* (1991). Among the books by French feminist theorists available in English are Hélène Cixous and Catherine Clement, *The Newly Born Woman* (1986); Luce Irigaray, *Speculum of the Other Woman* (1985), and *This Sex Which Is Not One* (1985); Julia Kristeva, *Desire in Language: A Semiotic Approach to Literature and Art* (1980); *The Kristeva Reader*, ed. Toril Moi (1986). On feminist treatments of African-American women: Barbara Christian, *Black Feminist Criticism* (1985); Hazel V. Carby, *Reconstructing Womanhood: The Emergence of the Afro-American Woman Novelist* (1987); Henry L. Gates, Jr., *Reading Black, Reading Feminist: A Critical Anthology* (1990). Feminist treatments of lesbian and gay literature: Monique Wittig, *The Lesbian Body* (1976); Eve Kosofsky, *Between Men: English Literature and Male Homosocial Desire* (1985), and *Epistemology of the Closet* (1990). Feminist film studies: Teresa de Lauretis, *Alice Doesn't: Feminism, Semiotics, Cinema* (1982), and *Technologies of Gender* (1987); Constance Penley, *The Future of an Illusion: Film, Feminism, and Psychoanalysis* (1989).

Influence and the Anxiety of Influence. Critics and historians of literature have for many centuries dealt with what has been called the **influence** of one author upon a later author who is said to adopt, and at the same time to alter, aspects of the subject matter, form, or style of the earlier writer. Among traditional topics for discussion, for example, have been the influence of

Homer on Virgil, of Virgil on Milton, of Milton on Wordsworth, or of Wordsworth on Wallace Stevens. The **anxiety of influence** is a phrase used by the influential contemporary critic Harold Bloom to identify his radical revision of this standard theory that influence consists in a direct "borrowing," or assimilation, of the materials and features found in earlier writers. Bloom's own view is that in the composition of any poem, influence is inescapable, but inescapably involves a drastic distortion of the work of a predecessor. He uses this concept of influence to deal with the reading as well as the writing of poetry.

In Bloom's theory a poet (especially since the time of Milton) is motivated to compose when his imagination is seized upon by a poem or poems of a "precursor," or father-poet. The "belated" poet's attitudes to his precursor, like those in Freud's analysis of the Oedipal relation of son to father, are ambivalent; that is, they are compounded not only of admiration but also (since a strong poet feels a compelling need to be autonomous and absolutely original) of hate, envy, and fear of the father-poet's preemption of the son's imaginative space. The belated poet unconsciously safeguards his sense of his own autonomy and priority by reading a parent-poem "defensively," in such a way as to distort it beyond his own conscious recognition. Nonetheless, he cannot avoid embodying the malformed parent-poem into his own doomed attempt to write an unprecedentedly original poem; the most that even the best belated poet can achieve is to write a poem so "strong" that it effects an illusion of "priority"—that is, an illusion both that it has escaped the father-poem's precedence and that it exceeds it in greatness.

Bloom identifies six distortive processes which operate in reading a precursor; he calls these processes "revisionary ratios" and defines them mainly on the model of Freud's defense mechanisms (see *psychoanalytic criticism*). He also equates the Freudian mechanisms with the devices by which the medieval Kabbalists reinterpreted the Hebrew Bible, as well as with various types of rhetorical *tropes,* or figurative language. Since in Bloom's view the revisionary ratios are the categories through which all of us necessarily read our precursors, his conclusion is that we can never know "the poem-in-itself"; all interpretation is "a necessary misprision," and all "reading is therefore misprision—or misreading." A "weak misreading" is an attempt (doomed to fail) to get at what a text really means, while a "strong misreading" is one in which an individual reader's defense mechanisms are unconsciously licensed to recast in an innovative fashion the text that the reader undertakes to interpret.

Since Bloom conceives that "every poem is a misinterpretation of a parent poem," he recommends that literary critics boldly practice what he calls **antithetical criticism**—that is, that they learn "to read any poem as its poet's deliberate misinterpretation, *as a poet,* of a precursor poem or of poetry in general." The results of such strong readings will be antithetical both to what the poet himself thought he meant and to what standard weak misreadings have made out the poem to mean. In his own powerfully individualistic writings, Bloom offers many examples of such antithetical criticism, applied to poets ranging from the eighteenth century through the major Romantics to Yeats and Stevens. He is aware that, in terms of his theory, he cannot himself escape adopting defensive tactics against his own anxiety concerning the influence exerted on him by precursor critics, hence that his own interpretations both of poets and critics are necessarily misreadings. His claim is that his antithetical interpretations are strong, and therefore "interesting," misreadings, and so will take their place in the ceaseless accumulation of misreadings which constitutes the total history both of poetry and of criticism, at least since the seventeenth century—although tragically, as time goes on, because of an ever-decreasing sector of strong imaginative possibilities.

A precursor of Bloom's theory was Walter Jackson Bate's *The Burden of the Past and the English Poet* (1970), which told the history of the struggles by poets, since 1660, to overcome the inhibitive effect of fear that their predecessors might have exhausted all the possibilities of writing great original poems. Bloom presented his own theory of reading and writing poetry in *The Anxiety of Influence* (1973), then elaborated the theory, and demonstrated its application to diverse poetic texts, in three rapidly successive books, *A Map of Misreading* (1975), *Kabbalah and Criticism* (1975), and *Poetry and Repression* (1976), as well as in a number of writings concerned with individual poets. See also the collection of Bloom's recent writings, *Poetics of Influence,* ed. John Hollander (1988). For analyses and critiques of this theory of literature see Frank Lentricchia, *After the New Criticism* (1980), Chapter 9; David Fite, *Harold Bloom: The Rhetoric of Romantic Vision* (1985); M. H. Abrams, "How to Do Things with Texts," in *Doing Things with Texts* (1989). For a feminist application of Bloom's anxiety of influence, see Sandra Gilbert and Susan Gubar, *The Madwoman in the Attic* (1980).

Marxist Criticism, in its diverse forms, grounds its theory and practice on the economic and cultural theory of Karl Marx (1818–1883) and his fellow-thinker Friedrich Engels, and especially on the following claims:

1) "In the last analysis," the evolving history of humanity, of its social relations, of its institutions, and of its ways of thinking are largely determined by the changing mode of its "material production"—that is, of its overall economic organization.

2) Historical changes in the fundamental mode of production effect changes in the social class structure, establishing in each era dominant and subordinate classes that engage in a struggle for economic, political, and social advantage.

3) Human consciousness is constituted by an **ideology**—that is, the beliefs, values, and ways of thinking and feeling through which human beings perceive, and by recourse to which they explain, what they take to be reality. An ideology is, in complex ways, the product of the position and interests of a particular class. In any historical era, the dominant ideology embodies, and serves to legitimize and perpetuate, the interests of the dominant economic and social class.

Ideology was not much discussed by Marx and Engels after *The German Ideology,* which they authored jointly in 1845–46, but it has become a key concept in Marxist criticism of literature and the other arts. Marx inherited the term from French philosophers of the late eighteenth century, who used it to designate the study of the way that concepts develop from sense-perceptions. In the present time, ideology is used in a variety of non-Marxist ways, ranging from a derogatory name for any set of political ideas that are held dogmatically and applied rigorously, to a neutral name for any ways of perceiving and thinking that are specific to an individual's race, or sex, or education, or ethnic group. In its distinctively Marxist use, the ideology that is dominant in any era is conceived to be, ultimately, the product of its economic structure and the resulting class-relations and class-interests. In a famed architectural metaphor, Marx represented ideology as a "superstructure" of which the contemporary socioeconomic system is the "base." Friedrich Engels described ideology as "a false consciousness," and many later Marxists consider it to be constituted largely by unconscious prepossessions that are illusory, in contrast to the "scientific" (that is, Marxist) knowledge of the economic determinants, historical evolution, and present constitution of the social world. A further claim is that, in the present era of capitalist economic organization that emerged during the eighteenth century, the reigning ideology incorporates the interests of the dominant and exploitative class, the "bourgeoisie," who are the owners of the material means of production and distribution, as opposed to the "proletariat," or wage-earning working class. It is claimed that this ideology, to those who live in and with it, seems a natural and inevitable way of seeing, explaining, and dealing with the environing world, but in fact has the hidden function of legitimizing and maintaining the position, power, and economic interests of the ruling class. Bourgeois ideology is regarded as both producing and permeating the social and cultural institutions and practices of the present era—including religion, morality, philosophy, politics, and the legal system, as well as (though in a less direct way) literature and the other arts.

In accordance with some version of the views just outlined, a Marxist critic typically undertakes to "explain" the literature in any historical era, not as works created in accordance with timeless artistic criteria, but as "products" of the economic and ideological determinants specific to that era; usually, the Marxist critic also examines the relation of a literary product to the actual economic and social reality of its time and place. What some Marxist critics themselves decry as "vulgar Marxism" treats a "bourgeois" literary work as in direct correlation with the present stage of the class struggle, and demands that such works be replaced by a "social realism" that will represent the true reality and progressive forces of our time; in practice, this has usually turned out to be the demand that literature conform to the official party line. More flexible Marxists, on the other hand, building upon scattered comments on literature in Marx and Engels themselves, grant that traditional literary works possess a degree of autonomy that enables some of them to transcend their bourgeois ideology sufficiently to represent (or in the frequent Marxist equivalent, to *reflect*) the "objective" reality of their time.

The Hungarian thinker Georg Lukács, the most widely influential of Marxist critics, represents such a flexible view of the role of ideology. He proposed that each great work of literature creates "its own world," which is unique and seemingly distinct from "everyday reality." But a master of realism in the novel such as Balzac or Tolstoy, by "bringing to life the greatest possible richness of the objective conditions of life," and by creating "typical" characters who manifest to an extreme the essential tendencies and determinants of their epoch, succeed—often "in opposition to [the author's] own conscious ideology"—in producing a fictional world which is a "reflection of life in the greatest concreteness and clarity and with all its motivating contradictions"; that is, their fictional world accords with the Marxist conception of the real world of class conflict, economic and social "contradictions," and the alienation of the individual under capitalism. (Georg Lukács, *Writer and Critic and Other Essays,* trans. 1970; the volume also includes Lukács' useful review of the foundational tenets of Marxist criticism, in "Marx and Engels on Aesthetics.")

Lukács, while lauding nineteenth-century literary realism, attacked modernist experimental writers as "decadent" examples of the exclusive concern with the subjectivity of the alienated individual in the fragmented world of our late stage of capitalism. (See *modernism.*) He thereby inaugurated a vigorous debate among Marxist critics about the political standing of formal innovators in twentieth-century literature. In opposition to Lukács, the "Frankfurt School" of German Marxists, especially Theodor Adorno and Max Horkheimer, lauded modernist writers such as James Joyce, Marcel Proust, and Samuel Beckett, proposing that their formal experiments, by the very fact that they fragment and disrupt the life they "reflect," establish a distance and effect a detachment which serve as an implicit critique—or yield a "negative knowledge"—of the dehumanizing institutions and processes of society under capitalism.

Two rather maverick German Marxists, Bertolt Brecht and Walter Benjamin, who also supported modernist and nonrealistic art, have had considerable influence on non-Marxist as well as Marxist criticism. In his critical theory, and in his own dramatic writings (see *epic theater*), Bertolt Brecht rejected what he called the "Aristotelian" concept of a tragic play as an imitation of reality that has a unified plot and a universal theme, and establishes an identification of the audience with the hero which produces a catharsis of the spectator's emotions. (See Aristotle, under *tragedy* and *plot.*) Brecht proposes instead that the illusion of reality should be deliberately shattered by the use of an episodic plot, by protagonists who do not attract the audience's sympathy, by emphasizing theatricality in staging and acting, and by other ways of baring the devices of drama so as to produce *estrangement effects* that will jar audiences out of their passive and complacent acceptance of modern capitalist society as a natural way of life, into an attitude not only (as in Adorno) of critical understanding of capitalist shortcomings, but of active engagement with the forces of change. Another notable critic, Walter Benjamin, was both an admirer of Brecht and briefly an associate of the Frankfurt School. Particularly influential was Benjamin's attention to the

effects of changing material conditions in the production of the arts, especially the recent technological developments of the mass media that have
promoted, he said, "a revolutionary criticism of traditional concepts of art."
In his essay "The Work of Art in the Age of Mechanical Reproduction,"
Benjamin proposes that modern technical innovations such as photography,
the phonograph, the radio, and especially the cinema, have transformed the
very concept and status of a work of art. Formerly an artist or author produced a work which was a single object, regarded as the special preserve of
the bourgeois élite, around which developed a quasi-religious "aura" of
uniqueness, autonomy, and aesthetic value independent of any social function—an aura which invited in the spectator a passive attitude of absorbed
contemplation in the object itself. The new media not only make possible
the infinite and precise reproducibility of the objects of art, but effect the
production of works which, like motion pictures, are specifically designed to
be reproduced in multiple copies. Such modes of art, Benjamin argues, by
destroying the mystique of the unique work of art as a subject for pure contemplation, make possible a radical role for works of art by opening the way
to "the formulation of revolutionary demands in the politics of art." (A useful collection of central essays by the Marxist critics Lukács, Brecht,
Benjamin, and Adorno is R. Taylor, ed., *Aesthetics and Politics,* 1977.)

In the last few decades there has been a resurgence of Marxist criticism,
marked by an openness, on some level of literary analysis, to other current
critical perspectives; a flexibility which acknowledges that Marxist critical
theory is itself not a set of timeless truths but at least to some degree an
evolving historical process; a subtilizing of the concept of ideology as applied
to literary content; and a tendency to grant an increased role to non-ideolog-
ical and distinctively artistic determinants of literary structures.

In the 1960s the influential Marxist Louis Althusser assimilated the *structuralism* then current into his view that the structure of society as a whole is
constituted by diverse "nonsynchronous" social formations, or "ideological
state apparatuses," including religious, legal, political, and literary institutions. Each of these is interrelated with the others in complex ways, but possesses a "relative autonomy"; only "in the last instance" is the ideology of a
particular institution determined by the material base in the contemporary
mode of economic production. In an influential reconsideration of the nature
of ideology, Althusser opposes its definition as "false consciousness"; he
declares instead that ideologies vary according to the form and practices of
each mode of state apparatus, and that the ideology of each mode operates by
means of a type of discourse which "interpellates" (calls upon) the individual
to take up a pre-established "subject position," which in each instance serves
the ultimate interests of the ruling class. (See *discourse.*) Within the particular
social formation of literature, furthermore, a great work is not a mere product
of ideology, for its fiction establishes for the reader a distance from which to
recognize, hence expose, "the ideology from which it is born . . . from which
it detaches itself as art, and to which it alludes." Pierre Macherey, in *A Theory
of Literary Production* (1966), stressed the supplementary claim that a literary
text not only distances itself from its ideology by its fiction and form, but also

exposes the "contradictions" that are inherent in that ideology by its "silences" or "gaps"—that is, by what the text fails to say because its ideology makes it impossible to say it. Such textual "absences" are symptoms of ideological repressions of the contents of the text's own "unconscious." The aim of Marxist criticism, Macherey asserts, is to make these silences "speak" and so to reveal, behind what an author consciously intended to say, the text's unconscious content—that is, its repressed awareness of the flaws, stresses, and incoherence in the very ideology that it incorporates.

In England the many social and critical writings of Raymond Williams demonstrate an adaptation of Marxist concepts to his humanistic concern with the overall texture of an individual's "lived experience." A leading theorist of Marxist criticism in England is Terry Eagleton, who has expanded and elaborated the concepts of Althusser and Macherey into his view that a literary text is a special kind of production in which ideological discourse—described as any system of mental representations of lived experience—is reworked into a specifically literary discourse. In recent years Eagleton has been increasingly hospitable to the tactical use, for dealing with ideology in literature, of concepts derived from *deconstruction* and from Lacan's version of Freudian *psychoanalysis*. Eagleton views such poststructuralist analyses as useful to Marxist critics of literary texts insofar as they serve to undermine reigning beliefs and certainties, but only as preliminary to the properly Marxist enterprise of exposing their ideological motivation and to the application of the criticism of literature toward politically desirable ends.

The most prominent American theorist, Fredric Jameson, is also the most eclectic of current Marxist critics. In *The Political Unconscious: Narrative as a Socially Symbolic Act* (1981), Jameson expressly adapts to his synthetic critical enterprise such seemingly incompatible viewpoints as the medieval theory of fourfold levels of meaning in the *allegorical interpretation* of the Bible, the *archetypal criticism* of Northrop Frye, *structuralist criticism,* Lacan's reinterpretations of Freud, *semiotics,* and *deconstruction.* These modes of criticism, Jameson asserts, are applicable at various stages of the critical interpretation of a literary work; but Marxist criticism, he contends, "subsumes" all the other "interpretive modes," by retaining their positive findings within a "political interpretation of literary texts" which stands as the "final" or "absolute horizon of all reading and all interpretation." This last-analysis "political interpretation" of a literary text involves an exposure of the hidden role of the "political unconscious"—a concept which Jameson describes as his "collective," or "political," adaptation of the Freudian concept that each individual's unconscious is a repository of repressed desires. In any literary product of our late capitalist era, the "rifts and discontinuities" in the text, and especially those elements which, in the French phrase, are its "non-dit" (its not-said), are symptoms of the repression by ideology of the contradictions of "History" into the depths of the political unconscious; and the content of this repressed History, Jameson asserts, is the revolutionary process of "the collective struggle to wrest a realm of Freedom from a realm of Necessity." In the final stage of an interpretation, Jameson holds, the Marxist critic "rewrites," in the mode of "allegory," the literary text "in such a way that the [text] may be seen as the . . . reconstruction of a prior histori-cal or ideological *subtext*"—that is, of the text's unspoken, because repressed and unconscious, awareness of the ways it is determined not only by current ideology, but also by the long-term process of true "History."

See *sociology of literature,* and for the Marxist wing of the current critical mode called new historicism, see *cultural materialism.* In addition to the writ-ings listed above, refer to: Georg Lukács, *Studies in European Realism* (1950); Raymond Williams, *Culture and Society, 1780–1950* (1960), and *Marxism and Literature* (1977); Peter Demetz, *Marx, Engels and the Poets: Origins of Marxist Literary Criticism* (1967); Walter Benjamin, *Illuminations* (trans., 1968); Louis Althusser, *Lenin and Philosophy, and Other Essays* (1969, trans. 1971); Fredric Jameson, *Marxism and Form* (1971); Lee Baxandall and Stefan Morawski, eds., *Marx and Engels on Literature and Art* (1973); Terry Eagleton, *Criticism and Ideology* (1976), and *Marxism and Literary Criticism* (1976)—the latter is a use-ful introduction to Marxist criticism in general; Chris Bullock and David Peck, eds., *Guide to Marxist Literary Criticism* (1980); Michael Ryan, *Marxism and Deconstruction* (1982); J. J. McGann, *The Romantic Ideology* (1983); J. G. Merquior, *Western Marxism* (1986). Various essays by Gayatri Chakravorty Spivak assimilate Marxist concepts both to *deconstruction* and to the view-point of *feminist criticism;* see for example her "Displacement and the Discourse of Women," in *Displacement: Derrida and After,* ed. Mark Krupnick (1983). For a sharp critique of recent theorists of Marxist criticism, see Frederick Crews, "Dialectical Immaterialism," in *Skeptical Engagements* (1986).

New Criticism. This term, made current by the publication of John Crowe Ransom's book *The New Criticism* in 1941, came to be applied to a theory and practice that dominated American literary criticism until late in the 1960s. The movement derived in considerable part from elements in I. A. Richards' *Principles of Literary Criticism* (1924) and *Practical Criticism* (1929), and from the critical essays of T. S. Eliot. It opposed itself against the prevail-ing interest of scholars and critics of that era with the biographies of authors, the social context of literature, and literary history by insisting that the proper concern of literary criticism is not with the external circumstances or effects of a work, but with a detailed consideration of the work itself. Notable critics in this mode were the southerners Cleanth Brooks and Robert Penn Warren, whose textbooks *Understanding Poetry* (1938) and *Understanding Fiction* (1943) did much to make the New Criticism the reigning method of teaching literature in American colleges, and even in high schools, for the next two or three decades. Other prominent writers of that time—in addition to Ransom, Brooks, and Warren—who are often identified as New Critics are Allen Tate, R. P. Blackmur, and William K. Wimsatt. An influential English critic, F. R. Leavis, in his focus on the detailed analysis of individual works and passages, shared some concepts and practices with these Americans.

The New Critics differ from one another in many ways, but the follow-ing points of view and procedures are common to many of them.

1) A poem, it is held, should be treated as such—in Eliot's words, "pri-marily as poetry and not another thing"—and should therefore be regarded as an independent and self-sufficient verbal object. The first law of criticism, John Crowe Ransom said, "is that it shall be objective, shall cite the nature of the object" and shall recognize "the autonomy of the work itself as existing for its own sake." (See *objective criticism*.) New Critics warn the reader against critical practices which divert critical attention from the object itself (see *intentional fallacy* and *affective fallacy*). In analyzing and evaluating a particular work, they eschew reference to the biography of the author, to the social conditions at the time of its production, or to its psychological and moral effects on the reader; they also tend to minimize recourse to the place of the work in the history of literary forms and subject matter. Because of this critical focus on the literary work in isolation from its attendant circumstances and effects, the New Criticism is often classified as a type of critical *formalism*.

2) The distinctive procedure of a New Critic is **explication**, or **close reading**: the detailed and subtle analysis of the complex interrelations and *ambiguities* (multiple meanings) of the components within a work. "Explication de texte" has long been a formal procedure for teaching literature in French schools, but the kind of explicative analyses characteristic of the New Criticism derives from such books as I. A. Richards' *Practical Criticism* (1929) and William Empson's *Seven Types of Ambiguity* (1930).

3) The principles of the New Criticism are basically verbal. That is, literature is conceived to be a special kind of language whose attributes are defined by systematic opposition to the language of science and of practical and logical discourse, and the explicative procedure is to analyze the meanings and interactions of words, *figures of speech,* and *symbols*. The emphasis is on the "organic unity" of overall structure and verbal meanings, and we are warned against separating the two by what Cleanth Brooks has called "the heresy of paraphrase."

4) The distinction between literary *genres*, although recognized and used, does not play an essential role in the New Criticism. The essential components of any work of literature, whether lyric, narrative, or dramatic, are conceived to be words, images, and symbols rather than character, thought, and plot. These linguistic elements are often said to be organized around a central and humanly significant *theme,* and to manifest high literary value to the degree that they manifest "*tension*," "*irony*," and "*paradox*" in achieving a "reconciliation of diverse impulses" or an "equilibrium of opposed forces." The form of a work, whether or not it has characters and plot, is said to be primarily a "structure of meanings," which evolve into an integral and free-standing unity mainly through a play and counterplay of "thematic imagery" and "symbolic action."

The basic orientation and modes of analysis in the New Criticism were adapted to the **contextual criticism** of Eliseo Vivas and Murray Krieger. Krieger defined contextualism as "the claim that the poem is a tight, compelling, finally closed context," which prevents "our escape to the world of reference and action beyond," and requires that we "judge the work's efficacy as an aesthetic object." (See Krieger, *The New Apologists for Poetry*, 1956, and *Theory of Criticism,* 1976.) The revolutionary thrust of the new mode had lost much of its force by the 1960s, when it gave way to various newer theories of criticism, but it has left a deep and enduring mark on the criticism and teaching of literature, in its primary emphasis on the individual work and in the variety and subtlety of the devices that it made available for analyzing the structure of its internal relations. This emphasis on close reading survives, for example, in the radical mode of current literary criticism known as *deconstruction.*

Central instances of the theory and practice of New Criticism are Cleanth Brooks, *The Well Wrought Urn* (1947), and W. K. Wimsatt, *The Verbal Icon* (1954). The theory and practices of New Criticism are privileged over alternative approaches to literature in René Wellek and Austin Warren, *Theory of Literature* (1973), which became a standard reference book in the graduate study of literature. Robert W. Stallman's *Critiques and Essays in Criticism, 1920–1948* (1949) is a convenient collection of essays in this critical mode; the literary journal *The Explicator* (1942 ff.), devoted to close reading, is a characteristic product of its approach to literary texts, as are the items listed in *Poetry Explication: A Checklist of Interpretation Since 1924 of British and American Poems Past and Present,* ed. Joseph M. Kuntz (rev., 1962). See also W. K. Wimsatt, ed., *Explication as Criticism* (1963); the review of the movement by René Wellek, *A History of Modern Criticism,* Vol. 6 (1986); and the spirited retrospective defense of New Criticism by its chief exponent, Cleanth Brooks, "In Search of the New Criticism," *American Scholar* 53 (1983–84). For critiques of the theory and methods of the New Criticism, see R. S. Crane, ed., *Critics and Criticism, Ancient and Modern* (1952), and *The Languages of Criticism and the Structure of Poetry* (1953); Gerald Graff, *Poetic Statement and Critical Dogma* (1970); and (on contextual criticism also) Grant Webster, *The Republic of Letters: A History of Postwar American Literary Opinion* (1979); Frank Lentricchia, *After the New Criticism* (1980), Chapter 6.

New Historicism, since the early 1980s, has been the accepted name for a mode of literary study that its proponents oppose to the *formalism* they attribute both to the *New Criticism* and to the critical *deconstruction* that followed it. In place of dealing with a text in isolation from its historical context, new historicists attend primarily to the historical and cultural conditions of its production, and also of its later critical interpretations and evaluations. This is not simply a return to an earlier kind of literary scholarship, for the views and practices of the new historicists differ markedly from those of former scholars who had used political and intellectual history as a "background" to account for the characteristic subject matter of literature at a particular time and place.

What is most distinctive in the new mode of historical study, marking it as poststructural, is mainly the result of concepts and procedures that it has assimilated from various recent theories of literary and other writings. (See *poststructuralism.*) Especially prominent influences are: (1) The views of the revisionist Marxist thinker, Louis Althusser, that *ideology* manifests itself in different ways in the discourse of each of the semi-autonomous institutions of an era, and also that ideology operates to position its readers as the "subjects" in the discourse, in a way that in fact "subjects" them—that is, subordinates them—to the interests of the ruling classes. (2) Michel Foucault's theory that the patterns of power-relations at any given era in a society constitute the concepts, oppositions, and hierarchies of its *discourse,* and in this way determine what will be accounted knowledge and truth, as well as what will be considered humanly normal and so serve to define and exclude what, in that era, is accounted to be criminal, insane, or sexually deviant. (3) The central concept in deconstructive criticism that all texts involve modes of signification that war against each other, merged with Mikhail Bakhtin's concept of the *dialogic* nature of many literary texts, in the sense that they present a number of independent and often conflicting voices. (4) Recent developments in cultural anthropology, especially Clifford Geertz' view that a culture is constituted by distinctive sets of signifying systems, and his use of what he calls **thick descriptions**—the close analysis, or "reading," of a particular social production or event so as to recover the meanings it has for the people involved in it, as well as to discover the patterns of conventions, codes, and modes of thinking that invest the cultural item with those meanings.

In an oft-quoted phrase, Louis Montrose described the new historicism as "a reciprocal concern with the historicity of texts and the textuality of history." This historical mode is grounded on the concepts that history itself is not a set of fixed, objective facts but, like the literature with which it interacts, a text which needs to be interpreted; that a text, whether literary or historical, is a discourse which, although it may seem to present, or reflect, an external reality, in fact consists of what are called **representations**—that is, verbal formations which are the "ideological products" or "cultural constructs" of a particular era; and that these cultural and ideological representations in texts serve mainly to reproduce, confirm, and propagate the power-structures of domination and subordination which characterize a given society. Within this overall perspective, we find considerable diversity and disagreements among individual exponents of the new historicism. The following claims, however, occur frequently in their writings, sometimes in an extreme and sometimes in a qualified form. All of them are formulated in opposition to views that, according to the new historians, were central ideological constructs in traditional literary criticism. A number of the historians assign the formative period of these traditional views to the early era of capitalism in the seventeenth and eighteenth centuries.

1) Literature does not occupy a "trans-historical" aesthetic realm which is independent of economic, social, and political conditions and is subject to timeless criteria of artistic value. Instead, a literary text is simply one of many kinds of texts—religious, philosophical, legal, scientific, and so on—all of which are subject to the particular conditions of a time and place, and among which the literary text has neither unique status nor special privilege. A related fallacy of mainstream criticism was to view a literary text as an autonomous body of fixed meanings that cohere to form an organic whole in which all conflicts are artistically resolved. On the contrary, many literary texts represent a diversity of dissonant voices, and these express not only the orthodox, but also the subversive forces of the era in which the text was produced. Furthermore, what may seem to be the artistic resolution of a literary plot, yielding pleasure to the reader, is in fact deceptive, for it is an effect that serves to cover over the unresolved conflicts of power, class, gender, and social groups that make up the real tensions that underlie the surface meanings of a literary text.

2)   History is not a homogeneous and stable pattern of facts and events which can be used as the "background" to explain the literature of an era, or which literature can be said simply to reflect, or which can be adverted to (as in an earlier type of *Marxist criticism*) as the "material" conditions that, in a simple and unilateral way, determine the particularities of a literary text. In contrast to such views, a literary text is said by new historicists to be "embedded" in its context, as an interactive component within the network of institutions, beliefs, and cultural power-relations, practices, and products that, in their ensemble, constitute what we call history. New historicists commonly regard even the conceptual "boundaries" by which we currently discriminate between literature and non-literary texts to be a product of post-Renaissance ideological formations. They continue to make use of such discriminations, but only for tactical convenience in critical discussions, and stress that one must view all such artificial boundaries as entirely permeable to interchanges of diverse elements and forces. The favored terms for such interchanges—whether between the modes of discourse within a single literary text, or between diverse kinds of texts, or between a text and its institutional and cultural context—are "negotiation," "exchange," "transaction," and "circulation." Such metaphors are intended not only to denote the two-way, oscillatory relationships among the components of a culture, but also to indicate, by their origin in the economic and monetary discourse of the marketplace, the degree to which the operations and values of modern consumer capitalism saturate literary and aesthetic, as well as all other social institutions and relations. As Stephen Greenblatt has expressed such a view, the "negotiation" resulting in the production and circulation of a work of art involves a "mutually profitable exchange"—including "a return normally measured in pleasure and interest"—in which "the society's dominant currencies, money and prestige, are invariably involved." ("Toward a Poetics of Culture," in *The New Historicism*, ed. H. Aram Veeser, 1989, p. 12.)

3)   The *humanistic* concept of an essential human nature that is shared by the author of a literary work, the characters within the work, and the audience the author writes for, is another of the widely held ideological illusions that, according to many new historicists, were generated primarily by a capitalist culture. They also attribute to this "bourgeois" and "essentialist humanism" the view that a literary work is the creation of a free, or "autonomous," author who possesses a unified, unique, and enduring personal identity. In the epilogue of *Renaissance Self-Fashioning* (1980) Stephen Greenblatt says that, in the course of writing the book, he lost his initial confidence in "the role of human autonomy," for "the human subject itself began to seem remarkably unfree, the ideological product of the relations of power in a particular society." A major area of contest among new histori-

cists is the extent to which an author, despite being a "subject" produced and positioned by the play of power and ideology within the discourse of a particular era, may be able to retain some scope for individual initiative and "agency." Those historicists who ascribe a degree of freedom and initiative to an individual author do so, however, not as in traditional criticism, in order to explain an author's literary invention and distinctive artistry, but in order to keep open the theoretical possibility that an individual can conceive and inaugurate radical changes in the social power-structure of which that individual's own "subjectivity" and function are a product.

4) Like the authors who produce literary texts, their readers are subjects who are shaped and positioned by the conditions and ideological formations of their own era. All claims, therefore, for the possibility of a disinterested and objective interpretation and evaluation of a literary text—such as Matthew Arnold's behest that we see a work "as in itself it really is"—are among the illusions of a humanistic idealism. Insofar as the ideology of readers chances to conform to the ideology of the writer of a literary text, the readers will **naturalize** the text—that is, interpret its culture-specific and time-bound representations as though they were the features of universal and permanent human experience. Insofar as the readers' ideology differs from that of the writer, they will **appropriate** the text—that is, interpret it so as to make it conform to their own cultural prepossessions.

New historians acknowledge that they themselves, like all authors, are "subjectivities" that have been shaped and informed by the circumstances and discourses specific to their era, hence that their own critical writings construct, rather than discover ready-made, the textual meanings they describe and the literary and cultural histories they narrate. To mitigate the risk that they will unquestioningly appropriate texts written in the past, they tend to stress that the course of history between the past and present is not coherent, but exhibits discontinuities, breaks, and ruptures; by doing so, they hope to "distance" and "estrange" an earlier text and so sharpen their ability to detect its differences from their present ideological assumptions. A number of historicists present their readings of texts written in the past as (in their favored metaphor) "negotiations" between past and present. In this two-way relationship, the features of a cultural product, which are identifiable only relatively to their differences from the historicist's own subject-position, in return make possible some degree of insight into the power-configurations—especially in the aspects of class, gender, race, and ethnicity—that prevail in the historicist's present culture.

The concepts, themes, and procedures of new historicist criticism took shape in the late 1970s and early 1980s, most prominently in writings by scholars of the English Renaissance. They directed their attention especially to literary forms such as the pastoral and masque, and, above all, drama; emphasized the role in shaping a text of social and economic conditions such as literary patronage, censorship, and the control of access to printing; analyzed texts as discursive "sites" which enacted and reproduced the interests and power structure of the Tudor monarchy; and were alert to detect within texts the voices of the oppressed, the marginalized, and the dispossessed. At almost the same time, students of the English Romantic period developed parallel conceptions of the intertextuality of literature and history, and similar views that the "representations" in literary texts are not reflectors of reality but "concretized" forms of ideology. Historicists of Romantic literature, however, in distinction from Renaissance historicists, often name their critical procedures **political readings** of a literary text— readings in which they stress quasi-Freudian mechanisms such as "suppression," "displacement," and "substitution" by which, they assert, a writer's political ideology (in a process of which the writer remains largely or entirely unaware) inevitably disguises, or entirely elides into silence and "absence," the circumstances and contradictions of contemporary history. The primary aim of a political reader of a literary text is to undo these ideological disguises and suppressions in order to uncover the historical and political conflicts and oppressions which are the text's true, although covert or unmentioned, subject matter.

In the course of the 1980s, the viewpoints and practices of new historicism spread rapidly to all periods of literary study, and were increasingly represented, described, and debated in conferences, books, and periodical essays. Some *feminist* critics adapted this historical mode to their concerns by stressing the role of masculine power-structures in forming ideological and cultural constructs, while many critics interested in *Black* and other ethnic literatures stressed the role of culture-formations dominated by White Europeans in suppressing, marginalizing, or distorting the achievements of non-White and non-European peoples. In the 1990s, it seems clear, new historicism has displaced deconstruction as the reigning form of *avant-garde* critical theory and practice.

Stephen Greenblatt inaugurated the currency of the label "new historicism" in his Introduction to a special issue of *Genre,* Vol. 15 (1982). He prefers, however, to call his own critical enterprise **cultural poetics,** in order to highlight his concern with literature and the arts as integral with other social practices that, in their complex interactions, make up the general culture of an era. In his writings on the Renaissance, one of Greenblatt's recurrent critical tactics is to inaugurate his essay by telling an anecdote, or by referring to a text or cultural object that seems remote from literature; to subject the selected item to a close reading (in Clifford Geertz's term, a "thick description") designed to bring out the beliefs, norms, and rhetorical ploys of power that are implicit in it; and to apply that analysis so as to reveal similar cultural elements and configurations in literary texts of the same period. For example, in an essay called "Invisible Bullets" Greenblatt reads a selection from Thomas Harriott's *A Brief and True Report of the New Found Land of Virginia,* written in 1588, as a representative discourse of the English colonizers of America which, without its author's awareness, serves to confirm "the Machiavellian hypothesis of the origin of princely power in force and fraud," yet nonetheless draws its "audience irresistibly toward the celebration of that power." Greenblatt also asserts that Harriott tests the English power-structure that he attests by recording in his *Report* the counter-voices of the

American Indians who are being appropriated and oppressed by that power. Greenblatt then identifies similar modes of power discourse and counter-discourse in the dialogues in Shakespeare's *Tempest* between Prospero the appropriator and Caliban the expropriated native of his island, and goes on, surprisingly, to find similar discursive configurations in the texts of Shakespeare's *Henry IV, 1 and 2* and *Henry V*. In Greenblatt's reading, the dialogue and events of the Henry plays reveal the degree to which princely power is based on predation, calculation, deceit, and hypocrisy; at the same time, the plays do not scruple to record the dissonant and subversive voices of Falstaff and various other representatives of Elizabethan sub-cultures. These counter-establishment revelations in Shakespeare's plays, however, serve to maneuver their audience to accept and even glorify the power-structure to which that audience is itself subjected. Greenblatt's general thesis is that, in order to sustain its power, any durable political and cultural order not only to some degree allows, but actively fosters subversive elements and forces, yet in such a way as more effectively to "contain" such challenges to the existing order. This view of the general triumph of containment over the forces of subversion has been criticized as "pessimistic" and "quietest" by new historicists who insist on the capacity of subversive ideas and practices—including those manifested in their own critical writings—to effect drastic social changes.

Cultural materialism is a term, used by the Marxist critic Raymond Williams, which has been adopted by a number of British scholars to indicate the Marxist orientation of their mode of new historicism. (See *Marxist criticism*.) They insist that, whatever the "textuality" of history, a culture and its literary products are always to an important degree conditioned by the real material forces and relations of production in their historical era. They are particularly interested in the political significance, and especially the subversive aspects and effects, of a literary text, not only in its own time, but also in later versions of the text in the theater and the cinema, and in its altering interpretation and treatment by later literary critics. Cultural materialists stress that their criticism is itself oriented toward political intervention in their own era, in an express "commitment," as Jonathan Dollimore and Alan Sinfield have put it, "to the transformation of a social order which exploits people on grounds of race, gender, and class." (Foreword to *Political Shakespeare: New Essays in Cultural Materialism*, 1985.) Similar views are expressed by those American exponents of the new literary history who are political activists; indeed, some of them claim that if new historicists limit themselves to describing social domination and exploitation in literary texts of the past, but stop short of a commitment to remake the present social order, they have been co-opted into complying with the politically aloof formalism of the types of literary criticism that they set out to displace.

Related to the new historicism is a recent but very rapidly growing cross-disciplinary enterprise called **cultural studies.** The name designates the critical analysis of both the production and reception of all forms of cultural institutions, processes, and products; among these, literature counts as merely one of many types of "symbolic constructions." A chief concern is to identify the role, and the historical changes, of the social, economic, and political forces and power-structures that produce, sustain, and propagate the meanings, "truth," value, and relative status of diverse cultural phenomena and their institutions—including the institutions of traditional literary production and study, and even of their own field of cultural study. One prominent tendency is to subvert the hierarchical distinctions between "high art" and "high literature" and the traditionally "lower" forms that appeal to a much larger body of consumers—or at any rate, to devote no more attention to élite *canonical* literature than to popular fiction and romances, magazine writing, journalism, and advertising, together with other arts that have mass appeal such as comics, film, television, video, and all forms of popular music. Prominent also is the undertaking to transfer to the center of cultural study such hitherto "marginal" or "excluded" subjects as the literary, artistic, and intellectual productions of women, the working class, ethnic groups, and colonial, postcolonial, and Third-World cultures. An associated and frequently expressed aim is to displace, in schools and universities, the central subjects of study and value systems (said to have been established by, and therefore to reflect, the special interests of white European males), or at least to pluralize what is taught so as to substitute a **multiculturalism** for what is claimed to be the monoculturalism of the traditional curriculum. And as in the new historicism, some advocates of cultural studies orient their writings and teachings toward the explicit political end of reforming the existing power-relations which, they claim, are dominated by a privileged gender, race, class, or ethnic group. See the journal *Cultural Studies,* 1987 and following; and Gayatri C. Spivak, *In Other Worlds: Essays in Cultural Politics* (1987); Andrew Ross, *No Respect: Intellectual and Popular Culture* (1989); Lawrence Grossberg, Cary Nelson, and Paula Treichler, eds., *Cultural Studies* (1991).

For writers especially influential in forming the concepts and practices of the new historicism, see Louis Althusser, *Lenin and Philosophy, and Other Essays* (1969, trans. 1971); Michel Foucault, *The Foucault Reader,* ed. Paul Rabinov (1986); and Clifford Geertz, "Thick Description: Toward an Interpretive Theory of Culture," in *The Interpretation of Cultures* (1973). *The New Historicism,* ed. H. Aram Veeser (1989), is a very useful collection of essays by Louis Montrose, Stephen Greenblatt, and other prominent historicists who focus on the Renaissance; see also Stephen Greenblatt, ed., *Representing the English Renaissance* (1988), and his *Learning to Curse: Essays in Early Modern Culture* (1990). For a feminist emphasis in new historicism, refer to Margaret W. Ferguson, Maureen Quilligan, and Nancy J. Vickers, eds., *Rewriting the Renaissance: The Discourses of Sexual Difference in Early Modern Europe* (1986). Treatments of Romantic literature that exemplify a new historicist orientation include Jerome J. McGann, *The Romantic Ideology: A Critical Investigation* (1983); Marjorie Levinson, *Wordsworth's Great Period Poems* (1986); Clifford Siskin, *The Historicity of Romantic Discourse* (1988); Alan Liu, *Wordsworth: The Sense of History* (1989); and Marjorie Levinson and others, *Rethinking Historicism: Critical Readings in Romantic History* (1989).

Jonathan Dollimore and Alan Sinfield present writings by British cultural materialists in *Political Shakespeare: New Essay's in Cultural Materialism*

(1985), as does John Drakakis in *Alternative Shakespeares* (1985); see also Raymond Williams, *Marxism and Literature* (1977), and Terry Eagleton, *Marxism and Literary Criticism* (1976). Walter Cohen, "Political Criticism of Shakespeare," in Jean E. Howard and Marion F. O'Connor, eds., *Shakespeare Reproduced: The Text in History and Ideology* (1987), interrogates new historicism from a Marxist point of view; while J. Hillis Miller, in his presidential address to the Modern Language Association on "The Triumph of Theory" (*PMLA*, Vol. 102, 1987, pp. 281–91), does so from the point of view of deconstructive criticism. Feminist critiques of new historicism are Lynda Bose, "The Family in Shakespeare Studies," *Renaissance Quarterly* 40 (1987); and Carol Thomas Neely, "Constructing the Subject: Feminist Practice and the New Renaissance Discourse" (*English Literary Renaissance*, Vol. 18, 1988). Critiques of new historicism from more traditional critical positions are Edward Pechter, "The New Historicism and Its Discontents," *PMLA*, 102 (1987); M. H. Abrams, "On Political Readings of *Lyrical Ballads*," in *Doing Things with Texts: Essays in Criticism and Critical Theory* (1989); Richard Levin, "Unthinkable Thoughts in the New Historicizing of English Renaissance Drama," *New Literary History*, 21 (1989–90), pp. 433–47; and Brook Thomas, *The New Historicism and Other Old-Fashioned Topics* (1991). For tendencies in the writing of general history closely parallel to the new historicism in literary studies, see Dominick La Capra, *History and Criticism* (1985); and Lynn Hunt, ed., *The New Cultural History* (1989).

Phenomenology and Criticism. The philosophical perspective and method called **phenomenology** was established by the German thinker Edmund Husserl (1859–1938). Husserl set out to analyze human consciousness—that is, to describe the concrete "Lebenswelt" (lived world) as this is experienced independently of prior suppositions, whether these suppositions come from philosophy or from common sense. He proposes that consciousness is a unified **intentional** act. By "intentional" he does not mean that it is deliberately willed, but that it is always directed to an "object"; in other words, to be conscious is always to be conscious of something. Husserl's claim is that in this unitary act of consciousness, the thinking subject and the object it "intends," or is aware of, are interinvolved and reciprocally implicative. In order to be free of all prior conceptions, the phenomenological analysis of consciousness begins with an "epoché" (suspension) of all presuppositions about the nature of experience, and this suspension involves "bracketing" (holding in abeyance) the question whether or not the object of consciousness is real—that is, whether or not the object exists outside the consciousness which "intends" it.

Phenomenology has had widespread philosophical influence since it was put forward by Husserl in 1900 and later, and has been diversely developed by Martin Heidegger in Germany and Maurice Merleau-Ponty in France. It has greatly influenced Hans-Georg Gadamer and other theorists concerned with analyzing the conscious activity of understanding language (see *interpretation and hermeneutics*), and has, directly or indirectly, affected the way in which many critics analyze the experience of literature.

In the 1930s the Polish theorist Roman Ingarden (1893–1970), who wrote his books both in Polish and German, adapted the general phenomenological viewpoint and concepts to a theory of the way we understand and respond to a work of literature. In Ingarden's analysis, a literary work of art originates in the intentional acts of consciousness of its author—"intentional" in the phenomenological sense that the acts are directed toward an object. These intentional acts, as recorded in a text, make it possible for a reader to re-experience the work in his or her own consciousness. The recorded text contains many elements which are potential rather than fully realized, as well as many "places of indeterminacy" in what it sets forth. An "active reading" responds to the sequence of the printed words by a temporal process of consciousness which "fills out" these potential and indeterminate aspects of the text, and in so doing, in Ingarden's term, the reading **concretizes** the schematic literary work. Such a reading is said to be "co-creative" with the conscious processes recorded by the author, and to result in an actualized "aesthetic object" within the reader's consciousness which does not portray a reality that exists independently of the work, but instead constitutes a "quasi-reality"—that is to say, a fictional world. See Roman Ingarden, *The Literary Work of Art* (1931, trans. 1973), and *The Cognition of the Literary Work of Art* (1937, trans. 1973); also, the exposition in Eugene Falk, *The Poetics of Roman Ingarden* (1981). For German critics strongly influenced by Ingarden, see Wolfgang Iser under *reader-response criticism,* and Hans Robert Jauss under *reception-theory.*

The term **phenomenological criticism** is often applied specifically to the theory and practice of the **Geneva School** of critics, most of whose members taught at the University of Geneva, and all of whom were joined by friendship, interinfluence, and their general approach to literature. The older members of the Geneva School were Marcel Raymond and Albert Béguin; later members were Jean Rousset, Jean-Pierre Richard, and (the dominant figure) Georges Poulet. J. Hillis Miller, who for six years was a colleague of Poulet at Johns Hopkins University, was in his earlier career (before turning instead to *deconstructive criticism*) the leading American representative of the Geneva School of criticism, and applied this critical mode to the analysis of a variety of American and English authors.

Geneva critics regard each work of literature as a fictive world which is created out of the *Lebenswelt* of its author and embodies the author's entirely unique mode of consciousness. In its approach to literature as primarily subjective, this criticism is opposed to the objective approach of *formalism,* both in its European variety and in American *New Criticism.* Its roots instead go back through the nineteenth century to that type of romantic *expressive criticism* which regarded a literary work as the revelation of the personality of its author and proposed that the awareness of this personality is the chief aim and value of reading literature. (As early as 1778, for example, the German critic Johann Gottfried Herder wrote: "This *living reading,* this divination into the soul of the author, is the sole mode of reading, and the most profound means of self-development.") In the course of time, however, Geneva critics assimilated a number of the concepts and methods of Husserl, Heidegger, and other phenomenologists. In the view of the Geneva critics the "cogito," or distinctive structures of consciousness, of the author—related to, but not identical with, the author's "empirical," or biographical, self—pervades a work of literature, manifesting itself as the subjective correlate of the "contents" of the work; that is, of the objects, characters, imagery, and style in which the author's personal mode of awareness and feeling imaginatively projects itself. (For a related critical concept see *voice;* also, refer to *objective and subjective.*) By "bracketing" all their personal prepossessions and particularities, the readers of a literary work make themselves purely and passively receptive, and so are capable of achieving participation, or even identity, with the immanent consciousness of its author. Their undertaking to read a work so as to experience the mode of consciousness of its author, and then to reproject this consciousness in their own critical writings, underlies the frequent application to the Geneva School of the term **critics of consciousness** and the description of their critical aim as "consciousness of the consciousness of another." As Georges Poulet put it in "Phenomenology of Reading" (1969): "When I read as I ought . . . with the total commitment required of any reader," then "I am thinking the thoughts of another. . . . But I think it as my very own. . . . My consciousness behaves as though it were the consciousness of another." (It should be noted that whereas the philosopher Husserl's aim was to describe the essential features of consciousness which are common to all human beings, the Geneva critics' quite different aim is to identify—and also to identify oneself with—the unique consciousness of each individual author.)

Within this framework, Geneva critics differ in the extent to which they attend to specific elements in the contents, formal structure, and style of a text, on their way toward isolating its author's "interior" mode of consciousness. A conspicuous tendency of most of these critics is to put together widely separated passages within a single work, on the principle, as J. Hillis Miller says in his book *Charles Dickens,* that since all these passages "reveal the persistence of certain obsessions, problems, and attitudes," the critic may, by analyzing them, "glimpse the original unity of a creative mind." Furthermore the critics of consciousness often treat a single work not as an individual entity, but as part of the collective body of an author's writings, in order, as Miller said of Dickens, "to identify what persists through all the swarming multiplicity of his novels as a view of the world which is unique and the same." Georges Poulet has also undertaken, in a number of books, to tell the history of the varying imaginative treatments of the topic of time throughout the course of Western literature, regarding these treatments as correlative with diverse modes of lived experience. In these histories Poulet sets out to identify "for each epoch a consciousness common to all contemporary minds"; he claims, however, that within this shared period-consciousness, the consciousness of each author also manifests its uniqueness. The influence of the criticism of consciousness reached its height in the 1950s and 1960s, then gave way to the explicitly opposed critical modes of *structuralism* and *deconstruction.* Many of its concepts and procedures, however, survive in current forms of *reader-response criticism* and *reception-aesthetic.*

Robert R. Magliola, *Phenomenology and Literature* (1977), deals with various types of phenomenological poetics and criticism in the context of an exposition of Husserl, Heidegger, and other phenomenological philosophers. Brief introductions to the Geneva School of criticism are Georges Poulet, "Phenomenology of Reading," *New Literary History* 1 (1969–70); and J. Hillis Miller, "The Geneva School . . . ," in *Modern French Criticism,* ed. J. K. Simon (1972). In "Geneva or Paris? The Recent Work of Georges Poulet," *University of Toronto Quarterly* 39 (1970), Miller manifests his own transition from the criticism of consciousness to the very different critical mode of *deconstruction.* A detailed study of the Geneva School is Sarah Lawall's *Critics of Consciousness: The Existential Structures of Literature* (1968); see also Michael Murray, *Modern Critical Theory: A Phenomenological Introduction* (1976). Among the books of Geneva critics and other critics of consciousness available in English are Georges Poulet, *Studies in Human Time* (1949), *The Interior Distance* (1952), and *The Metamorphoses of the Circle* (1961); Jean Starobinski, *The Invention of Liberty, 1700–1789* (1964); J. Hillis Miller, *Charles Dickens: The World of His Novels* (1959), *The Disappearance of God* (1963), and *Poets of Reality* (1965). Other critical works influenced by phenomenology are Paul Brodtkorb, *Ishmael's White World: A Phenomenological Reading of Moby Dick* (1965); David Halliburton, *Edgar Allan Poe: A Phenomenological View* (1973); and Bruce Johnson, *True Correspondence: A Phenomenology of Thomas Hardy's Novels* (1983).

Poststructuralism designates a variety of critical perspectives that in the 1970s displaced structuralism from its prominence as the radically innovative way of dealing with language and other signifying systems. A conspicuous announcement to American scholars of the poststructural point of view was Jacques Derrida's paper on "Structure, Sign and Play in the Discourse of the Human Sciences," delivered in 1966 to an International Colloquium at Johns Hopkins University. (The paper is included in Derrida's *Writing and Difference,* 1978.) Derrida attacked the quasi-scientific pretensions of the strict form of structuralism—derived from Saussure's concept of the structure of language and represented by the cultural anthropologist Lévi-Strauss—by asserting that the notion of a systemic structure, whether linguistic or other, presupposes a "center" that organizes and regulates the structure yet itself "escapes structurality." In Saussure's theory of language, for example, this center is assigned the function of controlling the endless differential play of internal relationships, while remaining itself outside of and immune from, that play. (See *structuralism.*) As Derrida's other writings make clear, he regards this incoherent and unrealizable notion of an ever-active yet always-absent center as only one of the many ways in which all of Western "logocentric" thinking depends on the notion of a self-certifying foundation, or absolute, or essence, or ground, which is ever-needed but never present. (See *deconstruction.*) Other contemporary thinkers, including Michel Foucault, Jacques Lacan, and (in his later phase) Roland Barthes, although in diverse ways, also "decentered" or "undermined" traditional claims for the existence of self-evident foundations that guarantee the validity of knowledge and truth, and establish the possibility of determinate communication. This *antifoundationalism*, conjoined with skepticism about traditional conceptions of meaning and knowledge, is evident in some exponents of almost all modes of current literary studies, including Marxist, feminist, new-histori-cist, and reader-response criticism. In its extreme forms, the poststructural claim is that the workings of language inescapably undermine the meanings that they make possible, or else that every mode of discourse constructs or constitutes the very facts or truths that it claims to discover.

Salient features or themes that are common to diverse types of post-structural thought and criticism include the following:

1) The primacy of theory. Since Plato and Aristotle, discourse about poetry or literature has involved "theory," in the traditional sense of a con-ceptual scheme, or set of principles, distinctions, and categories—sometimes explicit, but often only implied in critical practice—for identifying, classify-ing, analyzing, and evaluating works of literature. (See *criticism*.) In poststruc-tural criticism what is called "theory" has come to be foregrounded as the central and dominant issue, so that it becomes incumbent on every critic to "theorize" his or her position and practice. The nature of theory, however, is conceived in a new way; for the word **theory**, standing without qualification, often designates an account of the general conditions that determine all meaning and interpretation. In most cases, this account is held to apply not only to verbal language, but also to psychosexual and sociocultural signifying systems; as a consequence, the pursuit of literary criticism is conceived to be integral with all the other pursuits traditionally distinguished as the "human sciences," and to be inseparable from consideration of the general nature of human consciousness and "subjectivity," and also from reference to all forms of social and cultural phenomena. Often the theory of signification is afforded primacy in the additional sense that, when our common experience in the use or interpretation of language does not accord with what the theory entails, such experience is rejected as illusory, or else is accounted a wish-fulfilling or ideologically imposed concealment of the actual operation of the signifying system.

A prominent aspect of poststructural theories is that they are posed in direct opposition to standard and inherited ways of thinking in all provinces of knowledge and values. That is, they expressly "challenge" and undertake to "destabilize," and in many instances to "undermine" and "sub-vert," what they identify as the foundational assumptions, concepts, proce-dures, and findings in all the traditional modes of discourse in Western civi-lization (including literary criticism). In many instances, this adversarial stance toward established ways of thinking and of formulating knowledge is joined to an adversarial stance toward the established institutions and prac-tices of political power and social organization.

2) The decentering of the subject. The oppositional stance of poststruc-tural critics is manifested in a sharp critique of what they call "humanism"; that is, of the traditional view that the author—or more generally, the human "subject"—is a coherent identity, endowed with initiative and pur-posefulness, whose design and intentions effectuate the form and meaning of a literary or other written product. Structuralism had already divested the subject of any operative initiative and control, evacuating the purposive human agent into a mere location, or "space," wherein the differential elements and codes of a systematic *langue* precipitate into a particular *parole*, or signifying product. Derrida, however, by deleting the structural linguistic "center," had thereby also eliminated the possibility of a controlling code in language, leaving an unregulatable play of purely relational elements. In the view of many deconstructive critics, the subject or author or narrator of a text becomes itself a purely linguistic product—as Paul de Man has put it in *Allegories of Reading* (1979), p. 18, we "rightfully reduce" the subject "to the status of a mere grammatical pronoun"; alternatively, the subject-author is granted at most the function of trying (although always vainly) to "master" the incessant freeplay of the decentered signifiers.

Michel Foucault and Roland Barthes both signalized this evacuation of the traditional conception of the author by announcing the "disappearance of the author," or even more melodramatically, "the death of the author." (Foucault, "What is an Author," 1969, in *Language, Counter-Memory, Practice*, 1977; Barthes, "The Death of the Author," 1968, in *Image, Music, Text*, 1977.) They did not, of course, mean to deny that an individual is a necessary link in the chain of events that results in a parole or text. What they denied was the validity of the key "function," or "role" hitherto assigned in Western thought to a uniquely individual and purposive subject as the "cogito," or origin of all knowledge; as the initiator, purposive planner, and (by his or her intentions) the determiner of the form and meanings of a text; and as the "center," or organizing principle, of the matters treated in traditional literary criticism, literary scholarship, and literary history. (For a lively commentary on the announced death of the author, see Clara Claiborne Park, "Author! Author! Reconstructing Roland Barthes," in her *Rejoining the Common Reader*, 1991.) In addition, a number of current forms of psychoanalytic, Marxist, and new historicist criticism manifest a similar poststructural tendency to decenter, and in extreme cases to delete, the function of the author as a self-coherent, purposive, and determinative human subject. Instead, the human being is said to be a disunified self that is subjected to the uncontrollable workings of unconscious compulsions; or an unknowing conveyor of current forms of ideology; or a "site" traversed by the "cultural constructs" and the "discursive formations" engendered by the structures of power in a given era.

3) Reading, texts, and writing. The decentering or deletion of the author leaves the reader, or interpreter, as the focal figure in poststructural accounts of signifying practices. This figure, however, like the author, is stripped of the traditional human attributes of purposiveness and initiative and converted into an impersonal process called "reading." What this reading engages is no longer called a literary "work" (since this traditional term implies a purposive human maker of the product); instead, reading engages a "text"—that is, a structure of signifiers regarded merely as a given for the reading process. Texts in their turn (especially in deconstructive criticism) lose their individuality, and are often represented to be no more than manifestations of *écriture*—that is, of an all-inclusive textuality, or writing-in-general, in which the traditional "boundaries" between literary, philosophical, historical, legal, and other classes of texts are considered to be both artificial and superficial. See *text and writing (écriture)*.

The distinctive poststructural view is that no text can mean what it seems to say. To a deconstructive critic, for example, a text is a chain of signifiers whose seeming determinacy of meaning, and seeming reference to an extra-textual world, are illusory "effects" produced by the differential play and conflicting internal forces which, on a closer reading, turn out to deconstruct the text into an undecidable scatter of opposed significations. In the representation of Roland Barthes, the death of the author-function frees the reader to enter the literary text in whatever way he or she chooses, and the intensity of pleasure yielded by the text becomes proportionate to the reader's abandonment of limits on its signifying possibilities. In Stanley Fish's version of *reader-response criticism*, all the meanings and formal features seemingly found in a text are projected into the printed marks by each individual reader; any agreement about meaning between two individuals is contingent upon their belonging to a single one among many "interpretive communities." In his theory of the *anxiety of influence*, Harold Bloom is expressly anti-poststructural in his insistence on the centrality of the human author in effecting what is distinctive in any literary work, and is vehemently opposed to what he describes as the "dehumanization" of literature by deconstruction and other current theories of signification. Nonetheless, he shares with poststructuralists (although on his own distinctive psycho-rhetorical grounds) the denial that any literary work is invested with specific and determinable meanings or formal features:

> The sad truth is that poems *don't have* presence, unity, form, or meaning. Presence is a faith, unity is a mistake or even a lie, form is a metaphor, and meaning is an arbitrary and now repetitious metaphysics. What then does a poem possess or create? Alas, a poem *has* nothing, and *creates* nothing.
>
> (Harold Bloom, *Kabbalah and Criticism*, 1975, p. 122)

4) Discourse. Literary critics had long made casual use of the term "discourse," especially in application to passages representing conversations between characters in a literary work, and in the 1970s there developed a critical practice called *discourse-analysis* which focuses on such conversational exchanges. This type of criticism (as well as the *dialogic criticism* inaugurated by Mikhail Bakhtin) deals with literary discourse as conducted by human characters whose voices engage in a dynamic interchange of beliefs, attitudes, sentiments, and other expressions of states of consciousness.

In poststructural criticism, **discourse** has become a very prominent term, supplementing (and in some cases displacing) "text" as the name for the verbal material which is the primary concern of literary criticism. In poststructural usage, however, the term is not confined to conversational passages but, like "writing," designates all verbal structures and implies the superficiality of the boundaries between literary and non-literary modes of signification. Most conspicuously, discourse has become the focal term among critics who oppose the deconstructive concept of a "general text" that functions independently of particular historical conditions. Instead, they conceive of discourse as social parlance, or language-in-use, and consider it to be both the product and manifestation not of a timeless linguistic system, but of particular social conditions, class-structures, and power-relationships that alter in the course of history. In Althusser and other recent Marxist critics, for example, the discourses of the various state "apparatuses," or institutions, are constituted by modes of ideology which are diverse and quasi-autonomous, yet are ultimately attributable to the material conditions and class-hierarchy of an historical era. (See *Marxist criticism*.) In Michel Foucault, discourse-as-such becomes the central subject of analytic concern. Unlike traditional discourse-analysts, however, Foucault does not conceive of discourse as human conversational exchanges, nor as what he describes as the "expression" or "manifestation" of an individual as "a thinking, knowing, speaking subject." Instead, he conceives discourse to be totally anonymous, in that it is simply "situated at the level of the 'it is said' (*on dit*)." (*The Archeology of Language*, 1972, pp. 55, 122.) Foucault—together with those new historicists for whom he is a model—represents this circulating discourse as traversed by a variety of "discursive formations" that are generated by the configurations of power at a given time and place.

Many socially oriented analysts of discourse share with other poststructuralists the conviction (or at any rate the profound suspicion) that no text means what it seems to say. But whereas deconstructive critics attribute the subversion of the apparent meaning to the unstable and self-conflicting nature of language itself, social analysts of discourse—and also current *psychoanalytic critics*—view the surface, or "manifest" meanings of a text as a disguise, or substitution, for underlying meanings which cannot be overtly said, because they are suppressed by psychic, or ideological, or discursive necessities. By some critics, the covert meanings are regarded as having been suppressed by all three of these forces together. Both the social and psychoanalytic critic of discourse therefore interprets the manifest meanings of a text as a distortion, displacement, or total "occlusion" of its real meanings; and these real meanings, in accordance with the critic's theoretical orientation, turn out to be either the writer's psychic and psycho-linguistic compulsions, or the material realities of history, or the social power-structures of domination, subordination, and marginalization that obtained when the text was written.

The primacy of "theory" in poststructural criticism has evoked countertheoretical challenges, most prominently in an essay "Against Theory" by Steven Knapp and Walter Benn Michaels that was published in 1982. Defining theory (in consonance with the widespread current use of the term) as "the attempt to govern interpretations of particular texts by appealing to an account of interpretation in general," the two authors claim that this is an impossible endeavor "to stand outside practice in order to govern practice from without," assert that accounts of interpretation in general can have no consequences for the actual practice of interpretation, and conclude that all theory "should therefore come to an end." Such a conclusion is supported by a number of writers, including Stanley Fish and the influential philosophical pragmatist Richard Rorty, who (despite disagreements in their supporting arguments) agree that no general account of interpretation entails particular consequences for the actual practice of literary interpretation and criticism. (See W. J. T. Mitchell, ed., *Against Theory: Literary Studies and the New Pragmatism*, 1985, which includes the initiating essay and a supplementary essay by Knapp and Michaels, together with essays and critiques by Fish, Rorty, E. D. Hirsch, and others.) The French philosopher Jean-François Lyotard has also mounted an influential attack against all "theory," which he regards as an attempt to impose a common vocabulary and set of principles in order illegitimately to control and constrain the many independent "language-games" that constitute discourse; see his *The Postmodern Condition* (1984). One response to this skepticism about the efficacy of theory on practice (a skepticism that is often labeled the **new pragmatism**) is that, while no general theory of meaning entails consequences for the practice of interpretation (in the strict logical sense of "entails"), it is a matter of common observation that diverse current theories have in actual fact served both to foster and to corroborate a number of diverse and novel interpretive practices. (For a view of both the inescapability and practical functioning of literary and artistic theory in traditional criticism, see M. H. Abrams, "What's the Use of Theorizing about the Arts?" 1972, reprinted in *Doing Things with Texts*, 1989.)

For anthologies that include important poststructural essays and selections, see David Lodge, ed., *Modern Criticism and Theory* (1988); K. M. Newton, ed., *20th-Century Literary Theory* (1988); Robert Con Davis and Ronald Schleifer, eds., *Contemporary Literary Criticism* (rev., 1989). For discussions and critiques of poststructuralist theories and practices from diverse points of view, see: Howard Felperin, *Beyond Deconstruction: The Uses and Abuses of Literary Theory* (1985); Peter Drews, *Logics of Disintegration: Post-Structuralist Thought and the Claims of Critical Theory* (1987); Tzvetan Todorov, *Literature and Its Theorists* (1987); James L. Battersby, *Paradigms Regained: Pluralism and the Practice of Criticism* (1991); Fredric Jameson, *Poststructuralism; or The Cultural Logic of Late Capitalism* (1991); John McGowan, *Postmodernism and Its Critics* (1991).

Psychological and Psychoanalytic Criticism. Psychological criticism deals with a work of literature primarily as an expression, in fictional form, of the state of mind and the structure of personality of the individual author. This approach emerged in the early decades of the nineteenth century, as part of the romantic replacement of earlier mimetic and pragmatic views by an *expressive* view of the nature of literature; see *criticism*. By 1827 Thomas Carlyle could say that the usual question "with the best of our own critics at present" is one "mainly of a psychological sort, to be answered by discovering and delineating the peculiar nature of the poet from his poetry." During the Romantic Period, we find widely practiced all three variants of the critical procedures (still current today) that are based on the assumption that a work of literature is correlated with its author's distinctive mental and emotional traits: (1) reference to the author's personality in order to explain and inter-pret a literary work; (2) reference to literary works in order to establish, bio-graphically, the personality of the author; and (3) the mode of reading a liter-ary work specifically as a way of experiencing the distinctive subjectivity, or consciousness, of its author (see *critics of consciousness*). We even find that John Keble, in the series of Latin lectures *On the Healing Power of Poetry*—pub-lished in 1844, but delivered more than ten years earlier—proposed a thor-oughgoing proto-Freudian literary theory. "Poetry," Keble claimed, "is the indirect expression . . . of some overpowering emotion, or ruling taste, or feel-ing, the direct indulgence whereof is somehow repressed"; this repression is imposed by the author's sentiments of "reticence" and "shame"; the conflict between the need for expression and the compulsion to repress such self-revelation is resolved by the poet's ability to give "healing relief to secret men-tal emotion, yet without detriment to modest reserve" by a literary "art which under certain veils and disguises . . . reveals the fervent emotions of the mind"; and this disguised mode of self-expression serves as "a safety valve, preserving men from madness." (The emergence and the varieties of romantic psychological criticism are described in M. H. Abrams, *The Mirror and the Lamp*, 1953, Chapters 6 and 9.) In the present era many critics make at least passing references to the psychology of an author in discussing works of litera-ture, with the notable exception of those whose critical premises invalidate such reference. See *formalism, New Criticism, structuralism, deconstruction*.

Since the 1920s, a very widespread psychological type of literary criti-cism has come to be **psychoanalytic criticism**, whose premises and proce-dures were established by Sigmund Freud (1856–1939). Freud had developed the dynamic form of psychology that he called psychoanalysis as a means of therapy for neuroses, but soon expanded it to account for many develop-ments in the history of civilization, including warfare, mythology, and reli-gion, as well as literature and the other arts. Freud's brief comment on the workings of the artist's imagination at the end of the twenty-third lecture of his *Introduction to Psychoanalysis* (1920), supplemented by relevant passages in the other lectures in that book, set forth the theoretical framework of what is sometimes called "classical" psychoanalytic criticism: Literature and the other arts, like dreams and neurotic symptoms, consist of the imagined, or fantasied, fulfillment of wishes that are either denied by reality or are pro-hibited by the social standards of morality and propriety. The forbidden, mainly sexual ("libidinal") wishes come into conflict with, and are repressed by, the "censor" (the internalized representative within each individual of the standards of society) into the unconscious realm of the artist's mind, but are permitted by the censor to achieve a fantasied satisfaction in distorted forms which serve to disguise their real motives and objects from the con-scious mind. The chief mechanisms that effect these disguises of unconscious wishes are (1) "condensation" (the omission of parts of the unconscious mate-rial and the fusion of several unconscious elements into a single entity); (2) "displacement" (the substitution for an unconscious object of desire by one that is acceptable to the conscious mind); and (3) "symbolism" (the representation of repressed, mainly sexual, objects of desire by nonsexual objects which resemble them or are associated with them in prior experience). The disguised fantasies that are evident to consciousness constitute the "manifest" content of a dream or work of literature; the unconscious wishes that find a semblance of satisfaction in this distorted form are the "latent" content.

Also present in the unconscious of every individual, according to Freud, are residual traces of prior stages of psychosexual development, from earliest infancy onward, which have been outgrown, but remain as "fixations" in the unconscious of the adult. When triggered by some later event in adult life, a repressed wish is revived and motivates a fantasy, in disguised form, of a satisfaction that is modeled on the way that the wish had been gratified in infancy or early childhood. The chief enterprise of the psychoanalytic critic, in a way that parallels the enterprise of the psychoanalyst as a therapist, is to reveal the true content, and also to explain the effect on the reader, of a literary work by translating its manifest elements into the unconscious determinants that constitute their suppressed meanings.

Freud also asserts, however, that artists possess special abilities that differentiate them radically from the patently neurotic personality. The artistic person, for example, possesses to an especially high degree the power to "sublimate" (that is, to shift the instinctual drives from their original sexual goals to nonsexual "higher" goals, including the discipline of becoming proficient as an artist); the ability to elaborate fantasied wish-fulfillments into the manifest features of a work of art in a way that conceals or deletes their personal elements, and so makes them capable of satisfying the unconscious desires of people other than the individual artist; and a "puzzling" ability—which Freud elsewhere says is a power of "genius" that psychoanalysis cannot explain—to mold the artistic medium into "a faithful image of the creatures of his imagination," as well as into a satisfying artistic form. The result is a fantasied wish-fulfillment of a complex and artfully shaped sort that not only allows the artist to overcome, at least partially and temporarily, personal conflicts and repressions, but also makes it possible for the artist's audience "to obtain solace and consolation from their own unconscious sources of gratification which had become inaccessible" to them. Literature and art, therefore, unlike dreams and neuroses, may serve the artist as a mode of fantasy that opens "the way back to reality."

This outline of his theory of art was elaborated and refined, but not radically altered, by the later developments in Freud's theory of mental structures, dynamics, and processes. Prominent among these developments was Freud's model of the mind as having three types of functions: the **id** (which incorporates libidinal and other desires), the **superego** (the internalization of standards of morality and propriety), and the **ego** (which tries as best it can to negotiate the conflicts between the insatiable demands of the id, the impossibly stringent requirements of the superego, and the limited possibilities of gratification offered by the world of "reality"). Freud has himself summarized for a general audience his later theoretical innovations, with his remarkable power for clear and dramatic exposition, in *New Introductory Lectures on Psychoanalysis* (1933) and *An Outline of Psychoanalysis* (1939).

Freud asserted that many of his insights had been anticipated by great authors in Western literature, and he himself applied psychoanalysis to brief discussions of the latent content in the manifest characters or episodes of literary works including Shakespeare's *Hamlet, Macbeth, A Midsummer Night's Dream,* and *King Lear.* He also wrote a brilliant analysis of Fyodor Dostoevsky's *The Brothers Karamazov* and a full-length study, *Delusion and Dream* (1917), of the novel *Gradiva* by the Danish writer Wilhelm Jensen. Especially after the 1930s, a number of writers produced critical analyses, modeled on classical Freudian theory, of the lives of authors and of the content of their literary works. One of the best-known books in this mode is *Hamlet and Oedipus* (1949) by the psychoanalyst Ernest Jones. Building on earlier suggestions by Freud himself, Jones explained Hamlet's inability to make up his mind to kill his uncle by reference to his **Oedipus complex**— that is, the repressed but continuing presence in the adult's unconscious of the male infant's desire to possess his mother and to have his rival, the father, out of the way. (Freud derived the term from Sophocles' Greek tragedy *Oedipus the King,* whose protagonist has unknowingly killed his father and married his mother.) Jones proposes that Hamlet's conflict is "an echo of a similar one in Shakepeare himself," and goes on to account for the audience's powerful and continued response to the play, over many centuries, as a result of the repressed Oedipal conflict that is shared by all men. In more recent decades there has been increasing emphasis by Freudian critics, in a mode suggested by Freud's later writings, on the role of "ego psychology" in elaborating the manifest content and artistic form of a work of literature; that is, on the way that the "ego," in contriving the work, consciously manages to mediate between the conflicting demands of the id, the superego, and the limits imposed by reality. On such developments see Frederic C. Crews, "Literature and Psychology," in *Relations of Literary Study,* ed. James Thorpe (1967), and the issue on "Psychology and Literature: Some Contemporary Directions," in *New Literary History* 12 (1980). Norman Holland is the leading exponent of the application of psychoanalytic concepts not (as in earlier criticism) to the relation of the author to the work, but to the relation of the reader to the work, explaining each reader's individual response as the product of a "transactive" engagement between his or her unconscious desires and defenses and the fantasies that the author has projected in the literary text; see *reader-response criticism.*

The term **psychobiography** designates an account of the life of an author (see *biography*) that focuses on the subject's psychological development, relying for evidence both on external sources and on the author's own writings. It stresses the role of unconscious and disguised motives in forming the author's personality, and is usually written in accordance with a version, or a revision, of the Freudian theory of the stages of psychosexual development. A major exemplar of the mode was Erik H. Erikson's *Young Man Luther* (1958), in which Erikson stressed the importance of Luther's adolescent "identity crisis." Other notable instances of literary psychobiography are Leon Edel, *Henry James* (5 vols.; 1953–72), and Justin Kaplan, *Mark Twain and His World* (1974).

Prominent and diverse examples of a Freudian literary criticism are in the collections listed below. It should be noted, in addition, that most modern literary critics, like most modern authors, owe some debt to Freud; such major critics, for example, as Kenneth Burke, Edmund Wilson, and Lionel Trilling have assimilated central Freudian concepts into their overall critical views and procedures.

Carl G. Jung is sometimes called a psychoanalyst, but although he began as a disciple of Freud, his mature version of depth-psychology is very different from that of his predecessor, and what we call **Jungian criticism** of literature departs radically from psychoanalytic criticism. Jung's emphasis is not on the individual unconscious, but on what he calls the "collective unconscious," shared by all individuals in all cultures, which he regards as the repository of "racial memories" and of primordial images and patterns of experience that he calls *archetypes.* He does not, like Freud, view literature as a disguised form of libidinal wish-fulfillment that parallels the fantasies of a neurotic personality. Instead, Jung regards great literature as, like the myths whose patterns recur in diverse cultures, an expression of the archetypes of the collective unconscious. A great author possesses, and provides for readers, access to the archetypal images buried in the racial memory, and so succeeds in revitalizing aspects of the psyche which are essential both to individual self-integration and to the mental and emotional well-being of the human race. Jung's theory of literature has been a cardinal formative influence on *archetypal criticism* and *myth criticism.* See Jung, *Contributions to Analytic Psychology* (1928), and *Modern Man in Search of a Soul* (1933); also Edward Glover, *Freud or Jung* (1950).

A prominent phenomenon since the development of *structural* and *poststructural* theories has been a strong revival of Freud, although in diverse reformulations of the classical Freudian scheme. Close attention to Freud's writings, and frequently the assimilation of some version of Freud's ideas to their own views and procedures, are features of the criticism of many current writers, whether they are Marxist, Foucauldian, Derridean, or feminist in theoretical commitment or primary focus. Harold Bloom's innovative view of the anxiety of influence specifically adapts to the composition and reading of poetry Freud's concepts of the Oedipus complex and of the distorting operation of defense mechanisms in dreams; see *anxiety of influence.*

The very influential Jacques Lacan, "the French Freud," developed a "semiotic" version of Freud, recasting the basic concepts of psychoanalysis into formulations derived from the linguistic theory of Ferdinand de Saussure, and applying these concepts not to people, but to the operations of the process of signification. (See under *linguistics in literary criticism.*) Typical is Lacan's oft-quoted dictum, "The unconscious is structured like a language." Lacan reformulates Freud's views of the early stages of psychosexual development and the formation of the Oedipus Complex into a distinction between the pre-linguistic stage that he calls the "imaginary" and the stage after the acquisition of language that he calls the "symbolic." In the imaginary stage, there is no clear distinction between the subject and an object, or between the self and others. When it enters the symbolic stage, the infant subject assimilates the inherited system of linguistic differences, and thereby learns to accept its pre-determined "position" in such linguistic oppositions as male/female, father/son, mother/daughter. This symbolic realm of language, in Lacan's theory, is the realm of the law of the father, in which the "phallus" (in a symbolic sense) is "the privileged signifier" that serves to establish the mode for all other signifiers. In a parallel fashion, Lacan translates Freud's views of the mental workings of dream-formation into textual terms of the play of signifiers, converting Freud's distorting defense-mechanisms into linguistic figures of speech. And according to Lacan, all processes of linguistic expression and interpretation, driven by "desire" for a lost and unachievable object, move incessantly along a chain of unstable signifiers without any possibility of coming to rest on a fixed signified, or presence. (See Jacques Lacan, *Écrits: A Selection*, 1977; also Lacan's much discussed reading of Edgar Allan Poe's short story *The Purloined Letter* as an allegory of the workings of the signifier, in *Yale French Studies*, Vol. 48, 1972.) Lacan's notions of the inalienable split, or "difference," that inhabits the self, and of the endless chain of displacements in the quest for meaning, has made him a prominent reference in *poststructural* theorists. And his distinction between the pre-Oedipal, maternal stage of the imaginary and the "phallocentric" stage of symbolic language has been exploited at length by a number of French feminists; see Hélène Cixous, Luce Irigaray, and Julia Kristeva under *feminist criticism*.

Some of Freud's psychoanalytic writings on literature and the arts have been collected by Benjamin Nelson, ed., *Sigmund Freud on Creativity and the Unconscious* (1958). Anthologies of psychoanalytic criticism by various authors are William Phillips, ed., *Art and Psychoanalysis* (1957), and Leonard and Eleanor Manheim, eds., *Hidden Patterns: Studies in Psychoanalytic Literary Criticism* (1966). Useful discussions of "classical" Freudian literary theory are Frederick J. Hoffman, *Freudianism and the Literary Mind* (rev., 1957), which also describes Freud's wide influence on writers and critics; and Norman N. Holland, *The Dynamics of Literary Response* (1968). Elizabeth Wright, *Psychoanalytic Criticism: Theory in Practice* (1984), reviews various recent developments in psychoanalytic theories and their applications to literary criticism. For two major traditional critics who have to an important extent adapted Freudian concepts to their general enterprise, see Edmund Wilson, *The Wound and the Bow* (1941), and Lionel Trilling, "Freud and Literature," in *The Liberal Imagination* (1950). Frederic C. Crews, who in 1966 wrote an exemplary Freudian critical study, *The Sins of the Fathers: Hawthorne's Psychological Themes,* has more recently retracted his Freudian commitment; see his *Skeptical Engagements* (1986). Among *feminist* critiques and adaptations of Freudian theory are Juliet Mitchell's *Psychoanalysis and Feminism* (1975), and Nancy Chodorow's *Feminism and Psychoanalytic Theory* (1990). For feminist views and adaptations of Jacques Lacan, see Jane Gallop, *Reading Lacan* (1985), and Shoshana Felman, *Jacques Lacan and the Adventure of Insight* (1987).

Reader-Response Criticism does not designate any one critical theory, but a focus on the process of reading a literary text that is shared by many of the critical modes, American and European, which have come into prominence since the 1960s. Reader-response critics turn from the traditional conception of a work as an achieved structure of meanings to the ongoing mental operations and responses of readers as their eyes follow a text on the page before them. By this shift of perspective a literary work is converted into an activity on the part of the reader. In the more drastic forms of such reader-response criticism, matters that had been considered by traditional critics to be features of the work itself (including narrator, plot, characters, style, and structure, as well as meanings) are dissolved into an evolving process, consisting primarily of diverse kinds of expectations and the violations, deferments, satisfactions, and restructurings of expectations, in the flow of a reader's experience. Reader-response critics of all theoretical persuasions agree that, at least to some considerable degree, the meanings of a text are the "production" or "creation" of the individual reader, hence that there is no one "correct" meaning for all readers either of the linguistic parts or of the artistic whole of a text. Where these critics importantly differ is (1) in their view of the primary factors that shape a reader's responses, (2) in the place at which they draw the line between what is "objectively" given in a text and the "subjective" responses of an individual reader; and as a result of this difference, (3) in their conclusion about the extent, if any, to which a text controls, or at least "constrains," a reader's responses, so as to authorize us to reject at least some readings as misreadings, even if, as almost all reader-response critics assert, we are unable to demonstrate that any one reading is the right one.

The following is a brief survey of some of the more prominent forms of reader-response criticism:

The contemporary German critic Wolfgang Iser develops the phenomenological analysis of the reading process proposed by Roman Ingarden, but whereas Ingarden had limited himself to a description of reading in general, Iser applies his theory to the analysis of many individual works of literature, especially prose fiction. (For Ingarden, see *phenomenology and criticism.*) In Iser's view the literary text, as a product of the writer's intentional acts, in part controls the reader's responses, but always contains (to a degree that has greatly increased in modern literary texts) a number of "gaps" or "indeterminate elements." These the reader must fill in by a creative participation with what is given in the text before him. The experience of reading is an evolving process of anticipation, frustration, retrospection, reconstruction, and satisfaction. Iser distinguishes between the "implied reader," who is established by the text itself as one who will respond in specific ways to the "response-inviting structures" of the text, and the "actual reader," whose responses are inevitably colored by his or her accumulated private experiences. In both cases, however, the process of the reader's consciousness constitutes both the partial patterns (which we ordinarily attribute to objective features of the work itself) and the coherence, or unity, of the work as a whole. As a consequence, literary texts always permit a range of possible meanings. The fact, however, that the author's intentional acts establish limits, as well as incentives, to the reader's creative additions to a text allows us to reject some readings as misreadings. (For an application of phenomeno-logical analysis to the changing history of reader-responses to a text, see *reception-theory*.)

French *structuralist criticism,* as Jonathan Culler has said in *Structuralist Poetics* (1975), "is essentially a theory of reading" which aims to "specify how we go about making sense of texts" (pp. viii, 128). As practiced by critics such as Culler in the course of his book, such criticism stresses literary conven-tions, codes, and rules which, having been tacitly assimilated by competent readers, serve to structure their reading experience and so make possible, at the same time as they impose constraints on, the partially creative activity of interpretation. The structuralist Roland Barthes, however, in his later theory encouraged a mode of reading that opens the text to an endless play of alter-native meanings. And the poststructuralist movement of *deconstruction* is a theory of reading that subverts the structuralist view that interpretation is in some part controlled by linguistic and literary codes, and instead proposes a "creative" reading of any text as a play of "differences" that generate innu-merable, mutually contradictory, but totally "undecidable" meanings.

American proponents of reader-response types of interpretive theory usu-ally begin by rejecting the claim of the American *New Criticism* that a literary work is a self-sufficient object invested with publicly available meanings, whose features and structure should be analyzed without "external" reference to the responses of its readers (see *affective fallacy*). In radical opposition to this view, these newer critics turn their attention exclusively to the reader's responses; they differ greatly, however, in the factors to which they attribute the formation of these responses.

David Bleich, in *Subjective Criticism* (1978), undertakes to show, on the basis of classroom experiments, that any purportedly "objective" reading of a text, if it is more than an empty derivation from theoretical formulas, turns out to be based on a response that is not determined by the text, but is instead a "subjective process" determined by the personality of the individ-ual reader. In an alternative psychoanalytic analysis of reading, Norman Holland accounts for the responses of a reader to a text by recourse to Freudian concepts (see *psychoanalytic criticism*). The subject matter of a work of literature is a projection of the fantasies—engendered by the interplay of unconscious needs and defenses—that constitute the particular "identity" of its author. The individual reader's "subjective" response to a text is a "trans-active" encounter between the fantasies projected by its author and the par-ticular defenses, expectations, and wish-fulfilling fantasies that make up the reader's own identity. In this transactive process the reader transforms the fantasy content, "which he has created from the materials of the story his defenses admitted," into a unity, or "meaningful totality," which constitutes the reader's particular interpretation of the text. There is no universally determinate meaning of a work; two readers will agree in their interpretation only insofar as their "identity themes" are sufficiently alike to enable each to fit the other's re-creation of a text to his or her own distinctive responses.

In his theory of reading, Harold Bloom also employs psychoanalytic concepts; in particular, he adapts Freud's concept of the mechanisms of defense against the revelation to consciousness of repressed desires to his own view of the process of reading as the application of "defense mechanisms" against the "influence," or threat to the reader's imaginative autonomy, of the poet whose text is being read. Bloom applies Freudian concepts in a much more complex way than Holland; he arrives, however, at a parallel conclusion that there can be no determinate or correct meaning of a text. All "reading is . . . misreading"; the only difference is that between a "strong" misreading and a "weak" misreading. See *anxiety of influence*.

Stanley Fish is the proponent of what he calls **affective stylistics**. In his earlier writings Fish represented the activity of reading as one which converts the spatial sequence of printed words on a page into a temporal flow of experience in an "informed" reader who has acquired a "literary competence." In following the printed text with his eye, "there is a point at which the reader has taken in only the first word, and then the second, and then the third, and so on." At each point at which the reader stops, he makes sense of what he has so far read by anticipating what is still to come. These anticipations may be fulfilled by what follows in the text; often, however, they will turn out to have been mistaken. But since, according to Fish, "the meaning of an utterance" is not some final, corrected result, but the reader's "experience—all of it," and the reader's mistakes are "part of the experience provided by the author's language," these mistakes are an integral part of the meaning of a text. ("Literature in the Reader: Affective Stylistics," published 1970 and reprinted with slight changes in *Self-Consuming Artifacts: The Experience of Seventeenth Century Literature*, 1974, and in *Is There a Text in This Class?*, 1980.) Fish's analyses of large-scale literary works were designed to show a coherence in the kinds of mistakes, constitutive of specific types of meaning-experience, which are effected in the reader by the text of John Milton's *Paradise Lost*, and by various essayists and poets of the seventeenth century.

Fish's early claim was that he was describing a universal process of the competent reading of literary texts. In later publications, however, he introduced the concept of **interpretive communities**, each of which is composed of members who share a particular reading "strategy," or "set of community assumptions." Fish, in consequence, now presented his own affective stylistics as only one of many alternative modes of interpretation, which his earlier writings were covertly attempting to persuade his readers to adopt. He also proposed that each communal strategy in effect "creates" all the seemingly objective features of the text itself, as well as the "intentions, speakers, and authors" that we may infer from the text. The result is that there can be no universal "right reading" of any text; the validity of any reading, however obvious it may seem to a reader, will always depend on the assumptions and strategy of reading that he or she happens to share with other members of a particular interpretive community. See Fish, *Is There a Text in This Class? The Authority of Interpretive Communities* (1980).

Since the early 1980s, as part of a widespread tendency to stress cultural and political factors in the study of literature, reader-response critics have increasingly undertaken to "situate" a particular reading in its historical setting, in the attempt to show the extent to which the responses that constitute both the interpretation and evaluation of literature have been determined by *ideology* and by built-in biases about race, class, or gender. (See Peter J. Rabinowitz, *Before Reading: Narrative Conventions and the Politics of Interpretation,* 1987; and for *feminist* emphasis on the male biases in the responses of readers, Judith Fetterley, *The Resisting Reader* (1978); and Elizabeth A. Flynn and Patrocinio Schweikart, eds., *Gender and Reading: Essays on Readers, Texts, and Contexts* (1986).

A survey of a number of reader-response theories of criticism is included in Steven Mailloux's own contribution to this mode in *Interpretive Conventions* (1982); another survey from the point of view of deconstructive theory is Elizabeth Freund, *The Return of the Reader: Reader-Response Criticism* (1987). Anthologies of diverse reader-response essays: Susan Sulleiman and Inge Crossman, eds., *The Reader in the Text* (1980); Jane P. Tompkins, ed., *Reader-Response Criticism* (1980). Important early instances of a criticism that is focused on the reader are: Walter J. Slatoff, *With Respect to Readers* (1970); Louise Rosenblatt, *The Reader, the Text, the Poem* (1978); Umberto Eco, *The Role of the Reader* (trans., 1979).

In addition to the titles mentioned in this essay, the following are prominent exemplars of reader-response criticism: Stanley Fish, *Surprised by Sin: The Reader in "Paradise Lost"* (1967), and *Self-Consuming Artifacts: The Experience of Seventeenth-Century Literature* (1972); Norman Holland, *The Dynamics of Literary Response* (1968), and *Five Readers Reading* (1975); Wolfgang Iser, *The Implied Reader* (1974), and *The Act of Reading: A Theory of Aesthetic Response* (1978). For critiques of Fish's "affective stylistics": Ralph W. Rader, "Fact, Theory, and Literary Explanation," *Critical Inquiry* 1 (1974); Jonathan Culler, *The Pursuit of Signs* (1981); Eugene Goodheart, *The Skeptic Disposition in Contemporary Criticism* (1984); M. H. Abrams, "How to Do Things with Texts," in *Doing Things with Texts* (1989).

Reception-Theory is the historical application of a form of *reader-response* theory that was proposed by Hans Robert Jauss in "Literary History as a Challenge to Literary Theory" (in *New Literary History,* Vol. 2, 1970–71). Like other reader-response criticism, it focuses on the reader's reception of a text; its prime interest, however, is not on the response of a single reader at a given time, but on the altering responses, interpretive and evaluative, of the general reading public over the course of time. Jauss proposes that although a text has no "objective meaning," it does contain a variety of objectively describable features. The response of a particular reader, which constitutes for that reader the meaning and aesthetic qualities of a text, is the joint product of the reader's own "horizon of expectations" and the confirmations, disappointments, refutations, and reformulations of these expectations when they are "challenged" by the features of the text itself. Since readers' linguistic and aesthetic expectations change over the course of time, and since later readers and critics have access not only to the text but also to the published responses of earlier readers, there develops an evolving historical "tradition" of critical interpretations and evaluations of a given literary work. Following views proposed by Hans-Georg Gadamer (see under *interpretation and hermeneutics*), Jauss represents this tradition as a continuing "dialectic," or "dialogue," between a text and the horizons of successive readers; in itself, a literary text possesses no fixed and final meanings or value.

This mode of studying literary reception as a dialogue, or "fusion" of horizons, has a double aspect. As a **reception-aesthetic**, it "defines" the meaning and aesthetic qualities of any individual text as a set of semantic and aesthetic "potentialities" which become manifest only as they are realized by the cumulative responses of readers over the course of time. In its other aspect as a **reception-history**, this mode of study also transforms the history of literature—traditionally conceived as an account of the successive production of a variety of works with fixed meanings and values—by making it a history that requires an "ever necessary retelling," since it narrates the changing yet cumulative way that selected texts are interpreted and assessed, as the horizons of successive generations of readers alter in the passage of time.

See Hans Robert Jauss, *Towards an Aesthetic of Reception* (1982), and *The Aesthetic Experience and Literary Hermeneutics* (1982); and for a history and discussion of this viewpoint, Robert C. Holub, *Reception Theory: A Critical Introduction* (1984).

Russian Formalism. A type of literary theory and analysis which originated in Moscow and Petrograd in the second decade of this century. At first, opponents of the movement applied the term **formalism** derogatorily, because of its focus on the formal patterns and technical devices of literature to the exclusion of its subject matter and social values; later, however, it became simply a neutral designation. Among the leading representatives of the movement were Boris Eichenbaum, Victor Shklovsky, and Roman Jakobson. When this critical mode was suppressed by the Soviets in the early 1930s, the center of the formalist study of literature moved to Czechoslovakia, where it was continued especially by members of the **Prague Linguistic Circle**, which included Roman Jakobson (who had emigrated from Russia), Jan Mukarovsky, and René Wellek. Beginning in the 1940s both Jakobson and Wellek continued their influential work as professors at American universities.

Formalism views literature primarily as a specialized mode of language, and proposes a fundamental opposition between the literary (or poetical) use of language and the ordinary, "practical" use of language. It conceives the central function of ordinary language to be the communication to auditors of a message, or information, by references to the world existing outside of language. In contrast, it conceives literary language to be self-focused, in that its function is not to make extrinsic references, but to offer us a special mode of experience by drawing attention to its own "formal" features—that is, to interrelationships among the linguistic signs themselves. The linguistics of literature differs from the linguistics of practical discourse, because its laws are oriented toward producing the distinctive features that formalists call **literariness**. As Roman Jakobson wrote in 1921: "The object of study in literary science is not literature but 'literariness,' that is, what makes a given work a literary work." (See *linguistics in modern criticism*.)

The literariness of a work, as Jan Mukarovsky described it in the 1920s, consists "in the maximum of **foregrounding** of the utterance," that is, the foregrounding of "the act of expression, the act of speech itself." (To "foreground" is to bring something into the highest prominence, to make it dominant in perception.) By "backgrounding" the referential aspect and the logical connections in language, poetry makes the words themselves "palpable" as phonic signs. The primary aim of literature in thus foregrounding its linguistic medium, as Victor Shklovsky put it in an influential formulation, is to **estrange** or **defamiliarize**; that is, by disrupting the modes of ordinary linguistic discourse, literature "makes strange" the world of everyday perception and renews the reader's lost capacity for fresh sensation. (In the *Biographia Literaria*, 1817, Samuel Taylor Coleridge had long before described the "prime merit" of a literary genius as the representation of "familiar objects" so as to evoke "freshness of sensation"; but whereas the Romantic critic had stressed the author's ability to communicate his own fresh mode of experiencing the world, the formalist stresses the function of purely literary devices to produce the effect of freshness in the reader's sensation.) The foregrounded properties, or "artistic devices," which estrange poetic language are often described as "deviations" from ordinary language. Such deviations, which are analyzed most fully in the writings of Roman Jakobson, consist primarily in setting up and violating patterns in the sound and syntax of poetic language—including patterns of speech sounds, grammatical constructions, rhythm, rhyme, and stanza forms—and also in setting up prominent recurrences of key words or images.

Some of the most fruitful work of Jakobson and others, valid outside the formalist perspective, has been in the analysis of *meter* and of the repetitions of sounds in *alliteration* and *rhyme;* these features of poetry they regard not as supplementary adornments of the meaning, but as effecting a reorganization of language on the semantic as well as the phonic and syntactic levels. Formalists have also made influential contributions to the theory of prose fiction. With respect to this genre, the central formalist distinction is that between the "story" (the simple enumeration of a chronological sequence of events) and a plot. An author is said to transform the raw material of a story into a literary plot by the use of a variety of devices that violate sequence and deform and defamiliarize the story elements; the effect is to foreground the narrative medium and devices themselves, and in this way to disrupt what had been our standard responses to the subject matter. (See *narrative and narratology*.)

American *New Criticism*, although it developed independently, is sometimes called "formalist" because like European formalism it stresses the analysis of the literary work as a self-sufficient verbal entity, independent of reference either to the state of mind of the author or to the "external" world. It also, like the European formalists, conceives poetry as a special mode of language whose distinctive features are defined in terms of their opposition to practical or scientific language. Unlike the Europeans, however, the New

Criticism did not apply linguistic science to poetry, and its emphasis was not on a work as constituted by linguistic devices for achieving specifically literary effects, but on the complex interplay within a work of ironic, paradoxical, and metaphoric aspects around a humanly important "theme." The main influence of Russian and Czech formalism on American criticism has been on the development of *stylistics,* as well as *narratology.* Roman Jakobson and Tzvetan Todorov have been influential in introducing formalist concepts and methods into French *structuralism.* Strong opposition to formalism, both in its European and American varieties, has been voiced by some *Marxist critics* (who view it as the product of a reactionary ideology), and more recently by proponents of *reader-response criticism, speech-act theory,* and *new historicism;* these last three types of criticism all reject the view that there is a sharp and definable division between ordinary language and literary language.

The standard treatment is by Victor Erlich, *Russian Formalism: History, Doctrine* (rev., 1981). René Wellek has described *The Literary Theory and Aesthetics of the Prague School* (1969). Representative formalist writings are collected in Lee T. Lemon and Marion J. Reese, eds., *Russian Formalist Criticism: Four Essays* (1965); Ladislav Matejka and Krystyna Pomorska, eds., *Readings in Russian Poetics: Formalist and Structuralist Views* (1971); and Peter Steiner, ed., *The Prague School: Selected Writings, 1929–1946* (1982). A comprehensive and very influential formalist essay by Roman Jakobson, "Linguistics and Poetics," is included in Thomas A. Sebeok, ed., *Style in Language* (1960). Samuel Levin's *Linguistic Structures in Poetry* (1962) represents an American application of formalist principles, and E. M. Thompson discusses *Russian Formalism and Anglo-American New Criticism* (1971).

Semiotics. At the end of the nineteenth century Charles Sanders Peirce, the American philosopher, described a study that he called "semiotic," and in his *Course in General Linguistics* (1915) the Swiss linguist Ferdinand de Saussure independently proposed a science which he called "semiology." Since then **semiotics** and **semiology** have become alternative names for a general science of signs, as these function in all areas of human experience. The consideration of **signs** is not limited to explicit systems of communication such as language, the Morse code, and traffic signs and signals; a great diversity of other human activities and productions—our bodily postures and gestures, the social rituals we perform, the clothes we wear, the meals we serve, the buildings we inhabit, the objects we deal with—convey common "meanings" to members who participate in a particular culture, and so can be analyzed as signs which function in diverse kinds of signifying systems. Although the study of language (the use of specifically verbal signs) is regarded as itself only one branch of the general science of semiotics, *linguistics,* the highly developed science of language, in fact supplies the basic concepts and methods that a semiotician applies to the study of other social sign-systems.

C. S. Peirce distinguished three classes of signs, defined in terms of the kind of relation between the signifying item and that which it signifies:

(1) An **icon** functions as a sign by means of inherent similarities, or shared features, with what it signifies; examples are the similarity of a portrait to the person it depicts, or the similarity of a map to the geographical area it stands for. (2) An **index** is a sign which bears a natural relation of cause or effect to what it signifies; thus, smoke is a sign indicating fire, and a pointing weathervane indicates the direction of the wind. (3) In the **symbol** (or in a less ambiguous term, the **"sign proper"**), the relation between the signifying item and what it signifies is not a natural one, but entirely a matter of social convention. The gesture of shaking hands, for example, in some cultures is a conventional sign of greeting or parting, and a red traffic light conventionally signifies "Stop!" The major and most complex examples of this third type of purely conventional sign, however, are the words that constitute a language.

Saussure introduced many of the terms and concepts exploited by current semioticians; see under *linguistics in modern criticism*. Most important are the following: (1) A sign consists of two inseparable components or aspects, the *signifier* (in language, a set of speech sounds, or of marks on a page) and the *signified* (the concept, or idea, which is the meaning of the sign). (2) A verbal sign, in Saussure's term, is "arbitrary." That is, with the minor exception of *onomatopoeia* (words which we perceive as similar to the sounds they signify), there is no inherent, or natural, connection between a verbal signifier and what it signifies. (3) The identity of all elements of a language, including its words, their component speech sounds, and the concepts the words signify, are not determined by "positive qualities," or objective features in these elements themselves, but by *differences*, or a network of relationships, consisting of distinctions and oppositions from other speech sounds, other words, and other signifieds that obtain only within a particular linguistic system. (4) The aim of linguistics, or of any other semiotic enterprise, is to regard the *parole* (a single verbal utterance, or a particular use of a sign or set of signs) as only a manifestation of the *langue* (that is, the general system of implicit differentiations and rules of combination which underlie and make possible a particular use of signs). The focus of semiotic interest, accordingly, is not on a particular parole, but on the general system of the langue that the parole manifests.

Modern semiotics, like structuralism, has developed in France under the aegis of Saussure, so that many semioticians are also structuralists. They deal with any set of social phenomena or productions as "texts"; that is, as constituted by self-sufficient, self-ordering, hierarchical structures of differentially determined signs, of *codes*, and of rules of combination and transformation which make them "meaningful" to members of a particular society who are competent in that signifying system. (See *structuralist criticism*.) Claude Lévi-Strauss, in the 1960s and later, inaugurated the application of semiotics to cultural anthropology, and also established the foundations of French structuralism in general, by using Saussure's linguistics as a model for analyzing, in primitive societies, a great variety of phenomena and practices, which he treated as quasi-languages that manifest the structures of an underlying signifying system. These include kinship systems, totemic systems, ways of preparing food, myths, and prelogical modes of interpreting the world. Jacques Lacan has applied semiotics to Freudian *psychoanalysis*—interpreting the unconscious, for example, as (like language) a structure of signs. Michel Foucault developed a mode of semiotic analysis to deal with the changing medical interpretations of symptoms of disease; the diverse ways of identifying, classifying, and treating insanity; and the altering conceptions of human sexuality. Roland Barthes, explicitly applying Saussurean principles and methods, has written semiotic analyses of the constituents and codes of the differential sign-systems in advertisements which describe and promote women's fashions, as well as analyses of many "bourgeois myths" about the world which, he claims, are exemplified in such social sign-systems as professional wrestling matches, children's toys, cookery, and the striptease. (See his *Mythologies,* trans., 1972.) Barthes was also in his earlier writings a major exponent of *structuralist criticism,* which deals with a literary text as "a second-order semiotic system"; that is, it views a literary text as employing the first-order semiotic system of language to form a higher-level semiotic structure, in accordance with a specifically literary system of differential elements, conventions, and codes.

Introductions to the elements of semiotic theory are included in Terence Hawkes, *Structuralism and Semiotics* (1977); in Jonathan Culler, *The Pursuit of Signs* (1981); in Robert Scholes, *Semiotics and Interpretation* (1982); and in the anthologies, Thomas A. Sebeok, ed., *The Tell-Tale Sign: A Survey of Semiotics* (1975); and Robert E. Innes, ed., *Semiotics: An Introductory Reader* (1986). See also Umberto Eco, *A Theory of Semiotics* (1976); Roland Barthes, *Elements of Semiology* (trans., 1967); Thomas A. Sebeok, *Semiotics in the United States* (1991). Among the semiotic analyses of diverse social phenomena available in English are Claude Lévi-Strauss, *Structural Anthropology* (1968), and *The Raw and the Cooked* (1966); Roland Barthes, *Mythologies* (1972), also *Selected Writings,* ed. Susan Sontag (1983); Jacques Lacan, *The Language of the Self: The Function of Language in Psychoanalysis* (1968); and Michel Foucault, *The Archaeology of Knowledge* (1972), *Madness and Civilization* (1965), and *The Birth of the Clinic* (1973). On semiotics and literary analysis: Maria Corti, *An Introduction to Literary Semiotics* (1978); Michael Riffaterre, *Semiotics of Poetry* (1978); Barbara Hernstein Smith, *On the Margins of Discourse: The Relation of Literature to Language* (1978). For a critical view, see J. G. Merquior, *From Prague to Paris* (1986).

Speech-Act Theory, developed by the philosopher John Austin, was described most fully in his posthumous book *How to Do Things with Words* (1962), and was explored and expanded by other "ordinary-language philosophers," including John Searle and H. P. Grice. Austin's theory is directed especially against traditional tendencies of philosophers (1) to analyze the meaning of isolated sentences, abstracted from the context of discourse and of the attendant circumstances in which a sentence is uttered, and (2) to assume, in what Austin describes as a logical obsession, that the standard sentence—of which other types are merely variants—is a statement that describes a situation or asserts a fact and is judged to be either true or false. John Searle's expansion of Austin's speech-act theory opposes to these views about language the claim that when we attend to the overall linguistic and situational context—including the institutional conditions that govern many uses of language—we find that in speaking or writing we perform simultaneously three, and sometimes four, distinguishable kinds of "speech acts": (1) We utter a sentence; Austin called this act a "locution." (2) We refer to an object, and predicate something about that object. (3) We perform an illocutionary act. (4) Often, we also perform a perlocutionary act.

The **illocutionary act** performed by a locution may indeed be the one stressed by traditional philosophy and logic, to assert that something is true, but it may instead be one of very many other possible speech acts, such as questioning, commanding, promising, warning, praising, thanking, and so on. A sentence consisting of the same words in the same grammatical form, such as "I will leave you tomorrow," may in its particular verbal and situational context turn out to have the "illocutionary force" either of an assertion, a promise, or a threat. In an illocutionary act that is not an assertion, the prime criterion (although the utterance does make reference to some state of affairs) is not its truth or falsity, but whether or not the act has been performed successfully, or in Austin's term, "felicitously." A felicitous performance of a particular illocutionary act depends on its meeting "appropriateness conditions" which obtain for that type of act; these conditions are tacit linguistic and social (or institutional) conventions, or rules, that are shared by competent speakers and interpreters of a language. For example, the successful performance of an illocutionary act of promising, such as "I will come to see you tomorrow," depends on its meeting its special set of appropriateness conditions: the speaker must be capable of fulfilling his promise, must intend to do so, and must believe that the listener wants him to do so. Failing the last condition, for example, the same verbal utterance might have the illocutionary force of a threat.

In *How to Do Things with Words,* John Austin established an initial distinction between two broad types of locutions: **constatives** (sentences that assert something about a fact or state of affairs and are adjudged to be true or false) and **performatives** (sentences that are actions which accomplish something, such as questioning, promising, praising, and so on). As he continued his subtle analysis, however, Austin showed that this initial division of utterances into two sharply exclusive classes does not hold, in that many performatives also involve reference to a state of affairs, while constatives also perform an illocutionary act. Austin, however, drew special attention to the "explicit performative," which is a sentence whose utterance itself, when executed under appropriate institutional and other conditions, brings about the state of affairs that it signifies. Examples are "I name this ship the Queen Elizabeth"; "I apologize"; "I call this meeting to order"; "Let spades be trumps."

If an illocutionary act has an effect on the actions or state of mind of the hearer which goes beyond merely understanding what has been said, it is also a **perlocutionary act.** Thus, the utterance "I am going to leave you," with the illocutionary force of a warning, may not only be understood as such, but have (or fail to have) the additional perlocutionary effect of frightening the hearer. Similarly, by the illocutionary act of promising to do something, one may please (or else anger) the hearer; and by asserting something, one may have the effect either of enlightening, or of inspiring, or of intimidating the hearer. Some perlocutionary effects may be intended by the speaker; others occur without the speaker's intention, and even against that intention. For a useful exploration of the relations, in diverse cases, of illocutionary and perlocutionary speech acts, see Ted Cohen, "Illocutions and Perlocutions," in *Foundations of Language 9* (1973).

Since 1970 speech-act theory has influenced in conspicuous and varied ways the practice of literary criticism. When applied to the analysis of direct discourse by a character in a literary work, it provides a systematic but sometimes cumbersome framework for identifying the unspoken presuppositions, implications, and effects of speech acts which competent readers and critics have always taken into account, subtly though unsystematically. (See *discourse analysis*.) Speech-act theory has also been used in a more radical way, however, as a model on which to recast the theory of literature in general, and especially the theory of prose narratives (see *fiction and truth*). What the author of a fictional work—or else what the author's invented narrator—narrates is held to constitute a "pretended" set of assertions, which are intended by the author, and understood by the competent reader, to be free from a speaker's ordinary commitment to the truth of what he or she asserts. Within the frame of the fictional world that the narrative thus sets up, however, the utterances of the fictional characters—whether these are assertions or promises or marital vows—are held to be responsible to ordinary illocutionary commitments. Alternatively, some speech-act theorists propose a new version of mimetic theory (see *imitation*). Traditional mimetic critics had claimed that literature imitates reality by representing in a verbal medium the setting, actions, utterances, and interactions of human beings. Some speech-act theorists, on the other hand, claim that all literature is simply "mimetic discourse." A lyric, for example, is an imitation of that form of ordinary discourse in which we express our feelings about something, and a novel is an imitation of a particular form of written discourse, such as biography (Henry Fielding's *The History of Tom Jones*, 1749), or autobiography (Charles Dickens' *David Copperfield*, 1849–50), or even a scholar's annotated edition of a poetic text (Nabokov's *Pale Fire*, 1962).

For basic philosophical treatments of speech acts see John Austin's *How to Do Things with Words* (1962); John R. Searle's *Speech Acts: An Essay in the Philosophy of Language* (1970); and H. P. Grice, "Logic and Conversation," in *Syntax and Semantics 3* (1975). Among the attempts to model the general theory of literature, or at least of prose fiction, on the theory of speech acts are Richard Ohmann, "Speech Acts and the Definition of Literature," *Philosophy and Rhetoric* 4 (1971); Charles Altieri, "The Poem as Act," *Iowa Review* 6 (1975); John R. Searle, "The Logical Status of Fictional Discourse," in *Expression and Meaning* (1979), Chapter 3. A detailed application to literary theory is Mary Louise Pratt's *Toward a Speech Act Theory of Literary Discourse* (1977). For views of the limitations of speech-act theory when applied in literary criticism, see Stanley Fish, "How to Do Things with Austin and Searle: Speech-Act Theory and Literary Criticism," in *Is There a Text in This Class?* (1980); and Joseph Margolis, "Literature and Speech Acts," *Philosophy and Literature* 3 (1979). For Jacques Derrida's deconstructive analysis of Austin's views, and John Searle's reply, see under *deconstruction;* for Searle's speech-act theory of metaphor, see *figurative language.*

Structuralist Criticism. Almost all literary theorists since Aristotle have emphasized the importance of *structure,* which they conceive in diverse ways, in analyzing a work of literature. "Structuralist criticism," however, now designates the practice of critics who analyze literature on the explicit model of modern linguistic theory. The class includes a number of *Russian formalists,* especially Roman Jakobson, but consists most prominently of a group of writers, with their headquarters in Paris, who apply to literature primarily the concepts and analytic distinctions developed by Ferdinand de Saussure in his *Course in General Linguistics* (1915). This mode of criticism is part of a larger movement, French **structuralism,** inaugurated in the 1950s by the cultural anthropologist Claude Lévi-Strauss, who analyzed, on Saussure's linguistic model, such cultural phenomena as mythology, kinship relations, and modes of preparing food. See *linguistics in literary criticism.*

In its early form, as manifested by Lévi-Strauss and other writers in the 1950s and 1960s, structuralism cuts across the traditional disciplinary areas of the humanities and social sciences by undertaking to provide an objective account of all social and cultural phenomena, in a range that includes mythical narratives, literary texts, advertisements, fashions in clothes, and patterns of social decorum. (See *semiotics.*) It views these phenomena as a signifying structure—a combination of signs that have a set significance for the members of a particular culture—and undertakes to explain how the phenomena have achieved their cultural significance, and what that significance is, by reference to an underlying system (analogous to Saussure's *langue,* the implicit system of a particular language) that consists of the relationships among signifying elements and their rules of combination. The elementary cultural phenomena, like the linguistic elements in Saussure's exposition, are not objective facts identifiable by their inherent properties, but purely "relational" entities; that is, their identity as signs are given to them by their relations of differences from, and binary oppositions to, other elements within the cultural system. This system of internal relationships and of the "codes" of significant combinations has been mastered by each person competent within a given culture, although he or she remains largely unaware of its nature and operations. The primary interest of the structuralist, like that of Saussure, is not in the cultural *parole* but in the *langue;* that is, not in any particular cultural phenomenon except as it provides access to the structure, features, and rules of the general system that engenders its significance.

As applied in literary studies, **structuralist criticism** views literature as a second-order system that uses the first-order structural system of language as its medium, and is itself to be analyzed primarily on the model of linguistic theory. Structuralist critics often apply a variety of linguistic concepts to the analysis of a literary text, such as the distinction between *phonemic* and *morphemic* levels of organization or between *paradigmatic* and *syntagmatic* relationships; and some critics analyze the structure of a literary text on the model of the *syntax* in a well-formed sentence. The undertaking of a thoroughgoing literary structuralism, however, is to explain how it is that a competent reader is able to make sense of a particular text by specifying the underlying system of specifically literary conventions and rules of combination that has been unconsciously mastered by such a reader. The ultimate aim of classic literary structuralism, accordingly, is to make explicit, in a quasi-scientific way, the tacit *grammar* (the system of rules and codes) that governs the forms and meanings of all literary productions. As Jonathan Culler put it in his lucid exposition, the aim of structuralist criticism is "to construct a poetics which stands to literature as linguistics stands to language." (*Structuralist Poetics*, 1975, p. 257.)

Structuralism is in explicit opposition to *mimetic criticism* (the view that literature is primarily an imitation of reality), to *expressive criticism* (the view that literature primarily expresses the feelings or temperament or creative imagination of its author), and to any form of the view that literature is a mode of communication between author and readers. More generally, in its attempt to develop a science of literature and in many of its salient concepts, structuralism departs radically from the assumptions and ruling ideas of traditional humanistic criticism. For example:

1) In the structuralist view, what had been called a literary "work" becomes simply a "text"; that is, a mode of writing constituted by a play of component elements according to specifically literary conventions and codes. These factors may generate an illusion of reality, but have no truth-value, nor even any reference to a reality existing outside the literary system itself.

2) The individual author, or "subject," is allowed no initiative, expressive intentions, or design as the "origin" or producer of a work. Instead the conscious "self" is declared to be a construct that is itself the product of the workings of the linguistic system, and the mind of an author is described as an imputed "space" within which the impersonal, "always-already" existing system of literary language, conventions, codes, and rules of combination gets precipitated into a particular text. As Roland Barthes expressed, dramatically, this subversion of the traditional humanistic view, "As institution, the author is dead." ("The Death of the Author," in *Image-Music-Text*, trans., 1977.)

3) Structuralism replaces the author by the reader as the central agency in criticism; but the traditional reader, as a conscious, purposeful, and feeling individual, is dissolved into the impersonal activity of "reading," and what is read is not a text imbued with meanings, but écriture, writing. The focus of structuralist criticism, accordingly, is on the impersonal process of reading which, by bringing into play the requisite conventions, codes, and expectations, makes literary sense of the sequence of words, phrases, and sentences that constitute a text. See *text and writing (écriture)*.

In the 1990s, the strict application of structural premises and procedures continues mainly in two areas: the semiotic analysis of cultural phenomena, and the analyses of the limited number of formal structures that, in their combinations and variations, constitute the plots in the genre of the novel. (See *semiotics* and *narratology.*) In the late 1960s, however, the general structuralist enterprise, in its rigorous form and all-inclusive pretensions, ceded its central position to deconstruction and other modes of poststructural theories, which attacked the scientific claims of structuralism and subverted its view that literary meanings are made determinate by a system of invariant conventions and codes. (See *poststructuralism.*) This shift in the prevailing point of view is exemplified by the changing emphases in the lively and influential writings of the French critic and man of letters, Roland Barthes (1915–1980). His early work developed and helped disseminate the structuralist theory that was based on the linguistics of Saussure—a theory that Barthes applied not only to literature but (in *Mythologies,* 1957) to decoding, by reference to an underlying signifying system, many aspects of popular culture. In his later writings, Barthes abandoned the scientific aspiration of structuralism, and distinguished between the "readerly" text such as the realistic novel that tries to "close" interpretation by insisting on specific meanings, and the "writerly" text that aims at the ideal of "a galaxy of signifiers," and so encourages the reader to be a producer of his or her own meanings according not to one code but to a multiplicity of codes. And in *The Pleasure of the Text* (1973) Barthes lauds, in contrast to the comfortable pleasure offered by a traditional text that accords with cultural conventions, the *jouissance* (or orgasmic bliss) evoked by a text that incites a hedonistic abandon to the uncontrolled play of its signifiers.

A clear and comprehensive survey of the program and accomplishments of structuralist literary criticism, in poetry as well as narrative prose, is Jonathan Culler, *Structuralist Poetics* (1975); also Robert Scholes, *Structuralism in Literature: An Introduction* (1974). For an introduction to the general movement of structuralism see Philip Pettit, *The Concept of Structuralism: A Critical Analysis* (1975); and Terence Hawkes, *Structuralism and Semiotics* (1977). For critical views of structuralism see Frederic Jameson, *The Prison-House of Language* (1972); Gerald Graff, *Literature Against Itself* (1979); Frank Lentricchia, *After the New Criticism* (1980), Chapters 4–5; J. G. Merquior, *From Prague to Paris: A Critique of Structuralist and Post-Structuralist Thought* (1986). Some anthologies of structuralist writings: Richard T. De George and M. Fernande, eds., *The Structuralists: From Marx to Lévi-Strauss* (1972); David Robey, ed., *Structuralism: An Introduction* (1973); Richard Macksey and Eugenio Donato, eds., *The Structuralist Controversy: The Languages of Criticism and the Sciences of Man* (1970); and Josué V. Harari, *Textual Strategies: Perspectives in Post-Structuralist Criticism* (1979). Among the books of structuralist literary criticism available in English translations are Roland Barthes, *Critical Essays* (1964), and in Barthes' later poststructuralist phase, *S/Z* (1970), and *The Pleasure of the Text* (1973); Stephen Heath, *The Nouveau Roman: A Study in the Practice of Writing* (1972); Tzvetan Todorov, *The Poetics of Prose* (trans., 1977), and *Introduction to Poetics* (trans., 1981). Structuralist treatments of cinema are Christian Metz, *Language of Film* (1973); and Peter Wollen, *Signs and Meaning in the Cinema* (1969).

Stylistics. Since the 1950s the term **stylistics** has been applied to critical procedures which undertake to replace the "subjectivity" and "impressionism" of standard criticism with an "objective" or "scientific" analysis of the style of literary texts. Much of the impetus toward these analytic methods, as well as models for their practical application, were provided by the writings of Roman Jakobson and other Russian *formalists,* as well as by European *structuralists.*

We can distinguish two modes of stylistics, which differ both in conception and in the scope of their application:

1) In the narrower mode of formal stylistics, style is identified, in the traditional way, by the distinction between what is said and how it is said, or between the content and the form of a text. (See *style.*) The content is now often denoted, however, by terms such as "information," "message," or "propositional meaning," while the style is defined as variations in the way this information is presented that serve to alter its "aesthetic quality" or the reader's emotional response. The concepts of modern *linguistics* are used to identify the stylistic features, or "formal properties," which are held to be distinctive of a particular work, or else of an author, or a literary tradition, or an era. These stylistic features may be phonological (patterns of speech sounds, meter, or rhyme), or syntactic (types of sentence structure), or lexical (*abstract* vs. *concrete* words, the relative frequency of nouns, verbs, adjectives), or rhetorical (the characteristic use of *figurative language, imagery,* and so on). A basic problem, acknowledged by a number of stylisticians, is to distinguish between the innumerable features and patterns of a text which can be isolated by linguistic analysis, and those features which are functionally "stylistic"—that is, features which make an actual difference in aesthetic and other effects on a reader. See, for example, Michael Riffaterre's objection to the elaborate stylistic analysis of Charles Baudelaire's sonnet "Les Chats" (The Cats) by Roman Jakobson and Claude Lévi-Strauss, in *Structuralism,* ed. Jacques Ehrmann (1966).

Those stylisticians who aim for scientific precision employ quantitative methods to calculate the relative frequencies of stylistic features, and often use electronic computers to establish frequency tables of the features which are held to identify a distinctive style. Other analysts of style instead make use of concepts derived from language theory, such as the distinction between *paradigmatic* and *syntagmatic* relations, or the distinction between surface structure and deep structure in *transformational* grammar, or the distinction between the propositional content and the *illocutionary force* of an utterance in *speech-act theory.* For stylistic analyses of the ways a character's speech and thought are represented in narratives, refer to *free indirect discourse,* under *point of view.*

Sometimes the stylistic enterprise stops with the more or less quantitative determination, or "fingerprinting," of the style of a single text or class of texts. Often, however, the analyst tries also to relate distinctive stylistic features to traits in an author's psyche; or to an author's characteristic ways of perceiving the world and organizing experience (see Leo Spitzer, *Linguistics and Literary History,* 1948); or to the typical conceptual frame and the attitude to reality in an historical era (Erich Auerbach, *Mimesis,* 1953); or else to particular semantic, aesthetic, and emotional functions and effects (Michael Riffaterre and others).

Stanley Fish wrote a sharp critique of the scientific pretensions of formal stylistics; he proposed that since, in his view, the meaning of a text consists of its reader's total response to it, there is no valid way to make a distinction in this spectrum of response between style and content ("What Is Stylistics and Why Are They Saying Such Terrible Things About It?" in *Is There a Text in This Class?* 1980; see also under *reader-response criticism*). For extended critiques of traditional analyses of style, as well as of modern stylistics, based on the thesis that style is not a separable feature of language, see Bennison Gray, *Style: The Problem and Its Solution* (1969), and "Stylistics: The End of a Tradition," *Journal of Aesthetics and Art Criticism* 31 (1973). On the other side, the validity of distinguishing between style and propositional meaning—not absolutely, but on an appropriate level of analysis—is cogently defended by E. D. Hirsch, "Stylistics and Synonymity," in *The Aims of Interpretation* (1976).

2) In the second mode of stylistics, which has been prominent since the mid-1960s, proponents greatly expand the conception and scope of their inquiry by defining stylistics as, in the words of one theorist, "the study of the use of language in literature," involving the entire range of the "general characteristics of language . . . as a medium of literary expression." (Geoffrey N. Leech, *A Linguistic Guide to English Poetry*, 1969; see also Mick Short, "Literature and Language," in *Encyclopedia of Literature and Criticism*, ed. Martin Coyle and others, 1990.) By this definition, stylistics is expanded so as to incorporate most of the concerns of both traditional literary criticism and traditional *rhetoric*; its distinction from these earlier pursuits is that it insists on the need to be objective by focusing sharply on the text itself and by setting out to discover the "rules" governing the process by which linguistic elements and patterns in a text accomplish their meanings and literary effects. The historian of criticism René Wellek has described this tendency of stylistic analysis to enlarge its territorial domain as "the imperialism of modern stylistics."

On formal stylistics see Thomas A. Sebeok, ed., *Style in Language* (1960); Roger Fowler, ed., *Essays on Style and Language* (1966); Seymour Chatman, ed., *Literary Style: A Symposium* (1971); Howard S. Babb, ed., *Essays in Stylistic Analysis* (1972). For an exhaustive stylistic analysis of a twelve-line poem, see Roman Jakobson and Stephen Rudy, *Yeats's "Sorrow of Love" Through the Years* (1977).

In the practice of some critics, stylistics includes the area of study known as *discourse analysis*, which is treated in a separate entry in this *Glossary*. For inclusive views of the realm of stylistics, see: G. N. Leech and M. H. Short, *Style in Fiction* (1981); Roger Fowler, *Linguistic Criticism* (1986); Ronald Carter and Paul Simpson, eds., *Language, Discourse and Literature: An Introductory Reader in Discourse Stylistics* (1989).

Text and Writing (Écriture). Traditional critics have conceived the object of their critical concern to be a literary "work," whose form is achieved by its author's deliberate design and its meanings by the author's intentional uses of the verbal medium. French *structuralist* critics, on the other hand, depersonalized a literary product by conceiving it to be not a "work," but a "text," one species of the social institution called **écriture** (writing). The author is regarded as an impersonal agency in whom the action of writing precipitates aspects of the pre-existing linguistic and literary system into a particular text. The interpretation of this writing is effected by an impersonal "lecture" (French: process of reading) which, by bringing to bear expectations formed by earlier exposure to the functioning of the linguistic system, invests the marks on the page with what merely seem to be their inherent meanings and references to an outer world. Structuralists differ on the degree to which the activity of reading a text is governed by the literary conventions and codes that went into the writing; most *poststructuralists,* however, propose that any impression that a text has determinately-fixed meanings is illusory, and that all writing disseminates into an open set of diverse and opposed meanings.

The system of linguistic and literary conventions that constitute a literary text are said to be "naturalized" in the activity of reading, in that the artifices of a nonreferential "textuality" are made to seem **vraisemblable** (credible)—that is, made to give the illusion of referring to reality—by being brought into accord with modes of discourse and cultural stereotypes that are so familiar and habitual as to seem natural. **Naturalization** (an alternative term is **recuperation**) takes place through such uncritically habitual procedures in reading as assigning the text to a specific *genre,* or taking a fictional text to be the speech of a credibly human narrator, or interpreting its artifices as representing characters, actions, and values that represent, or accord with, those in an extra-textual world. To a thoroughgoing structuralist or poststructuralist critic, however, not only is the text's representation of the world an illusion, but the world is itself held to be in its turn a text; that is, simply a structure of signs whose significance is constituted by the cultural conventions, codes, and *ideology* that happen to be shared by members of a cultural community. The term **intertextuality**, popularized especially by Julia Kristeva, is used to signify the multiple ways in which any one literary text is inseparably inter-involved with other texts, whether by its open or covert citations and *allusions,* or by its assimilation of the formal and substantive features of an earlier text or texts, or simply by its unavoidable participation in the common stock of linguistic and literary conventions and procedures that are "always already" in place and constitute the discourses into which we are born. In Kristeva's formulation, accordingly, any text is in fact an "intertext"—the site of an intersection of numberless other texts, including those which will be written in the future.

Roland Barthes in *S/Z* (1970) proposed a distinction between a text which is "lisible" (readable) and one which, although "scriptible" (writable) is "illisible" (unreadable). Readable texts are traditional or "classical" ones—such as the realistic novels by Honoré Balzac and other nineteenth-century authors—which for the most part conform to the prevailing codes and conventions, literary and social, and so are readily and comfortably interpretable and naturalizable in the process of reading. An "unreadable" text (such as

James Joyce's *Finnegans Wake,* or the French *new novel,* or a poem by a highly experimental poet) is one which largely evades, parodies, or innovates upon prevailing conventions, and thus persistently shocks, baffles, and frustrates standard expectations. In Barthes' view an unreadable text, by drawing attention in this way to the pure conventionality and artifice of literature, laudably destroys the standard illusion that it represents social reality. In *The Pleasure of the Text* (published 1973), Barthes assigns to the readable text the response of mere "plaisir" (quasi-erotic pleasure), but to the unreadable text the response of "jouissance" (orgasmic ecstasy); as Jonathan Culler has put Barthes' view, jouissance is "a rapture of dislocation produced by ruptures or violations of intelligibility" (*Structuralist Poetics,* p. 192).

For related matters and relevant bibliographic references, see *structuralist criticism, poststructuralism,* and *semiotics.*

Index of Terms

The first number, in **boldface,** identifies the page of the text that contains the principal discussion of a term; in the text itself, that term is also printed in boldface. Succeeding numbers, in *italics,* identify other pages of the text on which the term occurs, in a context that illustrates its uses in critical practice; on such pages, the term is also italicized. The term in the text may be a modified form of the term listed in the Index; the forms "parodies" and "parodied," for example, are listed in the Index under "parody," and "structuralist" and "structuralists" are listed under "structuralism."

Some entries in the Index are followed by one or more references to related entries that supplement the exposition; thus: "courtly love. *See:* Platonic love." A number of comprehensive terms, such as drama, figurative language, or novel, are followed by a list of the entries that deal with the types of the general class or with the component features of the literary form.

Terms likely to be mispronounced by a student—many of these are borrowings from a foreign language—are followed (in parentheses) by a simplified guide to pronunciation. This guide marks the stress—in some instances, both the primary and secondary stresses—and also indicates the pronunciation of those parts of the word about which the student is apt to be in doubt. The following vowel marks are used:

ā (fate)   ĭ (pin)

ă (pat)   ō (rope)

ä (father)   ŏ (pot)

ē (meet)   oo (food)

ě (get)   ŭ (cut)

ī (pine)

Additional Terms

Additional Terms

Additional Terms

Additional Terms

Additional Terms

Additional Terms

Additional Terms

Additional Terms

Additional Terms